Eileen Chang

Eileen Chang

Romancing Languages, Cultures and Genres

Edited by Kam Louie

香港大學出版社
HONG KONG UNIVERSITY PRESS

This publication has been generously supported by the Faculty of Arts of the University of Hong Kong.

Hong Kong University Press
14/F Hing Wai Centre
7 Tin Wan Praya Road
Aberdeen
Hong Kong
www.hkupress.org

ISBN 978-988-8083-79-4 *(Hardback)*
ISBN 978-988-8083-72-5 *(Paperback)*

British Library Cataloguing-in-Publication Data
A catalogue record for this book is available from the British Library.

10 9 8 7 6 5 4 3 2 1

Printed and bound by Condor Production Ltd., Hong Kong, China

Contents

Notes on Contributors

Esther M. K. CHEUNG is currently Chair of the Department of Comparative Literature and Director of the Center for the Study of Globalization and Cultures at the University of Hong Kong. She is the author of Fruit Chan's *Made in Hong Kong* (Hong Kong University Press, 2009) and *In Pursuit of Independent Visions in Hong Kong Cinema* (Joint Publishing, 2010), as well as co-editor of *Between Home and World: A Reader in Hong Kong Cinema* (Oxford University Press, 2004).

Hsiu-Chuang DEPPMAN is Associate Professor of East Asian Studies at Oberlin College. Her research interests include the history of cinema, film adaptations, documentaries, and modern Chinese fiction. She is the author of *Adapted for the Screen: the Cultural Politics of Modern Chinese Fiction and Film* (University of Hawai'i Press, 2010). She has published widely on Chinese film and literature, most recently in *TV China, positions: east asia cultures critique, Journal of Narrative Theory,* and *Modern Chinese Literature and Culture.*

Nicole HUANG is Professor of Chinese Literature and Visual Culture Studies at the University of Wisconsin-Madison. She is the author of *Women, War, Domesticity: Shanghai Literature and Popular Culture of the 1940s* (Brill, 2005) and *Writing Against the Turmoil: Eileen Chang and Popular Culture in Occupied Shanghai* (Shanghai, 2010). She is also the co-editor of *Written on Water: A Collection of Essays by Eileen Chang* (Columbia University Press, 2005). Her current research deals with visual culture and daily practice in late Mao China.

Leo Ou-fan LEE is currently Wei Lun Professor of Humanities at the Chinese University of Hong Kong. He is the author of, among other books in both English and Chinese, *Shanghai Modern: The Flowering of a New Urban Culture in China, 1930–1945* (Harvard University Press, 1999). His wide-ranging interests include literature, film, music, and cultural criticism.

Jessica Tsui Yan LI is a Faculty Associate at the York Centre for Asian Research at York University. Her research areas are on modern Chinese literature and film and Asian North American studies. Her publications include "Self-Translation/Rewriting: The Female Body in Eileen Chang's 'Jinsuo ji,' *The Rouge of the North, Yuannü* and 'The Golden Cangue'" in *Neohelicon* (37.2, 2010) and "The Politics of Self-Translation: Eileen Chang" in *Perspectives: Studies in Translatology* (14.2, 2006). She is currently working on a book manuscript on Eileen Chang's self-translation.

Kam LOUIE is Dean of Faculty of Arts and MB Lee Professor of Humanities and Medicine at the University of Hong Kong. His diverse research interests cover interdisciplinary studies of language, literature, history, and philosophy in modern China. Recent publications include *Theorising Chinese Masculinity* (Cambridge University Press, 2002) and edited books *The Cambridge Companion to Modern Chinese Culture* (Cambridge University Press, 2009) and *Hong Kong Culture: Word and Image* (Hong Kong University Press, 2010).

Gina MARCHETTI is Associate Professor in the Department of Comparative Literature, School of Humanities at the University of Hong Kong. Her books include *Romance and the "Yellow Peril": Race, Sex and Discursive Strategies in Hollywood Fiction* (University of California Press, 1993) and *From Tiananmen to Times Square: Transnational China and the Chinese Diaspora on Global Screens* (Philadelphia: Temple University Press, 2006), as well as several co-edited volumes—most recently, *Hong Kong Screenscapes: From the New Wave to the Digital Frontier* (Hong Kong University Press, 2011).

Laikwan PANG is Professor of Cultural Studies in the Department of Cultural and Religious Studies at the Chinese University of Hong Kong, and she researches on a wide range of topics related to China, cinema, and modernity. She is the author of, among others, *Building a New China in Cinema: The Chinese Left-wing Cinema Movement, 1932–37* (Rowman and Littlefield, 2002), *The Distorting Mirror: Visual Modernity in China* (University of Hawai'i Press, 2007), and *Creativity and Its Discontents: China's Creative Industries and Intellectual Property Right Offenses* (Duke University Press, forthcoming).

Tze-lan Deborah SANG is Associate Professor of Chinese in the Department of East Asian Languages and Literatures at the University of Oregon. She is the author of *The Emerging Lesbian: Female Same-Sex Desire in Modern China* (University of Chicago Press, 2003), and co-editor of *Documenting Taiwan on Film: Issues and Methods in New Documentaries* (Routledge, forthcoming). Her current research projects include a study on Sinophone documentary and a book on popular fiction and urban culture in early-twentieth-century China.

Shuang SHEN teaches at the Department of Comparative Literature and Asian Studies Program of Penn State University. Her areas of specialization include Asian American and Asian diaspora literatures, modern Chinese history and literature, postcolonialist theories and literature. She is the author of *Cosmopolitan Publics: Anglophone Print Culture in Semi-Colonial Shanghai* (Rutgers University Press, 2009) and the editor of a critical collection on Eileen Chang, entitled *Eileen Chang Degree Zero* 零度看張 (The Chinese University Press, 2010).

David Der-wei WANG is Edward C. Henderson Professor in Chinese Literature, Harvard University, Director of CCK Foundation Inter-University Center for Sinological Studies, and Academician, Academia Sinica. His specialties are modern and contemporary Chinese literature, late Qing fiction and drama, and comparative literary theory. Wang's English books include *Fictional Realism in 20th Century China: Mao Dun, Lao She, Shen Congwen* (Columbia University Press, 1992), *Fin-de-siècle Splendor: Repressed Mondernities of Late Qing Fiction, 1849–1911* (Stanford University Press, 1997), *The Monster That Is History: Violence, History, and Fictional Writing in 20th Century China* (University of California Press, 2004).

Xiaojue WANG is Assistant Professor in the Department of East Asian Languages and Civilizations at the University of Pennsylvania, member of the Graduate Group in German Languages and Literatures and the Cinema Studies Program. Her main area of research is modern and contemporary Chinese literature and film and comparative literature, particularly Cold War German and Chinese cultures. Recent publications include "From Asylum to Museum: The Discourse of Insanity and Schizophrenia in Shen Congwen's 1949 Transition," *Modern Chinese Literature and Culture* (23.1, 2012). She is currently completing a book *Modernity with a Cold War Face: Re-imagining the Nation in Chinese Literature Across the 1949 Divide*.

Acknowledgements

In April 2009, the Faculty of Arts at the University of Hong Kong organized an international conference on Eileen Chang. Between 1939 and 1941, Chang had studied in the Faculty, and this symposium was held "to bring Eileen Chang home." The papers presented at the symposium were stimulating and shed new light on Eileen Chang, and many were revised over the next two years and now appear as chapters in this book. We greatly benefitted from the informative and enlightening papers by other presenters such as Ping-kwan Leung, Carole Hoyan, Karen Kingsbury, and Li-ling Huang. I am grateful to Haiyan Lee, Ngai-lai Cheng, Maureen Sabine, Q. S. Tong and Y. F. Yeung whose help in organizing the conference was invaluable. I am also grateful to all participants whose comments and suggestions greatly enriched the papers of all who contributed to this volume.

I am especially indebted to Fiona Chung, who guided this project to fruition from its very beginning. Fiona's superb organizational skills have made the work on getting the conference and the book together an enjoyable and fulfilling experience. I should also thank Michael Duckworth, Anne Platt, Chris Louie, Jessica Wang, Alan Walker, and the two anonymous readers for Hong Kong University Press for their advice and help. Finally, I would like to acknowledge the financial support that I have received from the HKU Arts Faculty's Louis Cha Fund, the China-West Strategic Research Theme, and the Hong Kong Research Grants Council's General Research Fund that enabled me to do my own research as well as organizing research workshops to stimulate research in this area.

Introduction

Eileen Chang: A Life of Conflicting Cultures in China and America

Kam Louie

Eileen Chang [Zhang Ailing 張愛玲] was born into a large Shanghai family in 1920 and died alone in Los Angeles in 1995. In accordance with the terms of her will, she was cremated and her ashes were scattered to the wind. Since her death, Chang's life and writings have been closely scrutinized and her literary work has extended its reach through translations and screen adaptations. Chang herself retold her personal stories in different languages and from different perspectives, times, and places throughout her life, so these recent renditions build upon a lengthy tradition of retellings.

Since Chang's death, her life and times have been accorded more critical and popular attention and significance than ever before. In recent years, the number of articles and books about Chang has continued to multiply. However, there is still relatively little written about her in English. This book seeks to go some way to correcting this imbalance. And this introduction provides a short summary of Chang's life, pointing to junctures that provided the impetus for her creative output. It pays tribute to this remarkable woman and will hopefully elicit many more studies that will give her further life. Eileen Chang's experiences and observations are worth telling, not only because she lived in exciting times and places, but also, as Eva Hung remarks, because "circumstances and temperament combined to make her an observer of the details of Chinese urban life at a time when the majority of writers felt that it was their obligation to look at the grand picture,"[1] and she was almost unique in the honesty with which she recorded her reactions to life around her.

The essays in this book reveal a highly observant young woman weaving tales of romance amid war and "fallen" cities. When she was older, during the latter part of her American sojourn, she seemed to live in deafening silence and isolation. But her inner life, harking back to her days in Hong Kong and

Shanghai, was still filled with stories of romance, this time more personal and complex. Despite a long writing career, Eileen Chang seemed obsessed with those few years in the early 1940s when she was one of the most celebrated writers in Shanghai. Her best creative works, whether written in China or America, center on that period. While she wrote some novels about Communist China in the 1950s, these novels, in keeping with the political requirements of the time, are about peasants, and Chang clearly did not write them with much personal knowledge or commitment. They had little impact then, and it is unlikely they ever will. In keeping with Chang's own focus, the essays in this book mostly relate to her observations and reminiscences of her Hong Kong and Shanghai years, although the rehearsals of these memories took place over the course of several decades. Because it is not the content but the way in which she expressed her memories that is most interesting, the chapters of this book are arranged so that Chang's major works are discussed approximately in the chronological order in which they were released.

Eileen Chang's penchant for evocatively recalling the lives of members of wealthy families in decline in occupied Hong Kong and Shanghai meant that there was no way her writings could thrive in the Mainland in the 1950s and 60s, no matter how dispassionately she expressed herself. However, her work continued to generate interest in Taiwan and Hong Kong. As well as critics such as C. T. Hsia and David Wang who though based abroad publish in Chinese and so exert an influence in the Greater China region, numerous critics who are based in Taiwan, Hong Kong, and increasingly Mainland China, such as Shui Jing (水晶), Tang Wenbiao (唐文標), Chen Zishan (陳子善), William Tay (鄭樹森), Joseph Lau (劉紹銘) and Zhang Jian (張健), continue to publish volumes on Chang's writings. More importantly, in Taiwan in particular, many creative writers have been influenced by Eileen Chang, to such an extent that several generations of "Chang School writers" are said to have emerged.[2]

Indeed several of her novels have been made into plays and films in the last few decades, and her popularity has increased as a consequence. But, as indicated above, she has remained relatively unknown among the lay reading public in the West, despite having written and published several novels in English. Until recently, only a few scholars in the West had researched her work in depth, and even this was mostly due to C. T. Hsia's claim in his authoritative 1961 book on modern Chinese fiction that she was "the best and most important writer in Chinese today."[3] But such praise only reached readers interested in contemporary Chinese literature, and they were few in number outside Hong Kong and Taiwan. However, in the last few years, thanks to the success of Ang Lee's film *Lust, Caution* (色，戒, 2007) and the controversies surrounding it, interest in Chang's work has received an international boost beyond Sinological circles. Given the truly modern concerns that Eileen Chang represented, this international recognition is timely.

In today's world where cultures collide and interact in so many different ways and places, Eileen Chang presents a fascinating study. She came from a distinguished family—her great-grandfather was Li Hongzhang (李鴻章), the eminent late-Qing official. As well as having suppressed several rebellions, Li Hongzhang was known to Westerners as the Superintendent of Trade— the chief architect of foreign policy in the late Qing. He was such a highly regarded figure that Queen Victoria made him a Knight Grand Cross of the Royal Victorian Order. Despite this pedigree, the family fortunes had declined considerably by the time Eileen was born. She was named Zhang Ying (張瑛), but her Europhile mother changed this to the English-sounding Zhang Ailing (i.e. Eileen Chang 張愛玲) when she was ten years old.[4] As Karen Kingsbury remarks, "even Eileen Chang's name speaks her dual heritage: a surname linked to the declining patriarchal world of the late imperial scholars and statesmen; and a maternally bequeathed, English-derived given name, with its associations of modern-style female assertiveness."[5] Indeed, her mother so admired things European that, when Eileen was only two, her mother left for the UK, and stayed there for five years. From a very early age, then, Eileen's life revolved around Chinese high culture and the imagined allure of Europe.

Despite being born into a privileged family with such a cosmopolitan background, Eileen Chang was not a happy child. Not only was her mother more concerned with personal liberation than with her children's happiness; her father, like so many of his class and generation, led a dissolute life, taking on a second wife and using opium. Her parents' irreconcilable differences and the consequent drawn-out estrangement and divorce embittered them both and had a lasting impact on the hapless child. Eileen recalls that "Dream of Genius" (天才夢, 1940), her first story, written at the age of seven, was about a family tragedy, and her second story was about a young woman who commits suicide. Her first published work, which appeared in her school magazine when she was only twelve, was appropriately titled "The Unfortunate Her" (不幸的她, 1932).[6] The story is only a few pages long, but the protagonist's lament—at seeing her best childhood friend with a loving family as an adult—that "I cannot bear to see your happiness, it only accentuates my sadness,"[7] already foreshadows the maudlin tone of her writings decades on. Indeed, Eileen Chang's descriptions of dysfunctional families such as the short story "The Golden Cangue" (金鎖記, 1943) stand as some of the best fictional pieces in modern Chinese literature. While "The Unfortunate Her" verges on pretentiousness and childish self-pitying sentimentality, it foreshadows many of the emotions and themes of Chang's later writings. The young protagonist may not be a likeable character, but her feelings are sincerely expressed and are far from insipid. Apart from the obvious envy she manifests for her friend's perceived existence, there is a sad yearning for a loving and harmonious family life.

"The Unfortunate Her" was published a year after Eileen Chang's parents divorced. In the same year, her mother again left for Europe, her father remarried, and Eileen's relationship with him deteriorated. In the spring of 1938, after a particularly vicious argument with her stepmother, her father beat Eileen heartlessly and isolated her in a room for several months before she was able to escape to join her mother, who had by then returned to Shanghai. While locked up, Chang suffered from dysentery and nearly died. She wrote about this incident and her unhappy childhood in an essay entitled "What a Life! What a Girl's Life" (1938), which was published in the English language newspaper *Shanghai Evening Post*. Thus, right from the beginning, Eileen Chang demonstrated that she was keen to reach out to both English and Chinese readers. She continued to refine and utilize her bilingualism and biculturalism during the course of her writing career. In her teenage years and earliest publications, Chang already portrayed the themes that were to be repeated throughout her writing career: the misfortunes that befall young women and the warped families of urban China at that time, which give rise to emotionally isolated and crippled personalities. That lingering sense of melancholy and desolation was to resonate throughout her creative works. By Chang's own reckoning, the word she used most often is "desolation" (荒涼), reflecting the mood that dominates her writings.[8] Indeed, Lin Zou argues that Chang was able to develop this feeling of desolation into a very successful aesthetics for the commercial consumption of the petty bourgeois.[9]

Despite her literary talent, Eileen Chang's family circumstances meant that for much of the time she was literally locked up, with nothing to do but dream and read, and as she grew older she became increasingly introverted. Unlike most of her contemporaries who were swept up in the New Culture and nationalist movements, her concerns were focused on personal rather than national salvation. The dramatic social upheavals taking place in China at the time were only background noise in her writings. In the midst of the Japanese invasion of Shanghai in 1937–38, Chang was recounting in her essay "Whispers" (私語, 1944) her misfortunes as a young girl struggling to survive her father's drug-induced violence and mother's self-indulgent bohemianism, even as some of the fiercest fighting in modern times was claiming hundreds of thousands of lives around her. The whole essay focused on the family violence at home, and we only hear of the war because "we were kept awake at night by the shelling." The only other mention of it is when Chang "wished a bomb would land on our home. I would have been happy to die along with them."[10] Eileen Chang's ability to write about very personal turmoil in the midst of great human upheavals as if such upheavals were happening elsewhere makes her unique in modern Chinese literature. It also meant that she was, as she intimates, not able or willing to parrot the nationalist or revolutionary slogans so prevalent in that era. Such isolationism in the midst of war and revolution was considered a great shortcoming in those days. Indeed, Chang's unhappy childhood meant that she became, as her brother recalls, "self-defensive, selfish and self-absorbed."[11]

Nonetheless, it was not all tragedy and unhappiness. In 1939, Chang went to study at the University of Hong Kong, with the understanding that she would proceed directly to Oxford for further study. She worked hard and did so well that she achieved very high grades and won two scholarships. Unfortunately, the Japanese occupation of Hong Kong after a short but brief battle in December 1941 and the consequent closure of the University meant that she was not able to graduate, and her plans to study in England were also dashed. Nonetheless, her years at the University of Hong Kong were pivotal in the evolution of Eileen Chang as an author. The University had an international faculty and student body. While there, she met a diverse range of people from different parts of China as well as Southeast Asia, many of whom she would draw upon for inspiration in her later writings. She also made a number of good friends, one of whom, Fatima Mohideen (Yanying 炎櫻), was a cheerful and intelligent woman. Their friendship was to last throughout their lives. In fact, Yanying was probably the only friend that Chang truly admired and loved. Yanying's wit and good humour can be glimpsed in the "Sayings of Yanying" (炎櫻語錄, 1944) that Chang collated and published.[12]

The University of Hong Kong also provided the linguistic environment that enabled Chang to perfect her English writing skills. In fact, she made a commitment to only writing in English during the time she was in Hong Kong, to the extent that when she returned to Shanghai in 1942 and tried to enroll in St. John's University she failed to get in because her Chinese grades were too low. But her English was so good that her early paid writings were film criticism pieces she wrote in 1942 for the only English language daily in Shanghai at the time, *Shanghai Times*. She also wrote essays for magazines for the English readership in China on aspects of Chinese life. Essays such as "Chinese Life and Fashions" (1943), published in *The XXth Century*, demonstrated her increasing awareness of how the mundane in Chinese culture could interest foreigners. Furthermore, the sojourn in Hong Kong enabled her to look at her native city from a distance—a crucial factor in developing her sensibility to Shanghainese culture. In her 1943 essay "Shanghainese, After All" (到底是上海人, 1943),[13] she shows how she came to really understand the Shanghainese by contrasting them with people from Hong Kong. Much like the present day, in Eileen Chang's time these were the two most cosmopolitan and exciting cities in Greater China. Clearly, her time in Hong Kong allowed her to gather much material and inspiration for her subsequent creative writing.

In the few years after she returned to Shanghai in 1942, Eileen Chang produced several short stories that catapulted her to celebrity status as a young fiction writer. Her hugely popular "debut work" "Love in a Fallen City" (傾城之戀, 1943) is rare among her fiction because it can be read as a romance with a happy ending. The story is also significant because barely a year after it was published, a script for "Love in a Fallen City" written by Eileen Chang was staged successfully, demonstrating her ability to write across a variety of genres. The first chapter of this volume is on male-female relations in "Love in a Fallen City," and Chapter 2 focuses on how the play has been rewritten for contemporary audiences in Hong Kong and cities in North America. In Chapter 1, I describe how the young Chang was quite different from other more "mainstream" writers of the time in her portrayal of romance and men, particularly Westernized men. Indeed, even though she saw her stories as "romances" (傳奇), her views were highly pragmatic and almost unromantic in terms of the characters' attitudes to love and marriage. The adaptation of the short story for the stage so soon after the former appeared is telling, but more significantly, in Chapter 2 Jessica Li demonstrates how its "new" version shows that Chang's works are, with few alterations, still highly relevant in a totally different culture and time. The changes to the story, while small, are significant: in contemporary Hong Kong, the female search for true love is paramount—diverging from the original story's emphasis on marriage as the ultimate goal.

While these romantic tales were influential and helped propel Chang to fame, her more tragic stories demonstrated to greater effect Chang's skills in character development and in portraying the stifling effects of family life. They are a cutting and merciless description of men and women and their relationships in a changing China. "The Golden Cangue" (1943) and "Red Rose, White Rose" (紅玫瑰與白玫瑰, 1944), published a couple of years after Chang's return to Shanghai from Hong Kong, reveal the moral disintegration of women (in the former story) and men (in the latter, also discussed in Chapter 1) caught up in a Shanghai on the cusp of transforming into a modern society in the early years of the twentieth century. There is no doubt that characters such as Cao Qiqiao in "The Golden Cangue" are some of the most memorable and iconic personalities in modern Chinese literature. Indeed, C. T. Hsia claims that Chang has successfully combined Chinese and Western styles of fiction writing in "The Golden Cangue," opining that this is "the greatest novelette in the history of Chinese literature."[14] Certainly, Qiqiao encapsulates very effectively the frustrations and destructiveness of a woman who is situated in a modernizing world but trapped in a stifling traditional family. According to Eileen Chang's brother Zijing, Cao Qiqiao is based on a real aunt, a capable village girl who was married into the Zhang family through marriage to an uncle who had rickets. Apparently, Eileen Chang's portrayal of this woman is accurate.[15]

Unlike her fictional creation Cao Qiqiao, Eileen Chang herself was not a victim of circumstance. She was determined to break free of the shackles of the family system that threatened to destroy her life, and at the same time to build her reputation as a writer. Following the success of "Love in a Fallen City" and "The Golden Cangue," Chang continued to produce a series of short stories such as "Shut Down" (封鎖, 1943), "Red Rose, White Rose," and "Waiting" (等, 1944). At around the same time, she also wrote a number of very influential essays such as "From the Mouths of Babes" (童言無忌, 1944) and "Whispers,"[16] expressing her innermost thoughts about her private life and the world around her. These essays invaluably document how a sensitive observer perceived everyday life in Japanese-occupied Shanghai. Even in occupied Hong Kong or Shanghai Chang's career blossomed, as indicated by the success of her stories. Her success in Japanese-occupied Shanghai showed that she was capable of operating easily in the Chinese-Western binary, but also in the milieu of Japanese occupation. As Nicole Huang shows in Chapter 3, she was an incredibly savvy operator who was able to bridge a variety of cultures and languages. Her popularity in Taiwan in later years suggests that she had pan-Asian tastes. This may be due to her ability to delight in the universal and sometimes sublime significance of the mundane, such as clothing. Not only did Chang have an eye for the everyday; her genius lay in her ability to delight in "romancing the ordinary"[17] even at times of social dislocation. As well as illustrating this point, Esther Cheung in Chapter 4 demonstrates how Chang's fiction and essays weave an intricate relationship between the literary, the mundane and gender. Cheung shows that this relationship is not just a "fashion show" that displays the surface of a shallow modern Shanghai, but can be traced to an ancient memory of Chinese antiquity.

With the publication of her early stories and essays, Eileen Chang won many admirers, one of whom was Hu Lancheng (胡蘭成), a cultured literatus who served in Wang Jingwei's puppet government. Holding an important government position as an undersecretary in the Ministry of Information, Hu had considerable influence in the cultural sphere. He was editor of the literary journal *Bitter Bamboo Monthly* (苦竹月刊), in which Eileen Chang had some essays published, including her response to critics of her work, most notably Fu Lei, who had earlier claimed that stories such as "Love in a Fallen City" were too ornate and lacking in substance.[18] When Hu met Chang he was already married. This did not stop him from pursuing her, and he published glowing essays in praise of his latest romantic interest. He describes Chang as a staunch upholder of individualism, and likens her to a goddess who places great value on both human beings and the material world.[19] A year later, he wrote another essay in which he compares Chang to the leftwing writers. He accuses the leftwing writers of promoting collectivism without understanding that collectives are made up of individuals and claims that in order to write about the masses well, one must know about relationships between individuals. That, he says, Chang does well.[20]

By the time this second essay was published in June 1945, Hu and Chang had already been married for nearly a year. Their courtship and ensuing doomed marriage would have been non-controversial had the times been normal. Indeed, Chang would have been happy with Hu Lancheng had he been a more devoted husband. But the times were abnormal, and though talented, Hu was powerful mainly because he was an official in the puppet regime that owed its existence to the invading Japanese. To make matters worse, when the Japanese were retreating and Hu had to go into hiding, he continued his womanizing ways and became romantically involved with other women even after Chang had sent him money to help him survive. Her deep sense of betrayal comes through in her recollections of this period. In Chapter 5, Shen Shuang points out that one reason the readership in the Mainland has been so fascinated by Eileen Chang in recent years could be because the Mainland is still feeling the effects of the Cultural Revolution, when stories of betrayal by family members and close friends were widespread. Shen uses Chang's narratives to explore the relationship between the sense of betrayal, historical memories, and the formation of the Chinese identity. She goes beyond the conventional perception of betrayal as immoral or unethical, and demonstrates how Chang's case shows that it is best understood in historical and personal contexts.

Even though her writings have experienced a revival in recent decades in the Sinophone world, including Mainland China, Eileen Chang's life as wife of a Japanese collaborator and her insistence on being "apolitical" made her unwelcome in Communist China after 1949, although her literary talents did help her to lead a reasonably successful life there for a couple of years under the new regime. In fact she published the novel *Eighteen Springs* (十八春) in 1950, and even participated in the inaugural Writers' and Artists' Conference in Shanghai in 1950. But in 1952 she went back to Hong Kong, where she worked for the United States Information Service, and wrote the novel *The Rice-Sprout Song* (1955) in English.[21] Produced in the opening stages of the Cold War, the novel could be considered a propaganda work showing the widespread suffering being experienced in China. In the same vein, Chang also finished the novel *Love in Redland* (赤地之戀), which she subsequently translated into English as *Naked Earth* (1956).[22] In these works she again demonstrated her ability to manage two entirely different languages and cultures. She then went to America in 1955, where, apart from a short spell in Taiwan in 1960–62, she remained until her death in 1995. In America, Chang spent some years immersing herself in classical Chinese literature. She loved English literature, but was also thoroughly conversant with traditional Chinese fiction, which she adored. When she obtained some short-term research positions at universities in America such as the University of California, Berkeley and Miami University in Ohio, she translated *The Sing-song Girls of Shanghai* (海上花列傳, 1894) and researched the novel *Dream of the Red Chamber* (紅樓夢, 1792). Such academic work was probably considered "safe" given the Cold War climate of the time. As Wang Xiaojue indicates in Chapter 6, Chang's *Dream of the Red Chamber* research and forays into screenwriting are best appreciated in the wider context of Cold War politics and how they affected diasporic writing across disparate languages and cultures.

In stark contrast to her self-proclaimed haste to publish and become famous when she was younger, the semi-autobiographical works Chang wrote in adulthood literally took years to appear. The most significant work (if only because it resulted in the film that launched her twenty-first century international fame) is "Lust, Caution,"[23] a short tale that underwent several revisions before being published in 1978. As noted above, the story twists the martyrdom of the beautiful secret agent Zheng Pingru (1918–40) into a tale of betrayal. Zheng failed to assassinate Wang Jingwei's security chief Ding Mocun; she was executed, but never betrayed her comrades. However, in "Lust, Caution," the heroine warns her lover/would-be victim moments before the assassination attempt, and he escapes. He quickly rounds up all the conspirators (including the heroine) and has them executed. Critics such as Cai Dengshan have written in depth about the historical events to reflect on Chang's complicated love affairs and marriages in complex political intrigues and times,[24] and other critics have also comprehensively explored the connections between and controversies surrounding Eileen Chang's story and Ang Lee's film.[25]

Neither the story nor the historical incident would have come to international attention but for the fact that Ang Lee chose to make a film based on this tale of multiple betrayals. And, to borrow a phrase from Lee Haiyan, Ang Lee's film successfully shows how the collaborator security chief gets "under the skin"[26] of the young protagonist Wang Jiazhi by way of a series of explicit sadomasochistic scenes in the movie. When he gives her an expensive diamond ring at the climactic point just before the assassination, she momentarily believes that this sadistic security chief is in love with her and warns him to escape; in so doing, she betrays her comrades, herself, and the nationalist cause. While Ang Lee has liberally reinterpreted the relationship between the heroine and her lovers/comrades, his film vividly captures the sexual-political dimensions of the story and makes explicit the many layers of betrayal that the story narrates.

The results of the "partnership" between two of the most talented artists in twentieth-century China in the production of the film is the focus of attention in Chapters 7 and 8 by Gina Marchetti and Hsiu-Chuang Deppman. Gina Marchetti's chapter plays on the idea of betrayal, showing how Lee's film goes beyond Chang and betrays its literary source. She shows how Lee appreciates the perspectives of all his characters, transforming Chang's anger toward Yi (and men of his ilk) into some form of understanding. Deppman by contrast shows that despite using different framing strategies, Chang and Lee "match" each other and in their different ways both present the issue of human cruelty extremely adroitly employing the resources at their disposal. Certainly, both the novel and the film are finely crafted works, and both are multi-layered, multi-vocal texts. However, even though the subtle psychological portrayals of the interplay between individual romantic reveries and the political demands of wartime nationalism may owe something to Eileen Chang's personal experiences, "Lust, Caution" is a work of fiction.

In real life, Eileen Chang actually married Hu Lancheng, even though the marriage did not last long. Despite a couple of attempts to save it, Hu Lancheng's infidelities and the collapse of the puppet regime that he served caused the couple to go their separate ways. After Japan surrendered, Eileen Chang was in danger of being officially charged with being a "cultural traitor"—indeed, this was a label she was given by some in Shanghai after the War ended—in the same way that Wang Jiazhi (and even the actress who played the role) in "Lust, Caution" has aroused unforgiving accusations of selling out. In June 1947, Eileen Chang divorced Hu Lancheng, who escaped to Japan in 1949. The story was published over thirty years after they separated, so if it was indeed a result of Chang's tumultuous marriage to Hu, it does seem he "got under her skin." Even though "Lust, Caution" underwent several revisions before it was published, it is a relatively short piece in the Chang oeuvre.

In the last decades of her life Eileen Chang was deeply involved in writing two long novels, one in Chinese and one in English. She began writing the Chinese work, the semi-autobiographical novel *Little Reunion* (小團圓), in the early 1970s. By July 1975, she had finished half of it. But the novel was only published posthumously in 2009. This was due mainly to the advice and intervention of her friend and quasi-literary agent Stephen Soong (宋淇), who feared that Hu Lancheng would profit from her fame or use her personal revelations to harm her.[27] Undoubtedly, fans will continue to speculate about the feelings Eileen Chang and Hu Lancheng had for each other or whether publishing *Little Reunion* before she died would have had any effect on Chang's reputation.[28] But as Pang Laikwan illustrates in Chapter 9, Chang's alter ego in the novel, Julie, seems to be most passionate towards the character in the novel that is Hu Lancheng's counterpart. Pang deftly looks at the dilemma of someone like Eileen Chang, who could be almost detached and merciless in her assessments of people but could at the same time create so lovingly and in such detail some of the most memorable characters in modern Chinese literature. Pang gives us a number of perspectives on the meaning of the term "*tuanyuan*" (團圓, reunion) and what it suggests about human relationships, especially those between the protagonist Julie and her mother and lover, who seem to be unambiguously modelled on Eileen Chang's own mother and Hu Lancheng.

Cold war politics and other world tensions might have created in Chang a sense of insecurity about the possibility of personal and political betrayal. But as Sang Tze-lan shows in Chapter 10, instead of radically revising the manuscript of *Little Reunion*, as suggested by Stephen Soong, Chang chose to delay and withhold the novel from publication, effectively demonstrating her lack of concern about her "moral" reputation or whether she would be bothered by the ageing Hu. In this way, Eileen Chang seems to have transcended the conventional ideologies of motherhood and nationalism. If she was insecure about human relationships, it could have been due as much to her parents—a mother who "abandoned" her twice to go to Europe when she was very little, and a father who sided with her stepmother and beat her savagely—as to her failed marriage to Hu Lancheng. It could even be argued that she looked for a parental figure in her relationships. Hu Lancheng was fifteen years her senior and Ferdinand Reyher (1891–1967), her second husband whom she married in 1956, was thirty years older. More significantly, while Chang had herself worked for the American Information Service, which at that time was mostly concerned with fighting Communism, Reyher was known to be leftwing and sympathetic to the Communists, and a close collaborator of Bertolt Brecht. Coming at the height of the Cold War and fears about the Red Peril, this suggests that Chang was unconcerned about whether her private affairs would harm her reputation politically.

Unless her unpublished papers, which Roland Soong is now gradually making public, tell us otherwise, Chang's main concern in America was literally how to survive with minimal fuss. There is little to indicate that she was involved in social action in America, and she was probably even less active politically there than she had been in China. Even though Eileen Chang spent more than half her life in America and was married to Reyher for over ten years, and despite the fact that in recent years there have been waves of "Eileen Chang fever" and her life and works have been subjected to minute examination in Taiwan, Hong Kong, and Mainland China, there has been nothing major written about her life in America or her marriage to Reyher, apart from an excellent book by Sima Xin. C. T. Hsia remarks that the absence of even one photo of Reyher in Chang's book *Mutual Reflections: Looking at My Old Photo Album* (對照記：看老照相簿, 1994) is a "strange" situation.[29] In fact, this "strange" phenomenon seems to characterize the second, "American" half of Chang's life. She became more and more introverted, and did not say much about America at all, but instead repeatedly revised what she had written about her life as a young woman in Shanghai and Hong Kong, or translated and interpreted traditional Chinese novels such as *Dream of the Red Chamber* and *The Sing-song Girls of Shanghai*. She became increasingly reclusive, and by the end of her life was taking great precautions to avoid being bothered by visitors. Her introspection did produce some extremely enlightening novels. As early as the 1950s, she began writing the novel *The Book of Change* in English. This project was so large that it eventually became two books, with the first part becoming *The Fall of the Pagoda*. The two semi-autobiographical novels that resulted recapture Chang's memories from her earliest childhood until she returned to Shanghai from Hong Kong. She was never able to find a publisher for these books, and only in 2010 did they appear with Hong Kong University Press amid great anticipation and acclaim.

In Chapter 11, which focuses on these posthumously published works, David Wang shows that the way in which Eileen Chang repeats herself has given rise to a peculiar poetics, one that highlights not revelation but derivation. Because she was a sensitive person living in times of tumultuous cultural transformation, her sensitivities are worth relating, and they are worth examining. At a time when most writers were obsessed with the idea of saving or changing the Chinese nation or Chinese culture, Eileen Chang presents a personal story, one that she felt compelled to rehearse many times. She manages to reveal her feelings and thoughts not via the theme of revolution or national salvation so prevalent at that time, but through a deliberate involution in the telling of her life. One thing is sure: this singular voice will continue to appeal to readers, who will no doubt respond to it in their own individual ways.

The contributors to this volume have given their responses from different perspectives to different aspects of Eileen Chang's life and work. This is just a beginning. I hope we have done Eileen Chang justice and that more research on Chang and her times will follow.

1
Romancing Returnee Men

Masculinity in "Love in a Fallen City" and
"Red Rose, White Rose" *

Kam Louie

In 1918, Lu Xun asserted that whenever the country seemed on the verge of collapse, Chinese men would thrust their women forward as sacrificial victims to obscure their own cowardice and helplessness in the face of the onslaught of aggressors and rebels.[1] Examples of such behavior abound in modern Chinese fiction. Throughout the twentieth century, Chinese men could be said to have suffered a crisis of masculinity, and often proved incapable of living up to the models of masculinity provided by traditional heroic narratives. Leftwing writers such as Lu Xun saw Chinese men as useless mostly because Chinese tradition, especially Confucianism, was outdated and constituted a stumbling block in the path to modernization. Modernity was seen as Western, and hence, according to the social Darwinist logic so popular at the time, traditional Chinese society was doomed, waiting to be replaced by a superior Western model. Such attitudes meant that even though the intellectual climate in the first half of the twentieth century was vibrant and exciting, with both new and conventional ideas circulating and doing battle, there was a high degree of anxiety about the future of China and Chinese culture. For the young and forward-looking, Europe and America (as well as a "Westernized" Japan) were the ideal sites for obtaining the most useful and up-to-date ideas to "save" the nation.

Unlike most young intellectuals of the time, Eileen Chang did not seek truths that had national significance, but she did have a hunger for new and Western things, and she would have gone to Europe, as her mother had done, had not the Japanese invaded. Indeed, given the circumstances under which she lived, it is hard to conceive how Eileen Chang managed to consistently display

* I would like to thank the Hong Kong Research Grants Council's General Research Fund for providing support for me to carry out the work for this paper.

an apparent lack of interest in large-scale political issues. Like Jane Austen, to whom she is often compared, she was more adept at dissecting in minute detail the mundane things in life that affect human relationships. However, whereas Austen lived in rural England, in her most creative periods Eileen Chang lived in Hong Kong and Shanghai, the two cities that during her lifetime underwent some of the most dramatic transformations in human history. In Chang's time, these were the most outward-looking cities in a China in which the modern and the Western were regarded by many as civilized, and as clear models to emulate. They were also two sites in China that were highly cosmopolitan, with people from all corners of the earth transiting or living there. In fact, Shanghai was occupied by Japan and Hong Kong was a British colony during Chang's time there. Given her penchant for describing male-female relations, and her preoccupation with both Chinese and Anglophone cultures, this chapter explores Chang's observations of Chinese men who had to varying degrees been "Westernized," Chinese men who were born or sojourned in Europe, and who returned to China in search of the good life.

Discerning readers generally agree that Eileen Chang's perceptive appraisals of the modern urban woman and her fate are among the finest in modern Chinese literature, and critics have understandably tended to concentrate on her women characters such as Qiqiao in "The Golden Cangue" (金鎖記, 1943). While Chang was perhaps at her best when she described women, I want to focus my discussion on the men in her fiction. Many critics claim or imply that the men in Chang's fiction tend to be mostly broken men addicted to opium and reliant upon family wealth to maintain their dissolute lifestyles. Zhang Junli for example begins her essay "The Masculine World in Eileen Chang's Fiction" by making the point that, in Chang's fiction, the men are usually depicted as useless old fogies and young diehards who spend their time bemoaning the loss of the good times of the Qing dynasty.[2] In fact, as noted above, this portrayal of Chinese men as self-indulgent, self-pitying, or self-absorbed was a common theme in Chinese literature throughout the Republican era. Through a discussion of Chang's depiction of Chinese men who had returned from Europe, I will examine whether the useless Chinese men syndrome was only applicable to indigenous Chinese men, or whether being Westernized was seen as having made any difference to their fundamental character.

Writers as diverse as Qian Zhongshu and Yu Dafu produced a gallery of returned overseas students with fake qualifications, whose vanity led them to chase after empty glory or whose insecurities led to paralysis. Such returnee male writers were certainly not flattering when describing their own kind. Did women have a more favorable impression of Westernized Chinese men or male returnees? I attempted to answer this question in my essay on Ding Ling's "Miss Sophie's Diary" (莎菲女士的日記), in which I suggested that in 1927 Ding Ling was already disillusioned with the slick, English-speaking returnee. Miss Sophie was infatuated with such a man, but as soon as she kissed him she found him revoltingly common and decided to abandon him.[3] In some ways, it could be argued that my analysis of Ling Jishi, the object of desire in "Miss Sophie's Diary," is flawed because he has returned not from "the West" but from Singapore, and the Chinese conception of *nanyang* (南洋, Southeast Asia) is full of contradictions. Thus, even though Ling Jishi speaks fluent English, he is not Western as such. In fact, Eileen Chang's stories, being mostly set in Hong Kong and Shanghai, are populated by ethnic Chinese who have returned from Europe, America, and Southeast Asia. Clearly, the degree to which the returnee is "Westernized" depends to a large extent on where he originated and how long he has been abroad. In this paper, I will try to clarify these points where they have an impact on the characterization of the men being examined.

Elsewhere, I have investigated to some extent the different perceptions of Chinese masculinity as it travels abroad. The piece on "Miss Sophie's Diary" focuses on how Chinese women might have looked at the returnee Chinese man in the context of the *wen-wu* matrix. By exploring Eileen Chang's writings, this chapter offers another look at how educated young women in China might have regarded Chinese men who returned to China from abroad, this time in the decade leading up to 1949. Unlike socially active May Fourth writers such as Ding Ling, Eileen Chang seemed apolitical, an individual who was only concerned with personal matters. Ironically, however, she was probably more worldly than most of the other writers of her time, and less constrained in her writing by the myriad "isms" that increasingly came to dominate China over the decades. Eileen Chang lived through some of the most tumultuous times in China's history, but while most writers such as Ding Ling took up the pen to describe great events such as revolution and national movements, Eileen Chang herself claimed that "all I really write about are some of the trivial things that happen between men and women. There is no war and no revolution in my works."[4] However, she uses the "trivial" to comment on human sensibilities during great social movements, and she is deservedly famed for her narrative strategy of using everyday objects as metaphors and providing a rich and detailed tapestry of Shanghai and Hong Kong life at a time of great social upheaval, when most other writers were concentrating on the grand and the abstract. Thus, Eileen Chang's approach to her art was very different, even in comparison to that of other women writers such as Ding Ling. But despite that difference, Ding Ling and Eileen Chang shared much common ground: they were almost contemporaries and their most influential works were written between 1919 and 1949. Most importantly, they were both educated young women who had an intense interest in and expressed well the modern relationships between men and women. Their radically different approaches to life only make their assessments of men all the more poignant.

Other chapters in this volume show that Eileen Chang was indeed very astute in her observations not only about mundane matters, but also about how these matters influenced and were a reflection of major political events of the time. I will show that her depictions of Westernized men also reflect her feelings about other aspects of life in China at that time: pity and despair. This lack of confidence in "Westernization" as a panacea for the low self-esteem experienced by Chinese male writers and low estimation of their men by female writers has important implications. It indicates that if Chinese masculinity had taken a battering in modern times, a Western veneer was not going to save it, at least in the eyes of Ding Ling and Eileen Chang, two of the best writers of the twentieth century. Solutions would have to come from within. Since space is limited, for clarity's sake, I will focus my analysis on "Love in a Fallen City" (傾城之戀, 1943) and "Red Rose, White Rose" (紅玫瑰與白玫瑰, 1944). These stories by Eileen Chang were produced at a particularly poignant time, with the country in the midst of Japanese invasion and occupation.

How does someone brought up overseas compare with the pathetic male specimens in China in Chang's estimation? This is demonstrated more clearly in "Love in a Fallen City," in which the protagonist Fan Liuyuan is a Sinicized Westerner, whereas the reverse is true of the male protagonist of "Red Rose, White Rose," Tong Zhenbao. Liuyuan is thus an even better model for a Western male culture in Chinese skin than Zhenbao. Here, social dislocation enables the dissolution and disintegration of all the standard dichotomies and cultural norms. So at least in terms of desirability, these two models of masculinity were ranked extremely highly by their contemporaries: Zhenbao was an "ideal modern Chinese man"[5] and Liuyuan was like "the prize the whole crowd was eyeing like so many greedy tigers."[6] By examining these two characters created by one of the most astute observers of human relations in modern Chinese literature, I hope to show that these "ideals" fall short of traditional or modern models. This is not surprising. Eileen Chang's ruthless and cynical examination of human weaknesses and self-interest is legend. In Liuyuan and Zhenbao, she again reveals that despite the social acclaim they both receive from their good social positions and university educations, their gentlemanly image is only a veneer. Beneath that desirable gloss are two men whose motivations and self-seeking behavior are no different from those of the other men Chang readily dismisses.

In my work on the ideal of Chinese masculinity, I have advanced *wen-wu* (文武, cultural attainment and physical prowess) as the dyadic ideal that Chinese men are meant to have achieved to be attractive.[7] *Wen* is generally attained through education, traditionally officially acquired through success in the civil service examinations, and *wu* through mastery of the martial arts or physical skills. The protagonist of "Love in a Fallen City," Liuyuan, has neither *wen* nor *wu* in the traditional sense. In fact, he is known as a man of leisure whose claim to fame is that he inherited a large fortune from his father's overseas businesses. Thus, it seems that *wen-wu* has no place in the story in terms of masculine ideals, which is demonstrated by the fact that the women all blatantly want to marry or have their daughters marry Liuyuan because of his money rather than his learning or physical attributes. And, surprisingly, it is Bai Liusu, a divorcee who is no longer young, who gets the prize. By the end of the story, Eileen Chang makes the point that the social dislocation brought about by the war has led to some unlikely marital pairings. Before war was declared in Hong Kong, the conspicuous competition for Liuyuan, the most eligible of bachelors, by the society women, and his subsequent surprise union with Liusu, the least likely bridal candidate, suggest that the world has indeed turned upside down, and things no longer come together as they are supposed to.

But is the war really the reason that this, of all Eileen Chang's stories, seems to have a happy ending? Chang herself describes the story as having a happy ending—and as a comedy, a genre that is rare for her. Is this purely a trivial romantic story that provokes a wry smile and nothing more? The ending has been found wanting by a number of critics, with Fu Lei describing the story as implausible soon after it first appeared. Fu Lei considered the story superficial because Chinese writers and readers at the time did not fully appreciate Western conventions of comedy.[8] A more recent Eileen Chang critic, Shui Jing, claims that the story is in fact a parody, reflecting classic novels such as *Dream of the Red Chamber* (紅樓夢) and *The Plum in the Golden Vase* (金瓶梅). It is probably true that most Chinese readers do not understand the concept of parody because it is a Western genre not often found in Chinese literature, traditional or modern, and "Love in a Fallen City" can be read as a parody of *chuanqi* (傳奇, traditional Chinese romances). To a large extent, this is a good reading, as Eileen Chang certainly goes to some lengths to invoke traditional tales of this sort, as other essays in this volume show. Here, Liusu's mimicking of the classical opera singer's postures certainly suggests tales of the classical femme fatale whose beauty causes empires to fall (thus the fall of the city), a theme so common in these operas. Yet, Liusu herself would have been amused by this vision, as she is acutely aware that, as a divorcee of twenty-eight, her desirability is fast fading.

But I believe we can generalize Eileen Chang's observations even further, as Chang herself was cynical about human motivations. It could even be said that the tale is a parody of life itself rather than just a parody of the *chuanqi* tales. Indeed, one of the adjectives Eileen Chang uses plentifully in her writings—and critics have often used to describe her—is *huangliang* (荒涼, desolation). Understandably, this word seems to describe Eileen Chang's attitude to life as full of solitary despair and she does describe women who end up living in almost tragic loneliness. But to me, desolation is Chang's perception of the human condition mercilessly described; humanity stripped and exposed. As noted earlier, in my work on the Chinese masculine ideal, I propose *wen-wu* as a construct by which men are measured. Since this dyad is applicable only to Chinese culture, it deems those outside this cultural context not fit to measure. In this way, *wen-wu* does not apply to Liuyuan, since he was born and raised outside China. But Eileen Chang does in fact give him a *wen* veneer, and he tries very hard to prove that he is a *wen* person in the traditional Chinese sense. Without discussing his motivations, he emphasizes that he is looking for a woman with traditional Chinese values. Even Liusu reflects that if that really were the case he would not be wooing a divorced woman, who was the only person in a party of women who could dance with him in the "lewd" modern style. Notwithstanding all this, perhaps he is genuinely sick of modern Hong Kong and Shanghai girls and wants to settle down. Maybe the mothers and other women at the time were not concerned about *wen-wu* accomplishments, but Liuyuan certainly is. He goes so far as to show off his *wen* skills by reciting a verse from the poem "Beating the War Drums" (邶風‧ 擊鼓) in *The Book of Songs* (詩經):

> 死生契闊 Facing life, death, distance,
> 與子成說 I still delight in your company.

執子之手 Holding your hand in mine,
與子偕老 I will grow old with you.[9]

Tellingly, he recites the second line differently from the original in *The Book of Songs*, using 與子相悅 rather than the original 與子成說.[10] This misquoted line has now become so common that many people write the quatrain in the way Eileen Chang wrote it here. This is understandable since 說 was an alternate character for 悅 (meaning happiness; both could be pronounced "yue"). But 與子相悅 and 與子成說 mean quite different things, with Eileen Chang's version implying that the lovers take pleasure in each other's company, whereas the original says that they make a promise to be true to each other. Liuyuan (or Eileen Chang) may have deliberately used the wrong word here, so that he says let's enjoy each other's company now, without the suggestion of a promise. Or maybe Eileen Chang, like so many other writers who cite classical poetry, had simply forgotten the verse and used the wrong words in the text when she wrote the story, even though she clearly knows the right version because she uses the correct words in her essay on writing this story, "Writing of One's Own" (自己的文章, 1944).[11] Whatever the intent, the story does show that Liuyuan gets the quote wrong, so he is not a "genuine" Chinese connoisseur of things Chinese as he tries to make out.

Fortunately for Liuyuan, Liusu does not correct him. Instead, even before he recites the lines, she says she does not understand. This is because he begins by saying that "In *The Book of Songs* there is a verse—"[12] and the mere mention of this classic is enough to cause Liusu to protest that she does not know about such things. In fact, while Liuyuan plays the role of man-of-the-world, she acts coy and ignorant, to display the virtues that traditional Chinese women are meant to possess (Liuyuan has already told her that he is after a real Chinese woman). These lines of poetry may have come from *The Book of Songs*, but they are standard lines quoted at weddings, and even people with no formal education would be familiar with them. It is very unlikely that someone like Liusu, who has already been married once, and who would give anything to be married again, would never have heard them. Yet, Liuyuan immediately accepts her declaration of ignorance and adopts the all-knowing masculine role, declaring "I know you don't understand . . . If you understood, I wouldn't need to explain!"[13] He proceeds to explain that the poem indicates that human beings are so pathetically small compared to the great forces in the world that they cannot really influence the course of events.

Some critics have pointed out that it is unlikely that Liuyuan, who was born and raised in England, would have been able to recite from *The Book of Songs*.[14] Granted, he may not have learnt the verse off by heart. However, as a playboy it makes sense that he has memorized these phrases associated with everlasting love and weddings in order to ingratiate himself with women. Eileen Chang uses this episode to illustrate the typical pattern of male-female interaction at the time. The man was supposed to have *wen* (文, literary) skills and the woman to be ignorant and impressed by learning, especially knowledge of traditional arts such as classical poetry. The episode also shows that "cultural" expertise such as reciting poetry was a common tool in the game of love in pre-war Hong Kong. Modern China was a place where "conquering" women was possible by reciting clichéd lines. Right on cue, Liusu plays the role of the uneducated woman and declares that she does not understand, giving Liuyuan an opportunity to expound on his learning and philosophy.

Liuyuan would not have used the poem as part of his seduction armory if he had known it well and remained true to its spirit. This poem from *The Book of Songs* relates the plight of a soldier who was unable to keep his vow to his beloved because he follows his general into battle. Although they win the battle, the soldier is left behind, unable to return, and will most likely die in the field instead of returning to hold the hand of his beloved as he promised. Taken as a whole, the poem has a tone of "pessimistic hopelessness."[15] And in this context, the lines cited by Liuyuan are tragic because they recall a promise that was made but was unable to be honored because of war. Most painfully, when the battle is won, the soldier is "betrayed" by his own side and cannot fulfill his promise. If Eileen Chang had really meant the story to be a happy one, these tragic lines would bring a sadness that was contrary to her intentions. On the other hand, it may be that just as Liuyuan does not really remember the words correctly, Eileen Chang herself has only remembered the oft-quoted lines rather than the whole poem. Ironically, in "Love in a Fallen City," the many layers of the poem ultimately become reality. There is a war, the lovers do hold hands, and they do marry. Whether they will live happily ever after is beyond the topic of our discussion here.

In the context of a playboy wanting to demonstrate his *wen* accomplishments to a "traditional Chinese woman" who simply does not understand or who feigns incomprehension, these poetic lines are uncannily appropriate. It is clear that Liusu's journey to Hong Kong was initiated and managed by Liuyuan so he could seduce her. And he stages the settings to display his "philosophical" concerns about constancy and eternity. Not long before he cites the verse from *The Book of Songs*, the flirtations between the two in this vein have played out, at the retaining wall of the Repulse Bay Hotel. At this spot, Liuyuan makes the observation that perhaps when human civilization has been completely destroyed, Liusu will care about him. It is unlikely that he has not used such natural objects as the moon, the sea, and an ancient wall before to target women's hearts. Sure enough, after his declaration at the wall that all he wants is to be understood, Liusu softens and believes that all he wants is platonic love, and that such love could lead to marriage. Thus, he has clearly succeeded in "conquering" Liusu.

But what is interesting is that here we have an overseas man portrayed as more knowledgeable about Chinese culture than the locals. As noted above, some critics consider this an indication that Eileen Chang has not painted a fully believable character. But as I have argued elsewhere, the mastery of popular jingles by foreign learners of Chinese is not an unusual phenomenon.[16] This twist in who can recite Chinese poetry is brilliant because it shatters the traditional understanding of *wen-wu* masculinity, in which foreigners, like women, are meant to be outside the realm of those who can achieve *wen-wu* excellence. This story destroys not only the concept of *wen-wu* masculinity, but the cultural norms as well. In contemporary Sinology in particular, the Chinese who come into contact with "foreigners" often proclaim exaggerated admiration for the latters' mastery of Chinese language and/or culture. Yet there is nothing unusual or abnormal in this kind of intellectual understanding. The idea that Chinese texts, no matter how ancient, can only be understood by indigenous Chinese living in China is absurd. In fact, Westernized Chinese, and even non-ethnic Chinese, can gain just as great an understanding as those who live in China. Besides, rote learning is not confined to any ethnic group.

As the story unfolds, Liuyuan is proven right. Humans are not entirely in control of events, but through natural turns of events and against all expectations, the couple gets married. Indeed, the story has a form of "happy ending" because this occurs in a city that has fallen. To use an oft-quoted line that Eileen Chang wrote about the Hong Kong bombings and her time at the University of Hong Kong during the eighteen-day siege of Hong Kong, "It was intolerable to most people, and that is why they were so anxious to grasp on to something solid, and that's why they got married."[17] Holding onto something tangible at a time of extreme uncertainty may be understandable, but it does not guarantee stability. By the same token, many marriages also fall apart and families break up in wartime. Thus, by the end of "Love in a Fallen City," Liusu has married Liuyuan as planned, and we can consider that this is a consequence of the world being turned upside down. As soon as the war is over, the situation will return to normal and it can be assumed that Liuyuan will no longer be the great lover he is portrayed as here.

However, it could be argued that understanding is something that is intuitive and not learnt. Liusu's understanding is much more down-to-earth and genuine. Her response to Liuyuan, after a thoughtful silence, is "just say, flat out, that you don't want to marry me, and leave it at that!"[18] Indeed, in the end, she has to all intents and purposes given up and decided to be his mistress, living in a house he has rented and with a maid he has hired. This would make her a lady of leisure, but she would have no legal status in modern China. Liusu is aware of this predicament, and asks Liuyuan to understand her position and adopt a more practical approach to their relationship. All the gentlemanly rituals of wooing her are simply that a courtship dance carefully choreographed but offering no more commitment than a "real" traditional Chinese man would make to a concubine or kept woman. After all, the concubine system was only outlawed in Hong Kong in 1970, and taking concubines was common in 1940s.

In Chen Bingliang's chapter on "Love in a Fallen City," Luo Xiaoyun points out that the old world—represented by Liusu's first husband—has died, never to return,[19] and that this is a story about how a woman survives in the new society. In fact, the fallen city is not just Hong Kong, but rather is representative of all of Chinese civilization. Scenes such as the Repulse Bay Hotel retaining wall and the promise to be true for eternity serve to highlight the transience of life, and how things disappear, with only nostalgia remaining. In this ever-changing world, how does one survive? According to Luo, Liusu hankers after constancy, which is evident in her observance of opera steps, mimicking the opera singer's postures when the huqin player in the street starts up. But Luo also claims that in contrast to Miss "Black," the Indian princess Saheiyini in the story (hei meaning "black" in Chinese), who really has no home to return to, Chinese women such as Miss White (Liusu's surname Bai means white) can still seek constancy and participate in traditional activities such as weddings and homemaking. Luo believes that in a similar manner, Eileen Chang, through little people such as Liusu, is trying to capture some stability and constancy in a collapsing world. But she is aware that this is not possible, and that is her "tragedy."[20]

It seems that everybody in this tale is after an illusory ideal. Liuyuan is a Chinese who is "not really Chinese," and that is why he chooses Liusu and vehemently insists that she is a traditional Chinese woman. Whether she is or not is irrelevant. He insists that she is making his "conquest" all the more satisfying. Because he resides mostly in Shanghai and Hong Kong, the people he meets are likely to be Westernized (modernized) to some extent. Liusu is thus deliberately cast (by him) as the original Chinese. And he claims to want to take her to the primitive natural environment of Malaysia, into the jungle. He is thus doing more than just juxtaposing China/West simplistically as dichotomies such as cultured/primitive and rational/passionate. Malaysia is neither China nor Europe: it is another colonized space that is neither East nor West, another British colony that is an in-between space. Eileen Chang exposes and deconstructs such dichotomies as farces. No matter how astute Liusu is, in the end Liuyuan wins out. He still wins her. However, even though the marriage certificate is obtained, the world is still in chaos, and chaos can take away as well as give. In the same way that a fallen city can give rise to an unexpected wedding, it can also render a marriage meaningless. Not long after the wedding, Liuyuan leaves for Southeast Asia and Liusu is left to live the life of a kept woman, in fact if not in law.

The in-between space of Hong Kong, at a time when the world was being turned upside down, provides the perfect location and time to situate this story. The choice of this particular location and this particular time makes the contrast between East and West even more stark. Here we have whites, Indians, and overseas Chinese. And, of course, later on the Japanese presence, though not seen, is also very much in evidence. This was a part of the world that Eileen Chang knew as a student at the University of Hong Kong. Here, differing cultures, and the old and the new, clash. Everyone is trying to understand how the other works. It is a place for those on the lookout for a "real" Chinese woman or those who are seeking to discover their own selves.

As Leo Lee points out, as a "playboy suitor" and womanizer, Liuyuan is by definition unlikely to want to marry Liusu.[21] Yet marriage is precisely Liusu's ultimate goal. In realistic terms, you could not find a more mismatched couple. Yet the whole story is about the reconciliation of their opposing wants. Other critics such as Fu Lei and Shui Jing simply claim that Chang's portrayals of the main characters are an indication that she did not really know how to develop the personality of the Casanova Liuyuan (as if Liuyuan were a real person!). Eileen Chang was only twenty-two when she wrote "Love in a Fallen City," and Fu Lei was almost condescending in his assertion that the author was flippant and did not know how to control the character—that what emerges is not a disciplined creation. Perhaps Fu Lei is right to assert that the characters are not fully developed and that what could have been a very good story was allowed to become shallow. But the popularity of the story, even before the release of the film *Lust, Caution* (色，戒, dir. Ang Lee, 2007), demonstrates that, whether Fu Lei was right or wrong, the story certainly appeals to readers.

Nevertheless, published in 1944, Fu Lei's was the first major critique of Eileen Chang's first significant literary piece, and it probably wounded her so much that she was very careful about what she wrote in future. In the story "Red Rose, White Rose," she seems to have made a deliberate effort at character development. If "Love in a Fallen City" shows the Westernized Chinese male as a Casanova with little substance, "Red Rose, White Rose" is even harsher in its judgment of the "modern" Westernized Chinese. The title and opening sentences of the story suggest that it is ostensibly about two types of woman. "There were two women in Zhenbao's life: one he called his white rose, the other his red rose. One was a spotless wife, the other a passionate mistress."[22] But there is no question that it is the life of the male protagonist Zhenbao that is primarily being examined in this story.

Eileen Chang wastes no time in introducing this "ideal modern Chinese man." Zhenbao, who received a university education in the West and now holds a high-level post in a foreign textile factory, is married to a pretty, gentle college graduate and has a young daughter. He is a filial son, a helpful sibling, and is true and generous to his friends and colleagues. In short, "Zhenbao's life was a complete success."[23] The critic Shui Jing describes the story as the only one of Eileen Chang's works to focus on the male character. Perhaps Chang wanted to respond to Fu Lei's charge that she did not delve deeply enough into characterization or character development in her earlier work "Love in a Fallen City," because in "Red Rose, White Rose" there is certainly much discussion of the state of mind of Zhenbao, to the extent that critics devote considerable attention to his Freudian state. And he does (superficially) change as a man during the course of the story. From being a perfect man, he makes the slow descent towards becoming a corrupt, useless man, who is "perfect" once again by the end of the story. In Zhenbao, Eileen Chang has created a male equivalent of the women in her stories, by portraying a man who is transformed by society from being a self-assured person into a warped individual with psychological problems. Other critics are also interested in Zhenbao because he is a good psychological study. But while these psychoanalytic readings are interesting in making sense of the seemingly oversimplified description of the two sides of a man, what Eileen Chang has done is to provide a parody not only of the simple dichotomies, but of the man himself.

Chang seems to have neatly adopted dichotomous personalities in her two returned Chinese men that match the neat female "red rose"/"white rose" distinction. This in turn matches the dichotomy between "Chinese" and "Western" in both men and women. The Red Rose is passionate and impulsive, while the White Rose is restrained and conservative. The Red Rose character Wang Jiaorui is a Singaporean who was educated in England, while Zhenbao's wife, the White Rose Meng Yanli, is a traditional Chinese woman from a good family. The story is almost neatly divided into two halves, with the first half describing Zhenbao's affair with Jiaorui and the second half his marriage to Yanli and his growing moral disintegration. Needless to say, Jiaorui is depicted as young, lively and exuding sexuality. Even though she is married, she boldly expresses her desires and is prepared to leave her comfortable home for Zhenbao. By contrast, Yanli is prematurely old, dull, and by the end of the story resentfully trapped in a very unhappy marriage with no one to comfort her.

However, as Rey Chow demonstrates, "if we simply concentrate on 'red rose' and 'white rose' as metaphors for the women characters, something crucial will be missed. The polarization of the two terms, Red Rose and White Rose, distracts attention from the fact that the women in Zhenbao's life are parts of a *series* of exchangeable, replaceable objects."[24] Chow's essay explores Eileen Chang's use of visual objects and metaphoric fantasy, thus prompting her perceptive comments on the objectification of women in the story. There is no doubt that Eileen Chang is best at revealing, even metaphorically, the relationship between the feminine and the social and political changes besetting China at the time. My focus in this essay, however, is firmly on the expression of masculinity, and the women characters are therefore seen here as an extension of Zhenbao's world.

As a Chinese man new to Europe, Zhenbao's first connection with a woman is with a prostitute; as he spends more time there, he goes out with the first Red Rose, a young woman whose father is a white Englishman married to a Cantonese woman. They live in Edinburgh and their Anglo-Chinese daughter is actually called Rose. Rose is full of passionate intensity and is deeply in love with Zhenbao. Had he stayed in Edinburgh longer, perhaps he would have changed and become more spontaneous. But he rejects Rose and returns to China. There, he aims to be seen as upright and respectable. But he gradually adopts a lifestyle presumably common to men at that time—hypocritical and dissolute—so that, by the end of the story, visiting prostitutes has become a way of life for him. Ultimately, Zhenbao transforms from a filial son, dutiful brother and supportive friend into an irresponsible father, disloyal husband, and dishonest brother and friend. He becomes morally bankrupt.

In this way, the male protagonist in "Red Rose, White Rose," though seemingly Westernized, is totally moribund in the Chinese moral framework. As soon as he gets back to China, the corruption and social dislocation surrounding him envelop him, and in the end he becomes no better than all the other immoral and pathetic men in Eileen Chang's fiction. Western education has made him a respectable man, but that respectability only serves to expose what lies underneath the pretensions of filial piety and being a good husband. The man is at best a fraud and at worst simply what is to be expected in Chinese society. I will show that while this stereotypical divide is superficial and clichéd, Chang provides sufficient subtlety in the characterizations that this formulation does not descend into simplistic binaries of irreconcilable "cultures" of East and West; male and female; moral and immoral; educated and uneducated—or, indeed, even the neat Red Rose-White Rose dyad. By the time the mixed-blood Rose is transformed into the Singaporean Jiaorui, who is not really "the East," neither is she "the West," as she is Southeast Asian. If anything, she is the symbol of the mixing, muddying and in-between states that colonial experiences produce.

In "Miss Sophie's Diary," the Westernized man, who is also Singaporean, becomes unlikable and not a "real man" almost as soon as Sophie kisses him. This instant of familiarity breeds contempt, and the Westernized Chinese is caught out, conquered by a Sophie who is about to be awakened to the warmer climate and politics of the south. However, Zhenbao and his women are already based in the south. He descends into corruption quickly, but his women descend even further, with Jiaorui divorcing and Yanli becoming a manic-depressive. There is no salvation for anyone. Zhenbao is, even with his Western education and time in the UK, just like every other Chinese man—morally corrupt and not only unable to protect, but positively harmful towards, his women. When Jiaorui courageously tells her husband of her affair with Zhenbao, hoping that the latter will marry her, Zhenbao unfeelingly discards her because he considers that marrying a divorcee under such circumstances would hurt his career. Eileen Chang's world is thus a truly desolate sort of place.

Interestingly, in Zhang Junli's analysis of Eileen Chang's representations of Chinese men, she discusses "Red Rose, White Rose" but does not mention

"Love in a Fallen City." Perhaps the male protagonist here, Liuyuan, is not quite Chinese, since he was born in Europe and it is said that his childhood was so irregular that it warped him. By contrast, Zhenbao is totally Chinese, and only studied overseas as an adult, so that the Western experience—though formative—only served to give him a Western education rather than forming his personality. It is here that "Red Rose, White Rose" provides an interesting observation. Here, the returned man is the opposite of Liuyuan, in that he lived in England for some years but it did not change him very much. Whereas Liuyuan can be said to be a Sinicized Westerner, Zhenbao is a Westernized Chinese. He still ostensibly upholds traditional virtues such as filial piety and hard work, but he betrays his friend and has an affair with Red Rose, thus fulfilling the prophecy that one is always bored with one's White Rose wife and seeks love interests outside marriage.

From beginning to end, Zhenbao's main concern is to be a "good person"—a "good person" (好人) as opposed to a "real person" (真人).[25] Can we say that White Rose is a good person, and Red Rose a real person? At the end of the story, as Chen Bingliang points out, Zhenbao becomes a "good person again." What is this good person? According to the story, it is a boring, stereotypical person, yet one who also represents "Chinese" in the scheme of things, whereas Red Rose, be it the Anglo-Chinese Rose or the UK-born Jiaorui, is a "real" person with passionate feelings and a passion for life in general. Thus, the dichotomy of the Red and the White—wildly passionate versus deathly restrained—is not only between two stereotypes of women; it is also between man and woman, Western and Chinese, and indeed within Zhenbao himself.

But Chen Bingliang's whole thesis is that Zhenbao, rather than suffering from a fetish as proposed by Shui Jing, is a narcissist. Everything about him is narcissistic. Here then is someone who is filial, fraternal and loyal, but is ultimately exposed as someone who is only focused on himself. Chen Bingliang also points out that "Red Rose, White Rose" is the only Eileen Chang story that is narrated from the perspective of a Chinese man. This presents a sorry indictment of men, if all this filial piety, being good to colleagues, and fraternal responsibility boils down to looking after Number 1. To say that Zhenbao suffers from a psychological pathology called narcissism is simply psychobabble for saying he is unambiguously selfish and callous. In Zhenbao's case, he also tries to fool the world that he is a good person. This completely self-absorbed narcissistic individual is ultimately incapable of caring for anyone but himself, making him a complete mockery of what a "good man" should be.

If the pursuit of goodness in Chinese culture only leads a man to become an empty shell, devoid of any passion or genuine human feelings, what is left? Certainly, all of Chang's other minor male characters, who are presumably neither real nor good, are drug addicts, gamblers, or just plain useless. This is worse than Ximen Qing in the classic novel *The Plum in the Golden Vase*, who in the process of moral decline at least has some fun. Liuyuan is, to a certain extent, an echo of the Ximen Qing figure, a womanizer who is capable of having fun while trying to run a business. Ximen Qing presides over the loss of his family fortune and the decline of his family, but he is not so concerned about his own moral reputation. By contrast, throughout the course of the story, Zhenbao wants to be seen as good and respectable. This is because he "came from a poor family. If he hadn't struggled to rise in the world, he probably would have had to stand behind a counter in a shop, and then his whole existence would have been one tiny round of ignorance and stupidity."[26] In short, it is obtaining a degree in the West that gives him the chance to be interesting in life. He is a modern poor scholar who has had success in the examinations and has made good. But alas, he is very unlike the poor scholar in traditional talented scholar and beautiful maiden tales. His talents only allow him to slide into moral decline and bourgeois deception.

What Eileen Chang has created is thus a man who is from a poor family and who wants respectability. He may get it, but at his core he is not capable of being an ideal man. In my work on *wen-wu* masculinity, I have argued that, in modern times, it is possible for a scholar to possess *wen* in the sense that the *wen* attributes are transformed from classical learning into knowledge about business management and economics. The material content of what is learnt can change. However, one principle for this ideal that cannot be changed is that of control: control of others (so that one is a leader), but more importantly, self-control. The centrality of controlling others and self-control is so pervasive that Zhenbao unconsciously invokes it. Thus, when he talks about his first visit to a brothel in Paris, he gives the impression that even as a "boy" he was nonchalant and in command, when in reality the whole episode left him feeling nauseated. This experience was a turning point in his life. Because his initiation into sex was not a satisfying affair as he had anticipated, he decided that from then on he would be in charge in any sexual relationship, and take advantage of the woman. He went on to extrapolate this from the sexual domain to life in general, and resolved that he was going to be the "absolute master" of his world (even if Eileen Chang's authorial comment is that it is "that little pocket-size world of his").[27] Later, in his romance with Rose, his "first love," the Eurasian girl who is passionate and surrenders herself to him, he keeps his cool and resists her sexual advances, so "even he was surprised by his self-control."[28] He clearly boasts, no matter how "discreetly," about this, because his friends regard him as "a regular Liu Xiahui, a man who could keep perfectly calm with a beautiful woman in his lap."[29]

This mastery of his emotions serves him well. By the end of the story, he has become physically abusive towards his wife, although he maintains the façade of being a calm and stable husband in public, and even in front of his brother, so that his wife is considered to be a liar when she complains about his behavior. This is a "victory" for him, in that he has mastered his emotions so well that he can humiliate his hapless White Rose at will. To a certain extent, then, Zhenbao has worked out the true significance of *wen* masculinity, and despite his origins in a poor family, he has learnt to master self-control to control others. But Eileen Chang does not allow him to "enjoy" that mastery. He might have humiliated and dominated his wife Yanli by the end of the story, and he might have "stood there laughing silently," but it is an empty laugh, and even though the next day "he made a fresh start and went back to being a good man,"[30] it is clear that both the author and the reader (as well as Zhenbao himself) are meant to look at him with disgust and revulsion. The poor boy imitating bourgeois respectability can only ape that behavior. He is not and cannot be an ideal man.

But the real tragedy for Eileen Chang is that while she can describe the men in her novels very astutely, even if mostly with disdain, her women characters cannot escape the sad predicaments in which they find themselves. Perhaps they have been sacrificed by the men but, at best, they fail to find the happiness they seek. Either they are "wild" and therefore do not fit comfortably into conventional Chinese life, like the Red Rose Jiaorui, or they are trapped within the confines of the "home" like the White Rose Yanli. These are Eileen Chang's "happy" stories—others such as the "The Golden Cangue" portray some of the most abject and desolate souls in modern Chinese literature. Her women are simply destroyed by exploitative older women. A very interesting comparison can again be made with Ding Ling's Sophie, who some seventeen years earlier also romanced a returnee who spoke English and was highly Westernized. By the end of the story, Sophie also perceived the returnee man as a good-for-nothing. But she ran away to the warm south of China, rather than pining to go abroad or to find a rich husband. Ba Jin's protagonist in *Family* (家, 1933), Gao

Juehui, also runs away, which is a revolutionary path that was taken by many other intellectuals in pre-1949 China. Of course, it is difficult to say who led the more tragic lives in reality, but the story of romance with hybrid Westernized Chinese men has yet to be told in a happy light.

Unfortunately, these stories in which Eileen Chang tries to dissect the psychology of the Chinese male are very damning statements indeed on Chinese men. As Chang declares in her "Frank Comments on 'Love in a Fallen City'" (關於〈傾城之戀〉的老實話, 1944) she has written the story from the perspective of Liusu. But Liusu never really fully understood Liuyuan, and Eileen Chang claims that that was why she had no need to understand the character of Liuyuan completely. But Liuyuan is unable to face life's upsets, and spends his entire life drifting in an empty shell. Such people were common in China, "and not necessarily only among overseas Chinese."[31] In Eileen Chang's desolate universe, there are no genuinely good Chinese men. The men who populate her stories are leftovers from a defunct dynasty, consisting mostly of drug addicts, gamblers, loafers and no-hopers. Taken together, "Love in a Fallen City" and "Red Rose, White Rose" show that even when these men are born or educated overseas, they sink into a moral vacuum when they live in China.

Eileen Chang's writings reveal another facet of Chinese life before 1949. Her extremely pessimistic outlook on the human condition in China also performed a perhaps unintended political role. Leftist writers in pre-1949 China often verged on the juvenile in their inflexible classification of men and women as exploiter and exploited. Their emotional outbursts appealed to the young and juvenile at the time. Eileen Chang seems to have veered away from the overtly political, but her devastating critiques of the hypocrisies and falsehoods underlying the fundamental human experiences of love, marriage, and family life have probably done more to turn people away from the prevailing political scene than have the vast majority of leftist writers who were her contemporaries. China in the first half of the twentieth century experienced much social unrest. If Eileen Chang had sensitively depicted these social problems as belonging to another era, her readers may have treasured what they had and not wanted another revolution. But Eileen Chang's world seemed to confirm the nastiness that the "revolutionary literature" vehemently, and less sensitively, conveyed. No wonder, then, that so many people welcomed the idea of overthrowing the entire system and creating a new society, intangible and utopian though that may have been.

2
From Page to Stage

Cultural "In-betweenness" in (New) Love in a Fallen City

Jessica Tsui Yan Li

Eileen Chang's novella "Love in a Fallen City" (傾城之戀 hereafter LFC) has been regularly adapted into stage and film productions in many cities since its publication in Shanghai in 1943. Its adaptations can be considered as ongoing cultural re-creations, based on re-evaluation and re-contextualization in different places and historical periods. After the story's first publication, Eileen Chang rewrote it as a script for stage production that was performed successfully in Shanghai in 1944, demonstrating its popularity in Shanghai during the wartime period. Forty years later, Hong Kong film director Ann Hui made it into a film in 1984, the year that the People's Republic of China and Britain signed the agreement for the 1997 handover of Hong Kong's sovereignty.[1] In 1987, 2002, and 2005, the Hong Kong Repertory Theatre (hereafter HKRT) adapted the story for stage performances, with elements of singing and ballroom dancing included in the latest version, signaling the prosperity of Hong Kong after the handover. In 2006, the HKRT even took the Cantonese performance to Shanghai, Toronto, New York, and Beijing, thus bringing this tale of the Shanghai and Hong Kong of half a century ago not only to several major cities in China, but also to those in North America, showcasing the international status and flourishing cultures of these two cities. In 2009, a thirty-four-episode TV drama series was aired, in which the story was transformed into a fairy tale. It was produced by the China Television Production Center and released to several channels in the Mainland, Taiwan, and Hong Kong. It was also released in the DVD format.

These ongoing adaptations of Eileen Chang's *LFC* speak to the story's enduring appeal and adaptability among Chinese communities. HKRT's stage productions, *(New) Love in a Fallen City* (新傾城之戀, hereafter *NLFC*), which have been repeatedly performed from 1987 to 2006, have to date not been widely discussed. This chapter focuses on the performance and reception of HKRT's *NLFC*. My analysis seeks neither to consider *NLFC* as a copy of the "original" text created by Eileen Chang, nor to examine whether the adaptation is faithful to the earlier version. Rather, it aims to see *NLFC* as a cultural re-creation, in which the stage production has both maintained and transformed the representations in Eileen Chang's *LFC*. I argue that a cultural "inbetweenness" can be constructed in the stage adaptation intertwined with both familiarity and novelty, thus producing the liminal space in which the boundaries between adapted texts and adaptations, femininity and masculinity, and the colonized and the colonizer are blurred. *NLFC* is neither a mere replica of Chang's text nor a completely new depiction independent of the former text. Instead, Chang's text and HKRT's stage adaptation are mutually implicated. In what follows, I will first discuss the theory and practice of adaptation that I will apply in my analysis. I will then adopt a feminist approach to investigate how the stage adaptation has re-evaluated the female sensibility embedded in Chang's text and re-appropriated the story as a quest for true love. Finally, but equally importantly, I will employ postcolonial theories to contextualize this stage adaptation in terms of contemporary Hong Kong society and its relationship to Shanghai.

The Theory and Practice of Adaptation

As collaborative creative modes of presentation, stage and film productions inevitably involve a combination of producers, playwrights or screenwriters, directors, actors and actresses, lighting, sound effects, costumes, editing, and so on. The discrepancy between the modes of telling and showing stories requires consideration of the advantages and limitations of both mediums. Adaptations of *LFC* may preserve the plot and characters of the earlier text, but they are not mere duplications of the previous version. However, these adaptations cannot be considered completely new creations because they only partially transform the adapted text. As Linda Hutcheon observes, "Adaptations—as both repetition and variation—are their form of replication. Evolving by cultural selection, traveling stories adapt to local cultures, just as populations of organisms adapt to local environments."[2] The paradoxical nature of the adaptations of *LFC* can, however, perpetuate and transform Eileen Chang's text while preserving the existing plot. Adaptations of *LFC* oscillate between the established discourses embedded in the earlier text and the counter-discourses constructed in the adaptations. A state of cultural "in-betweenness" is produced in the discrepancy between the conflicting discourses, and "[w]hat they are not is necessarily inferior or second-rate—or they would not have survived."[3] Eileen Chang fans or those with prior knowledge of her texts have often already formed images in their own minds of characters' appearances, speech mannerisms and facial expressions, the surrounding environment, and so on. As a result, when they see stage or film productions that depict the story in a way that differs from their interpretation, they may feel disappointed, although this is not always the case. I argue that Eileen Chang's text and its adaptations have an interdependent relationship. While Chang's *LFC* gives meaning to and exposes the significance of its adaptations, these adaptations derive meaning from and add value to her text. Their interdependent relationship breaks down the boundaries and hierarchy between them. In other words, when audiences see film and stage adaptations of Eileen Chang's *LFC*, they may have an image of her novella in their minds if they have read it. Their understanding of the adaptations may be affected by the mental image they have formed through their reading experience. In addition, their interpretation of Eileen Chang's *LFC* may in turn be influenced by the audio-visual representations in the film or drama. There are intertextual references in all versions.

As noted above, adaptations are not mere duplications of the "original" text with some variations. In fact, the very "originality" of Eileen Chang's *LFC* warrants further investigation. Several versions of Eileen Chang's own retelling of the story of *LFC* have complicated the issue of the tale's originality. In her essay, "Reflections on 'Love in a Fallen City'" (回顧傾城之戀, 1984), Chang relates that during the summer break in her studies at the University of Hong Kong in 1941 she often went to the Repulse Bay Hotel to visit her mother and her mahjong friends. Later, the members of the mahjong group all fled to Singapore and Hanoi. Two, however, stayed in Hong Kong and lived together. Chang claims that *LFC* is based on the story of this couple who remained in Hong Kong. In her words, "The motive for writing 'Love in a Fallen City'— at least in relation to their story—I think it was because they were the most affected by the war in Hong Kong among my acquaintances."[4] According to Chang, then, the "original" idea for the tale came from the real-life experience of a couple she knew. The couple's love story might in fact replicate conventional cultural codes of behavior and fictional or non-fictional historical episodes. Chang's *LFC* can therefore, to some extent, be seen as an adaptation of a true story.

Eileen Chang's narration of this story is further re-created in her autobiographical work of fiction, *Little Reunion* (小團圓, 2009). In this novel, Jiuli's
mother, Ruiqiu, stays in the Repulse Bay Hotel with her mahjong friends: a
couple named Mr. and Mrs. Nanxi, the divorcee Miss Xiangba, and Mr. Bi, who
is in his late sixties. In one episode, Miss Xiangba unexpectedly asks Ruiqiu to
go out with them, but Ruiqiu declines. Later, Miss Xiangba reappears with Mr.
Bi and intimately fixes his tie in public, displaying her possessiveness towards
him. Jiuli reflects that Miss Xiangba's invitation had in fact been a strategy to
suggest that it was Ruiqiu who had refused to join in with the others, leaving
Miss Xiangba and Mr. Bi alone. She is thus suggesting that Ruiqiu cannot
blame Miss Xiangba for seducing Mr. Bi, who once showed an interest in
Ruiqiu. Miss Xiangba eventually remains in Hong Kong to live with Mr. Bi.
Ruiqiu comments that "[T]hat's good—she [Miss Xiangba] was meant to find
someone to remarry."[5] Chang's revision of the story enriches the background to
LFC, providing more detail about the couple's interaction with Jiuli and Ruiqiu,
whose images resemble but do not duplicate Chang and her mother respectively. By rewriting the tale in *Little Reunion*, Chang deliberately highlights the
calculating and pretentious personality of Miss Xiangba, which resembles that
of Bai Liusu in *LFC*, but this time she shifts the focus from the couple's love
story to Jiuli's ambivalent relationship with her mother. Chang's revision of this
anecdote in *Little Reunion*, written in the 1970s but published in 2009, can be
considered yet another adaptation of the real-life story recounted in her essay
"Reflections on 'Love in a Fallen City,'" published in 1984, and *LFC*, published
in 1943. All of these versions of the story by Eileen Chang, along with later
stage and film adaptations by other artistic directors, are intimately related to
one another. This not only affects readers' response to each of these versions,
but also destabilizes the linear process of adaptation and interpretation.

Comparison of Eileen Chang's *LFC* and the HKRT's *NLFC*

Re-presenting Bai Liusu

Eileen Chang's female protagonist Bai Liusu has been depicted in the HKRT's
stage adaptation *NLFC* as a woman with a rudimentary education. In Chang's
LFC, Bai discloses to the matchmaker-relative Mrs. Xu that she has not received
any formal education. However, in *NLFC*, Bai's education has been slightly
amplified. Third Master recounts that Bai knows some English and Japanese,

and he expects her to help him with his business. In Chang's *LFC*, Bai is not educated, which echoes the old Chinese saying that "women without talent are virtuous." Traditional wealthy families such as Chang's family sometimes gave their daughters a good education. However, women's education was not a common phenomenon in China in the 1940s, even though gender equality had been advocated since the May Fourth movement of the 1920s. In *NLFC*, Bai is reconstructed as a slightly educated woman who even knows some foreign languages. When a woman receives an education, she is empowered with knowledge and the potential to achieve autonomy, and this is a view to which Eileen Chang's mother subscribed. This idea also echoes the broader thinking of modern feminist movements, which have been active in China since the 1920s. Women's right to education has been advocated by Mary Wollstonecraft in *A Vindication of the Rights of Woman* (1792). Wollstonecraft argues that most women of her time were deprived of education and professional opportunities, which affected their perspective on their social role. After a sea change in women's political, social and legal rights, the old Chinese saying about uneducated women is no longer widely accepted in the twenty-first century, particularly in Hong Kong, Shanghai, Beijing, Toronto, and New York, where female figures can be seen in high-ranking positions in all walks of life. The reconstructed Bai in *NLFC* appeals to the general way of thinking in modernized Chinese communities.

The female protagonist Bai in *NLFC* is a mild version of the aggressive protagonist of Chang's text. In Chang's *LFC*, although Bai is not formally educated she is a very aggressive woman. As Chang writes in her essay, "Liusu is indeed a very strong person, decisive and eloquent. Her only weakness lies in her education and experience."[6] One example of her derisive nature can be seen in the scene in which Bai performs in front of the mirror in her brother's house in Shanghai:

> She cast a fleeting glance and made a gesture. Because of her performance in the mirror, the huqin did not sound like huqin anymore, but rather the profound temple dance music played with pan pipes, flute and zither. She took a few steps to the left, and then a few to the right. Each step seemed to be in time with the beat of some lost, ancient music. All of a sudden, she smiled—an ominous malicious smile—and the music stopped. Outside, the huqin continued, but the distant moral tales the huqin was playing no longer had anything to do with her.[7]

Bai's examination of her body shows that she aims to use her physical appearance to achieve what she is expected to have in her situation—social status and financial stability. Her "ominous malicious smile" shows her determination to disregard the Chinese traditional moral code of conduct that has imprisoned her, symbolized by the "distant moral tales" played by the huqin. In *NLFC*, when Bai poses in front of the mirror she looks more self-pitying and admiring than "malicious." Bai's psychological traits are elaborately depicted in *LFC* but not in *NLFC*, making her appear less cunning and shrewd in the latter. The differences in Bai's portrayal in these two mediums can be partly explained by the limitations of stage production. As George Bluestone has discussed in relation to the confines of the mode of showing, "[D]reams and memories, which exist nowhere but in the individual consciousness, cannot be adequately represented in spatial terms."[8] Due to the difference between textual and visual presentations, Bai's thoughts and feelings as they are depicted in Chang's text cannot be similarly conveyed through the conceptual stage.

Innovative stage techniques that break through the limits of drama were used in *NLFC*. For example, the stage production uses singing and dancing to indicate characters' desire, frustration, and other circumstances. A female singer played by Liu Yali performs most of the theme songs that serve to articulate different levels of narration in the drama, particularly manifesting the self and the other of Bai. As Leo Ou-fan Lee has commented to Fredric Mao, "Now you have invented two Bai Liusu. One acts and the other sings. To use singing as a means of giving comments, the singer is like Bai Liusu but she is not totally Bai Liusu."[9] Lee appreciates Mao's dramatic technique of inserting a singer, which highlights a characteristic of Eileen Chang's novels—the voice of the narrator on different levels. The singer sometimes speaks from Bai's perspective and at other times from a narrator's point of view, commenting on Bai's psychological state and pragmatic situation. Dressed in a raincoat and singing in a man's voice accompanied by two male singers, Gao Hanwen and Liu Shouzheng, Liu Yali even delivers the lyrics from Fan's perspective.[10]

Fan Liuyuan's Quest for True Love

During his flirtation with Bai Liusu, Fan Liuyuan recites a poem from *The Book of Songs* (詩經), "Death, life, separation, with thee there is happiness; thy hand in mine, we will grow old together." (死生契闊，與子相悅，執子之手，與子偕老。)[11] Disregarding the different versions of this poem and their complexities that are thoroughly outlined by Kam Louie in Chapter 1, Fan interprets it as meaning that even though there are many difficulties in life we still insist on saying "I love you forever." In Chang's *LFC*, because Bai has not received any formal education, she cannot understand Fan's use of the metaphor of classical poetry or his personality and behavior. In "Frank Comments on 'Love in a Fallen City'" (關於〈傾城之戀〉的老實話, 1944), Chang says, "Perhaps this needs to be explained. I wrote this story [*LFC*] from her [Bai's] perspective; since she has not totally understood Fan, I do not have to understand him very much."[12] Regardless of whether Chang or Bai can understand Fan, the poem that Fan cites becomes the theme of *NLFC*, as the poem is used as the lyrics of its theme song, making the quest for love its focus.

Apart from quoting the poem from *The Book of Songs*, in *NLFC* Fan also urges Bai to love him regardless of economic and social concerns. In Chang's story, Fan accuses Bai of wanting to marry him for money rather than love. He says to her on the phone, "I'm not that stupid. It's not worthwhile for me to spend my money marrying someone with no feelings for me, someone who is going to restrict me. That's too unfair. It's not fair to you either. Hey, maybe you don't care. Basically you think marriage is just long-term prostitution . . ."[13] Although Fan may be right in pointing out that marriage is Bai's ultimate objective, he is too harsh in calling her a prostitute, and disregards the fact that it is in fact the patriarchal system in traditional Chinese culture that restricts her opportunities to achieve economic autonomy. As Virginia Woolf has argued in "A Room of One's Own" (1929), women need a sustainable financial income and private space in order to develop their subjecthood. In *NLFC*, however, Fan becomes a seeker of true love, and presses Bai to love him. As he says, "Why can't we be together just as long as we are able to? Why can't we love for love's sake, disregarding any consequences? Why do we have to worry about so many practical considerations?" (my translation) Fan's questions can be seen as an excuse for not marrying Bai because of his promiscuous nature. They can also be seen as indicating his emphasis on true love—a major concern in his relationship with Bai. In the 2005 adaptation by the HKRT in Hong Kong, Fan breathes heavily before he phones Bai and asks these questions, indicating his anxiety and desire. In the 2006 performance in Toronto, Fan steps to the front of the stage and gives this speech of true love with great sincerity in his facial expression and body language, further signaling his idealism about love and by extension the theme of the drama.

The focus shifts not only from Bai's struggle for economic security in *LFC* to Fan's search for love in NLFC, but also from the female to the male protagonist. One of the major reasons for this is the overwhelming popularity of Tony

Kar-fai Leung, the actor performing Fan, in comparison to Su Yuhua and Liu Yali, the actresses playing Bai and the singer respectively, among Chinese audiences. Leung has acted in numerous films and has received several Best Actor awards. In addition, he received awards in Hong Kong and Shanghai for his performances in *Election* (黑社會, dir. Johnnie To Kei-fung, 2005) and *NLFC* respectively. Much of the publicity and reporting on *NLFC* in newspapers focused on Leung.[14] These newspaper photographs and captions highlight the fact that Leung was the major selling point of *NLFC*. News reports also provided wide coverage of Leung's activities in Chinese communities.[15] Due to his fame, most of the activities related to *NLFC* were centered on Leung. Leung's publicity and popularity is likely to have overshadowed all of the other actors and actresses who contributed to *NLFC*, not to mention Eileen Chang, *LFC*, the theater, the director, and the playwrights.

In addition to his fame among Chinese communities, Leung's acting ability inevitably made him the focal point of *NLFC*, thus shifting attention in this stage adaptation from the female protagonists to himself. The audience's intertextual knowledge of Leung's acting career inevitably affects their reception of the stage adaptation. As Hutcheon has commented in *A Theory of Adaptation*, "If the audience knows that a certain director or actor has made other films of a particular kind, that intertextual knowledge too might well impinge on their interpretation of the adaptation they are watching."[16] While Leung has successfully portrayed a wide range of characters in his repertory career, his devilish charisma and aura of magnetism are well suited to the personality of Fan Liuyuan in *NLFC*. Compared with Su Yuhua, who performs a less shrewish version of Bai Liusu, Leung gives Fan, who constantly and skillfully flirts with women, the upper hand in his relationship with his prey, thus placing Bai at the mercy of either him or circumstance.

Leung's portrayal of a charismatic lover is perhaps best demonstrated in the French film, *L'Amant* (*The Lover*, dir. Jean-Jacques Annaud, 1992). Based on the autobiographical novel *L'Amant* (1984) by Marguerite Duras, the film adaptation of the same title tells of the sexual affair between a wealthy Chinese man, played by Leung, and a poor French teenage girl in French Indochina, now Vietnam, in 1929. In the story, although the Chinese man has financial power over the French girl's corporeal body, the French family and her own ego will not accept him as her lover because of the disparity between the unstable Chinese political situation and French colonial power at the time. The dynamics between the different dimensions of class, gender, and ethnicity interweave to produce the purchasable body politics but unattainable love in this story.

Rey Chow has criticized Third World intellectuals in her discussion of gender studies in modern Chinese literature in a globalized context: "As in this case of what I call masculinist positions in the China field, their resort to minority discourse, including the discourse of class and gender struggles, veils their own fatherhood over the ethnics at home even while it continues to legitimize them as ethnics and minorities in the West."[17] Chow warns Chinese intellectuals to read and write against these "lures of diaspora" that occupy both the colonizing and colonized positions towards Chinese women at home in particular. Such diasporic locations can be applied to analyze Leung's roles in *L'Amant* and *NLFC*. Leung plays the role of a playful but love-stricken man in both *NLFC* and *L'Amant*, albeit with different political connotations. Given their similar backgrounds in terms of wealth, class, and gender superiority, however, the two roles represent different manifestations of political power towards the Chinese Bai Liusu and the French girl. In *NLFC*, Leung plays Fan Liuyuan, an overseas Chinese who has grown up in Britain and has business in Southeast Asia. With offshore capital, overseas experience, and foreign connections, Fan has superior social status to his love object, Bai Liusu, who comes from an apparently respectable but actually financially troubled Chinese family in Shanghai, a city under Japanese occupation during the Second World War. On the other hand, in *L'Amant*, Leung plays the role of a rich Chinese man who falls in love with a poor French girl. Both characters in *L'Amant* lack specific names, thus reducing them to representations of the wealthy and the poor, an experienced man and a naïve girl, as well as Chinese and French, in French colonial Indochina in the 1920s. The class and gender supremacy of Leung's role is counteracted by the unequal ethnic power between the colonized and the colonial. The juxtaposition of the two couples, Fan and Bai in *NLFC* and the rich Chinese man and the poor French girl in *L'Amant*, demonstrates the ambiguous politics of Chinese masculinity—powerful to the Chinese woman in China but inadequate for the French woman in a French colony in the first half of the twentieth century.

A Tale of Two Cities: Shanghai vs. Hong Kong

The cultural displacement depicted in Chang's LFC provokes a sense of "unhomeliness" that uncannily blurs the boundaries between home and world as well as the private and the public. According to Freud, two German words that are apparently opposites, *unheimlich* (unhomelike, uncanny) and *heimlich* (homey, familiar), paradoxically share the meaning of concealed and secret. Based on Friedrich von Schiller's idea, Freud argues that "everything is *unheimlich* that ought to have remained secret and hidden but has come to light."[18] In Chang's *LFC*, Fan, a symbol of Sino-British cultural conflict, experiences the notion of unhomeliness. He is a Chinese who has grown up in Britain. His dreams of his hometown are completely shattered when he goes to China. As he confesses to Bai, "I know you've seen enough bad things and bad people around you, but if this is the first time you have seen them, it's even harder on you. I was just like that. When I first came to China, I was already twenty-four. I had dreamed of home many times. You can imagine how disappointed I was. I couldn't stand the shock."[19] What has remained the dark side of his hometown is revealed to him after his relocation. As Homi K. Bhabha further argues in *The Location of Culture* (1994), "The negating activity is, indeed, the intervention of the 'beyond' that establishes a boundary: a bridge, where 'presencing' begins because it captures something of the estranging sense of the relocation of the home and the world—the unhomeliness—that is the condition of extra-territorial and cross-cultural initiations."[20] The displacement of Fan leads to his cultural disorientation and ambivalent relationship between his personal psyche and colonial politics.

Entering a postcolonial condition, *NLFC* presents an indeterminate hybridity of nationality and identity, which emerges from what Bhabha calls a "Third Space." As Bhabha has suggested,

> The intervention of the Third Space of enunciation, which makes the structure of meaning and reference an ambivalent process, destroys this mirror of representation in which cultural knowledge is customarily revealed as an integrated, open, expanding code. Such an intervention quite properly challenges our sense of the historical identity of culture as a homogenizing, unifying force, authenticated by the originary Past, kept alive in the national tradition of the People.[21]

In *NLFC*, Fan's confession about his sense of unhomeliness is omitted. Fan represents Westernized Chinese and does not exhibit any signs of culture shock. He is neither totally Westernized nor completely Chinese, but located between two cultures. He can be seen as a symbol of Hong Kong in the twenty-first century—Hong Kong has both perpetuated and transgressed Chinese and British cultures, and situates itself in the liminal space.

LFC and *NLFC* also offer different depictions of Shanghai and Hong Kong, and the relationship between the two cities. As Bhabha has contended, it is crucial to focus on the articulation of cultural discrepancy in order to illustrate the identities of the self and society. In his words, "These 'in-between' spaces provide the terrain for elaborating strategies of selfhood—singular or communal—that initiate new signs of identity, and innovative sites of collaboration, and contestation, in the act of defining the idea of society itself."[22] In Eileen Chang's text, both Shanghai and Hong Kong are under military attack, and their social and moral systems are in disarray. However, an ordinary couple would still be able to survive in such a world. The text contains detailed descriptions of the conflicts between Bai and other members of her family in Shanghai, whereas the conflict in Hong Kong is not depicted in detail. In Shanghai, Bai is always under the critical gaze of her family, which upholds Chinese Confucian doctrines on women's behavior; while in Hong Kong she is relatively free from such oppression even though she is still under the constant gaze of Mr. and Mrs. Xu and others. The displacement of Bai from Shanghai to Hong Kong sheds light on the intersubjective and collective experience of these two cities, whereby their cultural values are collaboratively dialogical if not antagonistically negotiated.

The contrast between Shanghai and Hong Kong is portrayed more starkly in *NLFC*. This drama was performed by the HKRT from 1987 to 2006, with the last production almost nine years after Hong Kong's return to China. During this period, the city has been in increasing competition with Shanghai in the financial arena. The resulting contrast between the two cities is reflected in *NLFC*. In *NLFC*, when in Shanghai, Bai is surrounded by her judgmental family in a traditional household that is symbolized by an old clock that does not match the pace of the city. In Hong Kong, the stage changes to the Repulse Bay Hotel, where travellers come and go, symbolizing Hong Kong in the 1940s when many people moved in and out of the city due to the Second World War. When Bai dances with Fan in Shanghai, the whole family watches them from a corner, and Seventh Miss faints to indicate that Bai's behavior is socially unacceptable. By contrast, Bai enjoys greater personal space in Hong Kong because she can dance with Fan without any repercussions from her family. Although people in Hong Kong are relatively less restricted by traditional codes of conduct, Bai is still under the gaze of others in this city. For example, when Bai and Fan are dancing in the hotel, someone takes a photograph of them, signifying the constant social monitoring of their behavior. The amplification of the differences between these two cities illuminates the subject formation of Bai "in-between" the emergence of the competing interstices of communities, where tradition is under ongoing negotiation rather than in static condition in moments of historical transformation.

The Beginning and the End

The beginning and end of Eileen Chang's *LFC* and HKRT's *NLFC* show significant discrepancies in terms of theme. The beginning and end of *LFC* focus on the endless and sorrowful tale told by the *huqin*. In the end, even though Bai remarries, she remains a little disappointed. She aims to achieve social status and economic security, which are what society expects of her, but not perhaps what she really wants. The disparity between social expectations and hidden personal desires ultimately leads to her frustration, indirectly highlighting the oppressed situation of women in China in the 1940s. However, the beginning and end of *NLFC* focus on a Chinese classical poem about true love. At the end of the performance, Bai recites the poem, speaks of true love, and lives in the old family house in Shanghai watching the changes in the city. *NLFC* presents Fan's quest for true love, leading in the end to Bai's enlightenment. Bai is so strong in this version of the story that she is able to outlive the rest of her family members through all the political and economic changes taking place in China.

In her essay "Frank Comments on 'Love in a Fallen City,'" Chang claims that most people are mediocre, and very few are able to achieve sudden enlightenment. This explains the ending of *LFC*. After the war, Bai does not become a revolutionary woman; she just lives an ordinary life. As Chang says in "Writing of One's Own" (自己的文章, 1944), "In 'Love in a Fallen City,' Liusu escapes from her corrupt traditional family, but the baptism of the battle of Hong Kong does not transform her into a revolutionary."[23] The development of Bai's character in *LFC* matches Chang's philosophy of life and the situation of women at the time. Chang further argues that "[t]here are very few people, after all, who are either extremely perverse or extremely enlightened. Times as weighty as these do not allow for easy enlightenment."[24] She believes in desolation as a mode of revelation, rather than in tragedy, which is a kind of closure. Tragic heroes, therefore, give way to ordinary people as major characters in most of her literary works. Bai in *LFC* becomes an ordinary housewife with signs of the usual frustration with life in a down-to-earth marriage, rather than turning into a heroine to achieve enlightenment.

In *NLFC*, however, Bai is more self-assured in the end, showing that she is self-contained and satisfied with her degree of autonomy, which generally reflects the situation of women in Shanghai and Hong Kong today. The transformation of Bai into an independent woman in *NLFC* can perhaps be attributed to a certain extent to the contribution of the artistic director Fredric Mao. As Hutcheon has pointed out, "It is obvious that adapters must have their own personal reasons for deciding first to do an adaptation and then choosing which adapted work and what medium to do it in. They not only interpret that work but in so doing they also take a position on it."[25] In a dialog with Leo Ou-fan Lee, Mao claims that he was inspired by Lee's novel, *Confessions of a Profligate, Fan Liuyuan* (范柳原懺情錄, 1998), a sequel to *LFC* in which Fan confesses his love to Bai, intertwined with the voices of Lee and Eileen Chang, embedded in both personal and public history in the past, present, and future. In Mao's words, "The most inspiration for me is: that the novel (*Confessions of a Profligate*) not only tells a story, but also reflects the author's special perspective on that story, particularly on Fan Liuyuan. Therefore, I found a point of departure, a point of view, which stems from the feeling that Bai Liusu as having been baptized through the passage of time. It is not merely narrating a historical story."[26] Mao's inclusion of the new ending—in which Bai lives alone and contented in modern Shanghai—in *NLFC* shows his view of time, which has been greatly affected by his recovery from serious illness in 2002. In an interview, Mao stated that after his illness he realized that the passage of time and growing older are not a matter of regret or loss. As he says, "Time will make your life more fulfilling, which is like wine—the longer the time, the better the taste. For love affairs, in this drama, I do not explain too much about the ending of Bai Liusu because it is not important. I want to show that in a love affair the power struggle, passion and contradiction will become a memory in the end. People need to experience the pattern of love through memory."[27] In *NLFC*, after experiencing the full gamut of frustration, romance, and excitement in her love affair with Fan, Bai lives happily alone and with dignity in Shanghai, witnessing the changing history and landscape of the city, which is shown through photographs of its spectacular architecture at significant historical moments.

The title "Love in a Fallen City" alludes to the theme of the femme fatale. In the oft-cited passage from the *History of the Former Han Dynasty* (前漢書), it is asserted that "There is a beauty in the north. She is independent and no one else could be compared to her in this world. With just one look, she will make

a city fall; and with another look, she will make a nation fall." (北方有佳人，
絕世而獨立。一顧傾人城，再顧傾人國。)[28] The beauty here can be seen to
be Bai and the city of Hong Kong. The fall of Hong Kong allows Bai and Fan to
live an ordinary life, and thus indirectly brings about their marriage. As Chang
narrates in *LFC*, "The fall of Hong Kong had helped her achieve her aim. But in
this world, who knew which was the cause and which the result? Who knew?
Maybe just because the big city had wanted to help her accomplish her goal, it
had been destroyed. Thousands of people had died, thousands of people had
suffered, and what followed was an earth-shaking change."[29] Here Chang is
being sarcastic about making Bai the cause of the fall of Hong Kong, just like
any other femme fatale whose charm destroys a city or nation. Of course, there
are obvious historical reasons for the battle in Hong Kong and its subsequent
surrender, which had nothing to do with Bai's marriage. Simone de Beauvoir
has discussed the contradictory but constitutive relationship between the myth
of the Eternal Feminine and the experience of women in *Le Deuxième Sexe*
(*The Second Sex*, 1949). She contends that "essence does not precede existence."
However, the myth of female archetypes constructs women's experience and
becomes timeless essence, thus defining women as the absolute Other of men.
Julia Kristeva refuses to define female subjectivity: "In 'woman' I see something
that cannot be represented, something that is not said, something above and
beyond nomenclatures and ideologies."[30] Renouncing the myth of the femme
fatale, Chang writes, "Liusu felt that she didn't amount to a pinhole in history.
She just smiled and stood up, kicking the mosquito coil underneath the table."[31]
Chang's comment on Bai's influence over the fate of the city parodies the cliché
of the femme fatale and thus repudiates such misogynist traditional views,
making their unreliability apparent.

Conclusion

Eileen Chang's *LFC* is written from a Shanghai writer's perspective, depicting
Shanghai and Hong Kong for an audience in Shanghai in the 1940s. As Chang
says in "Shanghainese, After All" (到底是上海人, 1943), "The entire time I was
writing these stories [Hong Kong romances including *LFC*], I was thinking of
Shanghainese people, because I wanted to try to observe Hong Kong through
Shanghainese eyes. Only people from Shanghai will be truly able to understand
the parts where I wasn't able to make my meaning clear."[32] However, *NLFC* was
produced from a Hong Kong perspective,[33] and portrays Shanghai and Hong

Kong for audiences in Hong Kong, Shanghai, Beijing, and North America in the twenty-first century. The subjectivity of Bai in *NLFC* has been re-appropriated to make her ultimately more assertive, due to the re-evaluation and re-contextualization of Chang's *LFC*. The lasting popularity of *LFC* among Chinese communities speaks to the appeal of adaptation of Chang's text, which lies in its paradoxical nature of perpetuation and transformation, thus leading to the emergence of the space of "in-betweenness," a zone that destabilizes the boundaries between Chang's *LFC* and HKRT's *NLFC*, Bai's sensibility and Fan's love quest, as well as Hong Kong, Shanghai, and other Chinese communities in the process of historical transformation.

I would like to express my gratitude to the following people and institutions for their assistance in the completion of this paper: Fredric Mao, artistic director of "(New) Love in a Fallen City," who invited me to see one of the Hong Kong Repertory Theatre's performances at the theater of Ryerson University in Toronto from April 28 to 30, 2006; the Asian Institute of the University of Toronto that provided me with a DVD of NLFC and invited me to participate as a panelist, along with Fredric Mao, in the seminar on NLFC held on April 27, 2006; Hangfeng Hoyan, who shared with me her research materials on Hong Kong Repertory Theatre's adaptations of "Love in a Fallen City"; Stephen Siu, associate director of the Hong Kong Economic and Trade Office in Toronto, who shared with me the office's materials on NLFC; and Ann Hui, who shared with me her views on her film adaptation of "Love in a Fallen City" in an interview on November 27, 2008.

3
Eileen Chang and Things Japanese

Nicole Huang

Much has already been written about Eileen Chang's life and works. The mushrooming of publications in the Chinese language in recent years in particular speaks to the fact that Eileen Chang studies has indeed become a contemporary "distinguished school of learning" (顯學). However, it is my contention that Chang's wartime activities are one area that calls for further in-depth research. Gone is the time when Chang and other writers of her day were branded "collaborators" and their works banished from a literary historiography dictated by political imperatives. But wartime complexity is a weighty issue that ought not be excluded from our scholarly discussion of Chang altogether. Too often she has been represented as a literary genius who rose above her time, transcending political strictures, while miraculously surviving and thriving on hardly any material attachment. This characterization of Chang as a transcendental figure has its origin in Hu Lancheng's (胡蘭成) infamous autobiography *This Life, These Times* (今生今世, 1976), in which, by painting Chang as some sort of celestial being that survives on little, he created the prototype of the Eileen Chang myth.[1]

The historical Eileen Chang is, I argue, located elsewhere, and should be situated in a broader wartime map of the world, a world more deeply connected and intertwined than we have collectively been able to acknowledge or understand. When all of the pieces of the puzzle are reassembled, we will find an incredibly savvy figure who maneuvered across several different cultures—a kind of cultural traveling that undercuts the traditional binary of China versus the "West," and who played wartime politics just like other major cultural agents of her time. Close reading of the material world manifested in Chang's literary order also offers many insights into patterns of cultural consumption and imagination in wartime occupied Shanghai. Putting more pieces of the puzzle together to retrieve a historical Eileen Chang will help us to further understand the making of a unique literary style that drew on the rich soil of a transnational wartime popular culture.

Noting the conspicuous lack of scholarly attention to Chang's cultural connection with Japan, I begin this chapter by asking some basic questions.[2] Is there a place for Japan and things Japanese in Chang's literary order? How do things Japanese feature? What position do Japan and things Japanese occupy in Chang's cultural imagination? How did Chang, as an avid consumer of cultural products, consume things and themes Japanese? After all, Chang was a writer who rose to fame during the war, and in an occupied city. From the outset of her writing career, she was a quintessentially professional writer, in the sense that she had to sell her writings, court her readership, and market her individual style. She managed this role skillfully and made a decent living through war and occupation. This leads to further questions: Exactly how are we to characterize Chang's cultural self-positioning? In other words, how did she maneuver across cultural divides and play wartime politics to her own advantage? To address these questions, I have assumed the "old-fashioned" role of textual "detective," and plowed through some of Chang's relatively obscure works from the period, looking at them with a new eye, seeking to piece together a more complex picture of a writer's entanglement in a textual labyrinth that comprises Chinese, Japanese, and Western sources, and her ingenious navigation through it.

A Photographic Chang

I begin with the single most important piece of photographic documentation from Eileen Chang's Shanghai era. This photo was taken on July 21, 1945, less than a month before the Japanese surrender and the end of the Pacific War.[3] Readers who are knowledgeable about Chang and her time would recognize the occasion that gave rise to this photo. The image is known for featuring two of the most enigmatic figures from the war era; it is also known for its bizarre composition and visual awkwardness. Many readers might also see it as an uncanny portrayal of an unlikely reunion on the eve of the collapse of Japan's colonial empire. (Figure 3.1)

The well-known occasion was a Sino-Japanese cosponsored event engineered by the popular journal *Miscellany Monthly* (雜誌月刊). Chang is featured here with the singer/film actress Li Xianglan (李香蘭, a.k.a. Yamaguchi Yoshiko 山口淑子, or Ri Ko-ran, b. 1920), the chameleon-like figure who

Figure 3.1

Eileen Chang (left) and the singer/film actress Li Xianglan
(李香蘭), July 21, 1945

typified the slippery boundaries of ethnic and national identities in wartime
East Asia. A Japanese woman raised in Manchuria by a Chinese family, Li went
on to become the brightest film star and popular icon in Manchuria, and later,
in all of East Asia. She traveled between Manchuria and Shanghai as a cultural
ambassador in an effort to further the cause of Japanese colonialism, and to
instill a new system of political ideology and popular symbolism into the cultural industry of occupied China. For years, the image and singing voice of Li
reigned over the cultural scene of a new colonial order. She displayed a conspicuous freedom to travel and an ability to highlight her trail as she trekked
across Manchuria, Shanghai, Taipei, and Tokyo.[4]

Li's ties to Shanghai's film industry were further strengthened following the May 1943 release of the big-budget filmic epic *Eternity* (萬世流芳), directed by Bu Wancang, Ma-Xu Weibang, and Zhu Shilin, which was set during the First Opium War of 1839–42. Li shines even among a star-studded cast, playing a young woman who urges her lover to participate in the anti-opium campaign launched by Lin Zexu. Her megastar presence in the film is enhanced by a catchy screen song, "The Candy Peddler's Song" (賣糖歌), which her character sings in front of an opium den while selling a type of candy reputed to curb opium addiction.[5]

Li's rise to transnational fame coincided with Eileen Chang's path to literary stardom in the brief period between 1943 and 1945. Following the box office success of *Eternity* within China and abroad, Li's frequent visits to Shanghai were documented in both words and images. Her last visit on July 21, 1945, the occasion that is captured in the above photograph, was particularly well covered. Local media placed her center stage, side by side with the brightest local star. By all accounts, this was a star-studded event, a "one-stop shop" for catching a glimpse of the iconic figures of the day. It remains a mystery how the local media could have been so oblivious to Japan's imminent defeat as to orchestrate such a festivity on the eve of the collapse of the empire. The two symbols of a colonial Shanghai captured in this particular photograph seem to be inscribed in a bygone era, unaffected by the deteriorating present.[6]

Those sympathetic to Chang would argue that her expression should be understood as one of reluctance, as she had always been a reluctant participant in the extravaganza engineered by the occupying regime. In Chang's own rec-ollections, however, no such reluctance is ever suggested. She remembers this moment fondly, and claims, seemingly amused, that the photographer asked her to be seated while Li stood to the side, because Chang was so tall that she would have dwarfed her petite companion if she had stood next to her. But surely this seating arrangement makes it look as if Li was waiting on Chang?[7]

Viewed from any angle, the composition of the photograph is awkward. The seating arrangement for Chang by no means redresses the balance between the pair, and the photographer was apparently unable to get his subjects to direct their gazes in the same direction. Li is the one who diligently complies with the photographer's direction. She gazes at the camera attentively with her signature innocent, earnest look. Chang, of course, proves a difficult subject to set on film. Her posture disturbs the power of the camera and upsets the composi-tion of the photograph. Seated sideways, she chooses not to look directly at the camera. Her crossed legs, exposed from the knees down, point to the left, while her eyes cast a doubtful look to the right of the frame.

The awkwardness of the photo is enhanced by the two women's strikingly different styles of dressing. Li's hair is combed neatly back, showcasing a carefully defined face, so familiar and so accessible. She wears a conservatively tailored *cheongsam*, with a mid-calf hemline and square padded shoulders, her pearl necklace completing the formal look. Chang, however, wears a strangely tailored dress in a style that would have been unrecognizable in her time. It is short, loose, and informal. The fabric, as Chang would later explain to her readers, was an old quilt cover left by her long deceased grandmother—a family heirloom. The fabric was so old and fragile that it was likely to tear or shred easily, like withered grass (陳絲如爛草), she would tell her readers.[8] The dress was designed by her friend Yanying (炎櫻), and Chang had it custom made to fit her style and persona. Described as "Western-style clothes" (西式衣服) by the reporter, for lack of a better description, it looks nothing like the type of Western-style clothes that were popular at the time. The piece has a timeless quality that sets it apart from what fashionable women typically wore at the time. The trend Chang set could not be followed.[9] And her long hair, only barely held back by a pin, flows freely down the sides of her face. While Chang's peculiar posture and style seem to transcend the boundaries of the picture frame, the photograph strangely grounds Li Xianglan and marks her as stunningly local and present. Here Li looks almost like an ordinary woman one would encounter on the streets of Shanghai, with her wrinkled *cheongsam* suggesting a hard day at the office, perhaps, working away at the typewriter. Her pearl necklace, however, belies the "working woman" scenario. After all, what kind of female office worker would wear a pearl necklace in broad daylight?

This photograph of Chang and Li is not the only visual document produced on this occasion. A group photo, in which Eileen Chang is also seated, appears two pages earlier in the report. In fact, Chang is the only one of the seven people in the photo to be seated, with her aunt standing to her right, Li Xianglan to her left, and her friend Yanying behind her. The other three people in the group photo are Chen Binhe (陳彬龢), Jin Xiongbai (金雄白), and a woman merely identified as Ms. Chen, all of whom are standing.[10] Here Chang is pictured with almost exactly the same posture and expression as in the photo with Li Xianglan. And Li, too, maintains her signature innocent, earnest look. The decision for her to be seated in this group photo seems even more peculiar. Chang's explanation of the seating arrangement in the photo with Li Xianglan does not account for the awkwardness of this group photo. Precisely what happened might forever remain a mystery, but the photo has the effect of drawing visual attention to the one person who is seated. In a group photo in which all subjects look towards and smile obediently at the camera, the queen of pan-Asian cinema pales beside this seated woman who insists on casting her gaze downward and away from the camera. A reluctant Eileen Chang is thus captured with a great degree of deliberateness.

This is certainly not the only time Chang made a media appearance. Throughout the three years and eight months of the Japanese occupation, she made frequent appearances at public events orchestrated by various cultural agencies in the occupied city. On another occasion she was featured with the Korean dancer Choe Seung-hui (崔承喜, 1911–69), another cultural icon of the Japanese empire, better known under the Japanese pronunciation of her name, Sai Shoki. At a November 1943 event, several Shanghai women writers were featured with Sai Shoki and a Chinese dancer named Wang Yuan (王淵). Eileen Chang, who arrived fashionably late, is said to have worn a pink *cheongsam* with a copper-green vest. In the poorly reproduced photo that accompanies the report, Chang appears to be looking obediently at the camera, like the other women featured in the frame.[11] While Chang's engagement with the photographic art is yet another weighty subject that calls for further study and perhaps a separate paper, suffice to say here that to manipulate the camera and to fashion an unusual public persona must be a skill that she had perfected over a period of about three years. Images of Chang gazing directly at the camera would become a rarity by the end of the period. During the long summer of 1945, the trademark image of Eileen Chang is of someone who looks away from the camera and who strikes a deliberate pose on every photographic occasion, a brand of visual deliberateness that sets her apart from almost all of the other public figures of the era, including Li Xianglan, the woman who made a glorious living facing the cameras in Manchuria, Shanghai, and Tokyo.

Reluctance or intent, then, is in the eyes of the beholder. We can no longer confidently assume that Chang was a reluctant player in a series of engineered media images of the "Greater East Asian Co-prosperity Sphere." Nor can we ascertain precisely what her intent is. Chang's facial expression and body language might suggest reluctance or even defiance, but there is also little doubt that she directs the camera's gaze at the very deliberateness of each of her poses. She might look like someone who has been dragged into her seat, reluctant and disengaged, but every little detail of her appearance has been meticulously engineered.

Chang's deliberateness is carried into her textual world. If she had rendered Japan absent in her writings while appearing frequently at public events hosted by the occupying regime and its Japanese sponsors, it would have produced an interesting dichotomy. But a more careful look at Chang's writings from the period, particularly her essays, including some that have rarely been discussed, seems to suggest that Japan and things Japanese have a place somewhere in her literary order. At some moments, things and themes Japanese feature prominently. Perhaps the clues to Chang's Japanese connections can indeed be located on a textual level.

On Colors, Shapes, and Sounds

The essays collected in *Written on Water* (流言), Chang's first prose collection, which was published in 1945, are by no means all masterpieces. In fact, the collection is marked by an unevenness for which we have as yet no explanation. Some essays are exquisitely written and rightly considered to be examples of the greatest achievements of modern Chinese prose. These include "From the Mouths of Babes" (童言無忌), "Notes on Apartment Life" (公寓生活記趣), and "From the Ashes" (燼餘錄). But others are of poorer quality, glossing over a range of topics not necessarily organized under a unifying theme. Some examples are "Unforgettable Paintings" (忘不了的畫), "On Dance" (談跳舞), and "On Paintings" (談畫). It is in these latter essays that we often find laundry lists of things that make up the material world that Chang draws inspiration from. In fact, it is precisely the unevenness of her prose collection that provides a peculiar sense of materiality to her writings from this period.[12]

A taxonomy of the material world in Chang's writings in the 1940s, particularly some of the essays in which she tends to provide such laundry lists, is therefore in order. Such a detailed investigation will lead us to the revelation that Chang's occasional rendering of things and themes Japanese can be read as another act of deliberateness. In fact, we might proceed further to portray her as an avid consumer of things Japanese, and things Japanese played a discernible role in Chang's construction of an intelligible world caught in the midst of wartime uncertainty.

From the essay "From the Mouths of Babes," we know that for a while Chang frequented businesses in Shanghai's Hongkew District (虹口, which from the 1920s was an area populated by Japanese expatriates), including fabric stores and movie theaters. She would occasionally buy bolts of Japanese fabric there.

And she would frequent the famed Hongkew Cinema (虹口大戲院), the first movie theater in Shanghai, to watch new Japanese feature films. The image of a self-indulgent consumer emerges from Chang's accounts of these excursions.

Chang certainly makes no secret of the fact that she is fascinated with Japanese textile designs, describing window shopping at Japanese fabric stores in Hongkew as a feast for the eyes. Most of the time she only looked, but occasionally she bought. In a section entitled "Fashion" in "From the Mouths of Babes," she famously remarks that the art of color coordination that had been lost in China is miraculously preserved in contemporary Japanese textile designs. Each bolt of Japanese fabric is a piece of art, she writes, but it is a pity that detailed Japanese tailoring disrupts the patterns of their textile design. The perfect solution, she says, is to cut the fabric into the much more simple lines of the Chinese cheongsam. Chang's proposition would create a truly pan-Asian product—Japanese fabric combined with Chinese tailoring. Chang goes on to imagine Japanese textile designs as a further aestheticization of Chinese poetic motifs:

> Japanese printed fabrics, each bolt a painting. Every time I buy some fabric and bring it home, I repeatedly unroll it and bask in the image before finally handing it over to the tailor. A small Burmese temple half obscured by the leaves of a palm tree, rain falling incessantly through the reddish brown haze of the tropics. A pond in early summer, the water covered with a layer of green scum, above which floats duckweed and fallen purple and white lilac petals. Perhaps a fitting scene for a song lyric set to the tune "Lament for the Southland." And another bolt, set to "Flowers in the Rain": on a white background, big gloomy purple blossoms, dripping with moisture.[13]

The Japanese textile designs that are highlighted here seem untouched by the historical period. The trend in the 1940s was to wear propaganda. For instance, a Japanese woman's silk kimono of the period would display Nazi and Japanese flags in a subtle design that acknowledged the Axis alignment.[14] We find none of this in Chang's aesthetic order. She is mostly fascinated by traditional design motifs, detecting themes from China's distant past in traditional Japanese textile designs. The superimposition of two contrasting and yet intertwined cultural pasts creates a hybrid product that is not only in tune with the pan-Asian trends of her time but also utterly modern and characteristic of Chang's unique approach to tradition.

The transition from things Chinese to things Japanese in Chang's aesthetic order is often so subtle as to be barely detectable. In her textual world, the transition from Chinese references to Japanese references occurs seamlessly, and it takes a careful eye and much patience to notice that the subject has shifted. In the visual and material world surrounding Chang, this transition is even more seamless. In two photographic portraits she claims were taken by amateur photographer Tong Shizhang (童世璋), Chang appears in the first image dressed in an oversized Qing-style padded gown, apparently a family heirloom. Shot from a low angle, Chang is pictured upright, her left hand splayed against the wall, her torso slightly turned to the right, and her eyes casting a vague glance toward the upper right corner of the frame. She appears tall and almost statuesque, and once again looks away from the camera, simultaneously defying and engaging its gaze. In the second image, her gaze again avoids the camera but her body continues to grab its attention. She has metamorphosed into a much more humble squatting figure, with her arms folded and resting on her knees, her eyes cast downward, and her faint smile creating a more accessible air. Perhaps most striking in this second photo is the featuring of a Japanese kimono. Between the two portraits, Chang has taken off her padded Manchu gown and put on a *yukata* (浴衣), a casual style of kimono used as lounge wear or bathrobe, displaying a dramatic shift in persona.[15] (Figures 3.2 and 3.3)

There are also seamless transitions in Chang's grasp of sounds and voices in Japanese. First, she drops some hints about her knowledge of the Japanese language in some of her writings from this time. We know that at one point she learned Japanese, and there is evidence that she reached a level of some fluency and her Japanese was fairly functional.

It is most likely that Chang learned Japanese in wartime Hong Kong, when she was a student at the University of Hong Kong. We learn through her writing that Japanese was part of the curriculum in wartime Hong Kong. In the essay "From the Ashes," the narrator and her college friends take Japanese lessons in their leisure time as the war goes on around them and the city lies in ruins. These lessons are not offered by Japanese, but by a young Russian man, who uses the opportunity to flirt with his female students. The flirtation takes place through the medium of elementary Japanese.[16]

Needless to say, Russian proficiency in Japanese language was a product of a long history of military and cultural engagement between Russia and later the Soviet Union and Asia.[17] Not only were Russian expatriates teaching basic Japanese to students in Hong Kong, they were also doing so in Shanghai, offering Japanese lessons to make a living. Eileen Chang also writes about Japanese lessons offered by Russian teachers in her Shanghai narratives. In her essay "Notes on Apartment Life," she skillfully weaves a tapestry of apartment

Figure 3.2

Eileen Chang in an oversized Qing-style padded gown, apparently a
family heirloom

sounds: a servant boy fluent in German translates phone conversations into
German for his young master; a woman of unknown ethnic/national origin
plays Beethoven on the piano; and a Russian man gives Japanese lessons.
These soundbytes combine with the penetrating aromas of simmering beef
stew and Chinese herbal medicine being brewed somewhere in the apartment
complex, providing us with a peculiar glimpse of Shanghai cosmopolitanism set against the backdrop of war and occupation.[18] The peculiar scenario
also testifies to the fact that the incorporation of elements of Japanese culture
in occupied Shanghai was filtered through an existing pattern of cultural
cross-fertilization.

Figure 3.3
Eileen Chang in a yukata (浴衣), a casual style of kimono

Of Poetry, Painting, and Performance Art

The laundry list of Japanese things and themes continues. We know that Chang
was by no means a poet, and seemed to have no taste for symbolist poetry. But
she did not reject poetry altogether. The particular kind of poetry she preferred
is best represented by Japanese *waka*, like the poem cited in her essay "Poetry
and Nonsense" (詩與胡説, 1944). In the essay, she merely mentions that there
is a Japanese poem rendered by Zhou Zuoren (周作人, 1885–1967) as follows:

夏日之夜，有如苦竹，竹細節密，頃刻之間，隨即天明。[19]

In English, the Chinese translation of the Japanese poem would read: "Night of summer days, like bitter bamboo, slender stalks and tight joints, in a quick moment, swiftly brightening the morning sky."[20] Chang fails to mention here that the Japanese poet was none other than Saigyō Hōshi (西行法師, 1118–90), a late Heian and early Kamakura period poet who was best known for *waka* poetry that depicted themes of melancholy and loneliness. Entitled "Untitled" (題不知), the original poem reads:

夏の夜わ　篠の小竹の　節ちかみそよやほどなく　明くるなりけり[21]

The Chinese rendition is almost entirely faithful to the Japanese original, with the exception of the expression "little bamboo," which is rendered as "bitter bamboo" by Zhou Zuoren, perhaps because of his particular affinity for the associations of bitter bamboo. What Chang also fails to mention is that the original translation by Zhou Zhuoren was slightly different, and the version she relays is the revised version produced by Zhou's estranged former student Shen Qiwu (沈啟無, 1902–69).[22] The original source of the poem seems unimportant to Chang. The poem is cited here to highlight her poetic ideal. Language needs to be simple and elegant, and the image it captures should convey an understated profoundness: "Such is the charm of living in China of the moment—in the midst of the filth, the mess, and the sadness, there are precious discoveries everywhere, bringing joy to the whole morning, the entire day, and one lifetime."[23]

In Chang's aesthetic order, the "China of the moment" can only be captured in a fleeting style of poetry produced in a different time and by a different culture. Apparently Chang was not the only Chinese writer who seemed to be in awe of the simple beauty captured in Saigyō's four lines. The same poem was to appear as a design feature on the cover of the inaugural issue of Hu Lancheng's prose magazine *Bitter Bamboo Monthly* (苦竹月刊), published in October 1944, slightly after Chang's essay. Anecdotal evidence suggests that Chang enlisted the help of her closest friend Yanying, the woman who designed her famous dress in the aforementioned photograph with Li Xianglan, to help envision the cover for Hu's magazine. Yanying duly complied. The finished product had Saigyō's poem inscribed in a prominent position, appearing in small fonts, and in pale green, on the whitish stalk of a cluster of bamboo against a warm crimson background. Leaves and branches in darkish green are scattered across the abstract composition (Figure 3.4).

The small closely knit group surrounding *Bitter Bamboo Monthly* must have taken great pride in this striking visual statement. Praise for it appeared in the second issue, penned by none other than Shen Qiwu. Titled "Random Notes from My Southbound Journey" (南來隨筆, 1944), the essay strings together some personal observations of the author as he travels from Beijing, the northern capital, to Nanjing, the southern capital, and the season shifts from summer to autumn. Shen casually tells how he once recounted Saigyō's poem to an unnamed friend and indicates that the text has to be rendered in this particular way to capture precisely the liveliness crystalized in the simple image of bitter bamboo on a summer night. Shen must have been pleased to see that it is indeed his rendition of Saigyō's poem that adorns the cover of the inaugural issue of the magazine, and not Zhou Zuoren's original translation. He marvels:

> Recently I saw the cover of *Bitter Bamboo Monthly*. The design is fabulous, with a bright red background setting off shapes in pure green. The red is of a primary red and the green is of a primary green. The purity of the colors suggests elegance. Neither strange nor deviant, the colors are whole and natural. People tend to abuse the color red, and there is also the danger of excessive application of the color green. But there is none of that dangerous tendency here. The leaves are supple and large, scattering across the frame, with the red background highlighting the design's vibrancy and liveliness. The huge stalk is presented as white, diagonally drawn across the frame. A few green leaves fall on the white stalk, displaying a freshness in contrast to an otherwise rich and dense background. This sort of design always delights me—it simulates the style of woodblock painting, and is not something that could be created by our generation of anemic Chinese artists. The two Chinese characters for bitter bamboo were also done artistically, simulating the seal script but also departing from it. Scripts are inscribed in the visual design, as if they were additional leaves and branches growing out of the bamboo plant—a striking harmony between scripts and image. The word "bitter bamboo" then captures the oneness of this articistic design. In sum, the cover is charming, displaying an Eastern beauty that is pure and proper. The design might not have stayed true to [Saigyō's] poetic image of bitter bamboo on a summer night, but its spirit is healthy, mature, bright, charming, and calm. This could be the atmosphere of autumn, as summer must have already passed . . .[24]

The remainder of Shen's essay is a celebration of Eileen Chang's writing, hailing her as the most talented author this new magazine was able to feature. The transition is abrupt, and supports the suspicion that these supposedly random notes are not random after all. Shen's sketches are a testimony to the shared aesthetics of a small group of authors and editors of whom Chang was a highly respected member. What Shen calls so-called "Eastern beauty that is pure and proper" is after all not quite "pure." Yanying's cover design is at the very best a

Figure 3.4

The cover of the inaugural issue of Hu Lancheng's prose magazine *Bitter Bamboo Monthly* (苦竹月刊), published in October 1944

hybrid product that highlights contrasts rather than harmony. Bringing contrasting elements together into a harmonious whole was a visual strategy that served to illustrate the pan-Asian discourses that were prevalent at the time. Here the four lines of poetry by a late Heian poet became a strange vehicle of a particular kind of cultural blending that took place amidst wartime occupation. While we can reserve a place for Eileen Chang in the history of transmission of Saigyō's poem, we can only speculate on her involvement in the cover design. In citing a *waka* poem, albeit via Zhou Zuoren's rendition and Shen Qiwu's rewriting, and in facilitating a visual statement in the form of this cover design, Chang places herself squarely within a network of cultural transmission and blending in Shanghai under Japanese occupation.

Elsewhere, Chang's preference for short verses from Japan can be seen in the particular attention she pays to the tradition of Japanese figure painting. She writes at great length about her admiration for Japanese woodblock paintings. The essay "Unforgettable Paintings" is laden with Japanese references, and can almost be seen as a reading list of books on Japan and Japanese arts that Chang had been exposed to during that period. "There is a Japanese *bijin ga* called 'A Day in the Life of a Courtesan House in Twelve Pictures' that portrays the life of a geisha over the course of twenty-four hours," she writes. The work she references appears to be one of the works in Kitagawa Utamaro's (喜多川歌麿, 1753?–1806) series of portraits entitled "Twelve Hours of the Green House" (青樓十二時). In referring to Utamaro's works, Chang goes directly into a comparison of Japanese culture and Chinese culture:

> To be sure, China has its famous courtesans such as Su Xiaomei and Dong Xiaowan, who distinguished themselves from the ordinary run of painted faces and went on to great distinction. But in China, it is a question of individual distinction, while in Japan the phenomenon has already become a *system*—in Japan, *anything* can become a system. Geisha are rigorously trained and rule-bound sweethearts for the masses, and even the most trivial of their movements carries the weight of a tradition which brooks not the slightest deviation . . .[25]

Here Chang is clearly traversing the dangerous territory of gross generalization. It is also apparent that her understanding of the artistic traditions of Japan is only rudimentary. As one Japanese scholar politely points out, Chang has apparently confused two works by Utamaro in the same series and ended up describing a work that does not exist. Writing in haste and from memory, Chang did not go back to the album she was citing to check her accuracy.[26] Textual and historical accuracy is clearly not something that concerns her in this essay that strings together rambling thoughts that span different cultures and their artistic manifestations. But her lack of in-depth understanding does not prevent her from launching into a series of rambling comments on the so-called uniqueness of Japanese culture. With a few examples of *bijin ga* at hand and seemingly unaware of the context that gave rise to Utamaro's greatness, Chang goes straight to a conceptualization of a Japanese society that celebrates its harmony at the expense of its women, who are forever relegated to the pleasure quarters of Yoshiwara.

Her feminization of Japanese culture continues elsewhere, albeit combined with further attempts at a miniaturization of Japanese performance art in particular and an infantilization and aestheticization of Japanese culture in general. Chang paints herself as a fan of Tōhō Song and Dance Troupe (東宝舞踊隊), the famous group that frequented Shanghai and other Asian cities in the early 1940s. In her essay "On Dance," Chang talks at great length of her fascination with the fairyland-style miniature world created by Tōhō. In commenting on a dance score entitled "The Lions and the Butterflies," she writes: "This toy-like fright plays on a deeply held childhood fear. It is the Japanese who understand children the best, perhaps because they are children themselves."[27] Elsewhere in the essay, this staged toy-land becomes Japan itself:

> Japan is like a toy box with cardboard partitions. You clear a space and put the miniature teakettles and little toy soldiers inside, each in its own appointed enclosure. An individualist would naturally have trouble endorsing that kind of environment, but the fact of the matter is that the vast majority of people fit very nicely into their partitions, because very few really stand out. Even many of those who are considered exceptional, or at least consider themselves exceptional, are in fact quite unexceptionable. The stylization of society, unlike its mechanization, is a natural process, and has its benefits.[28]

The miniature teakettles and little toy soldiers are recurring images in Chang's random remarks on things Japanese. Seemingly fragmentary, these glimpses of things and themes Japanese add up to a fairly systematic compartmentalization of Japanese culture. In her apparently casual comments, drawn from unsystematic observations, Chang has prefigured a feminization of Japanese culture that was to take place in postwar years.

Tōhō's tour schedule indicates that between March and June of 1943 the group toured Shanghai and performed at the Nanjing Theater (南京大戲院) and Shanghai Theater (上海劇院).[29] The performance Chang refers to in her essay "On Dance," which portrays lions and butterflies, must have been part of this particular tour programme. In April 1943, Li Xianglan joined the Shanghai leg of Tōhō's tour. The spectacle at the Nanjing Theater included Li singing the theme song from *China Nights* (支那の夜, 1940) in both Chinese and Japanese. Accompanying her singing were Japanese dancers wearing costumes that had the Japanese flag (the rising sun) on the front and the Nationalist flag ("blue sky and bright sun") on the back. It is safe to assume that, as early as 1943, Chang had seen Li Xianglan on a Shanghai stage and had participated in this spectacle. Chang's efforts at feminizing, infantilizing, and miniaturizing

Japanese culture took place alongside her participation in the grand spectacle engineered by the empire, in which all of Asia is portrayed as artistically unified under one colonial order.

Eileen Chang and Pan-Asian Film Culture

The list of things Japanese could go on, but perhaps its most important feature is Chang's fascination with wartime Japanese cinema. Surely the photograph of her with Li Xianglan/Yamaguchi Yoshiko was no coincidence. In Shanghai of the 1940s, Chang's writings and tidbits of her personal life were consumed alongside films starring Li Xianglan, including *Song of the White Orchid* (白蘭の歌, 1939) and *China Nights*.

Chang was certainly not the first Shanghai writer to nurse a fascination for Japanese cinema. Japanese films had been shown for Japanese residents in the Hongkew District as early as in the 1910s. And in the 1930s, a generation of Chinese leftist writers and filmmakers frequented Hongkew to watch Japanese films, although none admitted to such "dangerous" pleasures in writing.[30] Chang, however, showed no sense of shame or guilt in writing about the time when she frequented Hongkew Cinema to watch a range of Japanese films. Her two favorites were both musicals—*Dancers of Awa* (阿波の踊子, 1941) and *Songs of Tanuki Goten* (歌ふ狸御殿, 1942).

Filmed just a few months before the outbreak of the Pacific War, *Dancers of Awa* was directed by the prolific Makino Masahiro (マキノ雅弘), who made nearly 300 films during his career and was widely considered a master of the musical. Filming on an elaborate set in Tokushima Prefecture, Makino revived and immortalized the Awa Dance Festival—part of the famous Obon Festival—held every August until it was interrupted by war in 1938. Makino's re-creation of a prewar festivity that provided a visual and auditory feast appealed greatly not only to his audience on the home front, but also to those residing in Japan's colonies. In Shanghai, it would not have escaped Eileen Chang's attention that Hasegawa Kazuo (長谷川一夫), the leading male actor in *Dancers of Awa*, was indeed a household name in occupied Shanghai, as he had starred as the dashing Japanese savior of the Chinese woman impersonated by Yamaguchi Yoshiko in the wartime hits *Song of the White Orchid* and *China Nights* (Figure 3.5).

The 1942 version of the Tanuki Goten film is one of the many versions of the Princess Raccoon legend rendered on the silver screen. Acclaimed director

Figure 3.5

Hasegawa Kazuo (長谷川
一夫) in *Dancers of Awa*
(1941).

Figure 3.6

Miyagi Chikako (宮城千賀子),
in *Songs of Tanuki Goten* (1942).

Kimura Keigo (木村恵吾) directed a series of these films, the earliest in 1939 and the latest in 1959. All were box-office successes, making Kimura one of the most popular film directors of wartime and postwar Japan. The particular Tanuki Goten film that Chang references is a musical, starring Miyagi Chikako (宮城千賀子), a highly versatile actress, in the role of the male lead. In prewar Japan, Miyagi was associated with the Takarazuka Song and Dance Troupe, the famous all-female group. She began her film career at the beginning of the war, and starred in a series of filmic melodramas of the period.[31] (Figure 3.6)

What Chang selects from the wide range of Japanese filmic offerings during the war years is consistent with her general aesthetic preference. She writes: "A Japanese acquaintance laughed contemptuously when I mentioned these two titles, saying that the former was made for children, and the latter for ignorant and uneducated young girls, but I remain unashamed."[32] Films by Mizoguchi Kenji and Ozu Yasujiro did not capture her imagination. What fascinated her were wartime melodramas, fantasy features, and musicals—that is, films that appealed to a middle-brow audience both at home and abroad. Chang has always portrayed herself as an avid consumer of middle-brow features. Her comments on her favorite Japanese films of the war period point to a transnational spectatorship of wartime melodrama. The genre of Japanese home-front cinema also became a smash hit elsewhere in Asia, including occupied

Shanghai. These films typically featured top stars and drew material from well-known legendary narratives that had been told over and over. Chang wrote about the guilty pleasure of actually enjoying these films. Seemingly removed from the war, often marking a festivity that is located in another culture and in a remote time, these activities of viewing and listening were in fact situated at the very center of a transnational wartime culture.[33]

Chang's admission of her taste for the musicals of the war years provides a unique perspective from which we can begin to piece together a more complete picture of cinematic culture in occupied Shanghai. To be sure, *Dancers of Awa* and *Songs of Tanuki Goten* were not the only Japanese films that appealed to the local Shanghai audience. Yau Shuk-ting, in her study of filmic relations between Japan and Hong Kong, also addresses the filmic connection between Japan and Shanghai during the war years. Hers is the first work I have encountered that underscores the importance of understanding the consumption of Japanese middle-brow features by a transnational audience.[34]

The impact of a whole range of Japanese films on a Chinese audience was diluted by postwar denial of widespread Chinese collaboration with the Japanese occupiers, but the consumption of Japanese films in occupied Shanghai is a subject that calls for further study. When Yamaguchi's true identity was revealed, she became a notorious reminder of a shameful past. By contrast, the romanticized version of Eileen Chang gained currency, and her connections with the wartime establishment became elusive. The image of a woman who possessed great talent and rose above her time took root in the minds of generations of Chinese-speaking readers.

Rediscovering these textual tidbits in Chang's relatively obscure works from this time brings us back to the layers of cultural life in occupied Shanghai. We can also begin to have a serious discussion about patterns of cultural consumption through war and occupation. It would not be an overstatement to say that Eileen Chang was a participant in a pan-Asian culture that characterized daily life in the occupied territories of China and other parts of Asia.

To be sure, Chang was no ordinary consumer of things Japanese in occupied Shanghai. Her animated world of little figurines that represent the essence of a much aestheticized Japanese culture came at a most peculiar time. While the colonial empire was striving to represent itself as grand and masculine, Chang's efforts seem to point to a whole different set of references and symbolisms. A feminization of China and Korea (and East and Southeast Asia) in general was a by-product of Japan's systematic reconceptualization of Asia.[35]

Here Chang appears to have reversed the order. The images in her writings of the war period that touch on things and themes Japanese seem to point in one direction—an unsystematic miniaturization, feminization, infantilization, animatization, and aestheticization of Japanese culture. Here I underscore the word "unsystematic," as Chang's comments on Japan often come at unexpected moments, presented in a fragmented form, and in a random fashion. Piecing together these fragments, we can see a "Japan" quite different from that portrayed by the propaganda machine of Japan's colonial empire.

In asking, and trying to answer, the "Japan question," we are by no means diminishing the importance of Chang's work or questioning the reputation of a phenomenal literary figure. In fact, by re-situating Eileen Chang in her own time, and by highlighting wartime politics as the condition of her rise to fame, we should be able to define the importance of her work on a whole new level, one that will allow us to be more in tune with the historical transformations of a turbulent twentieth century, and one that will allow us to rewrite a writer's journey that is closely intertwined with war, revolution, and urban transformations. Simply put, a more careful investigation of wartime complexities as expressed in Chang's writings of her Shanghai period will only make Chang and her writing career more interesting.

Coda: Mapping Japan, and Postwar Reflections

The question that remains is whether Eileen Chang's impressionistic sketches of things Japanese were purely a textual encounter with Japan. Did Chang ever go to Japan, or was her encounter with things Japanese merely on a textual level? The answers to these questions are yes and no, respectively. Chang visited Japan once, in 1952, soon after she bid farewell to Shanghai and returned to a postwar Hong Kong. Chang's Japan trip is sparsely documented and rarely discussed, and the details only began to surface recently. In a letter to C. T. Hsia dated May 7, 1966, Chang mentions this trip: "Barely one semester after I re-enrolled at Hong Kong University in 1952, and because Yanying was in Japan at the time, I had an opportunity to go to Japan. I thought it would be a short-cut to the US . . . I returned to Hong Kong after having spent three months in Japan."[36]

One month after this letter to Hsia, Chang wrote another letter, this time to the Education Officer in the British Embassy in Washington DC. Its purpose was to request a copy of her student file from her three years at the University of Hong Kong in 1939–41. She again mentions her brief visit to Japan in 1952: "My friend Fatima Mohideen was in Tokyo then and offered to help me get to Japan and find work. Anxious to get there before she left for the US—she has been in New York since 1953—I rushed over in November '52 before the end of the term . . . Unable to find employment in Tokyo but with a standing offer of translation work at the Hong Kong USIS, I returned in February . . ."[37]

Exactly what Chang did during her three-month stay in Japan might never be known, but shadows of Japan seemed to always loom in the background of her cultural imagination. Sometimes shades of Japan appear in her descriptions of Japan's other former colonies. Taiwan is one such locale, forever inscribed in a shadowy past in Chang's imaginary map of Asia.

In an essay in English that she published in the American journal *The Reporter* in 1963, Chang recounts her first and only visit to Taiwan in the fall of 1961 as well as a third trip to Hong Kong. Titled "A Return to the Frontier," the essay paints a gloomy picture of a colonial Hong Kong and a postcolonial Taiwan. Taiwan, in particular, is depicted as a land still in the shadow of the Japanese colonial presence, forever inscribed in a bygone era. In the essay, Chang remarks on the fact that Japanese is spoken "in the middle of nowhere," not just by "the early Chinese settlers" who were assimilated during the occupation, but also by "a surprising number of their young people." She goes on to note "how un-Chinese these people were . . ."[38]

A Chinese version of this essay was recently unearthed by Roland Soong (宋以朗) among the boxes of personal belongings Chang left to Soong's parents. The Chinese essay is by no means a translation of the English one, as Roland Soong rightly indicates; rather, it enriches the earlier version by providing a much more detailed reflection on the place of Hong Kong and Taiwan in a postwar world. In the newly discovered essay entitled "Revisiting the Border Towns" (重訪邊城, 2008), Chang remembers her first glimpse of the island of Formosa en route from an occupied Hong Kong to her equally occupied home of Shanghai in 1941:

> I had never been to Taiwan before, but en route back to Shanghai from Hong Kong following the Pearl Harbor Incident, the Japanese boat that I was on was re-routed to avoid the bombing. It zigzagged and looped around south of Taiwan island. The boat never docked, though the mountains in the distance were clearly visible. Two or three other passengers were also there looking, leaning against the railings on the deck. They quietly called to their friends to come and take a look. For some peculiar reason, nobody dared to speak loudly. I stood there motionless, not daring

to move even one step away. I feared that if I missed this, I would not encounter such beautiful scenery ever again.[39]

This impressionistic view of the island of Taiwan on an imaginary map of Japan's colonial empire is a final rehearsal of an earlier moment in Chang's prose writing from the war era. In a rambling essay entitled "Duet" (雙聲) written in 1945, Chang's prose takes the form of a mini roundtable talk, a prominent genre in the popular culture of that period. At the beginning of the essay, like most of the roundtable talks recorded in popular journals of the time, the surroundings and atmosphere are sketched in painstaking detail. While indulging in coffee and pastries in a coffee shop, Eileen Chang, the narrator, and Mo Meng (獏夢), the narrator's female companion and a persona of Chang's friend Yanying, begin their rambling discussion of disparate topics: "Having seated ourselves, we started chatting about a variety of things in great detail. When our topics became more weighty, she [Mo Meng] said: 'You know what, this seems a lot like a roundtable discussion.'"[40]

During the course of the essay, the two women discuss a wide variety of themes: the discourse on love in both China and the West, the construction of romance in different cultural contexts, gender relationships both inside and outside marriage, fashions for women of different ages, and the distinctiveness of the Japanese mentality. When the topic shifts to things and themes Japanese, the narrator tells her female companion:

> Three years ago I first saw their woodblock paintings, their designer fabrics, their pottery, and those innocent looking, red-faced toy soldiers. I also remember on the boat returning to Shanghai (from Hong Kong), that an elderly Japanese sailor brought out a picture of his three daughters to show us. Our boat passed through Taiwan. The charming mountains on the island, seemingly floating on the sea, like a blue-and-green Chinese landscape painting. Never had I imagined that mountains could look like that in real life! They say that the scenery in Japan is of a similar style. Gazing out from my cabin window, captured in the round porthole, in the darkness of the night, the bay was cloaked in a bluish grey. A quiet fishing boat appeared in the distance, a red lantern hanging high . . . How obsessed I was with this intoxicating scene![41]

If Taiwan appears to be a land of beauty and mystique, it is seen from the vantage point of the war and occupation. And on board a Japanese boat, and tracing the edge of a fading colonial empire, the Eileen Chang observing a wartime topography seems to belong to no land. Hers is a perspective that is suspended and hovering above, one that she carried with her into the postwar years. On her imaginary map of the war and places affected by the war, the world is surprisingly connected and yet places seem far removed from each other. This creates the most intimate kind of alienation. What, then, can be made of the connection between Eileen Chang and Japan? It is both distant and intimate, an entanglement that haunted the long course of her creative life.

I wish to thank the organizers of and participants in the following international conferences for their comments on earlier versions of this paper: "Eileen Chang: Romancing Two Cultures," the University of Hong Kong, April 2009; "The Culture of Emergency: Cultural Production in Times of Upheaval, 1937–1957," National University of Singapore, August 2009; and "Visuality and Cultural Literacy," National Central University of Taiwan, December 2009. Special gratitude goes to Leo Ou-fan Lee, Karen Kingsbury, Paul Pickowicz, Yiman Wang, Yvonne Sung-sheng Chang, Yeh Yueh-yu, Yau Shuk-ting, Chang Wen-hsun, Hsiu-Chuang Deppman, Fan Ming-ju, and Charo D'Etcheverry for their comments and support.

4
The Ordinary Fashion Show

Eileen Chang's Profane Illumination and Mnemonic Art

Esther M. K. Cheung

From Fashion Consciousness to Mnemonic Art

Reading Eileen Chang's fascination for clothing is a fascinating experience; reading her critics' fascination with her writings on fashion is even more enthralling. The existing body of scholarship on Chang's fashion consciousness can be regarded as a reading guide for our engagement with this enigma. Among the endeavors to decode Chang's semiotics of fetishism, one major strand of criticism reads Chang's feminine sensibility through her sensuous and meticulous description of details, especially those about clothing. Some critics even claim that this writing strategy plays out a "politics of details" that challenges the May Fourth notion of the self.[1] Others prefer to adopt a psychoanalytical approach informed by Chang's autobiography, arguing that Chang's fascination with fashion is a way of compensating for what she has lost in her personal life.[2] Another strand of thought focuses on the relationship between fashion and everyday life, without overlooking Chang's feminine sensibility. Critics believe that Chang's fashion consciousness provides a clue that assists readers to grapple with the relationship between everyday life, modernity, and her material aesthetics.[3]

It is this latter strand of discussion that has interested me most. As Nicole Huang succinctly puts it, Chang's "conceptualization of fashion as an everyday invention is another illustration of the distinctly material quality of her aesthetics." In this regard, literary writing can be regarded as the beginning of "a cultural history of things."[4] With a different focus, Leo Ou-fan Lee explores the notion of modernity and the time-consciousness inherent in Chang's everyday world of materiality.[5] Contrary to a teleological and epochal historical view, Chang's writings demonstrate an impressive kind of "quotidianization of thoughts," as Harry Harootunian would have put it.[6]

In Chang's writings, it can be observed that everyday life is both a space and a time from which illuminations for historical and philosophical reflection can be derived. In the quotidian space of the here-and-now, it is often the most mundane and ordinary objects and people that have inspired Chang to observe, think, and reflect. However, this is not to suggest that her idea of everyday life can be deciphered through a transcendental perspective. Instead, her approach to everyday life is an immanent critique because her inspirations are often drawn from the materialistic and anthropological dimensions in the mundane realm of everyday life. However philosophical Chang may sound in her writings, her observations are generated from within the immanent realm of possible experience and secular knowledge. This is close to what Walter Benjamin calls "profane illumination" when he discusses the continental avant-garde in Europe in the 1920s. If surrealist writers such as André Breton convert "everything that we have experienced on mournful railway journeys . . . into revolutionary experience,"[7] Chang's visions of everyday life focus on the colors, patterns, and textures of clothing. She probably would have smiled agreeably with Benjamin if she had had a chance to read his aphorism that "the eternal would be the ruffles on a dress rather than an idea."[8] Her fascination with clothing is of course only a metonym of her general preference for things and activities that are secular, earthbound, and mundane. These activities may include routines such as eating and leisure as well as individualistic and non-monumental events such as people's romances. By valorizing the presentness of the present, Chang seeks to transform the prosaic state of empirical, everyday reality into a form of literary imagination characterized by *huangliang* (荒涼), which is now commonly translated as "desolation." In this regard, unlike other critics who decode her fashion consciousness through a symptomatic and allegorical lens, I seek to explore the ways in which her views on fashion are metonymically and horizontally associated with other aspects of everyday life.

To fill the void in existing scholarship, this chapter focuses on how Chang's essays show us an intricate relationship between everydayness, gender, and literary imagination. While a lot of discussions have centered on Chang's fictional works, this chapter turns to the essays that mediate a literary subjectivity that differs from that of her fictional works. In her study of women's print culture in war-torn Shanghai, Huang notes that the print culture initiated by a group of women, including Chang, "took part in defining and transferring the structure of modern knowledge."⁹ These women writers promoted themselves as cultural commentators and public intellectuals. The modern essay form, also known as the informal essay (小品文), became a tool of self-representation for these writers. It has a long tradition in Chinese literary history, but Chang's adoption of this literary form is associated with the contemporary urban reality in war-torn Shanghai in the 1930s and 40s. Huang further suggests that it was through the essay form that Chang "was able to weave a complex inner life together with a mounting public persona."[10] It has been observed that, in Chang's fictional works, there is always an authorial stance at a distance from her female characters that are subordinated to oppressive tradition and patriarchy. The aesthetic distance between the narrative voice and her female characters produces a dualistic consciousness often described as Chang's style of "feminine writing."[11] In this way, her fiction renders her literary subjectivity indirectly, while her essays paint a portrait of the author as a public intellectual whose private, everyday experiences and philosophical reflections are made more immediately accessible to readers.

It has been argued that all Western modernist literature can be generally described as mnemonic art because of the shock impact of modernity. With reference to the nineteenth-century French poet Charles Baudelaire, Paul de Man maintains that literary modernity is associated with a sense of freshness and youthfulness:

> The human figures that epitomize modernity are defined by experiences such as childhood or convalescence, a freshness of perception that results from a slate wiped clear, from the absence of a past that has not yet had time to tarnish the immediacy of perception . . . of a past that, in the case of convalescence, is so threatening that it has to be forgotten.[12]

In this strand of Western modernism, mnemonic art aims to preserve what threatens to vanish and to be forgotten. In this regard, one easily recalls Baudelaire's famous maxim that suggests this interesting paradox: "By 'modernity' I mean the ephemeral, the fugitive, the contingent, the half of art whose other half is the eternal and the immutable."[13]

By contrast, Chang's mnemonic art does not celebrate a similar sense of youthfulness and freshness but traces secular illuminations of everyday life through an antiquated path. In "Writing of One's Own" (自己的文章, 1944), for example, Chang expresses her view on memory and modernity, arguing that although the present moment is brief and fleeting, it is the source of stability and placidity that enables her to recall "an ancient memory." She describes this ancient memory as "the memory of a humanity that has lived through every era." She thinks that being "closer to our hearts than anything," this ancient memory enables us to see things in the future.[14] "Days and Nights of China" (中國的日夜, 1946), originally published as an epilogue to *Romances* (傳奇增訂本, 1946), is another exemplary piece that depicts how moments of inspiration from everyday life are intimately associated with a writer's creativity.[15] The piece features a fascinating "fashion show" of ordinary people without glamorous embroidery, colorful lace, or figure-fitting *qipao* (旗袍). From the hawkers and poor children to the Daoist monk and the prostitute she saw in the streets, this quotidian procession is not merely a slice of the Shanghai urban phantasmagoria in the present; its familiarity and sociological triviality allow Chang to grapple with a long, antiquated memory concretized in the space of the everyday. Like Benjamin's famous "angel of history" in "Theses on the Philosophy of History" ("Über den Begriff der Geschichte", 1940),[16] Chang's face is always turned to the past, not only to witness how the wind of progress piles up debris on debris, but also to see uncanny familiarity in this antiquated memory. It is amazing to observe that Chang was only in her twenties when she wrote "Days and Nights of China"—not long after the end of the Sino-Japanese War (1937–45). Surely she was too young to be retrieving such an ancient memory?

Between the General and the Particular

In reference to this ancient memory in Chang's works, Liu Zaifu makes a controversial remark that is at odds with C. T. Hsia's established view. It is this comment that places the present discussion within the context of everyday life, gender, and literary imagination.

In his famous *A History of Modern Chinese Fiction, 1917–1957* (1961), Hsia hails Chang as "the best and most important writer in Chinese today,"[17] and her "The Golden Cangue" (金鎖記, 1943) as "the greatest novelette in the history of Chinese literature."[18] This has helped Chang to gain wider recognition in the serious literature since the 1970s. Hsia argues that the value of Chang's works lies in her "strong historical awareness." Unlike *Dream of the Red Chamber* (紅樓夢), which is a world reverberating "stable moral standards," Chang's fictions deal with a society in transition by showing "the persistence of the past in the present."[19] Nevertheless, Hsia praises Chang's satirical style, maintaining that her moral passion is not "less intense than that of the professed didacticist."[20]

Liu, on the other hand, argues that Chang is better seen as a philosopher than a historian. Citing Wang Guowei, he further suggests that Chang's works fall into the category of Chinese literature, like *Dream of the Red Chamber*, that is concerned with philosophy.[21]

> [S]he [Chang] inherits from *Dream of the Red Chamber* an understanding about the dilemmas in human existence and human nature that lurk behind family activities, love relationships, and marriages. In so doing, she consciously and unconsciously demonstrates a concern for the fate of humankind, an everlasting concern that transcends the boundaries of space (Shanghai and Hong Kong) and time (her own era).[22]

Undoubtedly, Liu is right to argue that Chang's historical reflections in famous works such as "The Golden Cangue" and "Love in a Fallen City" (傾城之戀, 1943) carry a strong philosophical awareness. As Liu remarks, "Love in a Fallen City," a love story of two passing visitors in Hong Kong during the Pacific War, tells us that the world is not "making progress;" instead it is "gradually entering a desolate wilderness," and "everything in reality . . . will turn into nothingness and death in the end."[23] Chang's musings over abstract issues such as human civilization and human nature demonstrate her ability to generalize and philosophize. To further illustrate her philosophizing, I quote a passage from "Writing of One's Own":

> All of us must live within a certain historical era, but this era sinks away from us like a shadow, and we feel we have been abandoned. In order to confirm our own existence, we need to take hold of something real, of something most fundamental, and to that end we seek the help of an ancient memory, the memory of a humanity that has lived through every era, a memory clearer and closer to our hearts than anything we might see gazing far into the future.[24]

I argue that "something real" and "something most fundamental" can mean the true feelings between people. The "help of an ancient memory" (the so-called "historical consciousness") is used as a pretext, but the real concern is how we can survive and how we can face our human predicament. In another instance, in "From the Ashes" (燼餘錄, 1944), Chang reflects upon the fleeting nature of human existence:

> What a shame that we occupy ourselves instead searching for shadows of ourselves in the shop windows that flit so quickly by—we see only our own faces, pallid and trivial. In our selfishness and emptiness, in our smug and shameless ignorance, everyone of us is like all the others. And each of us is alone.[25]

The image of the shop window may remind readers of the mirror in *Dream of the Red Chamber*. Whereas the mirror in *Dream of the Red Chamber* may suggest, among other things, the prophetic meaning and the elusiveness of human life, the image of the shop window depicts the inevitability of human weakness. Most importantly, the historical background of Hong Kong's colonial modernity was the source of inspiration for Chang.

As Liu has observed, Chang's fondness for distilling and abstracting the general from the particular at a fleeting moment is obvious. What she herself calls "an ancient memory" that "has lived through every era" is the "general" grounding of this double bind of the general and the particular. She attempts to derive the universal from the specific. To grapple with this duplicity, Chang claims that she is fond of "an intense and unequivocal contrast." Referring to colors metaphorically, she likes to create such contrast by way of matching "bright red" with "deep green."[26] The relationship between "the general" and "the particular" can be better understood, then, in terms of different colors against the background of each other.

There is no denying that this philosophizing tendency has given rise to an abundance of aphorisms in both Chang's fiction and her essays. Her readers are often led to follow her generalizations from transient, piecemeal, and trivial existences. The process of distillation and abstraction, in fact, is not uncommon among literary writers. What is being "sublimated" from the fleeting moment is close to Baudelaire's idea of "the other half of art" that is "the eternal and the immutable." In this case, it is more productive to claim that Chang's texts are double-coded with the general and the particular. One may observe that her works demonstrate a tendency to philosophize, but to diminish her historical awareness will restrict our understanding of her dual reflections on Chinese history in particular and human existence in general.

In this way any comparison of this kind should enable readers to grapple with different manifestations of the double bind of the general and the particular in varied historical and cultural contexts. As discussed below in the context of everyday life, "Days and Nights of China" illustrates a similar process of abstraction through which Chang as a creative writer derives her inspiration from the most immediate historical milieu and everyday experiences in Shanghai. It follows that the historicity of her writings should not be underestimated.

That said, the question of Chang's historicity is not an easy one to tackle. As observed by many critics, Chang's historical awareness is closely associated with her views of everyday life or a different understanding of history through "a critical method that operates with details."[27] However, in the essay mentioned above, Liu's remarks about the everyday life details in Chang's works also spark controversy. He claims that her female characters are "often selfish women living in a mundane world": "Feeling lost in a fast-changing society, these women are poles apart from the female revolutionaries. They never want to change society. All they manage to do is to carefully struggle with the details of life."[28] He argues that despite her literary achievements, the everyday life aspects of Chang's works have turned her into a less remarkable writer than Lu Xun. Chang, in his view, is inferior to Lu Xun because she is trapped within the domain of everyday life and is too preoccupied with her feminine sensibility. It is necessary to quote at length from him to acquire a clear grasp of his arguments:

> In twentieth-century China, only two writers had a genuine sense of despair: Lu Xun and Eileen Chang. When despairing, Lu Xun tried to overcome his despair and, as a result, his writings are characterized by anger and frustration; whereas Eileen Chang just felt despair and, as a result, her works are characterized by a feeling of desolation. Lu Xun saw through life, but he also confronted life and struggled hard with it, so his works display a masculine sublimity; whereas Eileen Chang could see through life but did not have the courage to face it.[29]

In Liu's view, "Lu Xun obviously goes further than Eileen Chang in his spiritual exploration." This claim, which concerns the debate on gender and authorship, is in fact not new. The opposition between the masculine sublime and feminist sensibility has been a major focus of feminist critiques from the First Wave to the Third. The oppositions between form and matter, sublimity and sensibility, intellect and body, and reason and emotion are some common topics in this debate. To critique this binary way of thinking, many Western critics have attempted to work "against the grain" by challenging the tendency to essentialize gender attributes. For those who focus on gender and textual politics, much attention has been paid to the construction of gender roles and literary tropes. Some of these approaches only provide partial and biased knowledge. Gilbert and Gubar's influential study *The Madwoman in the Attic* (1979) is a case in point. The narrowness of their literary focus notwithstanding, their claim that the madwoman is the biographical author's alter ego has reduced the subjectivity of the author to nothing but a literary trope.

In light of the history of Chinese literary criticism, Liu's arguments replay the familiar debates between the leftwing and rightwing approaches to the meaning of history and revolution in literature. The controversies over the value and significance of the fiction of Mandarin Ducks and Butterflies are clear cases in point.[30] When Liu reiterates the claim that Lu's anger, frustration, and despair are sublimated through the process of writing, he concludes that male writing is symbolic, metaphysical, and spiritual, while Chang's feminine sensibility is a blatant revelation of escapism.

In response to the above claims, this chapter seeks to discuss the relationship between a writer's everyday experience and her literary imagination. By questioning the everyday space as gendered, this paper aims to destabilize, if not shatter, the binary thinking of female sensibility and masculine sublimity. It examines how an insufficient appreciation of the nature of everyday temporality has restricted our understanding of Chang's historical and philosophical awareness. By deciphering Chang's "mnemonic art," it is hoped that the ways in which the universal and the sublimated originate from the trivial and the ordinary will be augmented.

The Everyday: Insights from Shanghai Streets

The notion of the everyday, which derives from *le quotidien* in French, is an important aspect of the study of modernity in Western scholarship. It is Henri Lefebvre's *Critique of Everyday Life* (*Critique de la vie quotidienne*, 1961) that drew our attention to the importance of the trivial details of everyday life outside the macro-social structures.[31] In fact, before this conception was developed by French Marxists and the Situationists, the earlier idea of the quotidian was referred to as a moment in a day for the distribution of bread to the poor in Medieval France. Central to this notion is the idea of the banal, trivial, and repetitive quality of life under capitalism. As Rob Shields recapitulates, "[m]odernization wrought rapid changes in the patterns and routines of daily life and highlighted the loss of individual control and sense of community with the acquisition of a materialistic lifestyle."[32] In other words, the space of everyday life produces alienation because of its routinized and mechanized nature. Quoting Lefebvre, Harootunian further articulates the relationship between modernity and everyday life by saying that "modernity is represented here as the new, and everydayness is seen as the durational present, incomplete but 'situated at the intersection of two modes of repetition: the cyclical, which dominates in nature, and the linear, which dominates in processes known as "rational"'."[33] It is indeed very productive to see everyday life as a durational present that is incomplete, ongoing, transitional, and even recurrent, but its recurrence is always repetition with a difference from a phenomenological and ontological perspective.

Undoubtedly, modernization has produced regularized and routinized patterns of everyday life. However, as our lived reality, everyday life is the measure of all things; it is where we can find fulfillment and non-fulfillment of human relationships. The French Situationists are instructive in asserting that an array of experiences can be derived from everyday life: daily routine, leisure, artistic experimentation, and revolutionary politics. The quotidian space is both empirical and utopian. On the one hand, it is empirical because a multiplicity and variety of personal and family activities ranging from routines of work to entertainment and leisure pursuits can be found. Due to its frivolous routines and domestic and personal nature, this empirical dimension is often feminized. It is often suggested that when literary writers write about such experiences, as Liu and others comment, they are frivolous and escapist. There is often a naturalized assumption. This naturalization is problematic. On the other hand, everyday life is seen as utopian because there is always the promise that a different use of the quotidian than the banal and the repetitive is possible. Its utopian potentialities lie in its open-endedness and incompleteness. It can then be further argued that the utopian dimension pertains to what is philosophical and universal. For a literary writer, this is the space where he or she sublimates his or her thoughts. We may even argue that sublimity and sensibility coexist in the same mundane space of everyday life. Since everyday life is recurrent, every durational present is a Benjaminian *jetztzeit*—a historical "now" whose fullness can counter the empty chronology of modern and calendar time.[34] It is through such a dialectic of the empirical and the utopian that alienation can be disarticulated. In the process of reconfiguring the everyday, both history (the particular) and human existence and civilization (the general) can be re-comprehended.[35]

"Days and Nights of China" presents an impressive case in which Chang navigates her literary subjectivity between the private and the public space to disarticulate the condition of alienation. It can be seen that sublimity and sensibility coexist in the mundane space of everyday life. Unlike a Marxist critic, Chang does not launch any explicit critique of capitalism to dis-alienate; instead, she immerses herself in the daily routines of this empirical space. On many other occasions, she admits her own secular orientations and money consciousness. The essay was written after the Sino-Japanese war when China was still in turmoil. The condition of alienation was more concerned with the war and destruction. Without irony or sarcasm, she begins "Days and Nights of China" by expressing both surprise and delight at living through the routines of everyday life. Chang can derive the greatest ecstasy from the smallest falling leaf. The first poem in the essay, "The Love of a Falling Leaf," depicts a serene moment when a falling yellow leaf from a French plane tree is touching the ground, trying to get in touch with its shadow. After a brief transient moment, the writer describes the quiet reunion of the leaf and its shadow as if in a dreamscape:

> In the autumn sun
> on the cement ground
> they sleep quietly together
> the leaf and its love.[36]

This fascinating moment of disarticulating alienation is achieved in an insecure world in which the sun's rays are "knifelike" and the most concrete building is but a dusty dream. However, any careful reader would observe that this reunion does not fall into the natural, organic cycle since the leaf ultimately lands on the impenetrable cement ground of the city.

In this dreamscape, without pointing to a specific calendar time, Chang describes the everyday space as a transitional, liminal in-between, somewhere between autumn and winter. One may even argue that the two poems in "Days and Nights of China" were sublimated after innumerable banal and repetitive daily trips to the market. Measured time is not necessarily a feature of modernity, but the exactness of clock time has produced forms of control and tyranny over urban city dwellers. Efficiency, punctuality, and exactness characterize the world under capitalism, as Georg Simmel explicated in "The Metropolis and Mental Life" ("Die Großstadt und das Geistesleben," 1903) more than a century ago.[37] In this case, the writer's time is indefinite and imprecise, almost acquiring a certain mythic and transcendental quality. To our amazement, this subjective time is not subject to any transcendent critique, as there are no projected answers outside both the individual and the social realm; nor are there religious reflections displaced onto an afterlife or another world. As noted at the outset, Chang's portrayal of time can be seen as an immanent critique in which the criticism of everyday life is turned inward and comes within the realm of possible experience and knowledge. More precisely, it is the preoccupation of a social class whose pursuit of the exceptional and the extraordinary is in fact "a criticism of their classes." This argument is based on Chang's two interrelated responses to modern speed. In the first instance, she seems to be most concerned with racing with modern time. In the preface to the second edition of her short story collection *Romances*, Chang famously writes,

> Even if I were able to wait, the times rush impatiently forward—already in the midst of destruction, with a still-greater destruction yet to come. There will come a day when our civilization, whether sublime or frivolous, will be a thing of the past. If the word I use the most in my writing is "desolation," that is because this troubling premonition underlies all my thinking.[38]

In another instance, Chang urges herself, "Make yourself famous as early as you can! If success comes too late, the pleasure of it isn't as intense . . . Hurry! Hurry! Otherwise it will be too late! Too late!"[39] She seems to be competing with time, but this feeling of urgency is better read as a critique of the modern, capitalistic concept of time that denounces its linearity and forecasts its destructiveness.[40] In contrast to this sense of hurriedness, the indefinite subjective time of contemplation and creativity in "Days and Nights of China" slows the writer down and nurtures a rejuvenating power in the space of everyday life. We all remember Chang's famous phrase that "[e]ven if I were able to wait, the times rush impatiently forward."[41] Let me twist her aphorism a bit in light of this everyday encounter: If everyday life is a durational present that is incomplete and ongoing, profane illuminations can only be generated when individuals wait for them.

Chang's experience in a sense echoes Richard Lehan's reflections on literary creativity and modernism. Referring to Western modernist literature, impressionistic art and Henri Bergson's psychological theories, Lehan sees a close connection between literary subjectivity and what he calls "intuitive intelligence." Contrary to reason as "outward intelligence" and instrumental rationality, intuitive intelligence turns inward. When Lehan analyzes the Baudelairean personae in poems such as "Crowds" ("Les Foules," 1869) and "The Swan" ("Le Cygne," 1857) he argues that "artistic subjectivity is grounded in the crowd, that the poet's imagination is fueled by cityscapes."[42] While this reference to Lehan's assertion does not seek to universalize the diverse experiences of modernity, one must admit that the space of everyday life in the city has become a source of inspiration for writers and artists, regardless of their gender, social background and nationality. As is the experience of many writers, Chang's sublimity is achieved as a result of serendipities and subsequent contemplation rather than escapism.

This notion of the inward turn, however, is not an affirmation of the Western Romantic notion of the self that turns inward or any metaphysical idea of transcendence. In Chang's case, it is "intuitive intelligence" grounded in the observation of "beauty," "tragedy," or "desolation" rather than "heroics" and "strength." As noted earlier, the "equivocal contrast" that Chang advocates turns outward as well as being a subtle critique of the dominant literary discourse of her time, articulated so well and clearly by Liu's idea of male sublimity and leftwing writers' preoccupations with political reform, revolution, and national unity.

In a tug of war between tyrannical objective time and subjective, esoteric time, Chang reconstructs the experience of war-torn Shanghai through an idiosyncratic history of everyday life. It is interesting to note that Chang depicts everyday life as both "phenomenologically familiar" and "sociologically residual," to borrow from Peter Osborne's articulation of the history of everyday life.[43] In "Days and Nights of China," the morning chores are repetitive and routine; the smell from the laundry on the bamboo pole is familiar; the colors and patterns of the padded cotton gowns of two children are similar. Chang meets an array of the most unrecognizable and least impressive inhabitants. Their activities are most mundane and ordinary—selling, begging, shopping, passing by, and so on. Their quotidian world opens up an arena in which the writer conjures up an intertextual reading of a world that is both far and near, bright and dark, ephemeral and antiquated. The happy tangerine hawker's enthusiastic selling reminds her of the ideological depiction of Chinese people in the comics by Sapajou, who published daily cartoons in the *North-China Daily News* from 1925 through the Japanese occupation.[44] A prosaic moment of daily selling and buying becomes a time for meditating cross-cultural imaginations and the urban personality produced by metropolitan Shanghai. The Daoist monk's presence in the city street sparks ontological reflections on the meaning of life. He is clad in a cloak of "faded black cloth"; his coiled hair reminds Chang of "the look of an embittered woman who's fallen on hard times";[45] his tall, gaunt, malnourished body recalls an ancient memory of a different time, retelling the familiar story of the dream of the yellow millet porridge. In a brief instant, the vibrant metropolitan city is once again depicted as a dreamscape: will one wake up one day and realize that one's entire, mortal life is but a dream, which lasts the time it takes to cook a pot of yellow millet porridge?

Chang's literary reflections on this ordinary fashion show demonstrate her tendency to transcend binary and hierarchical thinking. This essay records a moment when Chang's critical reflections on life, people, and nation are generated as she makes her way to the market. There is no distinct boundary between high and low, sublime and frivolous; nor is there a hierarchy between male and female. This temporal configuration is close to what Osborne calls "differential time," in which time is composite. While each era may have a unified type of time, differential understandings of time coexist in connection with other temporalities that demonstrate their own points of reference and logic. Spatially, Chang's thoughts move horizontally rather than vertically, somewhat in the manner of Zhuangzi's notion of "the equality of things" (qi wu 齊物). Events and thoughts on the national and universal levels coexist with the ordinary and the everyday. Chang attributes equal status to the mundane and the monumental. This reminds us of an interesting example in Franz Kafka's diary in 1914. This is what he wrote on August 2, 1914: "Germany has declared war on Russia—Swimming in the afternoon."[46] As a serious writer known for his earnest concern for humanity, Kafka shows us the coincidental occurrence of a mundane routine and an international affair. Whether or not this diary entry suggests an individual and universal desire to maintain stability in the midst of turmoil is open to interpretation; it does remind us that many national and international happenings are simply disruptive and unwelcome in one's everyday life.

In the above portrayal of the procession of ordinary people in "Days and Nights of China" we can catch a glimpse of the ordinary people as phenomenologically familiar and yet sociologically residual. Their activities are not monumental or macro-structural but belong to a historical vacuum—an in-between space for what is left over after all distinct, superior, specialized, and even heroic activities have been marked for formal historical analysis. If the sociologically residual history of everyday life has escaped historians, it is always a point of interest for Chang. In "Writing of One's Own," in response to Fu Lei's criticism of her serialized novella Chained Links (連環套, 1944) Chang argues that the basis of the "uplifting and dynamic aspects of life" is the "placid and the static." Critics and readers, in her view, are often fascinated by the parts on "struggle" but are critical of the placid:

> Very few works in the history of literature plainly sing in praise of the placid, while many emphasize the dynamic and uplifting aspects of human life. But in the best of these works, the uplifting aspects of human life are

still portrayed against the background of its inherent placidity. Without this grounding, uplift is like so much froth. Many works are forceful enough to provide excitement but unable to offer any real revelation, and this failure results from not having grasped this notion of grounding.[47]

The grounding for the heroic and uplifting aspects of human life is the placid and harmonious dimensions of life. For a writer, this grounding is of utmost importance because it is an open-ended space of revelation. Although Chang does not refer to the term "everyday life," the incomplete and open-ended nature of this placid grounding is very similar to the quotidian dimension of life. It is the lived space of everyday life for weak, ordinary people, like those portrayed in her fiction. It is not defined clearly in black and white, but by an "equivocal contrast." Without being able to "aspire to heroic feats of strength," the ordinary people serve better than the heroes as a measure of their times, just like everyday life is the measure of all things, of success and failure, of sadness and happiness.

Furthermore, it is interesting to note that this open-ended space of everyday life is the source for retrieving an ancient memory that is uncannily recurrent. I have discussed Chang's "Writing of One's Own" about the role of "an ancient memory" in one's survival. In the same passage, Chang makes it clear that this antiquated form of remembering is caused by abrupt transition from the old to the new:

> In this era, the old things are being swept away and the new things are still being born. But until this historical era reaches its culmination, all certainty will remain an exception. People sense that everything about their everyday lives is a little out of order, out of order to a terrifying degree.[48]

Chang argues that we begin to feel the awkwardness of the discrepancies between memory and reality, thinking that this ancient world is "absurd and antiquated," "dark and bright at the same time."[49] No doubt this ancient memory is familiar and real phenomenologically, but repetition in Chang's mnemonic art always recurs with a difference. The familiar quotidian space is lived and re-lived differently in a historical "now." Let me cite the uncanny recurrence of the bluish green color from "Days and Nights of China" as an example. At the sight of the mended blue cotton shirts that ordinary people wear in the streets, Chang is reminded of a bigger patch of bluish green on the cosmological level:

> Most of the blue cotton shirts you see people wearing on the streets have been mended so many times that they are a patchwork of light and shade, as if they had all been rinsed by the rain, leaving an eye-opening bluish

green. Our China has always been a nation of patches. Even our sky was patched together by the goddess Nüwa.[50]

In both Chang's essays and her fiction, the concrete, mundane details of everyday life often mediate her general abstractions of history. This association is not merely a casual one about seeing folk mythology in everyday life. In the second poem, which bears the same title as the essay, "Days and Nights of China," and is also the epigraph for *Romances*, the portrayal of China as a nation of patches depicts a world of imperfection disquieted by drumbeats of war, chaos, internal turmoil, and an uneasy clamor of voices. It is a space of alienation, where daily routines have also become weighty and burdensome. In Chinese mythology, the goddess Nüwa mends the sky with patches and makes the world more livable for ordinary people, who are visualized as a "patchwork" of "eye-opening bluish green."

In Chang's fiction, references to the bluish clothing that signify a sense of ordinariness are abundant. Readers may readily recall the anonymous performer in "Preface to the Second Printing of *Romances*" (傳奇再版自序, 1944). When musing over the importance of achieving instant fame, she describes her experience of watching an outdated Shanghai Hop Hop Folk opera performance. On stage there was a man dressed in a blue gown:

> A man in a blue gown beat the rhythm out with strong blows of a big bamboo stick: *kua kua! kua!* He came out to stage-front, close to the audience, and pushed the singer hard. *Kua! ke-jia! ke-jia!*—the pitiless pounding went on and on.[51]

Blueness signifies the universal connection with ordinariness in the Chinese context. The phrase "a man in a blue gown" conjures up an image of poor Chinese people and brings forth an association with the historical fate of Chinese society in an age of instability and turbulence. In another instance, "Steamed Osmanthus Flower: Ah Xiao's Unhappy Autumn" (桂花蒸：阿小悲秋, 1943) describes a special moment of encounter between Ah Xiao and an unknown man who wears a blue gown:

> Just now in the third-class compartment of the tram, she [Ah Xiao] has been jostled about so much she had barely managed to keep her feet. She has had her face pressed right up close against a tall man's deep-blue gown. Because it was so filthy, the cloth had a peculiar softness about it. It didn't look like cloth at all. Waves of heat emanated from its blue depths. This weather smelled just like that gown—but not one's own clothes, absolutely not. One's own dirt was a lot easier to live with.[52]

Chang's subtle depiction of Ah Xiao's feelings for the man in the blue gown is telling. It is close to a kind of repugnance for people of her class. Although she belongs to the lower stratum of society, her physical intimacy with the man does not bring her psychologically closer to people of the same class. Blueness is a useful signifier to highlight this ironic ordinary connection that is not acknowledged by the character.

The color blue occupies an important position in Chang's fiction and essays. As Tao Fangxuan observes, there is a wide spectrum of bluish light and shade in Chang's works: peacock blue, brilliant blue, cyan blue, aquamarine, marine blue, and tangerine blue.[53] In her personal life, the bluish green is a memorable detail that is associated with her mother and her own writing career. In *Mutual Reflections: Looking at My Old Photo Album* (對照記：看老照相簿, 1994), at the sight of her childhood portrait, one is struck by the impressive blue of the little girl's dress. According to Chang's commentary, this bluish color was painted by her mother, whose strong liking for the color blue is tacitly and mysteriously shared by mother and daughter. In her memory, her talented mother's oil painting of a still object was also in this bluish-green spectrum.[54] Because of her liking for this color, she chose it for the cover of the first edition of *Romances*. Without any pattern or elaborate design, the blueness serves to bring back an antiquated memory. It encompasses an embrace of the empirical and utopian dimensions of everyday life and a secret yearning for a female bonding—with the mythological Nüwa, the theatrical woman of the barbaric state dancing at the end of "Love in a Fallen City," her long lost mother, and her oft-mentioned Auntie. But one can perhaps say that this female bond is but a metonym of the quotidian space which, as Chang states in the poem, is populated by "a people of patched and colored clouds."[55]

Chang's world of "profane illumination" encompasses the huge array of personal, historical, cultural, and philosophical reflections outlined above, within the space of everyday life. This discussion reminds us that there is so much to discover in the world of fashion. As Chang claims in her often-quoted essay "Chinese Life and Fashions" (1943), it is possible to do a psycho-social study of clothing. The world of fashion is her habitat:

> Quick alterations in style do not necessarily denote mental fluidity or readiness to adopt new ideas. Quite the contrary. It may show general inactivity, frustration in other fields of action so that all the intellectual and artistic energy is forced to flow into the channel of clothes. In an age of political disorder, people were powerless to modify their existing

conditions closer to their ideal. All they could do was to create own atmosphere, with clothes, which constitute for most men and all women their immediate environments. We live in our clothes.[56]

While there may be different perceptions of how one may choose to act in times of turmoil, it can certainly be said that a "differential history" can be written through fashion and the experiences of everyday life.

Dialog with Lu Xun: From the Mauve Scarf to the Hula Vest

Let me end with the recent archival discovery of an interesting essay by Chang entitled "Yanying's Catalogue of Clothes" (炎櫻衣譜), which was originally published in 1945 in a Shanghai tabloid.[57] The ideas in this essay are not as widely known as those in her famous "Chinese Life and Fashions" since the essay was only recently re-discovered. In this essay, Chang's intertexual reference to Lu Xun seems to offer us an indirect and subtle rebuttal of Liu Zaifu's criticism that was presented in the earlier section of this chapter. Writing the preface for Yanying's new fashion catalog, she expresses her view that what is regarded as trivial and mundane can also be revolutionary: "I really do not understand why people commonly praise one's dissatisfaction with reality as revolutionary and admirable whereas they criticize one's dissatisfaction with fashion styles as fancy but weird dress." She describes in great detail different kinds of revolutionary new styles in Yanying's shop. With considerable subtlety, she cites Lu Xun's famous "everyone's mauve scarf" in "After Nora Walks Out, Then What?" (娜拉走後怎樣)—a talk he gave at the Peking Women's Normal College on December 26, 1923.

Speaking about the plight of liberated women in response to A Doll's House (Et dukkehjeme, 1879), Lu criticizes Ibsen's lack of political vision for changing the world. In passing, he mentions that the mauve woolen scarf, a popular style at the time, would have no value if women were awakened from their dreams without also being socio-economically empowered: "Dreams are fine; otherwise money is essential."[58] In a mild rebuttal, Chang claims that she and Yanying are making money from fashion, implying that they achieve some form of financial independence as a result. The catalog of clothing she wrote for Yanying was a means of achieving that goal. Most interestingly, she describes how Yanying has made revolutionary changes to the mauve scarf by turning it into a hula vest. Evoking the tropical Hawaiian ambience of a hula vest, the newly transformed woolen scarf signifies an embodiment of feminine passion, desire, and playfulness. If there is something revolutionary about it, it is a revolution on the level of everyday life, albeit without the radical quality that Lu Xun promoted. Chang's intertextuality evinces a rebellious disposition through the playful citation of a popular garment.

Along with the horizontal chain of details of everyday life, Chang's subversive use of fashion, as some feminist critics have described it,[59] has shaped not only a habitat for her "to live in" but also an idiosyncratic cosmos of its own. Her contemplation of even the smallest "ruffles on a dress" has activated and transformed the prosaic and the mundane into an illuminatory "historical now"—a Benjaminian *jetztzeit*, for broader and deeper historical reflection. Lu Xun is right to say that Ibsen is a poet in the realm of dramatic literature but not a social reformer; neither is Eileen Chang, whose poesy of fashion and everyday life has not caused an empire to collapse but has constructed an idiosyncratic genre of mnemonic art in Chinese literature. Her profane illumination, immanent critique, and abstraction of the everyday have woven a tapestry of "the general" and "the particular" within a quotidian space of color, pattern, and sensation.

5
Betrayal, Impersonation, and Bilingualism

Eileen Chang's Self-Translation

Shuang Shen

In March 2009, several articles that told previously unknown stories about well-known Chinese writers and artists who were sent by the authorities to spy on their friends and colleagues during the Cultural Revolution were widely circulated on the Internet.[1] The articles provoked intense debate over these acts of betrayal—whether these individuals could be forgiven, and what the proper approach to a traumatic historical incident such as the Cultural Revolution should be. Coincidentally, the same month, Eileen Chang's novel *Little Reunion* (小團圓, hereafter *Reunion*) was published posthumously in Chinese-speaking regions, stimulating a new round of discussion about this talented but controversial writer.[2] At around the same time, two English language manuscripts by Chang also came to light. As a bilingual writer, Chang's Chinese language works have been more popular than her Anglophone works. Before the publication of *Reunion*, her literary accomplishment was assessed mainly on the basis of a handful of short stories written in the 1940s while Chang was living in Shanghai. Her creative activities after she left China in the 1950s, particularly during her years of residence in the United States, have been less well known or considered to be less significant to Chinese-language readers than her earlier works. However, the publication of *Reunion*, along with the discovery of Chang's two English language manuscripts, suggests the need for a new evaluation of this writer.

This chapter suggests that the newfound enthusiasm for Eileen Chang among Chinese language readers is not an isolated phenomenon that is unrelated to contemporary cultural politics in the local contexts of different Chinese-speaking regions. In mainland China, it is the current widespread public interest in narratives of betrayal that partly inspired the renewed interest in Chang. Stories of betrayal, such as those of the writers who spied on their friends during the Cultural Revolution, do not just prompt questions about the moral character of individual public figures; they also make the general public wrestle with larger issues of historical representation and the formation of the Chinese subject. Although Eileen Chang's life and writings do not have any connection to the Cultural Revolution *per se*, she has long been considered a politically ambiguous figure due to her position in an earlier moment of Chinese history—the Sino-Japanese War. Chang came to fame as a young writer of popular romances in Japanese-occupied Shanghai in the early 1940s, during which time she had a short-lived marriage to Hu Lancheng (胡蘭成), an intellectual who collaborated with the Chinese puppet government headed by Wang Jingwei during the war. The label of collaborator accorded to Hu by the Nationalist government after the war rendered Chang guilty by association, and this history still affects Chang's reception in mainland China. For instance, the Chinese authorities ordered the cancellation of an academic conference devoted to Chang's works that was originally planned for Shanghai in 2005.

The controversy surrounding Chang does not only represent an anachronistic return to an earlier historical moment; it is also in many ways a reaction to the contemporary moment of globalization and the role of the Chinese diasporic subject in this process. In 2007, the success of Chinese-American director Ang Lee's film *Lust, Caution* (色，戒), which is based on a short story by Chang, led to accusations of betrayal being directed at both director and author.[3] The cultural politics revolving around *Lust, Caution*, discussed in detail in other chapters of this volume, suggests some implicit connections between diasporic subjects and the charge of betrayal.

The reception of Eileen Chang over the decades gives us cause to wonder whether there are more productive ways of understanding betrayal than perceiving it simply as a political label. Defenders of Chang tend to assert that betrayal is a non-issue in her case by insisting on the essentially apolitical nature of Chang's works.[4] This trajectory of reading, though consistent with the strong aesthetic inclinations Chang displays in her writing, de-emphasizes the multi-layered historical embeddedness of Chang's self in national and international politics. Underlying this reading strategy is an understanding of betrayal as a negation of certain essential truths about a historical period or the Chinese subject defined in historical representations of that period.

In contrast to both her critics and defenders, Chang herself does not avoid discussing betrayal in her writings, especially those composed after she had left mainland China. Writing about betrayal allows her to describe the complex contextualization of the diasporic subject vis-à-vis multiple nation-states in the context of the Cold War. Elsewhere I have discussed the theme of betrayal in relation to historical representation in Chang's newly published novel *Little Reunion*, a novel written in the United States over the last three decades of her life.[5] In this chapter, I focus on Chang's bilingual practice in her early essays published in Shanghai, her story "Lust, Caution" (1978), her English essay "A Return to the Frontier" (1963), along with its Chinese version (重返邊城, 2008), all of which foreshadow her later self-representation as betrayer in *Little Reunion*.

Asian American critics such as Crystal Parikh and Leslie Bow argue that betrayal bears testimony to the complexity of belonging. They suggest that betrayal should not be understood in terms of "deception, hypocrisy, or cynicism," because "all of these refer to a place of authentic self-presence from which the adequacy of (self)-representation might be evaluated."[6] Underlying their consideration of betrayal is a philosophically informed (via Lévinas and Derrida) understanding of the self, which considers the self as always dependent upon a non-assimilative Other or Others. Betrayal exposes exactly this relationship of the self and the Other, albeit in a violent and traumatic manner, by severing intimate bonds and emotional ties. This violence actually forces us to reconsider the historical construction of the sovereign subject. "[A]n ethical reading of betrayal discerns self-presence, the coherence of an autonomous, sovereign subject unto itself, as impossible," Parikh argues.[7] This ethical attitude toward betrayal, advocated by Parikh, is a more complex response than either moralist denunciation of or liberal forgiveness towards the traitor. It can translate into a critical self-reflection on the historical conditions that constitute the sovereign subject.

How does this critical reflection on the sovereign subject enabled by the figure of betrayal allow us to better understand Chang's linguistic and cultural self-representation in between the cultural and political worlds? By comparing Chang's writings with their translations, I notice that Chang's bilingual practice shows clearly the consciousness of the tension as well as mutual dependency of the worlds of Chinese and English. It is based on this awareness that Chang engaged in a self-performance through self-translation. This chapter argues that since the danger of betrayal always accompanies the author's negotiations between opposing political interests and different cultural worlds, betrayal can be used as a lens through which to consider the complex social formations that contextualize the self of the author. To access Chang's bilingual practice through the figure of betrayal implies that we need to be careful with unconditional celebrations of bilingual competence, cosmopolitanism, and even transgression. While it is easy to interpret the translator's license of betrayal as a liberatory act that brings diversity and new meanings to the native language and culture, the consideration of Chang's bilingual practice here complicates this assumption by drawing attention to the historical conditions of bilingual practices. My concern in this chapter extends beyond reaffirming the status of Eileen Chang within the Chinese literary canon or the canon of Asian American literature; rather, given Chang's importance in modern Chinese literary history, we should consider the significance of this iconic figure in terms of how her bilingual practice sheds light on those areas that have been neglected or "othered" by mainstream narrations of this history. Along this line, I will first situate Chang in the larger context of Chinese cosmopolitanism before moving on to discuss her essays and their translations.

Reconsidering Chinese Cosmopolitanism through Eileen Chang

The betrayal embodied by Eileen Chang is specifically related to the cosmopolitan-turned-diasporic subject and the historical memory borne by such a subject. I have argued elsewhere that discourses and practices of cosmopolitanism in early twentieth-century China are of various kinds, and due to the self-perception of belated Chinese modernity and China's history of colonialism, some versions of cosmopolitanism do not necessarily conflict with discourses and practices of nationalism.[8] The May Fourth tradition, which consists of various discourses of radical anti-traditionalism and Westernization, can be considered as a form of "discrepant cosmopolitanism" with a nationalist orientation, particularly as the threat of Japanese invasion intensified in the 1930s.[9] However, the May Fourth discourse by no means encompasses all cosmopolitan subjects, ideas, and practices. Writing in Japanese-occupied Shanghai in the early 1940s, Eileen Chang deviated from the May Fourth tradition at the beginning of her writing career, and as several critics have argued, this deviation is reflected in the evocation of a different genealogy—that of the Mandarin Ducks and Butterflies fiction, which was an alternative discourse of modernity and cosmopolitanism repressed by the May Fourth tradition.[10] What is less commented on, however, is how this deviation introduced a different perspective on Chinese cosmopolitanism, one that highlights the issue of power in relation to cosmopolitan subjects and cosmopolitan culture. Chang's fictional works from the 1940s consider power differentials in gender relations, particularly in Orientalist perceptions of Chinese women. In both "The Golden Cangue" (金鎖記, 1943) and "Love in a Fallen City" (傾城之戀, 1943), for instance, cosmopolitan male subjects as either a "returnee man" (Kam Louie's term) or an overseas Chinese man command power over their "authentically Chinese" female counterparts by invoking their cosmopolitan advantage and their self-Orientalizing Chineseness. This depiction of cosmopolitan subjects becomes more complicated in "Red Rose, White Rose" (紅玫瑰與白玫瑰, 1944), in which Zhenbao, the male protagonist who has studied abroad and returned to China, meets his match in some equally cosmopolitan Chinese women he met abroad. Zhenbao deals with this competition by reverting to a culturally con-servative position—marrying an "authentically Chinese" woman with a tradi-tional bent, who is barely capable of coping with the modern world. The ironic ending of the story confirms that cosmopolitanism as embodied by Chang's fictional male characters is far from an ideal hybridization of East and West. On the contrary, it is shot through with power differentials determined by the material condition of China's colonial modernity. Chang's critical representa-tions of cosmopolitan Chinese men can be read as a satirical comment on the high-minded cosmopolitan ideals championed by the May Fourth pioneers.

In the stories Chang wrote in the 1940s that depict the asymmetrical rela-tionship between male cosmopolitan Chinese subjects and their gendered Other, the cosmopolitan subject has already returned home. Home is depicted as a bordered space that excludes certain Others. What happens when the setting of the story is no longer within China? What happens when the cosmo-politan subject leaves home again for the diaspora? Existing studies of Chinese cosmopolitanism have been hesitant to go beyond the borders of the Chinese nation-state and discuss the connection between cosmopolitanism and exile, immigration, or other types of diasporic dislocation.[11] This reticence is reflec-tive of the disciplinary divisions among Chinese studies, Asian American studies, and the studies of "overseas Chinese," which results in insufficient consideration of the complexity of Chinese cosmopolitanism (i.e., the tension between "Chineseness" and cosmopolitanism and various cosmopolitan posi-tions and individuals), particularly during the Cold War period. The domi-nance of the nation-state and the binary opposition between capitalism and communism in the Cold War period turns cosmopolitanism increasingly into a state-sponsored project, with Chinese diasporic subjects situated in between opposing ideological poles.

Little attention has been paid to Chang's writings outside China, partly because how to approach transnational and multilingual cultural production during the Cold War period is a question that both Chinese studies and Asian American studies have not resolved. Chang's alienation in the United States does not mean that she had no connection with the US or did not attempt to participate in US public spheres before or after immigrating to the US. She published two English novels, *The Rice-Sprout Song* (1954) and *The Rouge of the North* (1955), in the 1950s and 1960s, and wrote a long article entitled "A Return to the Frontier" that was published in *The Reporter* in 1963. During the early stages of Chang's career outside China, she had intricate connections with US Cold War institutions such as the United States Information Agency (USIA). *The Reporter*, a magazine based in New York, "is every inch anti-Communist," according to its chief editor Max Ascoli.[12] In the context of polarized political and national interests during the Cold War period, betrayal can easily be understood as going over to the other side. However, if as Parikh suggests, betrayal is an "intersubjective" moment that "intimate(s) an-other knowledge, the knowledge of the Other, that is a nonknowledge, insofar as it can never be made transparent and communicable,"[13] Chang's putative betrayal should render a more complex description of the historical context of the Cold War, in which the diasporic Chinese subject is situated.

So far I have tried to suggest that the term "Chinese cosmopolitanism" may be too vague to describe the complex and various intercultural encounters and border-crossing activities of this period in a broadly defined modern Chinese context. The case of a single bicultural writer such as Chang already suggests that we need finer distinctions that differentiate "Chinese cosmopolitanisms" according to position (i.e., cosmopolitanism from above vs. from below), location (home or abroad, national subject vs. diasporic subject), gender, and other factors. An all-too-easy and unconditional celebration of a homogenous notion of "Chinese cosmopolitanism" could produce undesirable outcomes that contradict some original intentions of endorsing cosmopolitan worldviews and outlooks of life.

Although I begin this chapter from a Chinese perspective, my reading of Eileen Chang foregrounds what may be perceived as a disjunction in Chang's late career between living and writing in the United States and publishing mostly in Chinese-speaking regions. Chang's writings are set in this disjunctive space between the Anglophone and Sinophone worlds—the United States and Asia—a space of cultural production that some scholars refer to as the "trans-

Pacific" or the "Asia Pacific."[14] In Parikh's discussion of emergent American literature, this space has been conceptualized as one of diasporic betrayal, where diasporic difference figures as the ungraspable Other that is brought to light only by narratives of betrayal. Parikh claims that betrayal enables us to see "the diaspora [as] always already exist[ing] within the idea of the domestic, marking a fundamental repudiation that installs the division between the domestic and the foreign in national and minority discourses."[15] However, in order to account for Eileen Chang's utilization of the "Asia Pacific" as a space of cultural production, we have to come to terms with betrayal not just as a political concept, but as a linguistic and cultural concept that is always historically determined.

The space of the "Asia Pacific" is also a space of multilingualism, where the Sinophone practice of Chang gets continuous translations into English, and vice versa. Here we can evoke Shu-mei Shih's term "Sinophone articulation" while considering it as denoting not just the transformations and differentiations within the Chinese language. The Sinophone cultural imaginary, as Shih has defined it, pays close attention to the history of dispersion and migration of Chinese people in the world, their social positions in the nation-states of their settlement, and the transformations in immigrant communities over time.[16] It makes important corrections to both the conventional assumption that Chinese is a singular category in terms of ethnicity and language and the US focus on the Asian American imaginary.[17] Chang's case is particularly useful for us in describing the shape of the Sinophone imaginary at a particular moment of history and the ways in which this Sinophone imaginary has been incorporated into nationalist narrations of history. The Cold War period is a space of aporia in the reception of this writer in mainland China. In order to come to terms with this aporia, we need to revisit some earlier moments of Chang's career in which her implication in politically charged contexts of cross-cultural communication is manifested.

Self-Translation and Impersonation

Chang's early practices of self-translation in the 1940s anticipate her later portrayal of the spy and of spying as a mode of cross-cultural knowledge production. Before her Chinese writings gained popularity in the early 1940s, Chang wrote English-language essays for the Shanghai-based magazine *The XXth Century*. These essays were subsequently translated into Chinese by Chang and republished in Chinese-language magazines in Shanghai. Writing and

rewriting the same pieces in Chinese and English later became a habitual practice in Chang's career. Sometimes, an English version preceded the Chinese
version; at other times, they were produced the other way around. Published
in the politically charged context of Shanghai under Japanese colonializa-
tion, Chang's self-translation exercises of the 1940s should not be perceived as
purely linguistic exercises; they are the textual site of an identity performance
that I call "impersonation."

Thinking of translation as impersonation moves away from the conventional
approach to translation as the transfer of meaning and places more emphasis
on the different contexts that create the differences between the source text
and the target text.[18] The metaphor of impersonation allows us to consider linguistic, personal, and bodily performances together in translingual and cross-
border contexts. The fact that Chang did not present herself as a translator in
most cases, but intended her texts, whether published in English or in Chinese,
to be read as originals, suggests that there is an issue of "masking" in her self-
translation and bilingual practice. In other words, when the critic approaches
an "original" text from the perspective of translation, the prior life of this text
in another language that comes to light in this critical investigation has a dou-
bling effect on the original, trailing it like a shadow. The concept of the doubleness of translation as impersonation allows us to gain a better understanding of
the writer's migratory trajectory from one cultural context to another.

The double act of impersonation does not imply that it is by nature insincere
or deceitful. Tina Chen distinguishes between impersonation and imposture in
Double Agency: Acts of Impersonation in Asian American Literature and Culture
(2005). She argues that "impersonation makes the duality of its ontology manifest."[19] Chang's self-translation practice "makes manifest" the "duality of ontology" of Chineseness as defined and articulated in the semi-colonial urban
setting of Shanghai that shaped Chang's cultural position in important ways.

An analogy can also be drawn between Judith Butler's discussion of Barbara
Johnson's translation of Derrida and Paul de Man and Chang's self-translation. Here Butler makes the distinction between two different kinds of loyalty
that the translator has towards the original text: "faithfulness" and "fidelity."
Depicting translation as a tug of war between these two articulations of faithfulness, Butler highlights the scandalous nature of translation, how it necessarily needs to push against the limits of acceptability, even in its attempt to render
the original in a faithful manner. "In fact, it is unclear whether translation can
ever be other than 'bad' or at least have some badness in it, since the original

has to be crossed, if not partially mutilated, with the emergence of translation itself," Butler argues.[20] Chang's self-translation is "scandalous" particularly because by writing in English, she insinuated herself into a complex environment in which knowledge production was intertwined with political interests.

As Butler has noted, it is difficult to imagine translation as "other than bad." The magazine that published Chang's English essays in the 1940s, *The XXth Century*, was a publication that had a clear pro-Axis political agenda. Its editor Klaus Mehnert was a Russian émigré to Germany and taught Russian history and politics at several American universities before going to Shanghai. Most of the articles he wrote for *The XXth Century* were either scholarly analysis of Soviet politics or a defense of Fascism from an intellectual perspective. Mehnert was very much aware of the strategic importance of a global city such as Shanghai as a place for gathering and exchanging information. In one article, he writes that

> [o]ut of all the cities outside the Soviet Union—with the possible exception of Ankara—Shanghai is the best equipped for the study of the developments in the USSR. It is the only place in East Asia, and one of the few places in the world, where one can simply step into a bookstore and purchase literature—newspapers, magazines, novels, plays, pamphlets, scientific treatises—fresh from the Moscow presses; where three Soviet dailies (two in Russian and one in English) as well as three Soviet magazines (two in Russian and one in Chinese) appear; where Bolshevist editorials are frequently made verbatim to Shanghai readers and radio listeners within a few hours of their publication in Moscow; where a Soviet radio station transmits daily from morning to night in Russian, Chinese, German, and English.[21]

These statements remind us that, as in Hong Kong during the Cold War period, knowledge production in wartime Shanghai was anything but apolitical.

It is in this kind of setting that Chang engaged in discussions of Chinese culture and history through her depictions of everyday life matters, such as Peking Opera and fashion. Looking at Chang's English essays alongside her own Chinese translations, we can see that she was careful in negotiating between different language communities and intricate political divides. She made conscious adjustments to her writing based on the different demands of English and Chinese readerships. In her English essay "Chinese Life and Fashions," published in the January 1943 issue of *The XXth Century*, the opening sentence invites the outsider to enter the private sphere of the Chinese home and observe the Chinese ritual of clothes-sunning:

> Come and see the Chinese family on the day when the clothes handed
> down for generations are given their annual sunning! The dust that has
> settled over the strive and strain of lives lived long ago is shaken out and
> dancing in the yellow sun. If ever memory has a smell, it is the scent of
> camphor, sweet and cozy like remembered happiness, sweet and forlorn
> like forgotten sorrow.[22]

The balcony where the ritual of sunning clothes takes place can be considered a liminal space between public and private spheres, Chinese and foreign worlds. Chang pays attention to the lighting in this liminal space. Details such as dust dancing in the sun give this space a theatrical quality, making it inviting to the foreign spectator. The syntax of the imperative in the first sentence issues an invitation to the addressee, who is assumed to be an outsider to the typical Chinese family described here. In a subsequent Chinese rewriting of this essay, entitled "A Chronicle of Changing Clothes," (更衣記, 1944) due to the change of audience, the first sentence is changed to a tone that sounds less inviting and more detached: "If all the clothing handed down for generations had never been sold to dealers in secondhand goods, their annual sunning in June would be a brilliant and lively affair."[23]

The ritual of sunning clothes brings to mind the confessional act of disclosing one's private life in public, as conveyed in the colloquial expression "airing dirty laundry." Indeed, cultural chronicles such as "Chinese Life and Fashions" (1943) and "Still Alive" (1943) are intended to achieve complex goals that go beyond simply providing a sketch of Chinese life and customs from an objective perspective. These chronicles have an autobiographical effect and perform the work of self-representation for the cultural outsider. That this work of cross-cultural self-representation was viewed by Chang as to a certain extent "scandalous" can be seen in her translation of another English language essay "Still Alive" into the Chinese essay "Peking Opera through Foreign Eyes" (洋人看京戲, 1943). She finds it necessary to add an entire paragraph at the beginning of the Chinese essay, where she defends her observation of Chinese culture through foreign eyes. As in her translation of "Chinese Life and Fashions," here she also radically adjusts her relationship with the reader by adding or deleting several passages and changing the tone of several sections of the essay. The opening paragraph of "Peking Opera through Foreign Eyes," which exists only in the Chinese version, places the speaker in relation to the collectivity of Chinese by using pronouns such as "we" and expressions such as "our fellow Chinese." The paragraph goes like this:

> To see China through the eyes with which foreigners watch Peking Opera would be an exercise not entirely lacking in significance. Bamboo poles overhead from which children's cotton-padded split pants are hung out to dry; big glass jars on store counters full of "ginseng-whisker" wine; the loudspeaker from one house broadcasting the sound of Mei Lanfang singing Peking Opera; the wireless in another house hawking medicine for scabies; buying cooking wine under a shop sign that reads "The Legacy of Li Po": China is all of these things—colorful, shocking, enigmatic, absurd. Many young people love China and yet have only a vague notion of what this thing called China might be. Unconditional love is admirable, but the danger is that sooner or later, the ideal will run up against reality, and the resultant rush of cold air will gradually extinguish one's ardor. We unfortunately live among our fellow Chinese. Unlike Chinese overseas, we cannot spend our lives safely and reverently gazing toward our exalted motherland at a comfortable remove. So why not make a careful study of it instead? Why not revisit its sights through the eyes of a foreigner watching Peking Opera? For it is only through surprise and wonderment that we may be able to find real understanding and a steadfast, reliable love.[24]

In this passage, the pronoun "we" indicates that the author comes from the same community as the intended reader. "We" does not just indicate a rhetorical position; it also refers to the object of the essay, the Chinese collective or "the object of our love," which is supposed to be constructed through performing an exercise of cultural spectatorship—i.e., watching Chinese life through the eyes of a foreigner watching Peking Opera. "We" refers not to a starting point but to an end product. The use of "we" sets a task for the rest of the essay, which is to prove that adopting the perspective of a foreigner watching Peking Opera should produce not just a better understanding, but a greater love for Chinese culture. Yet it is exactly this connection between the mind and the heart, rational understanding and emotional identification towards China, that is not guaranteed by the essay.

This additional paragraph in the Chinese version radically changes the tone of the original English essay, turning what was originally a detached explication of Chinese characteristics into an engaged argumentative essay with a more ambitious agenda: the task of showing that the "surprise and wonderment" stemming from seeing China through the eyes of a foreigner can translate into "a steadfast, reliable" love for Chinese culture as a whole.

Self-translation starts from the role-switching of the author from a supposedly "authentic" Chinese informant addressing a foreign audience to a Chinese person adopting the perspective of a foreigner while addressing a Chinese readership. In this process of role-switching, the Chinese person is delinked from Chinese culture, as is a foreigner from a foreign perspective. Andrew Jones's English translation of the title of Chang's Chinese essay into "Peking Opera Through Foreign Eyes" already incorporates the separation of "foreign eyes" from foreign bodies. The original Chinese title (洋人看京戲) is less clear about this separation. Such phrasing implies that by adopting a foreigner's perspective, the author may indeed become a foreigner (洋人), a suggestion that sounds more dangerous and scandalous than Jones's translation. To think of self-translation as impersonation allows us to see that translation is more than a linguistic act; it is an intellectual performance as well as a bodily performance. Chang's Chinese essay pushes against the cognitive and bodily limits against which "Chineseness" is defined.

This opening paragraph that appears only in the Chinese version acknowledges that China is often seen through a series of stereotypical images that make it seem "colorful, shocking, enigmatic, absurd." The questions of how to see differently, and what to see and not to see, are central issues in this essay. Chang's description of Peking Opera should not be taken as an objective representation of Chinese life, but as a reflection on Chinese manners of seeing *in* and *through* Peking Opera as an art form that has mastered and perfected this art of perception. Spying, which according to Chang, is a common practice among the Chinese themselves, is introduced into the essay precisely because spying draws our attention to the social norms that define what we should and should not see under specific circumstances. Andrew Jones's English translation of Chang's description of spying in the Chinese essay goes like this:

> For Chinese people, there is no escaping onlookers. A woman of the upper classes, if she is of a traditional bent, lives in nominal seclusion, sequestered in her boudoir, but once she wakes up in the morning she lacks even the right to close her bedroom door. In winter, a quilted curtain blocks out the wind, but the door is left wide open, inviting the scrutiny of everyone in the household, great and small. To close a door in daylight hours would be to invite scandal. Even under the shelter of night, with the door closed and barred, an uninvited guest is able to see everything simply by licking the window paper with his tongue and peering in through the moistened spot.
>
> Marriage and death are above all else matters of public concern. Spectators hide under the bed in the bridal chamber, and a man breathes his last surrounded by a roomful of people waiting to hear his last words. It is not without reason that Chinese tragedies are loud, bustling, and showy. Grief in Peking Opera is rendered in bright tones and vivid colors.
>
> This lack of private life explains a certain coarseness in the Chinese temperament. "Everything can be spoken," and that which is left unspoken

> is almost certainly dubious and criminal in nature. Chinese people are always astonished by the ludicrously secretive attitude foreigners bring to completely inconsequential matters.[25]

The English original contains exactly the same passage as the Chinese version; however, subtitles and section breaks in the English text frame these paragraphs differently. Whereas in the Chinese text, the passages quoted above immediately follow a paragraph about the loudness of Peking Opera, the highly dramatic nature of this theatrical form and its explicitness of artistic representation, in the English version a section break and the subtitle "The Crowd and the Chinese Psychology" separate the discussion of Peking Opera from that of the crowdedness of Chinese life. This section break and subtitle are crucial framing devices that provide a separate identity to Chang's discussion of Chinese crowds, hinting to the reader that this description can be interpreted as a straightforward explication of "Chinese psychology." Without the section break and subtitle, the Chinese essay, by contrast, conveys a different message by placing emphasis on performance and spectatorship. The writer suggests that since the performance on stage (Peking Opera) corresponds to performances off stage (spying and being spied on), there is no clear boundary that separates stage and off-stage. The Chinese are always watching others perform while performing themselves. The prevalence of spying in everyday life only shows that there is no "safe" position hidden from other people's glances from which one can comfortably watch the Chinese performance.

If, at the beginning of the essay, China and Chinese life are passive objects waiting to be seen, towards the end of the essay the Chinese themselves play an active role in spectatorship and the production of spectacles. The perspective of the foreigner looking in at Peking Opera and Chinese culture is reversed and transformed into the Chinese looking with "surprise and wonderment" at each other and the things around them. This essay's conclusion—that there is no *unseen* position for seeing—is a powerful argument against the adoption of an "omniscient" perspective in cross-cultural knowledge production. By impersonating a foreigner watching Peking Opera, the author tries to prove that this unfamiliar and defamiliarized perspective on Chinese culture can indeed combine "real understanding" with "a steadfast, reliable love" for it. The writer suggests in the end that impersonation, like translation, is an important aesthetic strategy that makes us love ourselves and others more.

Whereas Klaus Mehnert saw the magazine and the city of Shanghai as strategic locations from which to gather and transmit useful knowledge about other cultures, Eileen Chang clearly understood that knowledge production about the Chinese in these locales was not an objective and disinterested exercise; rather, it was dependent on the perspectives from which one observed this culture. This politics of seeing, situated in the specific interracial and cross-cultural context of the colonial city, creates the complex figure of the spy, whose role goes far beyond the utilitarian goal of information gathering. Chang's Chinese and English essays in the 1940s thus foreshadow her consideration of spying, betrayal, and identity in the well-known short story "Lust, Caution."

"Lust, Caution" as a Failed Spy Story

Although Chang's short story "Lust, Caution" does not directly deal with the interlingual and international sphere, since the opposing sides in the story are the Nationalist government and the puppet Chinese government headed by Wang Jingwei, the story can be read as an allegory of knowledge production in this interlingual and international context, particularly if we look at the Chinese version in conjunction with a newly discovered English version of the story "Lust, Caution," composed in the early 1950s, almost two decades before the Chinese version was published.[26]

There are some critical differences between this English story and the Chinese version completed many years later. In the Chinese version of "Lust, Caution," the ostensible reason that the female protagonist Wang Jiazhi fails to perform her role as a spy is that she has fallen in love with her enemy, Mr. Yee. However, in the English manuscript, interestingly titled "The Spyring (*sic*) or Ch'ing K'e! Ch'ing K'e!", the conflict between underground activism and love interest is not at all clear. There is barely enough evidence to allow us to conclude that Shahlu (Wang Jiazhi) has any true feelings for Mr. Tai (Mr. Yee in the Chinese version). Consequently, the reason that Shahlu fails to complete her role in the assassination remains ambiguous. Since the English version contains little description of the female protagonist's inner life and provides no details about her prior participation in revolutionary activities, Shahlu appears to be a more instrumental character whose expressed feelings are a mere cover for the job she has undertaken. In fact, it is this excessive instrumentality that brings about her eventual downfall.

In *Spy Story* (1987), Cawelti and Rosenberg argue that the structure of a typical spy story manifests a cycle of clandestinity that reflects the alienated state of existence of every man in modern society. This cycle culminates in the appearance of the figure of the double agent, who represents "total isolation" because "there is no person with whom he can share his secret view of the world. He must lie to everyone."[27] At this point, Cawelti and Rosenberg imply that the double agent becomes a personification of clandestinity himself, since he could be "engaging in secret activities against the clandestine group."[28] This double-layered secrecy necessarily causes betrayal, but it is not betrayal in the conventional sense of violation of the interests of the individual or group that a spy supposedly serves, but self-betrayal in the sense that the spy has undermined her own identity and lost the sense of purpose of the spying activity.

The English manuscript tells a Kafkaesque story about wartime life in Shanghai, where spying is more than a profession or a form of political activism, it is a mode of seeing and a way of life practiced by everyone in the story, as the title "spyring" suggests. Shahlu finds herself surrounded by spies after she arrives in Tai's residence. For instance, before she leaves the house for a rendezvous with her lover/enemy Mr. Tai, "she made no attempt to find out if Tai had already left the house. The place swarmed with servants all too ready to inform on the guests and on each other."[29] A few lines down, Chang tells us that Shahlu feels pressured to carry out the assassination attempt early because she is afraid that her cover will be blown if she waits any longer. "Time was getting short. Mrs. Mar would tell on them. Shahlu had heard that Mrs. Tai had on one occasion hired somebody to throw a package of filth at an actress Tai was interested in. The least she would do would be to set men trailing them and that would be disastrous to Shahlu's plans."[30] It may be true that the people surrounding Tai do not suspect that Shahlu works for Tai's political enemy, but this does not make Shahlu less suspect in their eyes, because being vigilant and keeping a watchful eye on those around them is a mode of existence that applies to professional intelligence workers and ordinary civilians alike. As Chang tells us towards the end of the story, "Since the war began there has been this saying, 'T'eh wu pu fung chia, special agents are all one family,' because they could switch sides with ease."[31]

Whereas the detective may be linked to crimes in local or domestic settings, the spy is often connected to international relations and politics. Cawelti and Rosenberg argue that, in a spy story, "[w]hether the action all takes place in one country or the agent is sent on a secret mission from one country to another, the background is a conflict of international political interests."[32] Chang's story can be read as a depiction not of a specific location or historical period (Shanghai during the Anti-Japanese War), but of any moment in history when knowledge production across national borders oversteps sensitive political fault lines, rendering the knowledge bearer and transmitter into the figure of the spy. The English version of "Lust, Caution" can be read as a commentary on Hong Kong as a "family of special agents" during the Cold War period. The manuscript is dedicated to R. M. McCarthy of the United States Information Agency in Hong Kong, a significant American institution in Cold War history. Historians have discovered that one of the missions of the USIA in Hong Kong was to collect information about Communist countries such as China. Although situated in an environment of clandestine knowledge production, Chang's story should not be read realistically as a text filled with intelligence submitted to the USIA, thereby equating Eileen Chang with a spy. Neither should McCarthy be seen as Chang's contact in an intelligence agency. In fact, by exposing spying as a mode of utilitarian knowledge production, this story does not serve the interests of any political party well.

Walter Benjamin finds that the detective embodies a paradox of "on the one hand . . . feel[ing] himself viewed by all and sundry as a true suspect and, on the other side . . . utterly undiscoverable, the hidden man."[33] In the English manuscript, Chang takes her spy protagonist on a stroll through the market in the typical fashion of the Benjaminian flâneur, but in this process, she finds that her identity as a spy can no longer remain undercover, but is fully exposed. Self-disclosure as a spy has caused her to lose the ability to do spy work, a paradox that lies at the heart of a clandestine identity such as that of a spy. In a different context, Tina Chen demonstrates how Henry Park, the Korean American protagonist of Chang-rae Lee's novel *Native Speaker* (1995), cannot sustain the "fantasy of invisibility" demanded of a spy because the markedness of his racial identity gets in the way of his "disappearing act."[34] Likewise, the spy here can no longer sustain the paradox of seeing without being seen. As in the case of Henry Park, Shahlu's eventual betrayal of the political faction that employs her is caused by self-disclosure, which ultimately results in self-betrayal.

Shahlu's self-exposure is caused by her double identity as spy and woman. The English manuscript contains a seemingly unconnected but utterly crucial section that shows how Shahlu's betrayal of her comrades is also a self-betrayal of her identity as an assassin and spy. In this section, Shahlu runs into a street "lined with paper shops displaying brochade-trimmed gilt-patterned scarlet wedding certificates in their dark, unlit shopwindows (sic)."[35] This depiction of shops selling wedding goods on the dark street presents matrimony and domesticity as crime scenes revisited in a nightmare. Shahlu runs into one of the shops and invades "an incredibly homey scene" of dinner between a shop-keeper and his assistants. One of the men "took hold of her and tried to pull her back," "obviously trying to take advantage of her."[36] Shahlu turns around and hits him in the face, leaving a "vicious cut in his cheek." "She had forgot-ten that in all her haste she had thoughtfully turned her ring inward while she was running. She closed her fist right over the reassuring hard lump of stone for fear that the blow had loosened it from its setting."[37] This scene depicts a nightmarish vision of marriage, in which the diamond ring as a symbol of a romantic relationship is changed into merely a "hard lump of stone" that can be used as a weapon for self-defense. In Shahlu's nightmarish journey through the dark city streets, she is all too visible due to her gender for her to be able to lose herself in the crowd.

A nationalist narrativization of a female undercover emphasizes the serv-iceability of her sexuality in the nationalist course. The English version of "Lust, Caution" subverts this discourse by depicting the traumatic after-effects of her service. The Chinese short story "Lust, Caution" does not contain an equivalent scene, but one can still detect the eerie shadow of domestic vio-lence in the Chinese story. For instance, Jiazhi is raped by one of her classmates on the pretense of helping her to rehearse for the role of Mr. Yee's seducer. The theatricality of this rape and Jiazhi's self-consciousness as a participant in nationalist activism as theater prevent the traumatic after-effects of this sexual violence from being fully represented or registered in Jiazhi's consciousness. If, in *Native Speaker*, what causes Henry Park's betrayal is his self-awareness of his double identity as spy and Korean American, in Chang's story, it is her double-ness as spy and woman that causes Shahlu/Jiazhi to betray her comrades and ultimately herself. The spy story, a popular genre that often fails to delve into identity issues in any depth, is used here to explore the inherent contradiction within the self of the spy-spectator situated in the context of the war.

Returning to the Frontier

In the Chinese essay "Peking Opera through Foreign Eyes," spying is depicted as an aesthetic strategy similar to the modernist notion of defamiliarization. In the English story "The Spyring," however, this aestheticization of the under-cover agent does not work precisely because the political context of spying is intensified. In the essays Chang wrote in the United States, we find that the spy-observer situated in the sensitive political environment of the Cold War embodies the doubleness of being both an instrument serving a set of political interests and someone who has an agenda of his/her own. This kind of doubleness is analogous to Tina Chen's observation that, in some situations, "impersonation and imposture, even as their distinctions are acknowledged, become confused and confusing."[38] The confusion sets in when the impersonator performs "not in order to assume another, more desirable or 'known' public identity but when it is undertaken to perform into existence a public identity that has already been used to label you."[39] Under these circumstances, as Chen suggests, it is necessary to examine the context of this double performance "as a critical venue" in which identities are both pre-defined and performed.

Chang's 1963 travel piece "A Return to the Frontier" appears to conform to the propagandistic agenda of the Cold War era since the framework in which "Chineseness" is defined seems to be somewhat over-determining. According to Martin Doudna, the magazine held a liberal view of domestic issues, but "the two basic principles expressed in his (Ascoli's) foreign-policy editorials—his insistence on the need for American involvement in world affairs and his reiterated belief that freedom and Communism were philosophically and ethically irreconcilable—remained constant."[40] Chang's article fits well with the political agenda of the magazine since in Chang's descriptions of her travels to Taiwan and Hong Kong she constantly reminds her readers of the contrast between the "free world" and Communist China. However, it is ultimately the displacement of the traveler herself in both worlds that skews and complicates the geopolitical division of the Cold War period.

This English piece underwent a long process of translation and rewriting, which resulted in a Chinese manuscript that was probably completed after 1982 but remained unpublished until 2008, ten years after Chang's death. Considering that close to twenty years elapsed between the publication of the English piece and the composition of the Chinese work, it is surprising how much of the English original is retained in the Chinese piece. The English version contains some elements that could be construed as anti-Communist propaganda, such as stories of refugees who have just escaped from mainland China or descriptions of the harsh living conditions of those left behind. However, there are also elements of the essay that do not align with the neat divisions between the left and the right, Communist China and the so-called "free world." That this ambiguity can be retained in the essay owes a lot to the geographic positioning of the story on the "frontier"—the city of Hong Kong, where boundaries are less clearly defined and transgression is more possible.

The essay begins with an account of the writer's visit to Taiwan, an experience filled with seemingly arbitrary instances of misrecognition or non-recognition, which demonstrate the writer's anxiety about existing frameworks that defined Chineseness in the Cold War period. Chang relates a funny scene about being mistaken for Mrs. Nixon by someone who has come to greet her at Taipei airport. Although this turns out to be an innocent mistake, it makes Chang wonder whether it has something to do with "Formosa's . . . wistful yearning for the outside world, particularly America, its only friend."[41] Immediately after this scene, Chang's friend, Mr. Chu, asks her, "How does it feel to be back?" "Although I have never been here before, they were going along with the official assumption that Formosa is China, the mother country of all Chinese," Chang comments of this remark.[42] The over-identification in the second instance and the non-recognition in the first instance illustrate as much the awkwardness that the diasporic subject from the Chinese mainland feels towards Taiwan as Taiwan's failure to recognize her Chineseness within a proper frame. It is not until Chang hears the familiar Mandarin voices that she begins to accept Taiwan as China, remarking that here "really was China, not the strange one I left ten years ago under the Communists but the one I knew best and thought had vanished forever."[43] The essay thus begins with the mutual alienation of Chang and her hosts in Taiwan, each as the other's spectator and object of gaze. This instance of non-identification demonstrates the crisis of "Chineseness" brought about by the ideological rifts during the Cold War era.

Taiwan seen from Chang's eyes still bears the specters of Japanese colonialism and the Chinese Civil War. In her refusal to identify with Taiwan, Chang shows that Taiwan's "Chineseness" was in itself colonialist and exclusionary towards cultural and racial Others, while being over-determined by the ideological structure of the Cold War. This exclusion is demonstrated through an incident in which Chang and her friends encounter some indigenous Taiwanese, who are in turn portrayed as the exotic Other by Chang's mainland settler friends. "From time to time Mrs. Chu, sitting next to me in the bus, whispered urgently, 'Shandi, shandi!' I just caught a glimpse of a shandi, or mountain dweller, a gray little wraith with whiskers tattooed on her cheeks carrying a baby on her back and loitering outside a shop along the highway."[44] In contrast to her non-identification with Taiwan, Chang's description of her experience in Hong Kong emphasizes affective bonds between Hong Kong and mainland China that are sustained by the circulation of people, goods, and information across the borders between the Communist and the "free" world.

Her essay depicts Hong Kong as a passageway, the point of crossing between the "realms of the living and the dead." In this metaphor, we can see that the polarization of the free vs. the unfree, the rich vs. the poor is maintained, but, speaking from the point of view of a struggling immigrant herself, Chang also shows that the so-called "land of the free" is not entirely free from economic disparity and hardship. She writes, "It makes me impatient to hear westerners quibble about the free world not being really free. Too bad that many of us have to go back over that bridge when we can't make a living outside."[45]

Although Hong Kong was a "frontier" of the so-called "free world," it was also a place of exchange that allowed affective bonds to persist despite the barbed wire and ideological divisions that separated it from the mainland. This kind of affective bonding did not just take the form of material goods smuggled across the border to help poor relatives back home; it also existed on a spiritual level as a utopic yearning for a racial identification of Chineseness that cut across the barriers of politics. Towards the end of the essay, Chang recalls her own passage across the borders of Hong Kong when she first left China—on that very hot day, a young PRC soldier described as "a round-cheeked north country boy in rumpled baggy uniform" told anxious immigrants such as Chang to "[g]o stand in the shade." This detail touched Chang deeply, making her feel "the warmth of race wash[ing] over me for the last time."[46] Here the characterization of Chang's identification with the mainland soldier as a racial identification has to be interpreted in the context of the overall racial shadow under which the entire Chinese-speaking world is represented in the article. That Cold War divisions and the metaphor of the frontier are represented as racialized divisions and boundaries reflects the imprint of a dominant American ideological perspective on the author. Chang's essay, while influenced by the ideologies of race and politics, nonetheless conveys a complex psychology of anxiety about belonging, which ultimately undermines the political self-assuredness that is a prerequisite for propaganda.

Sidonie Smith and Julia Watson claim that "[w]hile travel writing is often presented as a genre distinct from autobiography, extending back to classical Greece and Rome in the West, it can in fact be read as a major mode of life narrative, in this case the reconstitution of the autobiographical subject in transit and encounter."[47] If Chang's English essay already demonstrates a process of self-construction "in transit and encounter," the Chinese rewriting of "A Return to the Frontier" adds another form of "encounter" to the original essay—that is, an encounter with the past. The Chinese version, much longer and more disjunctive, multiplies the act of remembrance by describing not one journey, but several undertaken in the past as well. For instance, visiting some parts of the Central District of Hong Kong this time reminds Chang of strolling through the same streets the last time she was in Hong Kong as a college student. She uses material objects such as a piece of colorful fabric or a gold ornament as mnemonic devices to string her memories of the multilayered past together, and these are always random objects, unexpectedly discovered by the author in unlikely locations. The traveler's diasporic sentiments are conveyed through a psychological structure of nostalgia and loss that colors Chang's passage home. Diaspora is conventionally conceived in terms of a "return." However, this diasporic narrative clearly tells us that the place to which one returns is a continuously receding past that is figured as an abject Other—just like the stench in the air that Chang detects, and finds endearing, before she leaves Hong Kong again.

The title "A Return to the Frontier" captures the paradox of return and departure, home and abroad. It offers a constant reminder that Chang's entire life was lived on the frontier of language, culture, and politics. Both in her writings and through her self-translation practices, Chang demonstrates a great deal of self-consciousness towards the self's identity performance, particularly her doubleness, on the frontier. Throughout her career, Chang's "return" to such a frontier has been repeated in one piece of writing after another, signifying the ever-present danger of betrayal accompanying the self-positioning of being on the frontier.

6
Eileen Chang, *Dream of the Red Chamber,* and the Cold War

Xiaojue Wang

The year 1949 witnessed the beginning of Communist rule on mainland China and the retreat of the Nationalist Government to the island province of Taiwan. With the Cold War bamboo curtain sealed along the Taiwan Strait, China was ideologically and territorially divided into various entities—the mainland, Taiwan, Hong Kong, and overseas—which concomitantly created a diaspora of millions of Chinese people. This divide changed the topography of modern Chinese literature significantly. Eileen Chang spent the first few years after the Chinese Communist takeover of mainland China in Shanghai. During this period, she wrote *Eighteen Springs* (十八春, 1951) and "Xiao'ai" (小艾, 1952), which carry the leftist message of the time. In 1952, Chang decided to leave her native city for Hong Kong. During her time there, from 1952 to 1955, she finished two English novels, *The Rice-Sprout Song* (1955) and *Naked Earth* (1956), sponsored by the United States Information Service. Whereas these two Cold War novels continue to focus on human frailty and thus to a certain extent dwell on Chang's unique notion of history, which is marked by temporal discrepancies and ruins as against any grand narrative of historical monumentality,[1] they nevertheless bear the clear imprint of the propagandistic anti-Communist novel and belong to the genre of *roman à these*. The following year, Chang left for the United States, where she attempted to restart her literary career as a writer of English language fiction, a goal she never seemed to achieve.

In an effort to better understand Eileen Chang's post-1949 writing career as it spanned the mainland, Hong Kong, and the United States, this essay will examine Chang's two endeavors to rework the Qing dynasty classic novel *Dream of the Red Chamber* (紅樓夢, also translated as *The Story of the Stone*, from one of its earliest Chinese titles, 石頭記; abbreviated hereafter as *Dream*) in the 1960s and 70s. In 1961 and 1962, Chang spent five months in Hong Kong writing a screenplay based on *Dream* for the film company Motion Picture & General Investment Co. Ltd. (MP&GI). Shortly after her return to the U.S., she embarked on a Redologist journey of *Dream,* which resulted in a series of research articles. In 1976, the Crown Press of Taipei published Chang's last major work, a study of *Dream,* which she playfully named *Nightmare in the Red Chamber* (紅樓夢魘; hereafter referred to as *Nightmare*). At a time when she planned to make a new start as a writer of English fiction, why would Chang suddenly put aside her own literary creation and choose to delve into the classical world of *Dream,* which seems to deviate from her original writing goal? Through an exploration of Chang's *Dream*-related endeavors, which consume a substantial portion of her later years, I seek to address how her diasporic writing career bespeaks Cold War cultural and political restraints and how in turn these affect her poetics and politics of writing. The first part of the chapter reads Chang's *Dream* screenwriting experience at the intersections of Hong Kong filmmaking histories and Chinese Cold War cultural diplomatic tactics that pertain to *Dream*'s adaptation to opera forms. The second part ventures a textual and contextual analysis of Chang's *Dream* research to reflect on her distinctive aesthetics of desolation and poetics of the quotidian. The last part places Chang's engagement with *Dream* in the wider context of her second writing career in the Cold War era, and considers the cultural significance of her seemingly compulsive practice of rewriting across disparate languages, genres, and media.

Dream's Adaptations

In November 1961, Eileen Chang arrived in Hong Kong to adapt the classical novel *Dream of the Red Chamber* into a film commissioned by MP&GI. This was not Chang's first collaboration with MP&GI. In 1955, during an earlier stay in Hong Kong, Chang had joined the script committee of MP&GI,[2] which comprised a group of exiled writers, including Sun Jinsan, Qin Yu, and Stephen Soong (宋淇).[3] After she settled in the United States, Chang completed a number of film scripts for MP&GI, and screenwriting actually became her major source of income during her first few years in the U.S. Most of the films Chang wrote are sophisticated comedies and urban romances that combined elements taken from what some critics called American screwball comedy and Chinese family drama with an ethical dimension.[4] She had already begun to experiment with this cinematic model in the late 1940s when she wrote two screenplays for Shanghai's Wenhua film studio, *Neverending Love* (不了情, 1947) and *Viva the Wife* (太太萬歲, 1947).

However, the assignment to adapt *Dream* differs considerably from Chang's earlier screenwriting projects. Rather than making yet another sleek, witty romantic comedy, Chang faced the challenge of adapting to a film script an epic work that she often claimed was the essential source of her literary inspiration.[5] Chang's *Dream*-related undertakings began much earlier. In her early teens, she was so captivated by *Dream* that she was unable to resist the temptation to write her own modern version. Composing five chapters under the title *Modern Dream of the Red Chamber* (摩登紅樓夢, 1934)—at the age of thirteen, Chang fabricated her own dream of a twentieth-century Prospect Garden much along the lines of late Qing dynasty *Dream* fantasy, particularly Wu Jianren's innovative utopian science fiction *New Story of the Stone* (新石頭記, 1908). While Wu reincarnated Jia Baoyu as an adventurer floating on air in an "aerial car" on a trip to central Africa, Chang sent Baoyu abroad to obtain a college degree.

After three months of hard work and numerous revisions, Chang's screenplay was rejected by MP&GI and the plan to make the film was shelved. As Chang's original screenplay for *Dream* has not survived, a textual analysis is not possible. Instead, I will venture a contextual and historical analysis to explore the poignant cultural and political implications of cross-generic and cross-media *Dream* adaptations in mainland China and Hong Kong in the 1950s and 60s.

It was not mere chance that MP&GI decided to shoot a *Dream* film in 1961. What prompted the decision was no doubt the tremendous success of the recent Yue opera performance *Dream of the Red Chamber* by the visiting Shanghai Yue Opera Company, starring Xu Yulan and Wang Wenjuan. The play was then filmed in a joint project by the Shanghai Haiyan film studio and the Hong Kong Phoenix studio in 1962. In the heyday of the Cold War stand-off, the visit of the leading Shanghai Yue Opera Company from a fledgling socialist state to Hong Kong, a frontier of the capitalist world, was by no means devoid of political implications. As Chairman Liu Shaoqi stated at a meeting with the Yue opera troupe, they were charged with the political mission of building a cultural United Front. To dispel the "rumor" that the country was facing famine as a consequence of the so-called Great Leap Forward, the troupe was even "ghettoed" for two weeks in a resort hotel in Guangzhou, where they were offered nutritious food to put them in the best physical condition before their departure for Hong Kong.[6] The *Dream* opera ran for eighteen consecutive performances and became an instant sensation in Hong Kong in 1960. Given its romantic plot, artistic sophistication, and poetic lyricism, the Yue opera may have seemed the best form of cultural promotion to allow the young government to demonstrate its spiritual superiority, to claim the high ground of culture and tradition, and to win public endorsement among the Chinese diaspora.

In the mainland historical context, the production of the Yue opera *Dream* involved political and cultural complications on a different level. The first decade of the People's Republic of China is often regarded as a golden age of Yue opera.[7] The Shanghai Yue Opera Company's performance of the Yue opera *Dream* premiered in mainland China in 1958, and became an instant classic in the Yue theater repertoire. Xu Jin served as its playwright. The play gained such popularity that the troupe was summoned the following year to perform in Beijing to celebrate the tenth anniversary of the Chinese socialist state. Given the time of its production, we may well wonder how such a drama of "feudal" scholar and beauty (才子佳人) could possibly have survived the volatile political and cultural climate, let alone become such an enormous success.

Indeed, this Qing dynasty classic was thrust into the limelight of the socialist cultural purges of the 1950s and 60s. In 1954, Li Xifan and Lan Ling, two recent graduates of Shandong University, wrote an article critical of Yu Pingbo's (1900–90) recent Redology anthology, *Studies on Dream of the Red Chamber* (紅樓夢研究, 1952). Instigated by none other than Chairman Mao Zedong, this seemingly esoteric academic event developed into the "Criticize Yu Pingbo Campaign," and the consequent criticism of Yu's mentor Hu Shi, the archetypical Chinese bourgeois intellectual and father of the New Redology.[8] In 1957, the *Dream* debate expanded to the nationwide Anti-rightist Campaign, which was aimed at the entire Chinese intelligentsia. As hundreds of thousands of people were accused and prosecuted, the irony of history is that the series of political movements triggered by the anti-Yu Pingbo campaign resulted in *Dream* being widely read in post-1949 socialist China. Between 1958 and 1962, 140,000 copies were printed, and *Dream* became one of the highest selling books apart from the *Selected Works of Mao Zedong* (毛澤東選集).

The 1958 Yue opera *Dream* by Xu Jin was the first drama to adapt the entire book rather than just excerpts. Distilling the intricacies of *Dream*'s epic dimensions was in itself a herculean task. However, fitting the drama into the political ethos of the time was even more challenging. During the *Dream* debates of the 1950s, how the work could be interpreted in line with the Marxist political and cultural discourse espoused by the newly founded socialist state remained a focal point. While Hu Shi and Yu Pingbo were rebuked for their approach that was informed by subjective bourgeois idealism, Mao Zedong, himself an enthusiastic reader of *Dream,* asserted that only from the viewpoint of class struggle could one truly appreciate both *Dream* and Chinese history as a whole. Accordingly, he considered anti-feudalist class struggles to be the leitmotif of the work: "severe class struggle, with the (sacrifice) of dozens of lives."[9]

An earlier attempt to rework *Dream* into a Yue opera within the thematic framework defined by the new political discourse had been made by none other than Su Qing, Eileen Chang's good friend who, much like Chang, achieved literary fame in occupied Shanghai for her work focusing on female space and subjectivity.[10] And much like Chang, Su Qing was also castigated by fellow writers after the end of the war for her suspicious political conformism during the Shanghai occupation. In the early years of the PRC, she had to switch from fiction writing to screenwriting for opera companies to make a living. In order to meet the dominant political criteria for the interpretation of *Dream,* Su Qing, in her play "Baoyu and Daiyu" (寶玉與黛玉, 1954) written for Fanghua Yue Opera Company, created the maid Huixiang, who overcame brutal oppression to expose serious class struggles in the Jia family.[11]

However, when Xu Jin set out to adapt *Dream* for the Shanghai Yue Opera Company, he sought to do so in a more ambitious but refined way. Xu treated the work as a love tragedy brought about by the suffocating patriarchal family system, and Baoyu and Daiyu as victims of feudal marriage arrangements encapsulated in the adage "the goodly affinity of gold and jade" (金玉良緣). In this light, this is not just another outdated beauty-scholar story, but a work that disavows feudal ethical and social codes and promotes the key values adopted by the May Fourth New Cultural Movement, including the courage to fight against familial oppression and pursue individual freedom. Opening with Daiyu's arrival in the Jia mansion, the play highlights episodes such as Baoyu being beaten by his father, Daiyu burying fallen flowers, Baoyu and Daiyu reading *Romance of the West Chamber* (西廂記) together, Baoyu's wedding, and Daiyu burning her manuscripts and her subsequent death. It ends with Baoyu mourning Daiyu's death and escaping from home, with the chorus singing the famous line "discarding the 'never lose, never forget' jade tablet, breaking the 'never leave, never abandon' golden locket; leaving the filthy place infested with flies, escaping the wealthy nest swarming with ants."[12] The finale stresses the main theme of the play, cursing the traditional marriage system and the corruption of the feudal household. In adopting the main plot of Gao E's forty-chapter sequel, whereby Baoyu is tricked into marrying Baochai by the scheming of Xifeng on the same evening that Daiyu dies a dreadful, lonely death, the play has effectively reduced *Dream* to a tragic romance and successfully packaged it for popular consumption. In foregrounding the anti-feudalist theme, the play has managed to remain within the ambit of the prevailing political ideology while at the same time preserving the poetic sophistication of the original work in its exquisite, lyrical arias, ensembles, and choruses.

It was under precisely such entangled political and cultural circumstances that Chang was invited by MP&GI to write a *Dream* film script for the Hong Kong market, which saw a surge of enthusiasm for *Dream* touched off by the performances of the Shanghai Yue Opera Company. While it was political restraints that tethered playwrights such as Su Qing and Xu Jin on the mainland, Eileen Chang in Hong Kong was confronted by a dilemma of a different dimension. Certainly, both Su Qing's and Xu Jin's plays were censored because of political violations. However, Chang's *Dream* adaptation did not even manage to pass the scrutiny of the film company. The letters Chang wrote during this time to Ferdinand Reyher, an American screenwriter she married in 1956, suggested two reasons for the rejection of her film script: The managers of MP&GI, who had never read the original work, were not able to appreciate her adaptation of *Dream*; and the Shaw Brothers studio, MP&GI's primary competitor in Hong Kong, had also launched a plan to make a *Dream* film.[13]

MP&GI's managers may have not read *Dream*, the Shaw Brothers studio may have acted more quickly and thus seized the market opportunity, but it was not because Chang was unaware of how to appeal to a mass audience that her screenplay was rejected. After all, from the beginning of her literary career, Chang was well known for her constant flirtation with popular culture. I would like to suggest a different explanation for her dilemma. Chang once noted that all of the drama in *Dream* is to be found in the last forty chapters. She writes, "in the original eighty chapters of *Dream*, there is no single important event . . . All the important events occur in the last forty chapters . . . What the first eighty chapters provide is the vivid and close texture of life."[14] How to deal with the outcome of *Dream*'s plot, or how to deal with the relationships between Baoyu, Daiyu, and Baochai at the end of the story must have been the crucial concern for Chang in her reworking of *Dream*. Although there is no copy of Chang's *Dream* screenplay available for examination, a close reading of her research work on *Dream, Nightmare in the Red Chamber,* pertaining to her speculation about the authenticity of the last forty chapters, which she started shortly after the failed screenwriting project, provides important clues to her vision of *Dream.* I will pursue this issue further in the next section.

Indeed, as Chang was making countless revisions to the screenplay in order to garner MP&GI's approval, the Shaw Brothers studio produced a Huangmei (黃梅, yellow plum) opera film version of *Dream,* which largely adopted the line of development of Xu Jin's opera version that ended with Daiyu's death on Baoyu and Baochai's wedding night, and with Baoyu's subsequent escape from home. Released in 1962 and starring Betty Le Di, the Shaw Brothers' *Dream of the Red Chamber* ultimately forced MP&GI to abort its plan. With Huangmei opera films being a mainstay of Hong Kong's Mandarin cinema in the 1950s and 1960s, this blockbuster film achieved huge box office success.[15] By the time the Shaw Brothers' Huangmei opera film *Dream* was enjoying wide circulation in the Chinese diaspora, the Shanghai Yue opera film *Dream,* which had been completed in the same year, had been censored in mainland China with the onset of yet another cultural movement on a grand scale, the Great Proletarian Cultural Revolution.

Nightmare in the Red Chamber

In 1963, shortly after she returned to the U.S. from the aborted *Dream* film-making project, Eileen Chang started her research on *Dream,* a project on which she worked for the next ten years. The result is a series of articles that can be found in a monograph entitled *Nightmare in the Red Chamber.* In her diasporic life in the United States, especially in her secluded later years after the death of her second husband, why did Chang choose to delve into the world of *Dream*? And in what ways do *Dream* and Chang's reading of *Dream* relate to her own literary work and aesthetics? Little attention has ever been paid to Chang's only scholarly work. By addressing the above questions, my exploration of Chang's *Nightmare* suggests a new perspective for reflecting on Chang's post-1949 writing career as well as providing a deeper look at her aesthetic world.

Chang's *Dream* study stands in a long and rich tradition of *Dream* scholarship, which started almost at the same time as the novel was written. In addition to the early *Dream* commentaries, Red Inkstone annotations being the most important of them, there have been two main schools of Redology:

the *suoyin* (索隱, exploring obscurities) school, which interpreted the entire novel as a narrative about the palace intrigues during early reigns of the Qing dynasty or as a veiled ethnic criticism of the Manchu regime; and the *kaozheng* (考證, textual analysis) mode of criticism, the so-called modern study of *Dream of the Red Chamber* initiated by Hu Shi, which sought to shift the focus onto the author of the novel and suggested the novel as an autobiographical work of Cao Xueqin. However, in spite of their disparate focuses on political allegories or authorial history, both *suoyin* and *kaozheng* schools of interpretation treated *Dream* as a historical document rather than a fictional work. As Haun Saussy pointed out, "both *suoyin* and *kaozheng* are modes of historical reading, only the assumptions about what constitutes history, or what is important in history, differ."[16]

In her preface to *Nightmare,* Chang notes that her study of *Dream* scrutinizes between the lines and between different hand-copied manuscripts and printed editions, a practice that she compares with experiences such as walking through a "labyrinth," assembling a "jigsaw puzzle," reading "a detective story," or following multiple possibilities as in *Rashōmon.*[17] Such a meticulous study, as I have argued in a recent article on *Dream*'s afterlife in modern China, combines both hermeneutic and philological approaches that characterize the *suoyin* and *kaozheng* schools.[18] *Nightmare* ploughs through layers of editions, marginalia, annotations, and commentaries, and brings these texts into complementary or contrastive dialogs. In her preface, Chang attributes her study of *Dream* to her thorough familiarity with the novel: "When I read different editions, even the slightest different usage of words would jump out at me instantly."[19] In her rigorous textual analysis, Chang draws heavily on previous scholarship, particularly on research done by *kaozheng* scholars including Hu Shi, Yu Pingbo, Zhou Ruchang, Wu Shichang, and Zhao Gang.

However, Chang's palimpsestic study of *Dream* deviates significantly from both leading schools. She never endeavors to propose yet another speculation about political allegories, dynastic secrets, or the family history and life of Cao Xueqin. Her research rather attempts to uncover how Cao's literary styles and techniques and aesthetic ideas have gradually matured over the span of more than twenty years of writing and numerous revisions until his death, and to ponder major permutations of character creations, plot arrangements as well as of central concepts of love and lust, desire and disillusionment. In discussing Chang's *Nightmare,* Guo Yuwen maintains that Chang's study treats *Dream* as a fictional creation rather than an autobiography or a mere social or historical source. It is thus inherently literary, whereas both the *suoyin* and *kaozheng* schools are historical.[20] Indeed, Chang's Redological pursuit is permeated by her female authorial voice and uniquely marked by her refined perspective as a woman writer. It comes as no surprise that in the field of *Dream* study, Chang is often regarded as a quasi-Redologist for her eccentric approaches.[21] As much as he appreciates Chang's talent and her devotion to *Dream*, Zhou Ruchang, the noted Redologist, regards Chang as an "eccentric talent" (怪傑) in the tradition of *Dream* study and observes that *Nightmare* regretfully does not contribute much to Redology as an objective, scientific field.[22]

Questions about the authorship and authenticity of various editions of *Dream* have been the focus of different stages of *Dream* scholarship, particularly the *kaozheng* school.[23] One of the main concerns of Chang's research is how to assess Gao E's contribution to *Dream*. Recollecting her reading experiences in her early teens, Chang writes, "When I reached the eighty-first chapter, everything suddenly felt unbearably stale and flat. The book stepped into an utterly different world thereafter . . . Many years later, I learned that the last forty chapters were actually a sequel."[24] Could it be possible that the last forty chapters might have contained some fragments from Cao Xueqin's original work? Could the composition of the last forty chapters be credited solely to Gao E or there might have been multiple authors for them?

Chang attempts to respond to the above questions by conducting a critical examination of the uneven literary quality of the last forty chapters and by seeking to account for the major changes made to *Dream*'s early editions.[25] Rather than focusing on mere textual comparisons between different editions, she explores inconsistencies in writing styles, character portrayals, and literary themes. One salient example would be Chang's analysis of the discrepancies in characterizing Daiyu's outward appearance. Chang observes that throughout the first eighty chapters, there are virtually no material depictions of Daiyu's countenance or clothes. The image of Daiyu is conveyed as timeless, celestial, never corporeal: "there is no single physical detail (about her), merely a posture, a voice."[26] In this way, Cao Xueqin configures Daiyu as transcending the earthy world, whereas Baochai, confined by the Confucian morality, is represented as a refined yet worldly character. Chang feels strongly upset when she reads an explicit illustration of Daiyu's clothes in Chapter 89: Daiyu is described as dressed in a rose-colored embroidered coat, with a golden pin in her hair, which notably sabotages the image of Daiyu as an intangible beauty. She thus comes to the conclusion that this must have been composed by someone other than Cao Xueqin.

Consequently, Eileen Chang argues that one has to take the eighty-chapter edition of *Dream* as an incomplete work in order to appreciate its genuine literary excellence. The last forty chapters penned by Gao E are nothing but "a dog's tail replacing a sable" (狗尾續貂), "an ulcer deeply rooted in bone" (附骨之疽).[27] Gao E's edition has only turned *Dream* into the mawkish story of a love triangle with a dramatic ending, and has therefore seriously corrupted Chinese reading tastes as well as literary criteria. Chang has noted elsewhere that the dramatization of life is not healthy.[28] In her *Dream* research, she is particularly concerned with one instance of controversy—the eventual outcome of the plot regarding the protagonist Baoyu. She strongly reproaches Gao E for his "vulgar" addition, in which Baoyu marries Baochai while Daiyu dies a gloomy death and Baoyu ultimately chooses a life of renunciation away from home. Rather, she is inclined to adopt the theory that in one of the early lost editions, Baoyu eventually marries Xiangyun, the cousin with whom he grows up before Daiyu arrives, after the decline of the Jia family, and the novel ends with the couple living an impoverished life. According to Chang's reading, such an ending attests to one of couplets in the title of Chapter 31, "The unicorn predicts that the twin stars will grow old together" (因麒麟伏白首雙星).

Chang spares no effort in extrapolating on this conclusion, which strikes her with such a tremendous impact as if "the stone broke and the sky thundered, the clouds tumbled down and the ocean soared up" (石破天驚 雲垂海立).[29] Evidently, she favors an ending that features the destitute couple Baoyu and Xiangyun to the melodramatic one embraced by Gao E. Chang observes that the former gives the work a "realistic and modern" feel.[30] At the same time, she admits that such a mundane, undramatic solution would not have satisfied the popular tastes of the reading public of the time. This is why, she argues, the author was obliged to revise it later to include a more dramatic closure when Baoyu cuts off all human attachments and becomes a monk, an ultimate gesture that would appeal to the majority of readers. In this light, the revision of the work follows a trajectory "from modern to conventional" with regard to narrative strategies.[31] Chang regrets that Chinese literature has thereby missed a moment of modernity.

Given Chang's preference for the early version of the story's ending, there is reason to assume that Chang may well have proposed the Baoyu/Xiangyun model in the screenplay she completed for MP&GI. When discussing the significance of the original ending in literary history, Chang speculates that "Even if such an ending was composed for a novel of a modern time, it wouldn't be any easier for modern readers to accept it."[32] If this is true of litera-ture, it would be even more so for the new medium of moving pictures. Like Cao Xueqin, Eileen Chang was forced to trim her script extensively to meet the public taste. But this time, the public taste had been shaped for two centuries by the Gao E version of the story.

In the preface to *Nightmare*, Chang notes, "These two works (i.e., *The Plum in the Golden Vase* 金瓶梅 and *Dream*) mean every source for me, especially *Dream*."[33] In modern Chinese literature, Chang is indeed the quintessential practitioner of *Dream*'s artistic sophistication and the finest interpreter of *Dream*'s idea about illusion and disillusionment, which is deeply rooted in the essential texture of the quotidian life. In reflecting on her own writing, Chang states, "So my fiction, with the exception of Cao Qiqiao in 'The Golden Cangue' (金鎖記), is populated with equivocal characters—They are not heroes, but they are of the majority who actually bear the weight of the times. As equivo-cal as they may be, they are also in earnest about their lives. They lack tragedy; all they have is desolation. Tragedy is a kind of closure, while desolation is a form of revelation."[34] The lack in tragedy and the emphasis on ambivalent yet true to life characters, which constitute the essence of humanity and life, is exactly what Chang appreciates in Cao Xueqin's *Dream*. From her point of view, this marks *Dream*'s literary modernity and renders this novel ahead of its time. According to Chang's study, the early version conceives the misfortunate of the main heroes as triggered by their character flaws (自誤), an idea close to *hamartia* in Greek dramaturgy. Only in later versions did the author add some overriding external force of fate such as the imperial concubine Yuanchun's order that Baoyu and Baochai shall marry. In analyzing Daiyu and Baochai's personalities, Chang acknowledges one of the Red Inkstone comments and further elucidates, "Daiyu is too bright and sensitive, which harms her health; and Baochai knows all and is erudite. Marrying a *Ms. Know-all* would inevi-tably harm the emotion between the couple."[35] The flaws and ambiguities in characters render them true. Herein, Chang shares a similar opinion with Lu Xun. As early as 1924, in his article "On the Historical Evolution of Chinese Fiction" (中國小說的歷史的變遷), Lu Xun acclaimed *Dream* as contribut-ing significantly to the school of fiction on "human sentiments" and asserted that *Dream*'s value lies particularly in "its depiction of characters in a true-to-life manner, without unnecessary trimmings, which distinguishes it from previous fictions, which describe good people as perfect, bad people as pure evil. Therefore, the characters in *Dream* are real."[36]

In her observations of the religious sentiment of the Chinese people, Eileen Chang remarks:

> The fact that Chinese literature is full of sadness is due to lack of belief in anything. It takes pleasure only in material details (hence *The Plum in the Golden Vase* and *Dream of the Red Chamber* set out the menus of whole banquets in exact particular and with unflagging interest for no other reason than fondness), because the details are normally pleasant, satisfying and absorbing, while the main theme is always gloomy. All general observation of human life points to emptiness.[37]

Chang's own literary writings are precisely characterized by a fascination with superfluous, sensuous, "feminine details" of everyday life and simultaneously by a deep penetration into human frailty and historical pathos.[38] Such a philosophy, or "religious sentiment," is best conveyed in her favorite notion of "aesthetics of desolation." In her literary world, an impending catastrophe looms large in human civilizations. In "Writing of One's Own" (自己的文章, 1944), she notes,

> In this era, the old things are being swept away and the new things are still being born. But until this historical era reaches its culmination, all certainty will remain an exception. People sense that everything about their everyday lives is a little out of order, out of order to a terrifying degree. All of us must live within a certain historical era, but this era sinks away from us like a shadow, and we feel we have been abandoned.[39]

Permeated with a profound sense of loss and grief, Chang's aesthetics of desolation attests to the dialectic of worldly desire and its renunciation, which, according to Wang Guowei's philosophical reading of *Dream*, makes the central theme of this classic novel.[40]

Ever since its publication in 1976, Chang's *Nightmare* has never been popular among *Dream* scholars or the large population of Chang fans in the Sinophone world. It is a fragmentary work composed of quotations, gleanings, extensive textual and edition comparisons, literary criticism, as well as recollections of her own reading and writing experiences. And, as Qian Min duly pointed out, there are no coherent connections between "rigorous and careful textual analysis and imaginative and daring fictional writings,"[41] which makes the book extremely hard to follow. In her recent article on *Nightmare*, Huang Xincun suggested that one reads *Nightmare* as a work of literature rather than a scholarly monograph. Accordingly, she regards it as Chang's ruminations on her own life filtered through examinations of her *Dream* reading practices at different stages of her life. Viewed from this angle, *Nightmare* provides yet another reflection on Chang's central themes in her early fictions and essays such as temporal and spatial displacements.[42] I would argue that inasmuch as it continues to explore topics in Chang's work during the Shanghai Occupation, *Nightmare* marks a clear deviation from her early writings, fiction or essay, with regard to her literary styles. The renowned Redologist Zhou Ruchang may not agree with many speculations Chang proposed in her *Dream* study, however, he is definitely right in describing Chang's writing style in this work as "unadorned, plain, and simple."[43] The embellished writing style infiltrated with elaborate vocabularies and exquisite imageries, which characterizes her early writings and makes her a literary star in occupied Shanghai, has completely vanished, which without doubt contributes to its unfavorable reception by the readers. Yu Bin suggests that such a change in style can be traced back to Chang's postwar writings before she ultimately left mainland China for Hong Kong. From my point of view, Chang's pursuit of a simple yet mature narrative and aesthetic style is best manifested in her 1950s novel *The Rice-sprout Song*. In his comments on *The Rice-sprout Song*, Hu Shi observes that the novel evokes a "realistic or natural artistic quality," the same remark he used thirty years earlier in his appreciation of Han Bangqing's late Qing courtesan novel *The Sing-song Girls of Shanghai* (海上花列傳, 1892).[44] Not coincidentally, Chang praised *Sing-song Girls* as the true follower of *Dream,* and spent years in translating this novel in Wu dialect first into Mandarin Chinese and then into English. *Nightmare* marks another effort by Chang to create a "realistic or natural" style in probing her favorite novel. Chang's endeavor to appreciate Cao Xueqin's incomplete work results in an incomplete work of her own. In defying a definite closure, a conventional narrative structure, and a distinct literary genre, *Nightmare* attests to a form of literary modernity initiated by *Dream*.

The Politics of Rewriting

Ever since the mid-1980s, works by writers such as Qian Zhongshu, Shen Congwen, and Eileen Chang, who literally vanished from post-1949 versions of modern Chinese literary history, have been resurrected in mainland China. In such a context, Ye Zhaoyan, a writer of the younger generation who came to prominence in the post-Mao era, made an interesting observation:

While Qian Zhongshu's giving up fiction writing might have something to do with the transformations in 1949, Shen Congwen was already mired in stagnation before 1949. The good thing is that both of them found substitution outside literary creation in the latter half of their lives. Qian Zhongshu finished his scholarly tour de force *Limited Views* (管錐編), and Shen Congwen became a pre-eminent expert in archaeology. Ba Jin and Shi Tuo didn't give up writing, to be sure. Yet they seemed to take more effort to say good-bye to their pasts and to seek to become a new type of writer that they were not familiar with. Why didn't Ba Jin continue writing down the road he trod with *The Fourth Ward* (第四病室) and *Cold Nights* (寒夜)? Why didn't Shi Tuo continue writing works like *Orchard Town* (果園城記) and *A Master in the Village of No Hope* (無望村館主)? A simple explanation is that the environment didn't allow them to continue writing like before. However, Zhang Ailing escaped the mainland and had way too much free time to write, yet still she did not produce any good works. During this long period, there did not appear a single writer, like Cao Xueqin, who could have written for ten years in the most arduous times and would die for a work that could reach later generations.[45]

Ye's remarks provide a useful point of departure for reflecting on the dilemma confronting Chinese writers at the Cold War divide. Ye argues that the "environment" may have been one of the factors that forced those writers who remained on the Chinese mainland to stop writing, or stop writing in the manner in which they had previously written. By "environment" he clearly refers to the political constraints imposed on intellectuals in the newly founded socialist state. However, in commenting that Eileen Chang did not produce any good works either, despite having "too much free time" after leaving the socialist camp, Ye fails to mention that writers on the opposite side of the Cold War divide also suffered intense political pressure.

In this regard, Eileen Chang's strenuous attempts to get published in the United States provide an intriguing case in point. In 1956, Chang completed her English novel *Pink Tears,* which was an English expansion and rewriting of her earlier novella "The Golden Cangue" (1943), but it was rejected by major publishing houses including Scribner, Knopf, and Norton.[46] Given the strident Red Scare in the era of Joseph McCarthy, it comes as no surprise that a work such as *Pink Tears* would not have met political expectations. Focusing on revealing human frailty, *Pink Tears* by no means belongs to the rubric of anti-Communist novels such as Chen Jiying's *Fools in the Reeds* (荻村傳, 1950) and Jiang Wen's *The Tune of Waves Scour the Sands* (浪淘沙, 1964), which appeared high on publishers' lists at the time. Ironically, both works were translated into English by none other than Eileen Chang. With her own literary efforts rejected, Chang was forced to rely on translation to make a living. The irony doesn't stop there. As apolitical as it is, *Pink Tears* was considered to carrying dubious political implications. The Knopf review says of the manuscript that "all characters are loathsome. If the old China was like this, wouldn't it make the Communist Party the savior?"[47]

Furthermore, Knopf's review contains an underlying message that points to a different issue. The editor is obviously disappointed with, or to be more precise, provoked by the China represented by Eileen Chang. The image of China conveyed in *Pink Tears* does not meet the Orientalist expectations of Western readers. In responding to such Orientalist anxiety, Chang remarks, "I always have a hunch, for those who love China, the China they love is exactly the China I intend to disavow."[48] She is well aware of the constructedness of China and Chineseness in the eyes of the West. Her fiction never lacks moments satirizing characters that fall in love with a China fabricated by their own imaginations. Fan Liuyuan in "Love in a Fallen City" (傾城之 戀, 1943) and Tong Shifang in "The Golden Cangue" are two conspicuous examples. In this light, Chang's China differs significantly from that depicted in popular novels such as *A Many-Splendoured Thing* (1952) by Han Suyin (Elisabeth Comber).[49] According to Chang's reading, Han's China is not only a world "ornamented with classical poetry," but one that features sentimental love stories between a Chinese girl and a Caucasian. It is a vision of China with which Western readers can easily identify.[50] Therefore, while Cold War cultural policy certainly imposed severe constraints on disaporic writers of the time, the negative outpouring of Orientalism was equally precarious.

I will now return to Ye Zhaoyan's analysis of the cultural predicaments confronting Chinese writers after 1949. After indicating that political coercion is not the only factor that led Chinese writers to stop writing, Ye maintains that "there must be something wrong with the desire and motive of literary creation embedded deep in the minds of our writers."[51] He continues to conjecture: "If only writing had become part of their biological mechanism, something involuntary, like sexual drive, like hunger, or like shitting, things would have been different."[52] If only these writers had possessed such a drive to write, they would have continued writing, even secretly in the manner of Cao Xueqin in imperial times, for later generations. Ye thus concludes that these writers deprived themselves of writing possibilities.

As noted earlier, Ye Zhaoyan asserted that "Zhang Ailing escaped the mainland and had way too much free time to write, yet still she did not produce any good works." Ye is certainly not the first to point out that Eileen Chang's writings after she left the mainland do not measure up to her pre-1949 literary achievements. Yet, when he attributes this literary degeneration to the lack of inner drive among post-1949 Chinese writers, he seems to be overlooking Chang's almost compulsive writing output in the second half of the twentieth century. To mention just the novels she completed during the 1950s: *Eighteen Springs, The Rice-Sprout Song, Naked Earth, Pink Tears,* which she then revised as *Rouge of the North.* Her output was remarkable, even more so for a writer who had never before written in the form of the novel. Her research on *Dream* and the project to translate *Dream's* late Qing follower *The Sing-song Girls of Shanghai* are just as remarkable. Indeed, whether in Chinese or in English, Chang never stopped writing.

Furthermore, Chang's post-1949 literary career is characterized by an intriguing degree of compulsive rewriting. Take the two works mentioned at the beginning of this article as an example: "Lust, Caution" (色，戒) was written as early as 1953, and then went through numerous revisions over a period of thirty years, and was not actually published until 1983. *Little Reunion* (小團圓), which Chang began to write in the 1970s, took another twenty years to write and rewrite, and Chang still didn't consider it ready for publication. The revision and reworking of "The Golden Cangue" serve as another conspicuous case. As noted earlier, the first novel Chang finished after arriving in the United States, *Pink Tears,* was an English reworking of "The Golden Cangue," which also has an English version translated by Chang.[53] After it was rejected by a number of mainstream publishers, Chang rewrote it as *The Rouge of the North,* which was eventually published by Cassell in England in 1967. At the same time, she translated it into Chinese under the title "Embittered Woman" (怨女, 1968), and had it serialized in literary journals in Hong Kong and Taiwan. Indeed, Chang's literary life in the United States was marked by constant rewriting and translation across languages and literary genres, and across a variety of media including literature, theater, film, and radio production. Her projects on *Dream* and *The Sing-song Girls of Shanghai* can also be considered in this framework.

Such literary and cultural practice needs to be examined in the larger context of the Cold War period. David Der-wei Wang suggests that using English provided a way for Eileen Chang to flee modern Chinese literature dominated by literary realism. He observes that "A foreign language was no more alien a medium than Chinese to transmit, or translate, her already alienated existence in the Chinese environment."[54] I would take this argument even further to suggest that Chang's translingual practices not only question the restraints of modern Chinese literary and political discourse but also bespeak the equally manipulative ideological and cultural control of the Cold War United States. Chang migrated from Communist mainland China, only to find herself trapped by McCarthyism on the other side of the Iron Curtain. Knowing all too well the political and cultural rationale that prevented her work from being accepted by major American publishers, she nevertheless maintained her literary and aesthetic stance. Her deep suspicion of ideological hegemony of any kind is not only revealed in her arbitrary vacillation between pro-and anti-Communist novels between 1949 and 1953, but more importantly, is brought to the foreground by her prolific repetitions, or to be more precise, her translingual and trans-generic fission of works devoted to the portrayal of epochal transitions. In this way, rewriting, or a kind of literary schizogenesis, became her strategy of deterritorialization, a way of avoiding any political dominion over literary creation by either side of the Cold War dichotomy—Communist or anti-Communist.

In Chang's case, literary schizogenesis provided a way of penetrating the apparently seamless fortress of Cold War totality. Indeed, her post-1949 literary practice asserts its standpoint by inducing the proliferation of the same yet differentiated subjectivity, a schizophrenic subjectivity not only of the poetic characters but also of the poet herself. Such a schizophrenic strategy seems all the more trenchant in Chang's last work, *Mutual Reflections: Looking at My Old Photo Album* (對照記：看老照相簿, 1994), which is more a self-presentation in photographs than a representation in the conventional form of written words. In 1994, Chang produced this family photo album for Chinese audiences across mainland China, Taiwan, Hong Kong, and overseas communities. Using dozens of photographs taken over the course of a century, she presented her life image as a multiply split self and subjectivity. What could constitute a more schizophrenic cultural production than this?

7
Eileen Chang and Ang Lee at the Movies

The Cinematic Politics of Lust, Caution

Gina Marchetti

Eileen Chang's "Lust, Caution" (色，戒, 1978) and Ang Lee's 2007 adaptation of the story deal with appearance, performance, betrayal, and the cinema. Wang Jiazhi (Tang Wei), a young actress (and avid movie fan), plays the part of a spy playing the part of the wife of a war profiteer who takes up the role of mistress to a Japanese collaborator during the occupation of Shanghai. The young woman presents herself to Mr. and Mrs. Yi (members of Wang Jingwei's collaborationist branch of the Guomindang) as "Mrs. Mai," who proves useful as a companion to the couple because of her ability to interpret from Mandarin or Shanghainese into Cantonese as the Yi entourage goes shopping in Hong Kong. However, Mr. Yi (Tony Leung), at least, has his doubts about "Mrs. Mai." In fact, the "caution" of the title underscores the fact that Mr. Yi has his suspicions about "Mrs. Mai," and Wang Jiazhi seems to be (as the Chang short story makes explicit) aware of Mr. Yi's suspicions.

By the end of the book as well as the film, Mrs. Mai has betrayed everyone. While Mr. Yi only cheats on his wife, "Mrs. Mai" cheats on her "husband" as well as her friend Mrs. Yi, and Wang Jiazhi betrays her entire group of co-conspirators/university classmates as well as Mr. Yi (whom she may have saved, but also "betrays" as an idiot who could not even spot a spy in his midst). The intrigue of the story revolves around the question co-scriptwriter James Schamus poses in his essay in a book that reprints a translation of the Chang story along with the English version of the script: "Why did she do it?"[1] This question, of course, as Schamus, who has a doctorate in English Literature would no doubt be aware, has many possible interpretations. These range from the obvious one of why Wang would tell Yi to run and foil the assassination plot, to why Chang would write this story about a failed political assassination when she did. I would add the question of why Ang Lee (and his collaborators) would take up this particular story when they did and adapt it the way they have. This chapter looks at the various political positions rendered in cinematic terms in both Chang's novella and Lee's film. A film critic and scriptwriter, Chang crafted Jiazhi as a creature and creation of a specific "style," using film fantasies and cinematic conceits. Lee takes this up visually by citing Shanghai, Hollywood, European, and Asian films set during the same era, dealing with similar issues of sartorial style and fascist politics.

From the women revolutionists associated with early Shanghai film to Hollywood's Anna May Wong and moving through Bernardo Bertolucci's take on Chinese as well as fascist fashion in films such as *The Conformist* (1970) and *The Last Emperor* (末代皇帝——溥儀, 1987), Lee's *Lust, Caution* revolves around images of tailored dark suits, cloche hats, and diamond rings. The film's sensitivity to the links between colonial Hong Kong and pre-1949 Shanghai also places it in direct competition with the similar evocation of the post-1949 world of Shanghai émigrés in Wong Kar-wai's *In the Mood for Love* (2000). Within this heady mixture of politics, fashion, and postmodern consumerism, *Lust, Caution* creates a pastiche of past film styles evoked through fashion choices to parallel transformations in ideological fashion that may or may not be on a par with seasonal wardrobe changes. The film's politics, then, hinge on how it takes up questions of style.

Political Fashion

Lust, Caution is a story about a split in the Guomindang (KMT). Given the KMT's policy of non-engagement with the Japanese before the Xi'an Incident in 1936 and the loss of Nanjing and Shanghai in 1937, inevitable schisms within Chinese politics complicate any picture of resistance to the Japanese during that period. Chiang Kai-shek, of course, long saw the Chinese Communist Party (CCP) as his principal enemy, and Eileen Chang, who became a staunch anti-Communist during the Cold War, living briefly in Hong Kong (working for the CIA-front USIA) and primarily in the United States, likely agreed. Chang wrote and rewrote in her story "Lust, Caution" her own emotions deriving from her marriage to Japanese collaborator Hu Lancheng (胡蘭成, Deputy Head of the Ministry of Propaganda) during the occupation of Shanghai and, possibly, her second marriage to the American Ferdinand Reyher (a fiction writer whose story, *The End of the World*, formed the basis for the Cold War-era, post-apocalyptic film, *The World, The Flesh, and The Devil*, 1959).

Given that both sides in the struggle "use" the story's heroine Wang Jiazhi with little regard for her personal safety or feelings, Chang's story appears to come to the conclusion that all KMT men are culpable. Chang wrote the story when the war was over, and Japan and its former colony Taiwan (now the home of Chiang Kai-shek's ROC) were on friendly terms. The Cold War, in fact, saw the United States orchestrating its interests in Asia by playing the PRC off against the USSR, and the ROC off against the PRC, while romancing Japan with promises of peace and prosperity. At home in the US, Chang could look back on the Allies and the Axis and wonder at her own "collaboration" with the "enemy" during this period. Although many critics point to the similarities between Chang and her heroine Wang because they both attended the University of Hong Kong and became involved with members of Wang Jingwei's regime, the parallels stop there. Chang may have wanted to see herself as the idealistic "spy" and seductress but, in fact, she had no plans to assassinate Hu Lancheng for political reasons (although she might have wanted to shoot the philanderer if she had had the chance) and no ties to Chiang Kai-shek in Chongqing.

In fact, this story about a Chinese spy who became the mistress of a high-ranking collaborator, but who failed on several occasions to assassinate him, is supposedly based on the "true story" of Zheng Pingru, a half-Japanese/half-Chinese KMT agent.[2] Zheng had as her target Ding Mocun, who may or may not have been a double agent himself.[3] Japanese female agents, including cross-dressing Manchu princess Yoshiko Kawashima, featured as "Eastern Jewel" in Bertolucci's *The Last Emperor*, were newsworthy after the war.[4] Many others associated with the film industry also have a politically complicated biography, including figures such as the star Shirley Yamaguchi/Li Xianglan, who was acquainted with Eileen Chang during the Japanese occupation and later appeared in Hollywood films.[5]

The level of suspicion surrounding members of Wang Jingwei's government extended beyond threats from the KMT in Chongqing. Wang had been a close comrade of Sun Yat-sen, and the rhetoric surrounding his government in Nanjing drew on symbols and slogans associated with Sun and apparent calls for Chinese nationalism. Sun's concept of "bo'ai" (博愛, universal brotherhood) could be seen as supporting the Japanese call for a Greater East Asian Co-Prosperity Sphere, but the connection was always rather tenuous. *Lust, Caution* includes several references to Sun's call for "bo'ai" including a copy of the quotation over Mr. Yi's desk and a screening of the film *Universal*

Brotherhood (博愛, 1942) that was made during the occupation. The Japanese, needless to say, suspected these quislings of waffling between Chongqing and Nanjing/Tokyo.

The film version of *Lust, Caution* contains more than a trace of Chang's ambivalent feelings about the KMT—from both sides of the anti-Japanese/ pro-collaboration (Chiang Kai-shek/Wang Jingwei) divide—and that may have been part of its attraction. Hong Kong New Wave and Taiwan New Cinema filmmakers have made several adaptations of Eileen Chang's stories about Hong Kong and Shanghai,[6] so it comes as no surprise that Ang Lee should pick up on this Chang story for his film. However, Lee's decisions in relation to the depiction of the KMT at a time shortly before the party returned to power in Taiwan with the election of Ma Ying-jeou in 2008 merit critical attention.

The politics of *Lust, Caution* and its portrayal of the Japanese occupation of Shanghai can too easily be eclipsed by the film's steamy scenes featuring Hong Kong star Tony Leung and questions of censorship because of its graphic sex. In fact, *Lust, Caution* has a "political unconscious," which Leo Ou-fan Lee has alluded to in his work on the adaptation of the novella, and this also merits attention.[7] The lingering effects of Eileen Chang's own turbulent political associations become part of the narrative fabric of the film, and the conversation Ang Lee establishes with his English/Chinese source material as well as with screenwriters James Schamus and Wang Hui-ling, as they construct a script based on translations between English and Chinese, need to be taken into account.

Like the fictional Mrs. Yi, Eileen Chang appeared to be "apolitical" during the occupation. Poshek Fu quotes a telling remark of Chang's from this period: ". . . political topics are rarely favored because our private lives are already packed full of politics."[8] Although Chang's husband was a collaborator, her popularity during that period came from her ability to work around issues of national sovereignty and the Greater East Asian Co-Prosperity Sphere. During her time with Hu, Chang wrote in English (for the pro-Axis journal *The XXth Century*) and in Chinese. However, she did not appear to write pro-Japanese propaganda, and a significant portion of her non-fiction prose consisted of movie reviews and articles on "fashion," "leisure," and "style."

"Lust, Caution," and "The Spyring" from which it evolved, come from a very different period in Chang's career. Even though it is set during the occupation of Shanghai (with some brief narrative information on Hong Kong before Christmas of 1941), this is not a story exclusively about the Sino-Japanese War.

Chang wrote it during the Cold War. As such, it may be as much about the political changes of the 1970s (when the story was finally published) as about the Japanese occupation. During this decade, the PRC gained international recognition at the United Nations and from the United States (with Richard Nixon's visit in 1972). The KMT gradually lost its Cold War iron grip with the death of Chiang Kai-shek in 1975 and, after the publication of Chang's story, the normalization of US-PRC relations in 1979. Born in 1954, Ang Lee came of age during the 1970s, and Lee's *Lust, Caution*, with its visual evocation of European films of that period, may be as much about the Cold War as it is about the Pacific War. In rewriting the past and blurring the line between the "good guys" and the "bad guys" of the Pacific War after the "end" of the Cold War, Lee takes up the question of how the political complications of Chang's time impact on mid-twentieth-century loyalties.

During the Cold War, Chang fully vented her anti-Communist sentiments in her English language fiction.[9] The Chinese version of "Lust, Caution" was not published during the McCarthy era—when suspicion of espionage involving Communists was at fever pitch and a novel that was so ambivalent about political commitment and so cynical about romantic love would probably not have been welcome. The cliché from that era ran along the lines that "true" love wins the Communist over to the "right" political position—and Cold War comedies feature Soviet Russians and some Red Chinese romanced and seduced by consumer goods and attractive anti-Communist mates.

A diamond ring and some satisfaction in bed could work wonders in Hollywood, but Eileen Chang was never taken in by the movies in the same way as Wang Jiazhi. As a film critic and scriptwriter who eventually married an American screenwriter, Chang knew all the Hollywood tricks. Her characters may fall for the glint of a diamond or the soft light on a man's face, but she never does. Ang Lee, however, tells a different story, and has been romanced by his own cinematic version of Chang's more jaded tale: "After *Brokeback* and this one, I do believe deeply inside that I am a romantic . . . I was never romantic in real life. That is why I have to make movies about it."[10]

Though born in Taiwan, Ang Lee is from a so-called "mainlander" family, and stories about his "traditional Chinese" father (who passed away while Lee was making *Brokeback Mountain*, 2005) link him to the generation that came to Taiwan with the KMT after the war. As a member of a different, diasporic generation of Chinese who "passed through" Hong Kong and/or Taiwan on their way elsewhere, Lee has made films (e.g., *The Wedding Banquet* 喜宴,

1993) about other displaced children of KMT mainlanders who establish lives away from both the PRC and the ROC. The reasons behind this move away from Taiwan may include feelings of "not belonging" because of anti-KMT sentiment or simply a belief in the West (often the US) as a land of greater freedom (less repression—far away from traditional Confucian values) and economic opportunity. Bypassing Taiwan (with a brief stop in colonial Hong Kong instead), Eileen Chang followed the same route. Anti-Communist, far from pro-KMT, sympathetic to the political "outsider," Chang writes a story and Lee makes a film about the KMT divided, prostituting itself to foreign powers. Perhaps Lee's experience growing up in Taiwan among the children of the Japanese "collaborators" made him more receptive to a character such as Mr. Yi in the same way that Eileen Chang's marriage to Hu Lancheng allowed her to create a character such as Jiazhi who could betray the "cause" of national liberation because a diamond ring made her think that her villainous collaborationist paramour might "love" her.

With KMT officials making pilgrimages to Nanjing to pay their respects at Sun Yat-sen's mausoleum, *Lust, Caution* seems to caution against political divisions while lusting after the greater Chinese film market. The politics of *Lust, Caution* cannot be divorced from the postmodern moment. As Ella Shohat and Robert Stam note: "The important point that postmodernism makes is that virtually all political struggles now take place on the symbolic battleground of the mass media."[11] This means that *Lust, Caution*—and any depiction it offers of Chinese politics and its history—exists within the media marketplace and remains subject to its rules.

Movies on Their Minds

Film critic Michael Wood has remarked on *Lust, Caution* that ". . . each character in the movie has a movie running in his or her head . . ."[12] The same could be said of the Eileen Chang source, which also depicts Wang as an avid movie fan and Shanghai cinema as an important institution for its characters. This opens up the question of what movies run through the heads of not only the characters in the story, but also Chang, Lee, Schamus, and all the others involved with *Lust, Caution*, as part of the story, in crafting the plot, or in translating the narrative across languages and media.[13]

Beginning in Shanghai and Hollywood in the 1930s and 40s, resistance to Japanese rule was imagined through romantic melodramas about glamorous

Chinese women serving as spies. This narrative theme goes back to early films such as Sun Yu's *Daybreak* (天明, 1933), made soon after Japan's 1932 attack on Shanghai, which features a prostitute-turned leftwing patriot who, like Jiazhi, dies with a smile on her face.[14] Film scholar Miriam Hansen's discussion of the protagonist Ling Ling (Li Lili) in *Daybreak*, in fact, could be used to describe Jiazhi in *Lust, Caution*:

> . . . Ling Ling's face becomes a façade, a mask, a cypher, a mystery; in fact, dissimulation, masquerade, and performance become her strategies of survival, even as she faces the firing squad . . . *Daybreak* achieves a translation, hybridization, and reconfiguration of foreign (and not just American) as well as indigenous discourses on modernity and modernization.[15]

Throughout *Lust, Caution*, Jiazhi does nothing but "translate" for others and act out the roles chosen for her—from her stage performance as a student in the patriotic drama presented at the University of Hong Kong to her final "role" as "revolutionary martyr" facing the firing squad. She must perform flawlessly to survive as a spy, but she may get too caught up in her "act" when she decides to save Mr. Yi at the film's climax.

None of the roles she plays is without cinematic precedent, and Wang seems to play her part through performances given by other actresses, from Li Lili and Ruan Lingyu to Anna May Wong and Ingrid Bergman. In the novel as well as the film, Jiazhi creates herself through the cinema, and Ang Lee takes full advantage of this very rich cinematic history to create the film's look as well as his actors' performances. Jiazhi/Tang Wei, in fact, does not freely fashion her performance; rather, a number of men mold her and direct her actions—from the leader of her patriotic acting troupe/amateur spy ring in Hong Kong (Kuang Yumin/Wang Lee-hom) to their KMT handler Old Wu (Tou Chung-hua). Mr. Yi directs her in the bedroom, and Ang Lee directs her on the set.

On and off screen, all seem to have Hollywood movies running through their minds. During the Pacific War, Hollywood quickly picked up on the prostitute-patriot formula with films featuring Anna May Wong, such as *Lady from Chungking* (1942) and *Bombs Over Burma* (1943). In *Lady from Chungking*, for example, Anna May Wong plays an upper-class KMT operative who seduces a Japanese commander in order to foil his military campaign. Where Wang Jiazhi falters, Wong's character succeeds, but after the assassination she is caught and suffers the same fate as Wang before a firing squad. By the time the war was over, the formula was set: a Chinese woman prostitutes herself to a powerful pro-Japanese womanizer in order to assassinate him. She dies—usually by firing squad—at the end, apparently because patriotic self-sacrifice could never completely expiate the transgression of prostitution. As a film critic and script-writer, Chang had seen it all, so writing "Lust, Caution" about a film fan must have brought to mind all these hackneyed movie plots.

Wang Jiazhi at the Movies

Poshek Fu has pointed out in his work on Chinese cinema that the line between collaborator and resistance fighter was a particularly porous one during the occupation of Shanghai. For those working in the arts (such as Chang), this line was even more delicate. Fu's characterization of occupation cinema in many respects parallels *Lust, Caution*'s navigation of past and present political sensitivities: ". . . the occupation cinema in China represented an ambiguous space in which boundaries between heroic and villainous, political and apolitical, private and public were rarely clear and constantly transgressed."[16] The film *Universal Brotherhood*, excerpted in the film *Lust, Caution*, is a case in point. In Lee's film, Jiazhi has a rendezvous with Kuang at a screening of this occupation film *Universal Brotherhood*. Although, as *Lust, Caution* accurately shows, American films continued to screen after the occupation of the foreign settlements in 1941 (in fact, Wang Jingwei did not officially declare war on the Allies until 1943), no new films were imported, and the slack was taken up by local productions and Axis imports (including films from Manchukuo).[17] *Universal Brotherhood* was produced under the auspices of the reorganized Shanghai film industry and directed by Bu Wancang (*Mulan Joins the Army*, 木蘭從軍, 1939; and *Eternity*, 萬世流芳, 1942, starring Li Xianglan, mentioned above) and Zhu Shilin. Both directors found themselves in Hong Kong after the war, and Eileen Chang collaborated with them on film projects during the Hong Kong phase of her writing career.

The characters "博愛" have a prominent place behind Mr. Yi's office desk in *Lust, Caution*. They are associated with Sun Yat-sen's famous saying, paralleling France's "liberty, equality, fraternity," calling for "universal love" (translated as "fraternity" or "universal brotherhood") as a founding principle of the Chinese Republic. Under the Japanese occupation, this could be interpreted ironically or taken literally as a call to co-operate with Japan's pan-Asian agenda on the basis of Asian "brotherhood" against European colonial aggression. However, *Universal Brotherhood*'s focus seems to be more on affairs of the heart than on affairs of state. Zhu's episode in the omnibus film, for example, deals with a man with a mistress who leaves him in the end.

In fact, this is precisely the plotline of the Hollywood film Jiazhi watches in Hong Kong, *Intermezzo* (directed by White Russian émigré Gregory Ratoff, 1939). In this romantic melodrama, Ingrid Bergman plays the mistress of a violin virtuoso, who sacrifices her own happiness for the sake of her lover's family. The film even makes a comic reference to China that links potentially murderous Mandarins to birthday parties. The film clip prefigures Jiazhi's own fate as Mr. Yi's mistress, connecting wealth, death, and mahjong parties. It also links China and Hollywood in the same imaginative sphere and establishes an intratextual link to *Universal Brotherhood*, which appears later in *Lust, Caution*. Jiazhi cries copiously during the screening, relating the loss of her father (who has just remarried and neglected to provide passage for her to follow his new family to the UK) with screen events set in Europe, made in America, and poking fun at Chinese violence.

Needless to say, Jiazhi's tears in the movie theater also conjure up similar scenes in European New Wave films—most notably, Jean-Luc Godard's *Vivre Sa Vie* (My Life to Live, 1962), in which the protagonist, Nana, prostitutes herself when her acting career fails. She cries as she watches Dreyer's silent classic *The Passion of Joan of Arc* (1928), about another executed female political martyr. Serving as a mirror for *Lust, Caution*'s spectators, this mise-en-abîme and its intertextual complications illustrate the political complexity Robert Stam and Ella Shohat associate with colonial viewership (clearly in operation in Jiazhi's case), but that is also applicable more generally to the situation of the film's postcolonial viewers: "Spectatorial positions are multiform, fissured, schizophrenic, unevenly developed, culturally, discursively, and politically discontinuous, forming part of a shifting realm of ramifying differences and contradictions."[18] Jiazhi sees herself in this Hollywood film, and her over-identification with these tragic heroines gives way to her "losing" herself in her role as Mrs. Mai.

She continues to go to movies in Shanghai after the first failed attempt on Yi's life in Hong Kong. The screening of *Penny Serenade* (1941) she attends there, however, is interrupted by a Japanese propaganda reel. Like *Intermezzo*, *Penny Serenade* has an Asian connection (not excerpted directly in *Lust, Caution*). The newlywed couple featured in this film (Cary Grant and Irene Dunne) goes to Tokyo, and the bride has a miscarriage during the Kanto earthquake of 1923. Again, the Asian reference in *Penny Serenade* may be marginal to the film, but it establishes an imaginative commonality linking Hong Kong/ Shanghai film-going in the 1930s and 40s with an awareness of spectatorship and the emotional vicissitudes of identification with the actors and actresses on screen. Just as Hollywood drew on an imagined "Orient" in the 1930s and 40s, *Lust, Caution* works through a catalog of American film classics to shape its characters and envision their world.

The *Suspicion* (1941) poster in *Lust, Caution* brings Alfred Hitchcock into the mix. Although *Lust, Caution* references *Suspicion*, which deals with a woman who suspects that her husband plans to murder her, it is another of Hitchcock's Cary Grant vehicles, *Notorious* (1946), that most resembles Lee's film. Although clearly Lee could not put a 1946 film into a film set in 1942, he does zero in on Hitchcock's *Notorious*, not only by including the reference to *Suspicion*, which combines Cary Grant and Hitchcock, but also through reference to another Grant vehicle *Penny Serenade* and an early Ingrid Bergman feature *Intermezzo*. Thus, Lee brings references to Hitchcock, Ingrid Bergman, and Cary Grant together to equal *Notorious*, which acts as a narrative double for *Lust, Caution*, with its plot about a woman who marries a Nazi in order to spy on him. Like Wang Jiazhi, who likely participates in the assassination plot because of her infatuation with Kuang Yumin, Alicia Huberman (Ingrid Bergman) really loves her handler, T. R. Devlin (Cary Grant), but prostitutes herself for the Allied cause.

Lee can, of course, build on the fact that Bergman's star presence as the "other" woman or the woman with divided loyalties in films such as *Casablanca* (1942) also found expression, after the war, in her personal life through her love affair with Roberto Rossellini. In fact, James Schamus, *Lust, Caution*'s co-scriptwriter, in his essay on the film, quotes a passage from Slavoj Žižek's book *Enjoy Your Symptom! Jacques Lacan in Hollywood and out* (1992) that refers not only to acting in general, but specifically to Ingrid Bergman (in a section entitled "Why Is Woman a Symptom of Man?"). Wang Jiazhi, and by extension Tang Wei, go to see Ingrid Bergman movies to learn how to act and seem to be ". . . annihilated and subsequently reborn (or not) . . ."[19] Schamus may have had other parts of Žižek's book in mind as well as he crafted his version of the character of Jiazhi. Žižek speaks, for instance, of Bergman's performative "mask" as follows:

> The path to an authentic subjective position runs therefore "from the outside inward": first, we pretend to be something, we just act as if we are that, till, step by step, we actually become it . . . The performative

dimension at work here consists of the symbolic efficiency of the "mask": wearing a mask actually makes us what we feign to be . . . the only authenticity at our disposal is that of impersonation, of "taking our act (posture) seriously."[20]

And what is the act if not the moment when the subject who is its bearer suspends the network of symbolic fictions which serve as a support to his daily life and confronts again the radical negativity upon which they are founded?[21]

As the character of Wang Jiazhi took shape, her resemblance to Ingrid Bergman during her Hollywood years may have been overlaid by the media persona of her time with Rossellini. In the aftermath of the Second World War and after decades of Mussolini's rule in Italy, Rossellini was no stranger to the "radical negativity" of the "act" and to the consequences of taking up the "mask" to hide the emptiness of the self. In fact, Rossellini set the stage for the imagination of fascism as a predatory sexual performance in his feature *Open City* (1945) through the character of the lesbian fascist Ingrid (Giovanna Galletti).[22] According to Žižek, Ingrid Bergman saw *Open City* in New York, prompting her to contact Rossellini to offer him her services as an actress/lover.

Eileen Chang's story includes elaborate descriptions of clothing and jewelry linked to her psychological profiles of characters living behind various "masks" in the fiction. In the film, Lee makes use of an aesthetic associated with screen depictions of fascist masks played out in its visual design. For example, Yi initially marches towards the camera flanked by guards in uniform, with glimpses of the KMT flag behind, and passes a walled enclosure patrolled by a German shepherd. The dog guards/imprisons the ladies within, including the spy Jiazhi, sitting on display, clothed in a silk qipao/cheongsam similar to the dress of the other ladies around the table. They play mahjong and compare diamonds as Yi—the hypnotic cynosure of power and sexuality—enters to survey the scene. However, before he goes to greet his wife, lover, and guests, Yi stops to check his hair in a hall mirror—a narcissistic gesture that hints that his virility may be a "pose."

Susan Sontag could be describing the aesthetic thrust of *Lust, Caution* when she writes in her seminal essay "Fascinating Fascism":

Fascist aesthetics . . . flow from (and justify) a preoccupation with situations of control, submissive behavior, extravagant effort, and the endurance of pain; they endorse two seemingly opposite states, egomania and servitude . . . The fascist dramaturgy centers on the orgiastic transactions between mighty forces and their puppets, uniformly garbed and shown in ever swelling numbers. Its choreography alternates between ceaseless

motion and a congealed, static, "virile" posing. Fascist art glorifies surrender, it exalts mindlessness, it glamorizes death.[23]

Yi exerts control, while Jiazhi submits and endures pain during their sadomasochistic trysts. She is a puppet at the mercy of contending forces—the
resistance and the Japanese collaborators—that use her sexuality for their own
purposes. Yi's egomania may prevent him from seeing his lover as a mole, but
Jiazhi understands the situation well, becomes enraptured, surrenders to Yi
fully, and dies a "glorious" death (ironically both loyal to her fascist lover and
a martyr to her political cause). Yi may or may not be in love with Jiazhi, but
she buys into the idea that they are in love and seals her fate as well as the fate
of her anti-fascist comrades. Although the film seems to suggest that she loves
Yi because she feels he may not really be a sadistic fascist, the fact remains that
she submits to him and to fascism in the end. The film, then, strikes a balance
between depicting Jiazhi as giving in to her fascination with fascism and celebrating her as holding on to individual passion above political ideals. The question, though, is not only why Jiazhi "does it," but also why Ang Lee continues to
be fascinated by the fashion of fascism.

Screen Lust, Political Caution

There is a strong historical association between theatricality and fascism in
world cinema. As Sontag observes:

> Between sadomasochism and fascism there is a natural link. "Fascism is
> theater," as Genet said. As is sadomasochistic sexuality: to be involved in
> sadomasochism is to take part in a sexual theater, a staging of sexuality.
> Regulars of sadomasochistic sex are expert costumers and choreographers
> as well as performers, in a drama that is all the more exciting because it is
> forbidden to ordinary people.[24]

Certainly, *Lust, Caution* is far from the first film to look at fascism and impe-
rialism through the lens of explicit/illicit sexuality. Building on *Open City*,
many films (e.g., Luchino Visconti's *The Damned* (1969), Liliana Cavani's
The Night Porter (1974), Lina Wertmüller's *Seven Beauties* (1975), Pier Paolo
Pasolini's *Salo, Or the 120 Days of Sodom* (1975), and Nagisa Ōshima's *In the
Realm of the Senses* (1976), among others) have used sexually explicit allegories to explore the pathology of fascism. China too has a significant example,
Ye Daying's *Red Cherry* (紅櫻桃, 1995). While the sadistic fascist has been a
staple in films since the rise of the Axis powers, films made in the late 1960s

through the 1970s (around the time Eileen Chang published her novella in Chinese) began to explore the boundary between pornography and film art through sadomasochistic relationships set against the backdrop of fascist Italy, Germany, and Japan.

James Schamus has called *Lust, Caution*, "the Chinese porn movie."[25] The film, in fact, cites a specific type of pornography—fascist-inspired sadomasochistic porn (e.g., *Ilsa, She Wolf of the SS*, 1975). However, it even more directly alludes to the European New Wave's treatment of fascism and sadomasochism and, specifically, the work of one filmmaker. Indeed, watching *Lust, Caution* can serve as a journey through the career of Italian director Bernardo Bertolucci, from *The Conformist* (1970)[26] through *Last Tango in Paris* (1972) to *The Last Emperor* (1987). Some similarities exist at plot level—*The Conformist* and *The Last Emperor* deal with political betrayal, treason, and the sexual dynamics of fascism, and are set during the same time period as *Lust, Caution*. Other similarities can be found in the mise-en-scène and cinematography. The empty room in *Last Tango* (Figure 7.1) resembles the site of Yi and Wang's first sexual encounter in *Lust, Caution* (Figure 7.2). The chiaroscuro lighting, use of backlighting, and silhouettes give the films' characters a mysterious and conflicted visual quality.

Sadomasochistic sex scenes punctuate the films' narratives and provide an appearance of "insight" into the development of the characters' relationships

Figure 7.1

The empty apartment in *Last Tango in Paris*

Figure 7.2

The empty apartment in *Lust, Caution*

in *Last Tango* and *Lust, Caution*. Lee's film even echoes specific erotic acts and sexual postures. Although Marlon Brando as Paul may pause to ask for butter, rear penetration has the same visceral impact in both films, and the sadomasochistic sex retains an ambivalent quality in both cases. The smile on Jiazhi's face after her first violent encounter with Mr. Yi may indicate triumph that she has done her job well by playing a mistress with a taste for rough sex or hint at the fulfillment of her own erotic desire. In *Lust, Caution*, Jiazhi eyes the gun during coitus, while Jeanne (Maria Schneider) ends up using it in *Last Tango*. Jiazhi saves her lover and Jeanne destroys hers, but both grapple with the consequences of their sadomasochism. Both Mr. Yi and Paul play with a reversal of roles, softening their approaches to their lovers, but with very different results. When Paul tries to romance Jeanne, she kills him. When Mr. Yi does the same, Jiazhi sacrifices herself to save him.

In fact, the films' common interest in style—from Paris to Shanghai—complicates the way in which the characters relate to one another as well as their environments. They are creations of very specific historical periods, but also creatures of film style. The clothing in *The Conformist*, *The Last Emperor* and *Lust, Caution*, and the careful attention to furniture and architectural details from the Forbidden City in Beijing to the main building at the University of

Hong Kong attempt to replicate an image of the period in Italy, China, and Manchukuo that is known from the films of the time. All of the films, in fact, situate their own vision of sadism, fascism, and sexuality against the backdrop of film history. *The Conformist* references Plato's cave as a metaphor for the cinema. *Last Tango in Paris* contrasts the sadomasochistic "movie" going on in the empty apartment with the cinéma-vérité film Tom (Jean-Pierre Léaud) is making of his fiancée Jeanne, unaware of her encounters with Paul. In *The Last Emperor*, Puyi (John Lone) finally recognizes that he is a traitor when he sees himself in a newsreel about the Japanese occupation of China.

Joan Chen, who plays Puyi's principal wife in *The Last Emperor*, provides the visual hinge that connects Lee's film with Bertolucci's work. Chen as Mrs. Yi even takes up the round sunglasses so much a part of the mise-en-scène of *The Last Emperor* (Figures 7.3 and 7.4), and wears them as a jaunty reminder of the many things the films have in common, from the characters' decision to occlude their vision to the filmmakers' casting choices.

The Last Emperor and *Lust, Caution* also appear to be in political dialog. Both films take up the metaphor of politics as theatrical shadow play, but each film develops this symbol for different ends. While *The Last Emperor*

Figure 7.3

Joan Chen (with Tang Wei and Wang Lee-hom) out shopping in *Lust, Caution*

Figure 7.4

Joan Chen with John Lone and Vivian Wu in *The Last Emperor*

sympathetically chronicles the rehabilitation of Puyi as a model "citizen" under the tutelage of the Communist Party with the assistance of propaganda films, *Lust, Caution* seemingly "rehabilitates" Mr. Yi through his encounter with Hollywood movie fan Jiazhi. Hollywood romance trumps political engagement, and Lee's film deviates dramatically from Bertolucci's New Left encounter with fascism and sadomasochism.

Back to the Bordello: *Street Angel*

Bertolucci's films may play a major role in the visual and thematic imagination of Lee's motion picture, but other sources should not be neglected. Ōshima's *In the Realm of the Senses* finds its echoes in the Japanese geisha house/bordello in *Lust, Caution,* but so does Yuan Muzhi's *Street Angel* (馬路天使, 1937). In the geisha house scene that has no parallel in Chang's story, Wang/Mrs. Mai begins to sing the famous song from the film *Street Angel*. Made on the eve of the Japanese capture of Shanghai and Nanjing in 1937, *Street Angel* depicts the lives of two sisters who come to Shanghai to flee the Japanese incursions in the north of China. One becomes a street singer and the other a prostitute. Although loosely based on the Hollywood original of the same name (directed by Frank Borzage, 1928, with Janet Gaynor), the Shanghai film is leftwing— anti-capitalist, anti-imperialist, anti-Japanese—confirmed by the fact that Yuan joined the CCP in 1940. The song, translated in the script as "Girl Singing from Earth's End," includes explicit references to the "north" (i.e., Japanese-occupied Manchuria, Manchukuo) and to the singer's search for a "soul mate" who understands her "heart" (presumably her political sentiments). The political message of the song may be veiled, but for cineastes in the audience, the film reference is crystal clear, and could completely transform the meaning of Yi and Wang's relationship. The scene seems to point to the fact that the pair recognize each other as putting on an "act," but the film does not answer the question of what "act" each sees the other performing.

Yi and Wang may feel some sort of deep anti-Japanese connection that the playacting of their current circumstances forces them to deny. Yi admits he feels like a "prostitute" in this scene, and the entire "meaning" of the film may change if this scene is read as a confession of his genuine loyalty to the resistance. On the other hand, Jiazhi could be admitting to Yi that she is, indeed, working against the Japanese—giving Yi a further sadomasochistic thrill by highlighting the fact that he really is in danger because of the affair. Or it could simply be seen as a nostalgic vehicle that enables the two to express a "love" that "transcends" the status of bought-and-paid-for mistress to a wealthy, powerful quisling for the Japanese rulers.

Whether as the spy Wang or the adulterous Mrs. Mai, Jiazhi cannot deny the fact that she has prostituted herself to Yi; and, as closet loyalist or committed fascist, Yi cannot refute the fact he has prostituted himself to the Japanese. Political identities aside, these two whores find themselves in a film that cannot recapture the political certainty of *Street Angel*. However, the question of whether this scene picks up on the other promise of the song that "love prevails" and that the lovers can remain entwined like "needle and thread" remains unanswered. *Lust, Caution*, certainly, can be read as a paean to romantic love over politics, individual passion over social responsibility, and universal humanism over Chinese nationalism. However, this meaning tends to implode as it spirals outwards through Chang's novel, Hollywood films of the 1930s and 40s, Shanghai leftwing cinema and later occupation features, and European New Wave imaginations of sadomasochism and fascism, and lands in front of Mexican cinematographer Rodrigo Prieto's camera.

In the Mood for Clothes: Sartorial Connections between *Lust, Caution* and *In the Mood for Love*

Although *Lust, Caution* seems to set up a particularly intimate intertextual relationship with Bertolucci's work, fashion extends far beyond Bertolucci's domain to embrace an auteur closer to Ang Lee's home turf. As much as Lee's film mirrors European, Japanese, and Hollywood images of fascism, it perhaps comes closest in visual design and detail to Wong Kar-wai's *In the Mood for Love* (花樣年華, 2000). Just as Joan Chen's look provides the visual link between Lee and Bertolucci, Tony Leung provides the physical connection between *In the Mood for Love* and *Lust, Caution*, with Maggie Cheung and Tang Wei's *qipao* making the relationship absolutely clear. Tony Leung may look like Jean-Louis Trintignant in *The Conformist*, but he also seems to be playing some darker version of Chow Mo-wan from *In the Mood for Love* and *2046*. Stepping away from the anti-fascist ramifications of *The Conformist*, Lee moves with Tony Leung into a more ambiguous political sphere in which style and consumption, as well as alienation and isolation, provide a material alternative to Communist China in colonial Hong Kong. The blue-grey business suit of the fascist Yi becomes the anonymous uniform of the salaryman Chow, and the flamboyant Shanghai or Hong Kong-tailored *qipao* concretizes their desire beyond fascist or colonial politics. They all dress the part, play their roles, and go off to dinner. The *qipao* take center stage. Postmodernism outfits these characters for very different performances in the spectacle of consumption of the twenty-first century.

Mr. Yi and Jiazhi arrange their first rendezvous without their "spouses" at a Hong Kong tailor shop. Jiazhi has orchestrated the excursion with her comrades, and the tailor treats her as a valued regular customer. She gives Yi advice on the cut of his suit, and they gaze at themselves in the mirror. The look and its reflection transform them into a "couple." (Figure 7.5) Yi recognizes this intimacy by saying to Jiazhi that "I'm in your hands." Jiazhi has a fitting for a new blue *qipao* made from material Mrs. Yi has rejected as too gaudy. Yi tells her to keep the outfit, which accentuates her figure. They have dressed each other for their new roles as lovers, recognized their portrait framed before them, and go off to seal their new relationship with a quiet dinner in a Western restaurant. At dinner, they talk about the movies. Jiazhi goes to the cinema because she has time to kill, but Yi does not like dark places (implicitly because of the possibility of assassination in the shadows).

Figure 7.5

At the tailor shop in *Lust, Caution*

Wong Kar-wai's segment in *Eros* (2004), "The Hand" (手), also eroticizes the activity of the tailor and presents the *qipao* as a fetish object. In that segment, the female protagonist, Hua (Gong Li), is a doomed prostitute who has a complex relationship with her tailor Zhang (Chen Chang). The tailor's work-shop, the cloth, the details of the *qipao*, all take on a sexual significance that can never be disassociated from commerce. Similarly, in *In the Mood for Love*, the Shanghai émigré Su Lizhen (Maggie Cheung), seemingly sewn into her *qipao*, never manages to free herself from the constraints of her circumstances as the wife of a philandering husband within Hong Kong's Shanghai expatriate community. Like Jiazhi, she flirts with a character played by Tony Leung in a Western-style restaurant in Hong Kong—he in a tailored suit, she in her *qipao*. Both couples blend into an environment that conflates illicit sexuality, roman-tic promise, Western décor, and tailored clothing with colonial politics. The *qipao* as a fetish object stands out in a world of manufactured commodities, defining certain roles for its wearers, constricting their gestures, and determin-ing their performances. The costumes not only contribute to the films' visual style; they also highlight the fact that the performances are as constructed as the garments. Indeed, clothing and accessories "make" the films and highlight their own manufactured qualities. The close-up of the diamond ring at the climax of *Lust, Caution* illustrates this point.

The "Ring" of Truth

In both the novella and the film, the drama builds to the moment in the jewelry store when Jiazhi decides to save Yi from assassination. However, unlike Chang, who fills in all the blanks in her novella, Lee leaves the film viewer with questions. No voice-over narration, no intertitles, no dialog spoken by other characters allows spectators into either Yi's or Wang/Mai's head at that critical moment in the shop. Lee keeps the film on the level of speculation— she loves him, she thinks he loves her, she has lost "faith" in the validity of her cause (maybe she simply can no longer see the Japanese as all that bad or the Nationalists as all that good). The film, after all, graphically depicts the violence associated with Kuang's group during the killing of his relative in Hong Kong. The blood on Kuang's hands is shown on screen, while Mr. Yi merely narrates his involvement with torturing KMT spies as a sort of sexual foreplay with Jiazhi.

Maybe Jiazhi has taken the role of Mrs. Mai too seriously and feels she "owes" Yi something for the ring. Or she may be overly sentimental and unable to bring herself to kill someone with whom she has had an orgasm. Perhaps she feels more like Yi's mistress than a spy. The film, however, remains silent, and her motives obscure.

Chang's story rationalizes the decision by pointing to Wang Jiazhi's love of cinema for at least part of the explanation:

> She examined the ring under the lamplight, turning it over in her fingers. Sitting by the balcony, she began to imagine that the bright windows and door visible behind her were a cinema screen across which an action movie was being shown. She had always hated violent films; as a child she had turned her back whenever a scene became grisly.[27]

For Chang, the ring and the feeling her character has of being in a movie she really does not want to watch provide the backdrop for Wang's reading of Yi's expression as "true" love rather than an act. However, the reader and the film viewer already know that the actress Wang knows very well that Yi is a consummate actor himself. In Chang's story, the repetitious nature of the act Yi puts on for his string of sexual conquests belies any genuine belief that Jiazhi could somehow be "different." Similarly, in the film, Wang confronts her handler Old Wu, with Kuang acting as a witness. She lashes out:

> He [Yi] knows better than you how to act the part. He not only gets inside me, but he worms his way into my heart. I play my part loyally, so

> I too can get inside him. And every time he hurts me until I bleed and scream before he comes, before he feels alive. In the dark only he knows it's all true.

Wang knows Yi knows she is acting as well, and the couple recognize each other as political whores and amateur actors. Jiazhi's blood in the fiction, and the chatter about whether Leung and Tang really "did it" in the film press, prove that the act is completely "true." The nature of this cinematic "truth," however, remains open to speculation.

The novella and the screenplay make it clear that Jiazhi buys Yi's act. Without fully acknowledging her own feelings for Yi, she sees (or projects) love in Yi's facial expression. Ultimately, she has been taken in by his performance in the same way she was taken in by Hollywood screen fantasies earlier in *Lust, Caution*. However, this information does not appear in the film. The mise-en-scène and cinematography (e.g., the glint of the ring, the quality of the light on Tony Leung's face, the intimacy of the close-ups) point in a certain direction. These images, however, could be read as a classical cinematic depiction of romantic transcendence or as clichés meant to point self-reflexively back to the cinema as the realm of spectacle, performance, and illusory desire. The film never says "why" because it is all an act. Ultimately, then, the film (true to the postmodern turn of which it is undeniably a part) stays mute, and the political implications of Jiazhi's actions remain obscure. *Lust, Caution* may be celebrating individual desire and the sanctity of human emotion over social/political/national imperatives, or it may all be an "act." The film may, in fact, manifest a postmodern suspicion of the master narratives of romantic love as well as Chinese nationalism and pan-Asianism.

As in any drama, after the climax, the denouement promises to tidy things up. In this case (faithful to the Chang story), Wang goes window-shopping. She and her co-conspirators had movie tickets to allow them to make their escape by blending in with the cinema patrons (what better place for escapism than the movie theater?). The assassination plot now in tatters, Wang, frustrated in her search for a taxi and presumably in shock, checks out the latest Shanghai fashions. This could be ironic—i.e., Jiazhi has been seduced by a fashionable ring to betray her cause because of the illusion of romantic love the jewel connotes. Perhaps shopping reminds her of her first intimate moment with Yi in the tailor's shop in Hong Kong, and she may have second thoughts about her betrayal of her comrades. However, the scene could also point to the fact that she is as vapid as the mannequins in the window, taking up the poses and postures of the elegant Shanghai demimonde, and forgetting that it is, after all, only an act. She shops for clothes—to define her identity or to hide it—to blend in with a crowd equally a part of a spectacle that belies political oppression.

In writing her essay "Fascinating Fascism," Sontag may have had Siegfried Kracauer's analysis of Weimar mass culture in mind. Karsten Witte has also noted the link between Kracauer's analysis of the "mass ornament" and the emergence of fascism:

> If the massive consumption of the ornamental figures distracts people from changing the current social system, it becomes understandable why, a short time later in 1933, the fascists were able to mobilize those ener-gies which lay devoid of meaning, substance and interpretation, so that the masses could actually claim to see their own triumph of the will in that megalomaniacally contrived and hypertrophically staged spectacle in Nuremberg.[28]

In *Lust, Caution*, the mannequins in the shop window are overlaid by the superimposed image of the anonymous masses of shoppers in the street. Jiazhi fades into the reflection, a dummy in the window mirrors the clothes she wears, and her individuality is cast into doubt as a duplicate of an empty commercial fashion design. (Figure 7.6)

Perhaps shopping is at the root of the film's politics. Political caution, after all, may not be political silence. The film reflects on the seduction of the

Figure 7.6
Window shopping in *Lust, Caution*

spectator through the spectacle of consumption, the glamor of old Shanghai, and the magic of the movies. As politics melts into performance, the film poses the question, albeit obliquely, of whether or not we have been bought off by the glitz and glamor of the ring, the light on Tony Leung's face, and the seductive properties of the cinema.

The "traitors" and the "patriots" do not seem all that different in the film. The two sides of the KMT, in fact, cancel each other out. The CCP (represented by the leftwing film *Street Angel*), Japan (more in the form of the bordello than any actual character controlling Yi's life), and the American presence (depicted through Hollywood movies) are at the film's margins. A geopolitical present and the historical past merge into ornamental, seductive images meant to conjure up an ersatz nostalgia, and give in to the illusion that lust and love may, in fact, transcend both.

When Jiazhi is finally picked up by a jovial pedicab driver, the revolving pinwheel on his vehicle does not bode well. A children's toy in the West, in the Chinese context the pinwheel resembles the wheels used in funerary and other religious observances. The execution scene reinforces the Ang Lee "brand" and his authorial mark. The condemned co-conspirators face a void that resembles the one Jen (Zhang Ziyi) dives into at the end of *Crouching Tiger, Hidden Dragon* (臥虎藏龍, 2000). The visual cue links the hit martial arts epic to box office hope as much as it shies away from any final words from any of the mute characters in the scene. This is not Li Lili (Ling Ling from *Daybreak*) or Anna May Wong as the "lady from Chungking" facing her executioners in the final scenes of those anti-Japanese political dramas. Jiazhi says nothing, exchanges glances with Kuang, and falls mute into a murky pit.

Conclusion

Lust, Caution's box office receipts and critical reception have been mixed. The film won the Golden Horse (not surprisingly, since viewers in Taiwan can either love or hate the KMT based on evidence from the film) and the Golden Lion at Venice (also, not surprisingly, given Marco Müller's love for Chinese language cinema and the clear "Italian" presence in the film, with its copious Bertolucci quotes and interest in the sexual pathology of fascism—Mussolini, after all, inaugurated the Venice festival in 1932). Eileen Chang also seems to move in and out of the picture as a factor in the film's reception.

The film goes beyond Chang, however, and betrays its literary source (as most, if not all, film adaptations do). While movie critic Chang writes a story about an avid moviegoer turned spy, Lee makes a film about other movies about fascism. However, this adaptation may not be an absolute betrayal of Chang. Neither Lee nor Chang seems to be very angry about politics (although both suffered from and through the political vicissitudes of the twentieth century). Rather, Lee has transformed Chang's anger towards Yi (and men of his ilk) into some sort of understanding, represented by the face of Tony Leung and the shadow of Mr. Yi on Wang's empty bed at the end of the film. Abandoning political differences and, perhaps, betraying them all, Lee appreciates the perspectives of all his characters: "When we were doing the movie, I used to joke that I carry the head and purity of the idealistic student Kuang Yumin, the heart of Wang Jiazhi, and the balls of Mr. Yi . . ."[29]

8
Seduction of a Filmic Romance

Eileen Chang and Ang Lee

Hsiu-Chuang Deppman

Ang Lee's adaptation of Eileen Chang's short story "Lust, Caution" (色，戒, 1978) into a film of the same title in 2007 has brought into mainstream culture new and provocative interpretations of an old topic: the politics of a wartime romance. Chang's original story is controversial because it offers no clear moral indictment of a womanizing Japan-sympathizer who executes a patriotic spy during the Sino-Japanese war (1937–45).[1] Her dense and gripping storytelling, however, presents a complex picture of human struggles with love, seduction, and betrayal in a way that captured Lee's cinematic imagination.

Studies of "Lust, Caution" abound. In addition to Cai Dengshan's biographical sketch, Leo Lee, Gina Marchetti, Peng Hsiao-yen, Chang Hsiao-hung, Lee Haiyan, and Robert Chi have all proposed lively and sensitive interpretations of the film and the story.[2] Few, however, have examined the cultural relations of the two artists and the interaction of their works from a formalist perspective. In this chapter, I consider Lee's adaptation as a cinematic "reading" that deepens our understanding of Chang's philosophy, style, and aesthetic. Exploring the reasons that the narrative of "Lust, Caution" has both brought together and also divided Lee enthusiasts and Chang loyalists, I begin with a brief introduction to Chang and Lee, suggesting that they share a critical interest in identity politics and psychoanalytical drama. Close analyses of selective passages and scenes show how they experiment with literary and filmic techniques by combining interior monologues, flashbacks, and close-ups to represent the traps of romanticism and materialism. In particular, Chang uses objectifying "close-ups" to magnify the loss of human autonomy. Lee is able to visualize such interwoven abstract emotions as anxiety, fear, pain, and regret—detailed in Chang's myriad interior monologues—through the effective use of emotive color scripts, shot-reverse-shots, and divided screen planes. Ultimately, the artists' mixed styles reflect their ambition to rewrite both generic boundaries and moralist cultural expectations.

Born more than three decades apart, Chang (1920–95) and Lee (b. 1954) are two of the most influential artists of their generations. Since the publication of her short stories in the magazine *Violet* (紫羅蘭) in 1943, Chang has remained a popular and critically acclaimed writer in Chinese-speaking communities. From her first collection of short stories *Romances* (傳奇, 1944) to her posthumous novels *Little Reunion* (小團圓, 2009), *The Book of Change* (易經, 2010), and *The Fall of the Pagoda* (雷峰塔, 2010), her work has created a Benjaminesque "aura," attracting Chinese writers, filmmakers, and critics eager to interpret her literary style and philosophy.[3] Equally compelling is Ang Lee's reinvention of Chinese cinema for the global stage. A versatile director, Lee has popularized a traditional Chinese film genre—martial arts cinema—to new audiences in a new century and continued to experiment with different film forms in diverse cultural contexts. From melodrama to Western to science fiction, Lee has created a track record that sets him apart as one of the most innovative directors to date.

At first glance Chang and Lee seem an unlikely pair, but a closer look shows that the two share an important border-crossing experience: Chang moved from China to Hong Kong in 1952 and from Hong Kong to the US in 1955. Lee left Taiwan for the US in 1977 and has since lived and worked in New York. Their transcultural journeys explain in part their intellectual commitment to representing broader, richer, and more complex human interactions with their environments. Chang, for instance, defines art as an expressive means that "provides a unique access to the kind of people to whom we would not have otherwise come close."[4] Similarly, Lee comments that a recurrent theme in his work is "people in a changing time."[5] They focus on morally ambivalent figures, searching for different aesthetic practices that allow them to express the emotional challenges of people transitioning between cultures and historical periods.

Chang and Lee are both well positioned to integrate these two art forms. As many studies have pointed out, Chang was a movie aficionado, film critic and screenwriter.[6] Her experience in the film industry gave her an insider's knowledge about the process of adaptation. Practicing such visual techniques as close-ups, montage, and contrasts of light and shadow early in her writing, Chang novelizes a unique cinematic vision to illustrate the psychological pitfalls of her characters.[7] By the same token, Ang Lee has been noted for his avid appreciation of popular literature. All nine of his most recent films are adaptations from fiction. He explains in interviews: "I need material that has the brilliance and research and the heart of other writers. I borrow them. I snatch them."[8] As a result, his films are steeped in such literary techniques as impersonal narration, flashbacks, and irony.

These intertextual practices are further fashioned by a shared interest in melodrama, romance, and other popular genres. Along with *Dream of the Red Chamber* (紅樓夢) and *The Plum in the Golden Vase* (金瓶梅), Chang reads Zhang Henshui, Somerset Maugham, John le Carré, and James Jones, and speaks often and openly about fame, money, and the other rewards of being a successful writer.[9] Although she is popular among critics and elites, she writes for the masses.

The same is true of Lee. His father-knows-best trilogy focuses on melodrama or family ethic film (家庭倫理片), a genre that has remained popular in Chinese culture.[10] Like Chang, Lee relishes commercial success and makes his films as accessible as possible to a vast international audience. An astute student of Hollywood, he writes and adapts scripts that appeal to critics and general viewers. From Jane Austen to Wang Dulu to Elliot Tiber, Lee has embraced a wide range of popular fiction and used camera movement, quick cut, and editing to build dramatic tension to enhance the entertainment value of his films.

That Chang and Lee "match" well in adopting a populist approach to art and in exploring the dubious moral boundary of good and evil is manifest in the controversial plotline of "Lust, Caution." The story is about a patriotic student, Wang Jiazhi (played by Tang Wei), who seduces a Japanese collaborator, Mr. Yi (played by Tony Leung), in order to assassinate him. In the end, her patriotic resolve falters because she suspects that Mr. Yi has fallen in love with her. However, Mr. Yi quickly disproves this assumption by capturing and executing her.

Although "Lust, Caution" is often considered a minor work in Chang's impressive literary output, she toiled on the story. She started working on the narrative in 1953, but did not publish it until 1978.[11] She continued to revise the plot for decades. Lee explains that he is especially struck by the cruelty and beauty of Chang's story, which ensnare the characters and the reader as well as the author herself. He compares Chang's compulsive revisions to a criminal who "might return to the scene of a crime, or as a victim might reenact a trauma, reaching for pleasure only by varying and reimagining the pain."[12] Lee's analogy draws attention to the psychological entrapment of the story and expresses his Barthesian writerly interest in investigating Chang's detailed construction of a "crime scene."

The criminality or cruelty of Chang's story becomes intelligible when we understand the depth of her critique of Chinese moralist posturing in the 1940s. Shanghai, as many scholars have pointed out, was an "orphan island" that fell to imperial Japan from 1937 to 1945.[13] According to Cai Dengshan and Zhang Zijing, Chang's marriage to the infamous Japan sympathizer Hu Lancheng (胡蘭成) in 1944 jeopardized her burgeoning career and subjected her to such insults as "cultural traitor" (文化漢奸) during the occupation period.[14] Unsurprisingly, Chang is sensitive to the political and ethical implications of a story that not only exposes the flawed logic of an impulsive patriotic act but also concludes with the triumph of a villain. Responding to critics who are morally outraged by her setting a traitor free, Chang asks: "Writing about an antagonist, should we not get into his mind rather than simply scorn or caricature him from an outsider's viewpoint?"[15]

Chang's rhetorical question reveals a bold vision, one that seeks to broaden and diversify the aesthetic representations of ethically dubious figures. From Qiqiao in "The Golden Cangue" (金鎖記, 1943) to Zhenbao in "Red Rose, White Rose" (紅玫瑰與白玫瑰, 1944), to Big Aunt in *The Rice-Sprout Song* (1954), she created a list of memorable characters and sophisticatedly presented their ignominious self-interest. "Lust, Caution" is no exception. Very systematically, Chang works into her narrative effective cinematic techniques to pinpoint and amplify the source of societal ailments—the loss of human agency in a materialistic environment in which only signs of affluence speak. Next she exposes the *hamartia* of a protagonist who, a poor reader of human psychology, tries but fails to transform a grisly spy movie into a romantic comedy. These structural elements are carried out stylistically, and both are immediately evident in the opening scene:

> Although it was still daylight, the hot lamp was shining full-beam over the mahjong table. Diamond rings flashed under its glare as their wearers clacked and reshuffled their tiles. The tablecloth, tied down over the table legs, stretched out into a sleek plain of blinding white. The harsh artificial light silhouetted to full advantage the generous curve of Chia-chih [Jiazhi]'s bosom, and laid bare the elegant lines of her hexagonal face, its beauty somehow accentuated by the imperfectly narrow forehead, by the careless, framing wisps of hair.[16]

Chang highlights the multiple sources of illumination in the house: daylight, lamp, glaring diamond rings, and blinding white tablecloth. The hot, flashing, cruel lights create a sense of urgency, over-exposure, and intensity, even as they raise questions about what may be hidden in the shadows. One answer seems to be the loss of human agency, for Chang's syntax—well caught by the English translator Julia Lovell—consistently uses physical objects as the subjects of active verbs: "The hot lamp was shining . . . Diamond rings flashed out . . . The tablecloth . . . stretched out," and so forth. This striking technique, reminiscent of passages in the European realism of Flaubert or Balzac, eliminates human subjectivity and hints at the subjugation of the characters by their material possessions. Chang's syntax also makes her description behave more like an objective camera than a third-person omniscient narrator, because it gives these objects such an unrelenting sense of autonomy. Chang is careful, for example, to say that the diamond rings "flashed" under the glare of the lamp "as *their wearers* clacked and reshuffled their tiles" (my italics). Rather than affirming human possession—and here the translator does take liberty by saying "their wearers," rather than "their diamonds" or "the diamonds they wear" [in Chinese the sentence reads: 一隻隻鑽戒]—this stylistic choice tacitly endows the gems with the power to possess the humans: people are not people, they are merely vehicles for glitter, i.e., diamonds' "wearers." Such a subject-object reversal *stylistically* anticipates the *narrative* peril of the heroine Jiazhi, who later seems enslaved and objectified by the diamond ring given to her by Mr. Yi.

In a similar vein, Chang's opening sequence constructs an analogy between precious stone and beautiful body, as the competing illuminations light up both the diamonds and Jiazhi. Moving again like a camera, the literary "close-up" blows up the details of her body in a way that seems to eliminate her subjectivity. It begins by showcasing the heroine's sensual bosom and then ascends, coming to rest on her face which, being cut in a hexagonal shape, morphs into a diamond. This analogy foreshadows the way in which Jiazhi will be a glittering plaything to Mr. Yi as a diamond is to these socialites.

Thus the opening close-ups and supersaturated lights both expose and conceal Jiazhi. In addition to her seductive curves and "hexagonal face," she has an "imperfectly narrow forehead" and "careless, framing wisps of hair." These visible signs of dissonance insinuate Jiazhi's Janus-faced existence, for she plays the money-minded Mrs. Mai—the border-crossing and trade-seeking wife of a Hong Kong businessman—as well as an ideologically driven patriot who becomes ambivalent about the purpose of her mission. Her playacting ulti-mately becomes so convincing that she fatally loses herself in the first role.

In the first paragraph Chang has already sketched out two key seductive forces—diamonds and the female body—that play off the contrast between light and shadow and cradle the inscrutable power of glitter and image.

Ang Lee captures Chang's objectifying cruelty but contextualizes it differ-ently: he emphasizes the loss of human autonomy in political history rather than in capitalist materiality. Instead of opening with Chang's object-laden, domestic interior, Lee starts his film with a series of outdoor shots that patch together a historical big picture and accentuate the physical and psychologi-cal imprisonment of the characters: it is 1942 in Japanese-occupied Shanghai. While Chang parodies the mundane comfort of merry-makers and hints at the darkness underlying a bright, well-lit household, Lee directly portrays the grim reality of a quartered society under siege. Opening the film with a German shepherd—itself an emblem of beauty and cruelty— Lee draws attention to the political crisis plaguing the city and the nation. All is under the watchful eyes of a trained foreign guard dog. (Figure 8.1) Lee's camera then moves upward to capture the steely expression of a guard on the ground. (Figure 8.2)

His sidelong glance and decentered position produce a devious, suspi-cious look that complements Lee's consistent use of a cheerless palette—dark

Figure 8.1
Close-up of a German shepherd

Figure 8.2
Guard #1 with a devious look

blue and grey—to accentuate the emotional gloom of the outdoor scenes. The blurred background further makes the shallow focus on the man's tilted face seem more oppressive and menacing: like the German shepherd, he is the attack dog of a rogue regime governed by power and greed. In this distinct close-up, Lee carefully divides the screen into two planes—foreground and background. But departing from a Jean Renoir-style deep focus that simultaneously presents different actions in two planes, a split that defies any monolithic view of integrated screen action, Lee's main strategy here is to make the viewer aware of how other narrative threads are deliberately suppressed, in order to emphasize the actor's threatening expression in the foreground. Cutting to a medium long shot of an armed guard patrolling the area from a balcony, Lee further sketches out a larger picture of a war-torn society divided by race, class, and political allegiance. (Figure 8.3)

Like Chang's stylized syntax, Lee's crisp montage illustrates the occupants' paralysis in Mr. Yi's residence under tight security. The irony is that for Yi his power in the puppet government both liberates and imprisons him. This double-edged situation (also a trademark of Chang's writing) is especially evident in the first shot of a later scene in which Yi emerges behind prison bars, where he has just completed the gruesome interrogation of suspected spies. (Figure 8.4)

Figure 8.3

Guard #2 patrolling on the balcony

Figure 8.4

Mr. Yi behind the bars

Here again we see a clear division of foreground and background, and the blurred background magnifies Yi's brooding expression, which registers his shady existence: he is literally and metaphorically a man behind bars, tortured by his own conscience and ambition. This is a point Ang Lee returns to again and again in the film and in his commentary. He compares Yi, for instance, to a prostitute working for the Japanese.[17] The surname "Yi" (易) carries such meanings as "trade," "change," and "easiness," words that suggest deal-making, instability, and shiftiness. By the same token, the fake surname of Jiazhi is "Mai" (麥), which explicitly rhymes with "sell" (賣), anticipating the tragic trade of her body for a romantic fantasy. Chang and Lee make both characters appear self-conscious about how their situations seem analogous to that of prostitutes.[18] Moreover, as Lee points out, the Chinese word for prostitute "chang" (娼) rhymes with "the kill of a tiger" (倀), a word play that suggests that a tiger's kill can be forced into working "for the tiger, helping to lure more prey into the jungle."[19]

These nuanced psychological entrapments are critical to the exposition by both Chang and Lee of the contradictions in human nature and the ambivalent master-slave dynamic that complicates the power structures in interpersonal relationships. But a key difference in their works is the way in which they construct the interaction between humans and spaces. Chang's narrative moves discursively from the inside outwards. Her opening scene blows up the details of the materialistic obsession that provides a fragmented, kaleidoscopic view of a city on edge. Lee moves in the opposite direction, showing that the private world gets smaller and more isolated because of the oppressive political climate.

Why does Lee begin by reconstructing a historical reality that is carried by quieter, more implicit means in Chang's story? Part of this is marketing: while Chang appeals to a Chinese-speaking readership knowledgeable about its immediate political history, Lee aims to attract a global audience in need of interpretive shots that aid contextual understanding.[20] Another point is that Lee stretches out Chang's 26-page short story (in Chinese) into a 157-minute film; transforming a vignette into an epic requires him to expand Chang's densely written introduction into three separate scenes. Their difference also speaks to their distinct visions of the relations between individuals and their environments.

Cutting to the interior of Yi's house in the second scene, Lee shows that Mrs. Yi and her guests are getting ready for another round of mahjong. The contrast between the first two scenes in the film is immediate, not only because of the differences in color and lighting (grayish blue outdoors vs. homey soft yellow indoors) but also due to the visible gender and class differences (male guards vs. female socialites). This shift takes place in the first shot: we see a maid carrying a tray of soup upstairs for the guests. (Figure 8.5)

This image sustains an illusion about the stability and continuity of an orderly, stratified world in which hunger, death, revolt, and many other

Figure 8.5

Interior scene—maid carrying bowls of soup for the socialites

disasters are hidden behind the wall. If Chang parodies the sense of excess by enumerating the sources of illumination, Lee accentuates the characters' sequestered affluence (and boredom) by illustrating their insatiable materialistic consumption. A close-up of several manicured hands on the table, for instance, gives a disembodied view of their obsession with gems and their symbolic value. (Figure 8.6) Like Chang, Lee uses close-ups for the dual purposes of exposure and concealment. Masquerading as one of them, Jiazhi shows her hands in the same way the others do. But in contrast to Chang's exclusive focus on the heroine, Lee gives equal attention to all four women: just as their polished nails morph into mahjong tiles, so do all four women function interchangeably as tokens. The blended visual equilibrium suggests that Jiazhi has successfully integrated herself into her staged role as a businessman's wife. This feat becomes more apparent in a medium close-up in which Jiazhi wears a theatrically bland smile to showcase her uniformity: she is a tile just like the others. (Figure 8.7)

Both Chang and Lee use the opening scene to illustrate the cruelty of an illusive, materialistic environment, and both then lay bare the tragic flaw of the protagonist, who is first blinded by narcissism and then beguiled by the glitter of the diamond, a simulacrum of romantic love. In both versions, Jiazhi's complacency peaks at the critical scene in the jewelry store in which she sees herself on stage, playing an authorial role and able to rewrite the conclusion of

Figure 8.6

Close-up of the bejeweled hands

But it seems like the truth.

Figure 8.7

Jiazhi's theatrically bland smile

her own story. She gains this confidence by holding on to the diamond ring, an object of power that momentarily gives her the illusion of control:

> She examined the ring under the lamplight, turning it over in her fingers. Sitting by the darkish balcony, she began to imagine that the bright windows and door visible behind her were a cinema screen across which

> a black-and-white action movie was being shown. She had always hated violent films and was especially terrified by the scenes of spies being tortured by their captors; as a child, she had turned her back whenever a scene became grisly.[21]

This is an extraordinary, hyperrealist moment: Jiazhi is fantasizing that she is both at a movie theater and on stage, playing the roles of a spectator and an actress. Although she confesses that she hates violent films, she herself is "acting"—or is it living?—in one that promises to end in bloodshed. Thus it is also a transformative moment, one that confirms the power of precious objects depicted in the opening scene: like the ring being examined under the lamplight, Jiazhi has turned into a diamond, being scrutinized by the camera, Mr. Yi, and the audience. Her childhood aversion to violent scenes anticipates her dramatic reaction to her own planned action, a plot she helps create and later destroy.

Attempting to rewrite the ending, Jiazhi changes the story midstream from a violent gun battle to a pseudo romance. But Chang's narrator makes it clear that Jiazhi misreads the situation, because the sparkle of the diamond so blinds her that she mistakes Mr. Yi's dutiful dullness for affection.

> He was an old hand at this: taking his paramours shopping, ministering to their whims, retreating into the background while they made their choices. But there was no cynicism in his smile just then, only a hint of sadness. He sat in silhouette against the lamp; his downcast eyelashes tinged the dull cream of moths' wings as they rested on his gaunt cheeks. He seemed to wear an expression, she thought, of tender affection.
>
> This person truly loves me, she realized all of a sudden. Inside, she felt a raw tremor of shock—then a vague sense of loss.
>
> It was too late.[22]

It is important to appreciate how desperately Jiazhi seeks to turn a mundane affair into the kind of heart-throbbing romance that can satisfy her cinematic imagination about how the boy must love the girl because the girl is so irresistible—a satirical reminder of the romantic dreams sold to the world by Hollywood in the 1940s. The narrator knows, however, that Jiazhi is just one of Mr. Yi's paramours and the trip to the jewelry store is his standard tactic for rewarding sexual favors. While he usually fades into the background and lets the women and their material desire take center stage, today he is put in the spotlight. Jiazhi scrutinizes his expression as closely as she examines the ring. Analyzing his face like a precious stone, her "point-of-view" description identifies in his smile a tragic sense of earnestness and in his fluttering eyelashes a tender feminine vulnerability. All of this appeals to her romantic notion that she is the one for whom he must have fallen.

But this diamond, like others in the story, is actually a difficult and ironic text, and Chang's Jiazhi is almost always wrong in making crucial judgments at critical moments. She lends herself, for example, to exploitation by the group of students with whom she works closely to hatch the patriotic assassination plot. After engaging in sex with one of the least likeable male students in preparation for her role as seductress, she doubts herself momentarily: "'I was an idiot,' she said to herself, 'such an idiot.' Had she been set up, she wondered, from the very beginning of this dead-end drama?"[23] Chang's narrator coolly represents Jiazhi as having learnt nothing from her past mistakes and seeing only what she wants to see—"This person really loves me." This false realization allows her emotional reality to override other larger political ideals of loyalty and patriotism.

Ultimately Jiazhi's downfall derives from her inability to differentiate illusion from reality, to tell lies from truths. Playing the role of seductress, she is seduced by her own power to seduce and hence fantasizes herself as an irrepressible romantic object. As Jean Baudrillard points out, seduction is a double-edged sword, because one "cannot seduce others, if one has not oneself been seduced."[24] Jiazhi is indeed captivated by the idea of being loved and hence utters the fatal warning "run" (or "go fast") (快走) to show that she has chosen the role of passionate mistress over and against that of patriotic assassin.[25] Baudrillard explains the conundrum of seduction that deludes others as well as self. "To seduce is to die as reality and reconstitute oneself as illusion. It is to be taken in by one's own illusion and move in an enchanted world. It is the power of the seductive woman who takes herself for her own desire, and delights in the self-deception in which others, in their turn, will be caught."[26] The jewelry store provides a perfect illusive setting for Jiazhi to plunge into the simulacra of desire in which the seductress is tripped by her narcissistic ambition to rewrite the ending.

Chang's narrative weaves in and out of the protagonist's consciousness to show the contradictions embedded in her ambiguous story. Combining filmic imageries with a literary sensitivity to emotions, these two paragraphs, I believe, provide Ang Lee with the most suggestive language for interpreting the author's vision for developing a trans-media narrative, experimenting with genre-mixing, and exploring an intense human anxiety about self-deception. Lee illustrates Chang's synthetic vision by first picturing Jiazhi's fear of violent action films and infatuation with romance in two separate lengthy scenes.

When the assassination plot in Hong Kong unravels because the Yis have to move back to Shanghai with Wang Jingwei's mock government, Lee adds to the film a grisly scene in which the group of frustrated college students stab and kill Mr. Yi's bodyguard, Lao Cao (played by Kar-lok Chin). This gruesome confrontation seems to take its cue straight from Chang's earlier description of Jiazhi in the jewelry store—a "dream" that comes true: "Sitting by the balcony, she began to imagine that the bright windows and door visible behind her were a cinema screen across which a black-and-white action movie was being shown."[27]

Indeed, an action-packed play-within-a-play is being staged right behind the "bright windows and door." Instead of imagining a violent film with the mind's eye as Chang's Jiazhi does, Lee visualizes her deepest fear cut by cut. In a short (Figure 8.8), Lee again works with a dark bluish color scheme to forecast the emotional turmoil of the conflict. Using the French window as a stage screen, Lee divides the shot into different planes and separates Jiazhi from the main action. Seeing and being seen, she plays the double role of a character and a spectator, petrified by the raw aggression of her cohorts. The next shot (Figure 8.9) reverses to Jiazhi's perspective. Viewing the intense event through the window panes as it unfolds, Jiazhi acts as a voyeur of her class-mates' dejected fear. This is also a de-romanticizing moment: rather than vali-

Figure 8.8
Jiazhi being separated from the main action

Figure 8.9

Jiazhi's POV from the balcony

dating their heroism in times of crisis, these students come across as terrified and incompetent.

In the next shot (Figure 8.10), Lee brings together the foreground and background by adding Jiazhi's reflection to the window panel, a composite view that confirms her status as an eyewitness. She is literally and metaphorically seeing the world through the looking glass, a reflective device that forces her to face the danger and futility of her classmates' actions. Notably, Lee blurs the indoor scene to make the focus on her reflection appear all the more ghostly and oppressively shallow—a technique he uses consistently throughout the film. Is this a nightmare or a reality? Jiazhi's shadowy and ethereal expression suggests that this is a sight that she would have preferred not to have seen or remembered. The murder brings the viewer very close to understanding the horror and regret in Jiazhi's mind: perhaps their plan is too irresponsible, her sexual sacrifice meaningless, and their nationalism born out of ignorance.

This scene also conveys most effectively Lee's interpretation of the complex meanings of cruelty in Chang's story. Visually, Lee exposes the students' gratuitous violence and savagery; intellectually, the killing makes both Jiazhi and the viewer question whether patriotism is simply a lofty slogan, a pretense to play a dangerous game. Generically, it reveals Jiazhi's precarious existence as a character caught simultaneously in the very different narrative arcs of a thriller and a romance.

Figure 8.10

A composite view of Jiazhi on the French window

Both Lee and Chang use the anticlimactic ending to mock the conventional expectations of an action thriller. While Lee's lead-in scene to the jewelry store promises a grand shoot-out, the indoor sequence draws attention to the unfolding of a psychological drama. From medium close-ups to close-ups, Lee's camera slowly moves in to highlight the seduction of a romantic gesture. It all begins with the storeowner's display of the majestic ring. (Figure 8.11) Born to be showy, the ring looks beautiful, expensive, and complex. It takes center stage in a way that seems ready to bait and seduce. Leo Lee points out that the words "ring" and "caution" use an identical Chinese character (戒), and hence draws attention to how Chang blurs the distinction between the two.[28] Translating "jie" as "caution," Lee's film underscores the allegorical meanings of a story that highlights the pair's sexual indiscretion. It also justifies Lee's decision to add three intense sex scenes to demonstrate the characters' lust for love. This directorial interpretation signals a key philosophical difference between the two artists. Chang's Chinese title ironically embraces the moral overtone of "caution" and the seductiveness of the ring in equal measures. As a result, the ring in her text takes on a life of its own, embodying the various desires that possess the characters. Lee, however, presents the ring in a more humanistic and sentimental context. A romantic at heart, he sees the stone not as an autonomous entity but as emblematic of the lovers' delicate emotional interdependence. Following the initial presentation of the ring, he uses a series of

Figure 8.11

Shop owner's presentation of the ring

shot-reverse-shots to manifest his vision of how the precious object connects the two lovers on an affective level.

This starts with a reaction shot of the protagonist, whose downward glance shows a restrained but emotive appreciation of the ring. (Figure 8.12) This close-up perfectly captures Jiazhi's Janus-faced existence. Negotiating between acting and being, she performs resistance and submission to the seductive script of romance. Lee carefully situates her face in a controlled setting in which her expression is shaped by soft lighting and an affective color scheme. (Figure 8.13) He reinforces the emotional significance of the mise-en-scène in the following shot, in which Mr. Yi, sitting beside an ornate lamp, is shown with a look of sly contentment. His downcast glance and above-the-fray detachment appear, nonetheless, ambivalent. Does he seem to wear a self-congratulatory smirk, celebrating his sexual prowess? Or is he simply bored by the routine payment for a prized conquest? As with Jiazhi, his smile reveals an overestimation of his power and position. He basks in the euphoria of a narcissistic stupor. Jiazhi, on the other hand, is eager to verify the symbolism of the gift, so she nudges him to take a closer look at the ring.

This pair of symmetrical shot-reverse-shots (Figures 8.14 and 8.15) best displays Lee's (mock) attentiveness to the conventions of a romantic genre that relies on the actors' nuanced facial expressions, lighting, color script, and an atmospheric soundtrack to cue the viewer's emotive response to a "love" scene.

Figure 8.12

Jiazhi's refrained but coveted look at the ring

Figure 8.13

Mr. Yi sitting by a lamp

While they do not engage each other with their gazes, their tender expressions and gentle glances show a shared perspective. A cut to a close-up of the ring draws attention to the pseudo-matrimonial moment. Notably, the ring appears not by itself but in the context of a hand-holding close-up that suggests the completion of a binding union. (Figure 8.16)

Figure 8.14

Mr. Yi's renewed interest in the ring

Figure 8.15

Jiazhi's tender look at the ring

Lee's ring now initiates a bond that urges Jiazhi and the viewer to see beyond its face value, validating instead its more textured and complex significance. But Lee concludes this romantic interlude with another pair of shot-reverse-shots to signal a tricky turn of events. (Figures 8.17 and 8.18) He uses close-ups of their faces to express two different desires: Mr. Yi wants to remain in a love scene in which he is invariably cast as Mr. Right, while Jiazhi—a closet writer

Figure 8.16
A matrimonial handholding

Figure 8.17
Close-up of Mr. Yi's affection

and aspiring action hero—anticipates the imminent threat of genre-mixing and anxiously seeks to rewrite the ending. Taking up more than two-thirds of the screen and larger than life, the two symmetrical close-ups strengthen the literal and symbolic meanings of their face values. Ultimately, these striking images raise fundamental questions about the depth of cinema's surface, a face/ text that hides as much as it reveals.

Figure 8.18

Close-up of Jiazhi's panic look

In his adaptation, Lee presents the emotional struggle of his characters in a way that "matches" the psychological angst of Chang's story. Chang constructs different narrative realities by juxtaposing a detached, omniscient storyteller with a sentimental, self-delimiting first-person narrator. This juxtaposition teases out the disjuncture between emotional reality and social reality, a conflict that draws attention to the competing voices of romanticism and postrealism in Chang's writing. But Chang's boldest move, perhaps, is to systematically rework the generic boundary between spy thriller and pop romance. Her splicing, synthetic narrative is transformative on at least two levels: it insinuates the complex duplicity of Jiazhi on the one hand and anticipates the cinematic adaptability of her story on the other. Lee's film also internalizes generic tensions and delves into an interdisciplinary exchange. Using jump cuts and quick editing to mimic the suspense of an action movie, Lee also makes lavish use of expressive close-ups to dramatize and at times efface the promise of a romantic tale. This generic incongruity echoes the unsettling relation between the couple. The question at the end is not whether they love each other, but rather why one believes in being loved by the other. While Chang employs free indirect discourse to track such multilayered mind games, Lee uses contrasts of light and shade, foreground and background to nuance the characters' internal struggles. Chang begins her tale with an interior scene whose details embody the socio-historical tensions of an era. By contrast, Lee starts his film with the historical big picture and then slowly retreats to the inner world of Chang's psychological narrative. Despite these different framing strategies, both artists ultimately solve the problem of presenting human cruelty by pitting the formal and stylistic resources of different genres against one another.

9
"A Person of Weak Affect"

Toward an Ethics of Other in Eileen Chang's Little Reunion

Laikwan Pang

> She is a person with weak affective sensibility and strong defenses. In reality, only her mother and Zhiyong have given her a hard time.[1]

In the above extract from her autobiographical novel *Little Reunion* (小團圓, 2009), Eileen Chang describes the book's protagonist, Julie Sheng (Jiuli Sheng)—Chang's literary alter ego—as someone who is not *duochou shangan* (多愁善感, sentimental). "Chou" means sorrow, worry, and apprehension, and *duochou shangan* literally means "prone to sorrow." The term is often used to describe women who are oversentimental about nature, people, and events around them. *Duochou shangan* has an implicit gender tag, and clearly implies excess, as well as bearing the negative connotations of ignorance and indulgence. This concept is not easily translated into English, but I think the word "affect" best sums it up, as this psychological term also signifies womanly passion, sensation, and inward disposition. When I was reading *Little Reunion*, this short description caught my attention, as I find it an intriguing depiction of a self that is both introverted and engaged, and therefore intricately related to my reading of *Little Reunion* as an autobiographical novel.

If Julie is understood to be Chang herself, then I believe many readers would agree that Eileen Chang, too, was not *duochou shangan*. Chang does not seem attached to her characters, and she writes in a way that displays little ardor or anguish. The most naïve relationships and emotional responses, as penned by Chang, become calculated—if not malicious—and many of her characters are gloomy, feeble, and detestable. Chang's lover Hu Lancheng (胡蘭成, whose counterpart in *Little Reunion* is Zhiyong) describes her thus: "She is not a benevolent person. She shows no care for others, and she has no mercy or compassion . . . She is very selfish, and she can be vicious. Her selfishness can be visualized as an individual attending a big festive event, where her existence is especially noticeable."[2] Chang is typical of a girl growing up in a declining noble family—she despises both herself and others.

Hu's cruel description of Chang can easily be applied to Julie in *Little Reunion*. Julie's earliest memory is of the tug-of-war between herself and her nurse Nanny Han over a spoonful of baby food. She remembers being fed with a copper spoon that had a fishy smell of iron that she hated. She pushed the spoon away repeatedly until it hit the ground loudly: "She knew it was a bad deed. She had won, but was now lost."[3] Even in her infancy she understood self-other relationships in terms of battle and victory, rather than love and attachment. Julie does not lament, even at the outbreak of the Second World War: neither life nor death is heavy, and their differentiation is unclear. Julie is also concerned with money. After returning to Shanghai from Hong Kong, Julie worked hard to repay the tuition money she owed her mother; she also made sure she gave whatever she could to Zhiyong to assist him in his flight. This strong urge to repay her debts is intended only to free her of any connection to her mother and lover.

The question is this: Can someone who does not connect with people be a writer? This indifferent Eileen Chang was actually one of the twentieth century's most influential Chinese writers, and one who influenced masses and elites alike. Despite her aloofness, she has also written of many tender and touching relationships, and one cannot ignore the tremendous amount of care and love she invested in her own creation. Although Chang tended to see only the darker side of human nature, the characters she created have touched many readers. In traditional Chinese literature, the prototype of the sentimental female writer is clearly Lin Daiyu in *Dream of the Red Chamber* (紅樓夢). Writer Su Tong has noted that Eileen Chang reminds him of Lin Daiyu,[4] and many other critics have also connected the characters created by Eileen Chang with Lin Daiyu— an ironic association, given that the writer confessed to having little capacity for affect.[5] Chang's lover describes her as malicious and merciless, while her fans see her more affectionate and sensitive side in the characters she created. Her coldness provides a stark contrast to the Eileen Chang fever that has never subsided in Chinese literary circles.

The pivotal question of this essay is almost naïve: Can an impassionate person write about passion? Can a forlorn soul understand other folks? It is true that, in *Little Reunion*, Julie does not show great passion to those around her; this is conditioned by her own detachment. But we cannot, then, endorse a structure of opposition between "self" and "other" in this novel. This is a question of particular pertinence to our understanding of writing: In writing, does the author enclose herself within the writing, or does she expose herself and her loves and hatreds to the world? Much of the criticism of this book relates to the question of genre: whether the book should be read as fiction or autobiography. To my mind, it is precisely at the intersection between the two genres—between authenticity and falsity—that we are able to understand the complex dynamics between writing about oneself and writing about others. There is always the notion of "otherness" imbricated within the self, and my relationships with other people also always overlap with my own subjectivity. In this chapter I discuss my reading of *Little Reunion* in a way that allows me to see both the narcissism and the benevolence of Eileen Chang. My reading begins with the title of the book, as the term "reunion" (團圓) suggests the Chinese people's humble wish for fulfilled human relationships.

The Meanings of Reunion

Little Reunion is an autobiographical novel published in 2009, fourteen years after Eileen Chang died alone in her Los Angeles apartment. In a letter to her lifelong friend Stephen Soong (宋淇), who would become the executor of her estate, Chang demanded that the manuscript be destroyed. But Roland Soong (宋以朗), Stephen's son, decided to publish it after his parents passed away, and supported his decision by citing other letters by Chang that indicate that she had always wanted to publish it, and had spent two decades writing and rewriting the manuscript.[6] The novel begins one morning at the colony's Victoria University, where Julie and her dormitory mates are waiting anxiously to take the year-end examination. The narrative jumps back and forth in time and space—introducing Julie's mother, Rachel (Ruiqiu), her aunt Jody (Chudi), and many other people and events both related and unrelated to Julie's university life.[7] Because of the Japanese invasion of the colony later that morning, the examination never takes place, and Julie goes back to Shanghai, where she begins a writing career. There Chang recounts how Julie deals with the divorce of her parents and its lingering impact, and how she has to once again face the tangled affairs of both her mother's and her father's families. She also meets two of her lovers, Zhiyong and Yanshan. It is generally believed that the story of Julie corresponds loosely to Eileen Chang's own life.

The notion of reunion in *Little Reunion* clearly relates to Zhiyong's possessiveness in romantic relationships. At a time when Julie and Zhiyong are madly in love, Zhiyong develops another relationship, with teenage nurse, Ms. Kang. Speculating on how Zhiyong deals with his departure from Ms. Kang,[8] Julie thinks: "According to the formula of three-person reunion, this, as souvenir, is essential; its function cannot be fulfilled by any vow, however firm."[9] "This" refers to the sexual relationship between Zhiyong and Ms. Kang. Throughout his relationship with Julie, Zhiyong is constantly in love with or having sex with other women who take care of him, including the stepmother of his friend Mr. Yu, a Japanese housewife, his own niece, and Julie's close friend Wenji. Worse yet, Zhiyong later admits that his relationship with Ms. Kang involved rape. Julie recognizes that Zhiyong cannot love only one person at a time—she does not despise these women, although she never wants to deal with these relationships in a direct fashion.

It is true that Eileen Chang neither admires nor glorifies Zhiyong, but Zhiyong is described in the book more tenderly and passionately than any character other than Julie, and Julie's feelings for him are also described in the most detailed and unbounded ways. I disagree with those critics who argue that Zhiyong is only a minor character.[10] Instead, I believe that the relationship between Julie and Zhiyong is one that Chang presses herself to rationalize and tease apart. At the novel's end, Julie is dreaming:

> Standing on a green mountain is an Indian red cottage; a bright blue sky is in the background. On the ground we find shadows of the trees and their fluttering leaves. There are a few children running around, and they are all hers. Zhiyong appears, pulling her into the cottage with a smile. Hilariously, she becomes shy. The hands of the two pull into a straight line, and there she wakes up . . . She was so happy after awakening, for a long, long time.[11]

This is a traditional and conservative family image, reiterating the running theme of "reunion." However, Julie admits she does not like children, and according to Hu Lancheng, neither did Eileen Chang.[12] It is therefore difficult to imagine why Chang would choose to end her book with this vision.[13]

But there is a similar scene earlier: a dark room replaces the open air, and it is populated not by children, but by Zhiyong's lovers. The vision overtakes Julie just before she has sex with Zhiyong:

> He stood up after sitting for a while; with a smile on his face, he pulled her to the bed, and their hands became a straight line. In the dim light, she suddenly saw five or six women whose faces were hidden behind masks, and who wore Islamic or ancient Greek dresses. They lined up as dark silhouettes, one after another, walking before her and Zhiyong. She knew

that they were all ex-lovers of his. Although terrified, she also felt safe, knowing that she was one among many.[14]

This image gives us another perspective on what "little reunion" might mean in the book. If romantic love is frightening, so is Zhiyong—but at least there are other women with her, which makes her feel safe as she gives herself to Zhiyong sexually. Although Julie is ultimately unable to tolerate Zhiyong's appetite for other women, and admits that she cannot live with half the human race as her enemy, we cannot conclude that what Julie wants is a traditional monogamous relationship; nor can we assume that she feels total devotion to her lover. We should resist a hackneyed dichotomization of Julie's love for Zhiyong and Zhiyong's philandering—aficionado versus playboy. There are many overlapping and meeting points between the two characters, and their relationship is never understood by either to be exclusive or permanent.

Chapter 9, which depicts Julie and Mrs. Yu attending a performance in the village, is very important to the book, although the chapter does not relate well to the rest of the story and stands out awkwardly, much like the distant and self-conscious Julie. First, this very short chapter depicts an act of performance, which, allegorically, echoes the relationships and identities painstakingly established in the autobiographical novel, as everyone is performing one way or another. No matter how hard Julie and those around her try, their performances, like the show depicted in this chapter, are heckled by audience members, who keep repeating the line, "Why is everyone so ugly?"[15] In another chapter, as Chang describes the moment when her love for Zhiyong is the most intense, she can think only of performance: "Her face turned red and she lowered her head. Immediately she thought of the clichéd line in traditional novels, 'No matter how hard she tries she cannot raise her head, which weighs one thousand jin.' Neither can her head be lifted. Is this real, or is she performing?"[16] After breaking up with Zhiyong, Julie falls for Yanshan, a beautiful male actor. She really wants to tell Yanshan her first impression of him, but is afraid it might outrage him. "I saw you backstage after your performance in Jin Bixia. You were still in character after the show. You were just like him."[17] It is widely believed that Yanshan represents Sang Hu, another of Eileen Chang's lovers. In reality, Sang Hu was a film director, but in the book Yanshan becomes an actor (although he also directs).[18] Julie's mother, Rachel, is also aware that Yanshan is an actor, and Rachel knows that this relationship is not based on sincerity.[19] In a flash forward, Julie also confesses that her feelings for Rudi—her third lover in this autobiographical novel—are based on her youthful obsession with Hollywood films: Rudi worked in Hollywood for many years as a screenwriter.[20]

Secondly, the opera depicted in Chapter 9 is the story of a man falling in love with two women. Julie enjoys the show very much, but she has to leave before the opera ends to avoid keeping Mrs. Yu waiting:

> She couldn't stay any longer, and she stood up and moved out by pushing through the audience. Dismayed, she knew that she wouldn't see the exchange of vows between the lovers, or witness the reunion in the finale—after passing the imperial examination and launching a splendid career the man returns to marry both women.[21]

What does this passage represent—Julie's wholehearted commitment to a traditional happy ending, or Eileen Chang's sardonic attitude toward patriarchal fantasy? We might raise this question and link it to our understanding of the word *xiao* (小, little or small) as a prefix for *tuanyuan*. Many readers, including Chang's closest friend, Stephen Soong, believe that "little reunion" is an ironic twist on the traditional concept of a great reunion (大團圓, *datuanyuan*), the happy ending in most traditional operas in which the male hero realizes his ultimate dream, marries all the women he loves, and lives happily ever after.[22] I do not question the satirical dimension of the book's title, but I also see it as more than a send-up of a hackneyed concept. The autobiographical novel ends as it begins: with Julie's tremendous sense of anxiety as she waits to take the examination; Julie associates her unease with the scene in Stanley Kubrick's *Spartacus* (1960) in which the revolting slaves are helplessly waiting for the Roman Army to attack. I believe that Chang's idea of "little reunion" is located in such a temporal threshold—in which one waits for that which will never happen. *Xiaotuanyuan* might not be a mockery of *datuanyuan*, but a sincere and humble personal wish. But this suffocating air of yearning, anticipation, and desperation cannot easily emanate from the soberness associated with sarcasm.

Apart from the romance between Zhiyong and Julie, there are many intriguing relationships depicted in the novel. For example, there is a triangular bond between Julie, her paternal aunt Jody, and her cousin Brother Xu. Despite their aunt-nephew relationship and their age difference, Jody and Xu are in love with each other, and Xu is also fond of Julie. Julie reflects, "I remember clearly those summer evenings when the apartment was too hot and we had to go out on the balcony to catch a breath of cool air. Auntie Jody would talk to Brother Xu; I just loved to listen to their conversation. I really like the atmosphere when the three of us are together."[23] This scene is recalled on different occasions, and Julie is always content, gentle, and compassionate: "There is always a most fundamental mutual understanding between her [Julie] and Brother Xu."[24]

Triangulated relationships are manifested at other points in the novel. For example, Zhiyong and Yanshan both confess to Julie that if they were to marry her, they would be willing to live with Jody as well. Chang highlights the presence of Jody in Julie's romantic affairs. Although Jody is always the sober, detached third party, she physically or psychologically participates in most of the intimacy between Julie and her lovers.[25] And the ultimate archetype of the triangulated relationship in the novel might be that of Julie, Rachel, and Jody. Rachel and Jody are at some points lesbian lovers, and Julie also always considers the two as one.[26] Although at the novel's end Rachel and Jody are no longer on intimate terms, and Julie is disillusioned after seeing them so polite with each other over a small biscuit tin that Jody wants from Rachel,[27] the multifaceted relationship between the three permeates the whole book and serves as the basic foundation into which Julie's many other intricate relationships are interwoven. In *Little Reunion*, romance is never just between two people. If the reader adopts a voyeuristic position vis-à-vis the love and sex between Julie and Zhiyong, the reader will inevitably overlook, as Chang herself describes, the many meandering pathways romantic love takes.[28]

Zhiyong does not appear until halfway through *Little Reunion*, and those readers who mainly want to read about the romantic relationship between Julie and Zhiyong (Eileen Chang and Hu Lancheng) may be disoriented and confused by the many characters depicted in the first half of the story. Julie's relationship with Zhiyong also overlaps with many other types of relationship, thereby weaving a complex human network that goes far beyond what we normally understand to be heterosexual romantic love. The book does not adopt a linear approach to either time or space, and so many characters appear in the book—students, teachers, and nuns at Victoria University; and friends, relatives, maids, and servants of the Sheng, Zhu, and Bian families—that the reader is often confused about who is who. Eileen Chang also uses pronouns liberally,[29] making this book perhaps the most challenging read in her oeuvre thus far.

"In reality, only her mother and Zhiyong have given her a hard time."—we can say that *Little Reunion* is about the tortuous love affair between Julie and Zhiyong, as well as the relationship between Julie and her mother. But these relationships are established in a complex web of human affairs. Eileen Chang loved traditional Chinese novels, particularly *Dream of the Red Chamber* and *The Sing-song Girls of Shanghai* (海上花列傳), in which human relations play out in multiple plot developments and are therefore never clear-cut, and the fates and emotions of different women are particularly entangled. There are no simple one-to-one relationships in these traditional novels. At the end of Chapter 9, Chang describes Julie's recognition of the heaviness of her own existence while pushing through the crowd to leave the audience:

> In mathematical terms, these people are all points: only positions, without length or width. The only exception is Julie, who wears a heavy blue cotton overcoat: she has length and width, but occupies no position. In this picture composed of dense points and dotted lines, she stands out as a volumi-nous piece of greenish blue, pushing through the seats preposterously.[30]

This section echoes Hu's description of Chang that was quoted above. Perhaps Eileen Chang/Julie Sheng is really a person with little passion and strong defenses, but we cannot as a result see her self-protection as being constructed upon her rejection of people. She might be acutely aware of her embarrassing existence among people, but it is only within a collective that she is aware of the concreteness of her own being. If this novel depicts the growth of Julie, Eileen Chang makes sure to remind her readers that this life story is entangled with many others. Her self-awareness and shyness are tied to her affection for and sensitivity to other individuals.

Between Intersubjectivity and Self-Reflexivity

I am most touched by this novel's delineation of the complex relation between the individual and the collective, and between subjectivity and human rela-tionships. On the one hand, Julie needs to be alone: "No matter what hap-pened, she would feel fine after being alone for a moment. It is a sense of muddiness developed from her childhood experiences; but it is also a kind of stabilizing force."[31] On the other hand, Chang painstakingly describes and confronts the many characters who accompany her growth and who make up her personal history. Autobiographical writing involves not only detachment, but also full participation, demanding that the author come into contact with the past in order to be, perhaps, healed. Weaving through a picture of dense spots and dotted lines, she also re-experiences her own existence in terms of the color blue: in another piece of writing, Chang admits that among the very few things she inherited from her mother is her affinity with the color greenish blue.[32]

In fact, Chang's exploration of the different kinds of relationship that lead to, arise from, and are associated with romance illuminates our further investigation of the relationship between subjectivity and intersubjectivity. Two interrelated sets of questions emerge. First, *Little Reunion* invites us to reconsider the meanings of romantic love: Does romance originate entirely in self-love, or does it connect to other kinds of group relationship? The two-person union of Zhiyong and Julie could be seen as an archetype and point of departure for the author and readers to engage with other self-self (intrapsychic) and self-other (intersubjective) relationships. As we have been repeatedly reminded, romantic love is often understood and experienced as a form of narcissism. The alterity of the loved one is effaced in order to facilitate one's self-love. As psychoanalytic theorist Mladen Dolar describes and understands the most heightened moment of romantic love—"when their eyes meet"—"it emerges as the firm rock of positivity on which to build one's existence, the authoritative and commanding presence by which to rule one's life, the steadfast support of one's being against all odds. Therefore Lacan can say that love is always returned."[33] Love can always be returned because the one in love sees only him/herself in the other. But let us take a look at how Chang describes the electrifying moment when the eyes of Zhiyong and Julie meet:

> They were lying on the sofa, and in the sunset he looked into her eyes for a long time. "Suddenly I find you very much like a female fox spirit from Strange Tales of Liaozhai."
>
> He told her that his wife was infatuated with him, so much so that she was possessed by a fox spirit. Because of this, she dreamt of him every night, and ultimately she died from tuberculosis.
>
> He really believed in fox spirits! Julie felt the entire Central Plains between the two of them, and the distance greatly distressed her.
>
> That wooden bird still stands atop the door.[34]

In Julie's eyes, the way Zhiyong believes he is seen by his lovers only reveals the narcissistic dimension of his love. For Zhiyong, romantic love is a device for exploiting others for his own survival, which does not allow any room for engagement with the strangeness of his lover. Zhiyong can feel no distance between them, because he sees only the fox spirit, and not Julie. But Julie sees the fox spirit as an indication of the tremendous distance between the two; this spatial emphasis is striking, and also underscores their failure to communicate.[35] For Zhiyong, the fox spirit represents his own power, his allure for the women around him. But to Julie, the fox spirit is real otherness—something she does not believe in, and something that makes Zhiyong strange to her. *Little Reunion* investigates how the notion of the "other" can still be comprehended and practiced, not only in the form of Zhiyong as Julie's lover, but also in the other lovers (or fox spirits) of Zhiyong with whom Julie cannot personally associate. Trying to come to terms with these strangers is, as Lévinas reminds us, at the core of human ethics.

The wooden bird described above is associated with Julie's abortion. It first appears in the book shortly before this event, as the two lovers cuddle on the same sofa.[36] Immediately a temporal and spatial rupture brings the readers to a New York afternoon many years later, as Julie takes a bath in preparation for an abortion. After the doctor comes and performs the induction, she waits anxiously to deliver, echoing the frightening wait for the start of the examination depicted at the beginning and end of the book. Many hours later, after horrendous pain, Julie sees the male fetus floating in the toilet bowl, resembling the wooden bird, which Zhiyong always considered was watching them.[37] The romantic relationship between Julie and Zhiyong has always been traversed and scrutinized by this wooden bird, which, as her unborn son, represents an ultimate otherness, but one that is also closest to Julie. The bathing scene is reprised many years later, as Julie is submerged in hot water and the pain Zhiyong has caused her returns and drowns her.[38] Zhiyong, her unborn son, the wooden bird, and water are clearly associated, and make up Julie's self-awareness. We can consider that Julie's recognition of her self is always accompanied by some kind of radical alterity, and by pain, both physical and psychological.[39]

This exploration of the self-other relationship necessarily leads to my second question about *Little Reunion*: To what extent are the multiple interconnections between human beings relevant to autobiographical writing, and to author Eileen Chang's self-conception? Let us go back to the notion of the other, one of the most widely and loosely used terms in contemporary critical discourse. In Western philosophy, the concept of otherness can be traced back to Plato's *Sophist*, in which a Stranger participates in a dialog on the ontological problems of being and non-being. And the concept is constantly revisited afterwards, such as in the cases of Hegel's reflection on master-and-servant relationships, and Lévinas's theological discussions of one's responsibilities to others. It is Lacan (and to a lesser extent Freud) who brings about an internal turn of the notion of the other, which is no longer an external concrete entity but an internal otherness that makes up the subject, which is always de-centered.[40]

Many contemporary psychoanalytically informed studies of human subjectivity are indebted to Lacan's reading of the intrapsychic split, but I find Jessica Benjamin's distinction between "intrapsychic" and "intersubjective" more useful to an understanding of the relationship between the internal other and the external other.[41] Benjamin explains that intrapsychic theory concerns how we uncover the unconscious, whereas intersubjective theory explores the representation of self and other as distinct but interrelated beings.[42] The two theories should not be seen as being in opposition, and Benjamin reminds us to consider them as complementary ways of understanding the psyche. "Without the intrapsychic concept of the unconscious, intersubjective theory becomes one-dimensional, for it is only against the background of the mind's private space that the real other stands out in relief."[43] Benjamin is more interested in analyzing the ways of recognizing the concrete other rather than the deconstruction of the split subject, but she finds fruitful interactions between the two positions. The negativity that the other sets up for the self corresponds to and contrasts with the self's own negativity, and one's productive recognition of the self is made possible by the interaction between the two types of negativity: "The query into the obligation or possibility of sustaining respect for difference without reducing the other to the same . . . obliges us to avoid the ultimate escapism of moralism, of denying the monster, the Other, within."[44] Violence is often a result of failed attempts to come to terms with these two kinds of otherness.

We should not, therefore, conflate the external other with the internal other, as their distinction makes each meaningful. Recognizing the intrapsychic and the intersubjective that *Little Reunion* connects, we might amend and diverge from what are currently common readings of this book, which focus mostly on the relationship between the text and reality—the investigation of Chang's own life.[45] It is true that Chang writes about herself and her life, but not in such a way that her fictional characters correspond to actual ones. The book is not a documentation of her life, but represents the author's poetic efforts to revisit the outstanding fragments of her being. Zhiyong, as I have tried to explain, is less the persona of Hu Lancheng than that of the "Other," whose autonomy and strangeness help Julie to recognize herself.

Here we also need to differentiate Zhiyong's narcissism from Chang's self-reflexivity in the writing of the book. Chang might be critical of Zhiyong seeing nothing but himself, but she writes not in order to criticize Zhiyong but to explore herself: the differences between the two kinds of identification reside in the differences between "ego" and "self." Jessica Benjamin differentiates these thus: the conception of "ego" is established by its incorporation of the "object," whereas the conception of "self" is conditioned by its recognition of the "other."[46] To Benjamin, the object is indispensable for the subject in the making of the ego, but the self is formed through its constant confrontation with the outside other, external to its own projections and identifications. An essential step in the process of self-making is recognizing this presence of the other as subject, not object. In the aforementioned moment when their eyes meet, Zhiyong constructs his own "ego" by loving Julie as an "object," whereas Julie sees Zhiyong as an external "other" whose alterity must be recognized before she can make up her "self." Benjamin might be running the risks of dichotomizing ego and self, as the two define each other, and we should not hold onto any romantic view of a selfless self that can be constituted without any conception of the object. Precisely because of this, we can see Chang's efforts at coming to terms with the internal and external otherness as an impossible task, but one that must be taken up. *Little Reunion* can be seen as an attempt by Eileen Chang the writer to recognize the other in the making of the self, in the sense that she maintains that both the external and internal otherness are autonomous and beyond her control. It is in Chang's exploration of herself in line with or in favor of her characters and their otherness that the ethical dimension of the book, as well as autobiography in general, emerges: Chang both creates and destroys herself in *Little Reunion*, in order to bring others to life.

Let us consider the passage that immediately follows the abortion scene, in which Chang records the moment when Julie meets Zhiyong and his wife—all caught unaware.[47] Julie and her friend, Bibi, go to visit the home of the painter Xu Heng to see his work. Not knowing that Julie will be there, Zhiyong also goes to visit Xu, making everybody ill at ease. When Julie and Bibi decide to leave, they bump into a mahjong table in the hallway. The next day Zhiyong tells Julie that his wife was playing mahjong there, and Julie recalls seeing an angry-looking woman. Seeing her husband's lover in the same house, his wife is furious, and she actually slaps his face during the ensuing quarrel. Because Bibi is not able to communicate freely with Xu in Chinese, Julie has to do a lot of

translation and talking to ease their embarrassment. Julie also wears a particularly colorful and stylish outfit, which makes her presence in Xu's home particularly imposing. Similar situations can be found in many of Chang's works: the
female protagonist's outstanding appearance, both visually and verbally, make
her both powerful and powerless—she controls the scene, but she is also being
looked at and despised. On this particular occasion, Julie is forced to confront
herself retrospectively, but the deep reflection is made possible only because
she is informed of the strong emotions Zhiyong and his wife experienced after
seeing her. And the love among the three seems to be more entangled than ever
after this incident. Everybody is humiliated, yet everybody also comes closer to
themselves and others.

The construction of one's subjectivity is therefore always connected to
one's intersubjective space, allowing one to recognize the clear differentiation between "other" and "object," and resist the reduction of the former to the
latter. The notion of intersubjectivity rests on an otherness that remains beyond
one's control, and on seeing the other as an other, something that does not fall
under one's control. Subjectivity is not a given; it is preceded by our awareness
of and responsibilities for others. It is our relationship to the other that we must
come to grips with before we can speak of the self. The self and the other must
be understood together, mutually constituting one's subjectivity. Let us take a
look at a poem Julie writes about Zhiyong:

> There is no me in his past.
> Years pass in solitude.
> The backyard remains unfathomable.
> The empty room is filled with sunlight,
> And it is the ancient sun.
> I have to run into it,
> Yelling: "I am here.
> See, I am here."[48]

Julie knows that Zhiyong does not like this poem, as he views his past as
rich and rewarding, not as empty and simply a prelude to meeting her.[49] But
we can read this poem as being about Julie herself. She shouts in order to
confirm Zhiyong's recognition of her, as well as to realize her own recognition
of him. The ancient sun implies an undifferentiated moment in which there is
no her and no him, and she must plunge into this otherness in Zhiyong before
she can establish herself. The empty room is Julie's intersubjective space,

which, as Benjamin reminds us, constitutes subjectivity. In confronting the other, the self is both established and transformed. It is into this empty room that Julie must run.

Between inter-individual and intra-individual relationships, connections may be myriad and disordered. This is also where the correlation of intersubjectivity and self-reflectivity can be realized, specifically in autobiographical writing. We all live in an age of control: not only subordination of the powerless, but also subordination of self to oneself. In response to this alienation, Martin Heidegger argues that the world has been turned into a picture that can be studied and controlled—and mankind, as the viewer, is now the center of it. But in this age of the world picture, not just the world, but the subject himself, is objectified. By turning the world into knowledge, the subject also turns himself into a piece of knowledge, so that, according to Heidegger, the more objectively the object appears, the more subjectively the subject emerges.[50]

In my reading of *Little Reunion*, I resist positing Julie as the transparent representation of Chang's self-reflection, just as I avoid concluding that Chang's investigation into Julie leads to a supposedly conclusive, disinterested, and objective knowledge of herself. Chang does not want to represent herself to herself, and the "I" reflected here is not an object-self with absolute lucidity; this kind of thinking only endorses the omnipotence of the writer-subject. Instead, we can read the relationship between Chang and Julie as mediated by many kinds of otherness. In the process of writing, what Chang finds is not only Julie, but also Julie's (Chang's) unborn son, the fishy smell of the copper spoon, the gawking wooden bird, Zhiyong's many other lovers hidden behind masks, and the ridiculous politeness between her mother and aunt over a common biscuit tin. These are all strangenesses that Chang is not able to organize neatly into Julie's life story, but they also stand out distinctly, constituting both Julie's and Chang's subjectivity.

The writing of *Little Reunion* began in the 1970s, and Chang still considered it not yet ready for publication at the time she died. During this period Chang resided in the United States, and struggled painfully with her writing career—what language she should use, for which audience she should write, with which genre she was most comfortable, and whether she should give up fictional writing altogether and embark on a research career. Rather than experimenting with something entirely new, she chose to return to her personal life again and again. In addition to *Little Reunion*, she wrote *Mutual Reflections: Looking at My Old Photo Album* (對照記：看老照相簿, 1994) and two English language manuscripts, *The Book of Change* (2010) and *The Fall of the Pagoda* (2010); all are autobiographical to varying degrees. Perhaps Chang chose to repeatedly go back to herself in search of creative inspiration, but she also demonstrates the existential impulse of self-probing. Her untidy sentence structure, whirlwind temporal and spatial changes, as well as the confusing relationships between characters that puzzle so many readers, can also be understood as necessary gestures that relate to Chang's investigation of her self.

To return to the opening quotation, I think the novel gives us a new understanding of affect and otherness. Julie may not be someone who is *duochou shangan*, but that does not mean that she is incapable of affect, or of engaging with other people. If *duochou shangan* implies a (female) person's excessive emotional investment in and identification with people and things around her, then *Little Reunion* demonstrates a simultaneous embracing and renouncing of this attitude. The relationship between a person's own self-probing power and social embeddedness should not be reduced to a simple dichotomy. The emotive stasis of Chang/Julie cannot be detached from her sumptuous affective sensibility, and the defense mechanism she develops is inextricable from her obsessions with other people. The self described in *Little Reunion* is not only able to reflect upon itself, but also to "account for the possible transformation made by the intervention of an other whose negativity is fully independent of the subject."[51] I prefer to investigate the sentimental-ethical dimension of Chang than her sober and detached side—at least this is a reading of my own.

10
Romancing Rhetoricity and Historicity

The Representational Politics and Poetics of Little Reunion

Tze-lan Sang

After the Star Falls

With the discovery of Eileen Chang's unpublished manuscripts after her death, there is a need for us to revise our picture of her creative activities in the decades after her relocation to the United States in 1955. Unlike the previous assumption—that her creativity declined precipitously after her move to the United States, resulting in a limited output that consisted mainly of rewritings of her own old works from Shanghai and Hong Kong, some translations (including self-translations), a few screenplays, miscellaneous essays, and a scholarly study of the great eighteenth-century novel *Dream of the Red Chamber* (紅樓夢)[1]— we now know that she also worked on at least three new full-length novels, two in English entitled *The Book of Change* (2010) and *The Fall of the Pagoda* (2010), and a third in Chinese entitled 小團圓 or *Little Reunion*.[2] *The Book of Change* predates *Little Reunion* and served as the blueprint for the latter.[3] *Little Reunion*—written in 1975 and 1976—was published posthumously, in Hong Kong and Taiwan in February 2009, and then in April 2009 in mainland China, causing something of a sensation.

Given these recent discoveries, it is high time to explore the fruits of Eileen Chang's creative labor during her years in the United States in order to understand her literary practice—especially her autobiographical practice—in this later phase of her career. Towards this end, this chapter will focus on the Chinese novel *Little Reunion*, which is key to interpreting the series of self-fashioning performances Chang directed at Chinese reading publics as her imagined spectators, confessors, and adjudicators.[4] As an autobiographical text, *Little Reunion* brings the intersubjective politics of representation into high relief. Chang's desire for self-articulation and self-fashioning contends with the inscriptional authority of her former lover Hu Lancheng (胡蘭成), a versatile and accomplished man of letters in his own right. Moreover, her desire to search for her roots, and in particular to construct a group portrait of her extended family, creates tension with the traditional Confucian expectation that respectful children/descendants should speak only selectively and positively about their parents/ancestors. Complicating her bid for access to inscriptional and cultural authority is the traditional marginality of women's self-representation. As a female autobiographical subject who seeks to publicly interpret herself and the significant others in her life, Chang ineluctably needs to confront the gender bias of reigning literary, political, and social values. Through an examination of the publication history of *Little Reunion*—taking into account Chang's confessions about her state of mind while creating the novel, her confidants' objections to the finished manuscript, and one pronounced difference between *Little Reunion* and a later autobiographical text *Mutual Reflections: Looking at My Old Photo Album* (對照記：看老照相簿, 1994)—I show that both self-censorship and censorship haunt her autobiographical practice. However, ironically, the fact that Chang chose to withhold the "problematic" manuscript of *Little Reunion* from publication instead of radically revising it effectively preserves her resistance to several dominant discourses and ideologies, including the myths of motherhood, liberal individualism, and nationalism.

It would be to overlook the essence of *Little Reunion,* however, to only read it in terms of representational politics and ignore its poetics. And we cannot fully comprehend its poetics, I submit, without a more general consideration of Chang's literary practice and theoretical reflections in the 1970s. In this regard, two other texts are seminal: the short story "Lust, Caution" (色，戒), first written in the 1950s but not published until 1979 after repeated revisions, and an essay Chang published in 1974, "On Reading" (談看書).[5] Based on these key works from the 1970s, I argue that a fundamental paradox runs through Chang's literary practice and thinking in this period.[6] On the one hand, in keeping with the characteristics of her early works, she continues to be dedicated to the craft of fiction writing, paying great heed to technique. On the other hand, she places an increasingly high premium on the unexpected drama and rich texture of incidents that occur in real life, as opposed to stories spun largely from fantasy. This leads her to prize what she calls "a faithful documentary style" (忠實的紀錄體). Indeed, she goes so far as to provocatively assert that "[all] good works of literature are fundamentally biographical."[7] The paradoxical desire for both aesthetic and technical mastery and a high level of factual accuracy, I argue, leads Chang to focus her gaze on herself and her friends and kin as mnemonic and mimetic objects. It also explains why she was never able to bring herself to arbitrarily disguise the characters in *Little Reunion*—to transform them beyond recognition—as recommended by her friend and quasi literary agent Song Qi (宋淇, Stephen Soong) after she sent him the completed manuscript of *Little Reunion* in 1976. For Chang, autobiographical fiction called for a unique and delicate balancing act between rhetoricity and historicity, imagination and factuality. An autobiographical text is neither a simple verbal construct of indeterminable referents, nor the mechanical recording of indisputable facts, but rather a process of self-recollecting and self-enactment repeated with an inescapable difference over time.

(Auto)biographical Desire and Representational Politics

Since its publication in early 2009, *Little Reunion* has affected readers in the Chinese-speaking world like a veritable bombshell, not only because, by all indications, it is a thinly veiled autobiographical novel, but, perhaps more significantly, because it radically challenges many readers' preconceptions about Chang's family upbringing, romantic relationships, and literary style. Narrated in minimalist plain language with few of Chang's signature metaphorical flourishes, it depicts the life of Chang's fictional incarnation Jiuli in a decidedly desolate light, characterized by loneliness, betrayal, and unrequited love. Some readers might even cringe with surprise, or puzzlement, at why Chang would paint such a revealing and less-than-flattering portrait of herself and the significant others in her life. After all, in the autobiographical writings published during her lifetime, such as her personal essays "Whispers" (私語) and "From the Ashes" (燼餘錄) from 1944 and the collection of photos and short essays published a year before her death, *Mutual Reflections*, she never presented herself as quite so alienated as she appears in *Little Reunion*.

Adding to the mystery is the issue of whether Chang intended to publish the novel at all. Three days after its release in Taiwan, a well-known Taiwanese critic, Hsiao-hung Chang, published an indignant article in a major newspaper to protest the publication of this reputedly unfinished novel, calling the publisher's act a form of "legal piracy" against the author's will, and concluding her protest by declaring that, as "a faithful fan of Eileen Chang's works, [she] would boycott buying, reading, and commenting on the novel."[8] The basis for her indignation, she proclaimed, was Eileen Chang's wish for the novel to be destroyed, expressed in a letter that gave instructions for the disposition of her possessions after her death. However, as revealed by Stephen Soong's son, Song Yilang (宋以朗, Roland Soong)—who became the executor of Chang's literary estate after the death of his parents, Chang's longtime confidants and informal literary agents—Chang had at one time considered the novel finished, and was anxious to publish it in 1976. What's more, in 1992, when Chang expressed the wish for the manuscript of the novel to be destroyed, she did so only in a noncommittal fashion in a letter, rather than in her notarized last will. In the letter, which was addressed to Soong's parents, not only did Chang put the sentence "the novel *Little Reunion* should be destroyed" in parentheses; she further mitigated its force as an illocutionary act with the following sentence: "I haven't had time to think about these matters carefully. We'll talk about them another time."[9] Therefore, in an afterword to *Little Reunion* published on the *ESWN* website he has established, Song Yilang poses this hypothetical question to his real and imaginary critics: "If you were to receive such instructions—'(*Little Reunion* should be destroyed). I haven't had time to think about these matters carefully. We'll talk about them another time'—what would you do? Would you look for a match right away to set the novel to fire? Or 'wait to discuss the matter another time?' I don't believe you would dare to burn *Little Reunion* even if you were emboldened with a gall bladder borrowed from heaven!"[10]

To answer harsh critics such as Hsiao-hung Chang who are skeptical about the literary quality of *Little Reunion* and convinced that the decision to publish the novel amounts to the greedy exploitation of a dead literary icon, Song even began a blog devoted to *Little Reunion*, posting evidence culled from Chang's numerous letters to his parents to show that the novel was far from an unfinished work. According to Song, Chang had begun to write about her life and family in English as early as 1957, and when she wrote *Little Reunion* in the 1970s, she closely followed a chapter outline she had first described to the Songs in a letter in the 1950s. In other words, the novel had a twenty-year gestation period. In 1976, when Chang sent her completed manuscript to Song Qi and Kuang Wenmei (Mae Fong Soong) in Hong Kong, her instructions were to seek simultaneous serialization in Hong Kong and Taiwan. She was dissuaded from publishing it immediately only by the strong objections of Song Qi, who worried that the political sensitivity of the novel would destroy Eileen Chang's literary reputation and popularity in Taiwan. He averred that her descriptions of the female protagonist Jiuli's relationship with a collaborationist official in wartime Shanghai would make Chang an easy target for malicious attacks and political suppression in KMT-controlled Taiwan, given her past connections with Hu Lancheng, a key cultural official in the erstwhile Nanjing collaborationist government during the Sino-Japanese War. Song Qi and Chang exchanged many letters in the late 1970s discussing how to revise the novel so that readers would not identify the female protagonist Jiuli with Chang, and Jiuli's lover Shao Zhiyong with Hu Lancheng. However, Chang never completed—or possibly never even embarked upon—the revisions, for no revised version was ever found in her apartment upon her death in 1995, despite the fact that in the early 1990s she repeatedly told her editors at Huangguan Publishing Company who were working on her collected works that she would definitely keep her promise to readers to complete the novel soon.[11] Ultimately, Song Yilang emphasizes that the version that went to print in 2009 is none other than the version that Chang had originally intended to publish in 1976. In a sense, he is merely allowing the novel to see the light of day after a thirty-three-year delay.

The truth is that, even before completing the novel in 1976, Eileen Chang was already keenly aware of the degree to which *Little Reunion* entailed unsettling disclosures about herself. In her letters excerpted by Song Yilang, she claims to be "unmerciful" (不客氣) when writing about herself in this new work. She also predicts that some of the depictions in the novel will make Song Qi and his wife feel embarrassed for her.[12] That she was undecided about whether to publish the novel in the years before she died suggests that she may have felt conflicted about the novel until the very end. Nevertheless, the fact remains that she did make these self-disclosures and never categorically ordered her manuscript to be destroyed. Why?

Why did she write the novel in the first place? Was it simply to get back at her first love Hu Lancheng, and to set the record of their relationship straight? Her disagreement with Hu was no doubt a motivating factor, but Chang claimed it was not the main reason. In a letter to Song Qi and Kuang Wenmei dated November 6, 1975, she writes, "*Little Reunion* is about things past. Even though I've always wanted to write about them, I'm now terribly conflicted because I'm reluctant to give Hu Lancheng, who is currently in Taiwan, anything to brag about."[13] In another letter dated April 4, 1976, she writes, "I did not write *Little Reunion* to vent my anger. I've always believed that the material you know most deeply is the best material. However, because of the sanctions imposed by nationalism, for a long time I was unable to write about it."[14] She continues,

> After reading my preface to *Chang's View* (張看), C. T. [Hsia] wrote me
> a long letter suggesting that I write about my paternal grandparents and
> my mother since, fortunately, there is no clear distinction between fiction
> and biography nowadays. I replied, "The novel you've placed an order for
> is *Little Reunion*." Later I wrote him another letter telling him that, after
> the euphoria passed, I realized that there were many inconvenient descrip-
> tions, so I had to process and shape the facts and use them flexibly. I asked
> him to soft-pedal the point that the novel was based on facts. But word
> must have already gone out.[15]

In other words, the novel is not merely or chiefly about Chang's relationship
with Hu Lancheng. It is, rather, more generally about "things past," including
the experiences of her family. Her impulse was both biographical and autobiographical—she had a strong desire to remember and record the stories of
herself, her mother, and her paternal grandparents, among others.

This is not to say that Chang had a naïve optimism about the degree to which
she could approximate life through writing. On the contrary, if her remarks
to C. T. Hsia are any indication, no sooner had she experienced the "euphoria"—the exhilaration—of embarking on a mnemonic journey and unburden-
ing herself on paper than she was overtaken by an uncomfortable presentiment
about "inconvenient descriptions" (妨礙).[16] Her reference to inconvenient
descriptions, while deliberately vague, signals an acute awareness of the constraints of writing, the impossibility of using it to mirror life exactly. And she is
expressing concern less about the indeterminacy of meaning or the unreliability of memory than about the conflict with certain prohibitions. What were the
prohibitions she alluded to? What might have inhibited her from writing freely?
Here, political taboos were undoubtedly pertinent, for she had to refrain from
setting off an alarm among the Nationalist regime in 1970s Taiwan when revisiting the activities of herself and her family in Japanese-occupied Shanghai in
the 1940s. Probably also in play were sexual taboos—the demands of decorum
that a woman writing for a Chinese audience concentrated in Taiwan and Hong
Kong during the 1970s could not but be cognizant of when touching on sexual
love, especially her own. And yet political and sexual taboos were probably not
Chang's only concerns. There was also the traditional expectation of "making
omissions for one's close kin" (為親者諱)—the Confucian precept that one
should speak about one's close kin—above all, one's parents—only in a positive
light, and avoid defaming or embarrassing them by writing about their wrong-
doings or the ignoble aspects of their lives. In *The Biography of Gongyang* (公
羊傳), one of the earliest commentaries on *The Spring and Autumn Annals* (春

秋) by Confucius, it is said that "In *The Spring and Autumn Annals* Confucius avoids mentioning certain facts about his superiors, his close kin, and virtuous men" (《春秋》為尊者諱，為親者諱，為賢者諱).[17] In later centuries, this kind of self-imposed prohibition on making unreserved revelations about those to whom one should show respect is reflected in a pattern whereby biographies, whether written by the subjects' friends and family or by commissioned writers, are usually written for the purpose of honoring the dead and are thus laudatory in nature.[18] Needless to say, it would be highly inappropriate in such a biography to mention the subject's perceived mistakes and shortcomings. According to the Confucian principle of "making omissions for one's close kin," not only should one hide or erase one's parents' mistakes; one should also leave some other aspects of their lives as private territory to be shielded from public scrutiny. Following this Confucian dictum, then, a child's written reminiscences of his/her parents can only amount to a eulogy, often uninformative and predictable, if not outright ritualistic. A filial son or daughter has no choice but to exercise self-censorship when writing about his/her parents.

Comparing *Little Reunion*, a text that Chang withheld from publication during her lifetime, with the autobiographical texts that she did publish, there is reason to believe that she may have been inordinately influenced by the Confucian precept of "making omissions for one's close kin." And the influence is evident mainly in her treatment of her mother, rather than her father and stepmother, with whom she broke off relations early on. In *Little Reunion*, Chang drew a complex and ambivalent picture of her mother. By contrast, what she provided of her mother in *Mutual Reflections*, published a year before Chang died, was a simple outline tinged with unalloyed affection. She sketched out her mother's artistic talent, her self-confidence and courage, her beauty, and nothing more. Could it be that in the waning years of her life, Chang had forgiven her mother her mistakes? Or is it the case that *Mutual Reflections* was a restrained, filial rewrite, a cleaned-up version, of *Little Reunion*? Chang may have temporarily overcome the orthodox Confucian prescription of "making omissions for one's close kin" when describing her mother in *Little Reunion*, but ultimately have been unable to disregard her inhibitions and send the novel to press. Instead, what she did as her life drew to a close was to publicize a romanticized, respectable, yet arguably cosmeticized and disguised image of her mother in *Mutual Reflections*.

The specter of self-censorship that is palpable in Chang's rewritings and concealments is fascinating, I argue, less because it serves to reinforce some well-known poststructuralist theoretical claims about the fictive nature of autobiography—such as Paul de Man's famous assertion that autobiography is defacement, or Philippe Lejeune's observation that, internally, there is no difference between autobiographical fiction and autobiography[19]—than because it brings into sharp relief the intersubjective politics of representation in autobiographical acts. An autobiographical text is never just about the author's self; it is also about the significant others in her life. As the lives are intertwined, so inevitably are the stories. The autobiographical subject, then, wields enormous power over those who are turned into mnemonic and mimetic objects in the construction of her self-narration. That such power may be limited by social constraints, as evinced by the pronounced difference between *Little Reunion* and its revisionist double, *Mutual Reflections*, is a sobering reminder that no one has unlimited freedom in self-fashioning, not even in myth-making. As frequently as autobiographical acts are the subject's dialogs with her former self in order to achieve deeper self-knowledge, they are also fierce struggles with the overdetermination of one's social identity. The resulting texts carry battle scars.

Tragically, Chang's self-censorship in the case of *Little Reunion* was in a very tangible way also an extension of an instance of policing and censorship performed by another. The novel was shelved for many years not only because of Chang's own qualms, but, equally significantly, because of the advice she received from Song Qi immediately after the novel's completion. Song's advice to Chang to radically revise it before publication, though perhaps given with the best intentions, amounted to heavy-handed censorship, from one of her most trusted friends and critics. He reacted negatively in particular to Jiuli's "unconventional" and "unsympathetic" character traits, which manifested themselves in her knowing acceptance of Shao Zhiyong, a collaborationist and philanderer, as her lover.[20] Surmising that nosy readers could easily identify Jiuli with Chang, he urged Chang to better disguise herself by changing Zhiyong's profession in the novel. What he found particularly worrisome, to put it bluntly, was Jiuli's suspect political allegiance coupled with her unorthodox sexual morality. Even if he personally did not blame Chang for political disloyalty and sexual immorality, at the very moment of identifying these problems he had already assumed the moralistic stance and voice of Chiang Kai-shek's Nationalist regime and the self-righteous, conservative majority. His verdict could very well have given Chang an uncanny feeling of *déjà vu*, of being transported back in time to postwar Shanghai where she was tried publicly in the media as a cultural traitor (文化漢奸) for her association with Hu.[21] The effect of Song's negativity was far from negligible, for Chang never again actively sought to publish *Little Reunion* during her lifetime.

Female Autobiographical Practice: The Subversion of Political and Cultural Scripts

Exactly how can we be certain that *Little Reunion* is an autobiographical narrative? Its autobiographical status is established, first of all, by Song Yilang's foreword to the novel, in which Chang's own letters remarking on the personal nature of the narrative are quoted, illustrating what Philippe Lejeune calls "the autobiographical pact"—an explicit license for the reader to read the text as concerning the author's own life.[22] It is further reinforced by the many similarities between Jiuli's existence and Chang's life as we know it from other sources. Read alongside Chang's earlier personal writings such as the essays "Whispers" and "From the Ashes," as well as her final work, *Mutual Reflections,* Jiuli's story bears an unmistakable resemblance to Chang's own. Although the novel is narrated in the third person rather than the proverbial first person typical of classic autobiographies, and although there is no equivalence between the principal character and the author at the level of the proper name, its content nevertheless establishes it as an autobiographical work of fiction concerning the author's own existence, "where the focus is [her] individual life, in particular the story of [her] personality."[23] The novel is ruthlessly revealing, laying bare the psychological scars that Chang may have sustained because of her tenuous relationship with her harsh and unpredictable mother and her repeated disappointments in love.

Although Chang never commented on this, *Little Reunion* and her other autobiographical acts in fact place her firmly in an important genealogy of modern Chinese women writers. As Lingzhen Wang and other scholars have shown,[24] autobiographical writing has been a major mode of meaning-making among Chinese women writers since the turn of the twentieth century. It is a prominent, if unspoken and unconscious, textual tradition. The number of modern Chinese women writers who have in one way or another written autobiographical fiction or fictionalized autobiography is astounding. The list includes Qiu Jin, Bing Xin, Feng Yuanjun, Lu Yin, Xie Bingying, Ding Ling, Guan Lu, Bai Wei, Xiao Hong, Su Qing, Ling Shuhua, Yang Mo, Yu Luojin, Zhang Jie, Wang Anyi, Lin Bai, Chen Ran, Lin Haiyin, Zhu Tianxin, and Zhu

Tianwen, to name but the better-known examples. Now we find that Eileen Chang—who for years has been considered by readers to be the most detached from her fictional characters, who readers presume has hidden herself so well—has after all written three full-length autobiographical novels, giving a mercilessly incisive analysis of herself.

Seen in the larger context, Chang's autobiographical practice is yet another example of the modern Chinese woman's feminist desire to make her life known, to give public testimony of her existence. For too many centuries, women's existence has been inscribed within the confines of dominant cultural codes, and too many of women's experiences have been marginalized, distorted, and silenced. As Sidonie Smith observes of the Anglo-American tradition, one of the significant changes that the female autobiographer may accomplish is to establish "the discursive authority to interpret herself publicly in a patriarchal culture and androcentric genre that have written stories of woman for her, thereby fictionalizing and effectively silencing her."[25] The Chinese female autobiographer faces a similar, if not even more restrictive, patriarchal culture and androcentric literary tradition than the Anglo-American one; thus the road she must travel to achieve the discursive authority to interpret herself publicly is doubly tortuous and treacherous. In late imperial China, although talented women of the scholar-gentry class (才女) gained greater access to authorship and publishing than ever before in Chinese history, they could refer to their own lives in public writing using only highly formulaic poetic language and very limited scripts of female sentiment and virtue. Any woman who overstepped these marks was very much in the minority.[26] It was only in the twentieth century, with the advent of Western literary and cultural influences, that Chinese women began to write and publish prose narratives of significant length that attempted to interpret their individual lives, including their sexuality, a subject formerly under strict prohibition. Although, as noted earlier, the shadows of censorship and self-censorship often plague an individual's acts of self-narration and self-fashioning, and even though the process of articulating the self is always already a process of "negotiating" with dominant cultural and political discourses (to borrow Lingzhen Wang's preferred term), numerous Chinese women writers since the late Qing have confronted these challenges squarely and found ways to enunciate self-identities that resist total co-optation by dominant ideologies and narratives.

Precisely because Eileen Chang withheld *Little Reunion* from publication as a problematic text rather than radically revising it to make it acceptable, the text ironically keeps her struggles with certain powerful discourses intact. When Song Qi read her manuscript in 1976, he was made uncomfortable by the female protagonist Jiuli's unconventional sexuality, and by Chang's heedless self-disclosure through such a character. In other words, he worried that the novel failed to protect Chang with a mask of respectability. His discomfort certainly had its grounds, but I believe his reading barely scratched the surface of the text's subversion of accepted cultural scripts and ideologies. In my assessment, it is not only because the female protagonist forms a close relationship with a philandering collaborationist that the novel has a disconcerting effect. It is also not merely because Chang chose to exhibit rather than hide her wounds. The novel is disquieting, I argue, also because it challenges three major cultural and political narratives: the myth of motherhood, the lofty tale of liberal individualism, and the monolithic definition of nationalism.

The most important theme in the first half of *Little Reunion* is Jiuli's relationship with her mother. The mother-daughter relationship, as Lingzhen Wang, Sally Lieberman, and others have shown, is one of the most important intersubjective relationships to appear again and again in Chinese women's writings in the 1920s and 1930s. Moreover, many depictions are based on personal experience. The May Fourth generation of women writers provided pluralistic portrayals of their mothers. Some eulogized the natural, caring mother as the antidote to an oppressive patriarchy; others dis-identified with their traditional mothers and experienced profound guilt at disobeying and betraying them; still others looked to their mothers as models of strength and self-liberation. The interest in exploring mother-daughter relationships continued into the 1940s and the Mao era, as seen, for instance, in Guan Lu's and Yang Mo's works.[27]

Although until now no scholar has situated Eileen Chang in this representational tradition centering on the mother-daughter relationship, I believe it is time to place Chang in this larger context given how much weight she places on Jiuli's relationship with her mother in *Little Reunion*. Jiuli adored, even worshiped, her mother since she was a child, only to experience a profound disillusionment with maternal love in young adulthood. Although her mother Ruiqiu supports her college education, Ruiqiu also belittles her scholarly achievement by recklessly gambling her fellowship money away, is critical of Jiuli's gawkish mannerisms, her lack of practical skills, and almost everything she does, and bitterly resents the financial and personal sacrifices she has to make because of her daughter.[28] All of this, combined with the mother's romantic personality and unorthodox sexuality, little by little chips away at the perfect image that Jiuli constructed of her mother during her childhood. Here, the character of Ruiqiu fits neither the mold of the virtuous wife and wise mother dictated by Confucian kinship ideology, nor the image of the idealized liberated New Woman once advocated by May Fourth male intellectuals (whose interest in the woman question, as many have noted, was fueled not so much by a genuine concern about the problems facing women as by their own need to define themselves as modern subjects against the shadow of an oppressive tradition).[29] Departing from the simplistic equation between personal liberation and social progress drawn by May Fourth advocates of individualism, what Chang reveals instead is the complexity of individualism and women's liberation. She shows the hefty emotional price exacted from the younger generation by an individualistic Chinese Nora who walks out of her husband's cage-like bourgeois home, and who, not surprisingly, is also self-centered in her relationship with her children. As such, Eileen Chang's depiction of a cold, unpredictable mother goes beyond cultural scripts—not only that dictated by traditional patriarchal morality but also that provided by the May Fourth masculinist discourse of feminism.

Seen in light of *Little Reunion*, Eileen Chang's subtly sarcastic exposure of the naïveté and hypocrisy of May Fourth discourse in her short stories such as "Stale Mates" (五四遺事, 1957) and "Yin Baoyan Visits My Apartment, With a Bouquet" (殷寶灩送花樓會, 1944)—in which young married men try to disentangle themselves from their old commitments in order to pursue modern love relationships with New Women—becomes supremely understandable. She is a cynic when it comes to the May Fourth cult of free love and new womanhood, because she has already witnessed the dark underside of individualistic emancipation and desire. Her feelings for her mother, a quintessential New Woman, are marked by deep ambivalence. Describing her mother as a "fan of schools" (學校迷), Chang is all too aware that she is the direct beneficiary of her mother's infatuation with the idea that modern women have a right to a formal education.[30] At the same time, however, the harsh, willful, promiscuous and ever-wandering mother also leaves terrible scars on Chang, for Chang adores her and wants her acceptance and approval. In a telling scene in *Little Reunion*—which occurs some time after Jiuli successfully escapes her imprisonment in her father's home for having shown disrespect to her stepmother (which closely parallels an episode Chang describes in her personal essay "Whispers")—Ruiqiu says to Jiuli, "I know that your father has hurt your feelings," to which Jiuli fumes angrily in silence: "How could he have hurt my feelings? I have never loved him."[31] What is left unstated here is that the mother, unlike the father, has the power to devastate Jiuli, because Jiuli loves her deeply.

In addition to the myth of motherhood and the May Fourth narrative of individualism, another powerful script that *Little Reunion* resists is the Kuomintang's definition of patriotism. After the Sino-Japanese War, Eileen Chang was denounced by the popular press during the returning Nationalist government's anti-collaborator campaigns as a "cultural traitor," partly because she actively published in Japanese-controlled Shanghai, but mainly because of her romantic relationship during the war with Hu Lancheng, who once served as the Vice Minister of Culture in Wang Jingwei's collaborationist government.[32] This was guilt by association at best. In comparison, Chang's "incrimination" of herself in *Little Reunion* was much more serious, for she nonchalantly shows Jiuli to be a disbeliever in nationalism. Jiuli thinks of nationalism as "a common religion in the twentieth century," and yet "she does not believe in religions."[33] To make matters worse, Jiuli is fundamentally indifferent to the legitimacy of Chiang Kai-shek's regime, and fails to embrace Chiang's regime as the sole lawful representation of China. This political attitude has taken shape even before she meets Shao Zhiyong—it stems from her childhood and adolescent experience, for, besides her grandfathers, many elders in her extended family once held positions in Qing officialdom; some even worked in the Beijing warlord government and, worse, the Manchukuo government supported by the Japanese.[34] At heart, they have never acknowledged Chiang's Nationalist regime as the most legitimate and competent government, a political attitude that Jiuli accepts without question and without passing judgment. Significantly, when Zhiyong tells her one afternoon that the Second World War is about to end, after reading newspaper reports about the Potsdam Conference (held in occupied Germany between the leaders of the Soviet Union, the United Kingdom, and the United States from July 17 to August 2, 1945), Jiuli replies, "I wish the war would continue." She knows only too well that Zhiyong will have to become a fugitive once the Japanese are defeated, and she cares more about being able to stay with him than about China's victory under Chiang's leadership.[35] The novel does not jibe with "monolithic nationalism," as Eileen Chang herself points out.[36]

By adhering to the life experiences of herself and her family as raw material, Eileen Chang creates a story that goes against the grain of several powerful cultural and political narratives. Although her interpretation of things past may have a disconcerting effect on the reader, that effect in itself is a sign of her true originality. As an autobiographer and family historian, she poignantly conveys the difficulty of knowing right from wrong, truth from falsehood, asking again and again: What constitutes responsibility, freedom, and loyalty?

At the Meeting/Mating Ground between Rhetoricity and Historicity

Having considered the challenges that *Little Reunion* poses to powerful cultural and political scripts, we have now cleared the ground for considering the philosophical and aesthetic foundations on which the work is built—in other words, its poetics, rather than its representational politics.

As an autobiographical novel, *Little Reunion* embodies the perfect synthesis of rhetoricity and historicity, two values that consistently concerned Chang from the early days of her career through the 1970s. To understand this, it is necessary to look closely at Chang's reflections on realism, documentarism, and historicity, a conceptual cluster that she develops to assert the possibility of closely approximating reality through writing. I will then read her story "Lust, Caution," to demonstrate that a meticulous attention to the details of technique, such as the use of symbolism and narrative voice, pace, and structure, continues to preoccupy Chang in practice even as she decidedly privileges factuality over craft and rhetorical prowess in theory. *Little Reunion* is born, then, in the meeting or mating ground between her dual concerns—rhetoricity and historicity. In other words, it is the fruit of her lifelong romance with both rhetoricity and historicity.

Chang was never one to shy away from theorizing about literature in general and her own literary practice in particular. And a concern with realistic representation was evident from the very beginning. "Writing of One's Own" (自己的文章), an essay she wrote in 1944 in response to an austere critique of her fiction by the leftist critic Xun Yu (Fu Lei), is probably the best-known example. In the essay, Chang defends her own penchant for writing about the love and hate relationships of ordinary people by arguing that these are the real people who carry the burden of the times on their shoulders. She claims: "All I can ask myself to do is write more realistically" (我只求自己能夠寫得真實些).[37] Even though she had long been known for her technique—her felicity of expression, her fresh imagery, and her unerring narrative perspective and pace—she avers that she values realism, in the sense of a high verisimilitude rather than an ideologically dictated critical realism (if we are to believe, that is, that she was speaking the truth rather than simply borrowing a category fashionable among leftists in order to appease her critics).

Later in her career, Chang's reflections on literature can be gleaned from a steady stream of essays such as her commentaries on *Dream of the Red Chamber*, her afterword to her Mandarin translation of Han Bangqing's novel in the Wu dialect, *The Sing-song Girls of Shanghai* (海上花列傳), her essay reminiscing on interactions with Hu Shi, whom she regarded as a mentor, and so forth. In my opinion, her 1974 essay "On Reading" is a seminal but neglected text in which she sets out some of her most cherished convictions about literature. It also provides a window onto Chang's literary tastes and values just before she began to work seriously on *Little Reunion*. The essay opens with a forthright confession: "Most of the books I've read in recent years are documentary-style" (紀錄體). By documentary style, Chang means nonfiction works such as histories and biographies that purport to engage in factual recording as opposed to imaginary creation. In the essay, interspersed with lengthy and unassuming discussions on Western works of history, ethnology, anthropology, and sociology are her comments on what she values in literature. She claims to have a fondness for reading the facts as opposed to imaginative fabrication. Her favorites are the "social novel" genre in 1920s China and nonfiction works in the recent West. Discussing the Chinese genre of "social novels" (社會小說) popular between the 1920s and 1940s,[38] she professes to prefer novels that seem to record facts spontaneously and truthfully to those that contain a significant amount of imaginative elaboration and are thus, in her opinion, confined by the limits of fantasy and often overly "sentimental." She argues that at the height of the genre's popularity, editors-cum-novelists were obliged to write for more than one entertainment newspaper (小報) at a time. Under daily pressure to produce, they jotted down things they had seen or heard or what had happened to their acquaintances, without much time to "chisel and polish" (琢磨). What they hastily churned out, as a result, "contained a high degree of truthfulness" (倒比較存真).[39]

Chang further speculates that social novels may have been all the rage in China at the time because they satisfied a common epistemological and psychological need that imaginative fiction could not: "Might it be that, in a transitional age when society was in violent transformation, fabricated stories could not keep up with real events, and that the masses got curious about what was happening around them?"[40] However, hesitant to hypothesize that social novels always reflected social change, she attempts to rationalize the genre's erstwhile popularity from yet another angle—its appeal to writers. She muses: "As a form, fictionalized notations of goings-on (小説化的筆記) would afford a writer the greatest convenience and freedom . . . So long as he changed people's names to fake ones in the novel, he did not have to worry about stepping on taboos as he wrote, since in China people were not quick to sue for libel as in the West."[41] She then pronounces axiomatically:

> Someone in the modern West once remarked, "All good works of literature are fundamentally biographical." Of course, real people and incidents are merely the raw material. I am a fastidious critic of artistic creations but have a great weakness for the raw material. It is not because I "respect the facts," but because I am partial to their special flavor, which is in a word the flavor of life. This quality is as tender as a plant—it dies easily during transplantation.[42]

Here, Chang tantalizingly evokes the imagery of "transplantation." But transplanting from where to where? It seems that what she is positing here is a creative process whereby a writer would transpose or transform real people and incidents into a fictional representation, which nonetheless still retains the special poetic and dramatic essence of real life. In other words, the mode of representation she lionizes here is not nonfiction per se, but rather a special kind of fiction that is rooted or rich in facts.

In the essay, she claims that she has recently found in Western documentary works what she loved about Chinese social novels in the 1920s and 1930s. She loves both "for the real people and real events, not literariness."[43] Her reading taste has not changed. She also loves "reliable historical novels, for occasionally one can find some details of life that cannot be found in formal histories and biographies. They capture and trigger the reader's imagination, enabling the reader to come into touch with the texture of another age."[44] It is highly paradoxical that, in order to find the least expected details of the everyday life of a past age, she would rather rely on historical fiction than formal histories and biographies. But this is not the first time that she has trusted historical fiction to render the facts. For instance, much of her knowledge about her paternal grandparents' relationship comes from Zeng Pu's historical novel, *A Flower in the Sea of Sins* (孽海花, 1905).[45]

Even though Chang is primarily interested in seeking out the facts as a reader, she is thoroughly aware that "even a faithful documentary style can still be subjective and distortional."[46] Nevertheless, she has clearly taken a side; and her preference is to read accounts of society and history that are as free of subjective judgment and feelings as possible. She reveals this by commenting on the controversy surrounding the "new journalism" movement in the United States in the 1960s and 1970s, pointing out that it has been attacked for being too sentimental because of the authors' strongly subjective views and ideological tendencies.[47]

These theoretical musings, I argue, form the philosophical foundation for the creation of *Little Reunion*. Although Chang had begun to write autobiographical fiction in the 1950s, the essay "On Reading" offers us an opportunity to ascertain her latest thinking on literature at around the time she seriously set to work on *Little Reunion*. Given how highly she claims to value the flavor of real life, it is no surprise that, when Song Qi suggested that she revise the novel to better disguise herself, she simply shelved the manuscript rather than following his advice. She preferred to be faithful to the key personalities, scenes, and emotions in her life than to transform them beyond recognition. Such is her commitment to factuality, or historicity.

Nevertheless, even as her theoretical reflections privilege a spontaneous approach that involves little ornamentation and fantasy, and even if such values seem to have found a perfect expression in her autobiographical novel, she remains highly dedicated to the perfection of the fictionist's craft. This dual concern with documentary faithfulness and formal technique constitutes the paradox of Eileen Chang's literary practice in the 1970s.

On the opposite end of the spectrum from the faithful-to-life documentary aesthetics articulated in "On Reading" is Chang's story "Lust, Caution." Inspired by a real incident,[48] the technically brilliant story features an intricate narrative structure and highly sophisticated use of figurative language that can only be the creation of a powerful imagination. The deceptively simple story incorporates multiple layers of carefully arranged metaphors and ironies. Compressed and economical in form, the story's dramatic and emotional force is produced in major part by its ability to contrast, and yoke together, seemingly incongruous things, such as the gravity of murder and the levity of gambling and chatter. The story's main action consists of former college student Wang Jiazhi's attempt to lure the intelligence chief Mr. Yi into a death trap. However, temporally, the assassination attempt is sandwiched between two scenes in which witty yet insipid conversations take place around a mahjong table among the wives of collaborationist officials. Here, mahjong does not so much signify a domestic space far removed from the world of political intrigue as function as a trope for politics. In the first mahjong scene, the women joke about an absent character's blemished complexion while trying to outdo one another in showing off their expensive diamond rings, before Jiazhi excuses herself from the game in order to meet Yi outside the house. In the second scene, the gambling women, now without Jiazhi, clamor for Yi to take them out to dinner, while Yi quietly relishes his narrow escape from death a few hours earlier and the fact that Jiazhi, who has by now been executed on his orders, along with her co-conspirators, will forever belong to him. In both scenes, intense psychological drama takes place just beneath the surface of raucous merriment. The reader is given a distinct sense of his/her privileged perspective, being in the know about the deep irony of the situation.

Eileen Chang, of course, is an experienced writer of repartee, having written at least nine comic screenplays, such as *Viva the Wife* (太太萬歲, 1947), *The Battle of Love* (情場如戰場, 1957), and *The Greatest Wedding on Earth* (南北一家親, 1962), between the late 1940s and early 1960s.[49] It is therefore perhaps unremarkable that she puts her comedic craft to effective use in "Lust, Caution," conjuring up two scenes animated by the rapid-fire exchange of jests and taunts among tile-clacking mahjong players. What is indeed remarkable is that, through the juxtaposition of surface events and hidden psychological drama, Chang draws a suggestive parallel between gambling and Jiazhi's act of taking chances with her own life, for it is indeed risky business for her to act as bait in the assassination plot, a dangerous move that can lead as easily to irrevocable loss as to victory. Moreover, by framing the political assassination plot with the mahjong scenes, Chang draws another comparison—between the mahjong players' frivolous competition and the deadly political rivalry between the KMT leaders Chiang Kai-shek and Wang Jingwei. The association of the bloody political battle between Chiang's and Wang's governments with a mahjong game undoubtedly trivializes the ideological differences between the two governments. It is as if, just as the essence of a mahjong game may be more social interaction than pure strategy, the nature of the conflict between Chiang and Wang may be more personal than based on political conviction or principle. In other words, what Eileen Chang constructs through mahjong is not an alternative space far removed from politics, but rather a trope that comments on the nature of national politics.

The ability to see the domestic in the political, and the political in the domestic, is quintessentially Eileen Chang. She puts human faces on two competing political factions, imbuing them with human frailties and less than lofty motives. Seeing through the maze of grand slogans and moralistic pronouncements common in politicians' rhetoric, she gets right down to the underlying emotions and interpersonal dynamics. In "Lust, Caution," there are hints early on about the highly ambivalent relationship between Chongqing and Nanjing. Even though the two governments are in a bitter battle for moral legitimacy, each claiming to be defending China's sovereignty and best interests with its strategy in the face of Japanese militarist aggression and complex international politics, the wives of the officials in the Nanjing collaborationist government have come to favor black capes, which, the narrator points out, may be the result of their "following the lead of Chungking [Chongqing], the Chinese Nationalist regime's wartime capital, where black cloaks [are] very much in vogue among the elegant ladies of the political glitterati."[50] Although this description could be read as articulating a domestic space that operates as a heterotopia that disrupts and resists the force of national politics, I submit that the domestic here, far from being isolated from politics, is shot through with political valence, and that it functions precisely as national politics in miniature to demythologize and deflate exalted political doctrines. The description deftly implies that the relationship between the Nanjing and Chongqing governments borders on love-hate, and that their battle is akin to a fight between two brothers or intimate friends that have fallen out with each other, as a subterranean emotional attachment lingers even after their formal severance from each other.

Apart from mahjong, another extended metaphor that runs through the story is of course the already much discussed trope of playacting. Jiazhi, a former amateur actress in college, looks at her role in the assassination plot as a stage performance. The theatricality of the whole episode is foreshadowed by the very first lines of the story:

> Though it was still daylight, the hot lamp was shining full-beam over the mahjong table. Diamond rings flashed under its glare as their wearers clacked and reshuffled their tiles. The tablecloth, tied down over the table legs, stretched out into a sleek plain of blinding white. The harsh artificial light silhouetted to full advantage the generous curve of Jiazhi's bosom, and laid bare the elegant lines of her hexagonal face, its beauty somehow accentuated by the imperfectly narrow forehead, by the careless, framing wisps of hair.[51]

The "harsh artificial light" spotlights Jiazhi as if on stage. Yet her beauty is accentuated, rather than compromised, by the strong lighting. She is, in other words, born for the stage. Later, in the middle of the story, before a full flashback to Jiazhi's student life in Canton begins, Eileen Chang makes the comparison between her actions and playacting even more explicit with these lines: "She had, in a past life, been an actress; and here she was, still playing a part, but in a drama too secret to make her famous."[52] Then, before the story's climax and denouement, the narrator's description of Jiazhi's state of mind again turns to acting: "Her stage fright always evaporated once the curtain was up."[53]

But if Chang had merely succeeded in making the domestic and the political mirror each other and in presenting an interesting philosophical problem about the conflation of life and theater, "Lust, Caution" would not have been the chilling and unnerving story that it is. Chang also arranges for Jiazhi, the heroine of the story, to abandon the assassination scheme that has taken two years of her life to set up, just at the moment it is about to succeed. Thinking that "this person [Yi] really loves me," at the crucial moment Jiazhi abandons the assassination plot for which she has sacrificed a great deal, including her virginity and psychological well-being. Here, Chang has obviously taken up a difficult task—writing a dramatic yet improbable story. Perhaps it is even the kind of "overly sentimental" story that she has criticized elsewhere, in "On Reading." Within the diegetic world, Chang tries to prepare the reader for Jiazhi's sudden change of mind by hinting at her alienation from her former college friends, her naïveté and vanity, and her penchant for theatricality. She likes to indulge in theatrical illusion, and is loath to exit her role in the attic of the jeweler's shop. Indeed, when she sees the six-carat diamond ring, "she [registers] a tinge of regret that it [is] to be no more than a prop in the short, penultimate scene of the drama unfolding around it."[54] She wants the illusion to continue. Her love for the mirage overpowers her political convictions. She has a tragic flaw.

In light of the well-wrought "Lust, Caution," perhaps we can conclude that Chang's enduring dedication to technique is the reason she chose the novel rather than the classic autobiography to tell her life story. She was too fascinated with the games of language, imagery, and structural design to forsake them. Instead of being a straightforward chronological narrative, *Little Reunion* is constructed like a maze, with multiple temporal and dramatic lines weaving in and out of one another. Its language is cryptic and understated, deliberately requiring laborious decoding rather than easily ingested and consumed. It is not, as some critics claim, a shoddy, unfinished work. It is, rather, one of the last formal experiments Chang undertook. The evidence is unmistakable if we read *Little Reunion* against its precursors in English—*The Fall of the Pagoda* and *The Book of Change*, two linear narratives depicting, respectively, Chang's life before eighteen and her life between the ages of eighteen and twenty-two. Rather than follow the chronological designs of *Pagoda* and *Change* (much less translate them verbatim into Chinese), Chang deliberately chooses to start *Little Reunion in media res*, with Jiuli's college life in Hong Kong and some of her experiences during the Japanese invasion of Hong Kong. Then the narrative cuts to Jiuli's return to Shanghai, the beginning of her literary career, and her love affair with Zhiyong, all the while giving constant flashbacks to Jiuli's childhood and adolesence, and occasional fastforwards to Jiuli's life after leaving Shanghai permanently. Freely associating, or cutting back and forth between, events from Jiuli's distant past and more recent pasts, the novel is told in the manner of Jiuli's remembrance of time lost, who now resides outside China. In the third-person narrative voice, it is Jiuli's inner voice that we hear—an often pensive and introspective voice, which assumes a degree of familiarity with the reader that is not seen in either *Pagoda* or *Change*. It is as if the moment Chang switched from English to Chinese as her language and medium, she raised the bar for herself and her readers, expecting herself to tell the story of her life in one go, and expecting her readers to be accepting and patient enough to put the jumbled pieces together like a puzzle. She trusted, in other words, her Chinese readers to meet the challenge of understanding the gnarled complexity of her upbringing, relationships, loves, and hurts, conveyed enigmatically and fragmentarily though they may be. With *Little Reunion*, she tried to create a unique and precious marriage between imagination and factuality. Neither a mere verbal construct of indeterminable referents, nor the mechanical recording of indisputable facts, it is the progeny of her lifelong romance with rhetoricity and historicity.

11
Madame White, *The Book of Change*, and Eileen Chang

On a Poetics of Involution and Derivation

David Der-wei Wang

One aspect yet to be explored in studies of Eileen Chang is her penchant for rewriting existing works in multiple iterations and languages. This essay discusses Chang's aesthetic of revision and bilingualism by examining her two English novels, *The Fall of the Pagoda* and *The Book of Change,* which were discovered in 2009 and published in 2010. These two novels were written in the late 1950s, when Chang had just settled in the United States. In many ways, they provide a missing link in Chang's (re)writing of her life story, from English to Chinese and vice versa, from essay to fiction and photo album, and from autobiographical "whispers" to dramatized exposé. The titles of these two novels, one referring to the Leifeng Pagoda (雷峰塔) of the White Snake legend, and the other to the esoteric classic *The Book of Change* (易經), suggest Chang's effort to integrate her writings with a broader cycle of Chinese discourses and temporalities.

Through a comparative reading of the two novels and other texts, this chapter seeks to make the following observations:

1. Insofar as mimetic realism was the canonical form of modern Chinese literature, the way in which Chang repeats herself by traversing rhetorical, generic, and linguistic boundaries has given rise to a peculiar poetics, one that highlights not revelation but derivation, not revolution but involution.

2. Through the multiple versions of her story, Chang tries to challenge the *master* plot of her family romance by proliferating it, and to dispel her past by continually revisiting it. More provocatively, to write is to translate memory into art, an effort to re-member pieces of the past in a mediated form.

3. The circular, derivative inclination in Chang's writing also points to a unique view of (literary) history. It has at least two models—*The Sing-song Girls of Shanghai* (海上花列傳, 1894) and *Dream of the Red Chamber* (紅樓

215

夢, 1792). When she was rewriting her life story in various formats over the last four decades of her career, Chang was at the same time engaged in two parallel projects: translating *The Sing-song Girls of Shanghai* from the Wu dialect, first into Mandarin Chinese and then into English; and annotating *Dream of the Red Chamber* by means of textual analysis, philological verification, and biographical research.

Writers and critics of the revolutionary discourse would not welcome Chang's vision. But insofar as her writing entertains a negative dialectic of history and progress, Chang has provided a sobering perspective from which to detect Chinese literary modernity at its most convoluted.

In 1938, the *Shanghai Evening Post*, a Shanghai English language newspaper, published an essay entitled "What a Life! What a Girl's Life!"[1] Its author was an eighteen-year-old Chinese girl by the name of Eileen Chang. In the essay, Chang described her life as a girl growing up in a decaying aristocratic family, her tense relationship with her father and stepmother during her teenage years, and the recent ordeal of being locked up (on her father's orders) in a bare room for months. Denied medication for typhoid, Chang nearly died during her incarceration. She eventually escaped only because of her nanny.

The essay marked the literary debut of Eileen Chang, arguably the most talented woman writer in twentieth-century China.[2] In hindsight, the essay foreshadows the leitmotifs that would haunt Chang's writing in the decades to come: skewed family relationships, traumatic childhood memories, and decadent, gothic obsessions. The fact that the essay was written in English also anticipated the bilingual shuttling in Chang's career. Six years after its publication, "What a Life! What a Girl's Life!" was rewritten as the Chinese essay "Whispers" (私語, 1944); it also left imprints in other essays of the same period, such as "From the Mouths of Babes" (童言無忌). In the late 1950s, these essays became the source texts for Chang's English novel, *The Book of Change*.[3]

The Fall of the Pagoda

The Fall of the Pagoda constituted the first part of *The Book of Change*, and was later considered by Chang to be an independent piece. In the process of writing *The Book of Change* in English, Chang eventually wrote a Chinese counterpart. The result was *Little Reunion* (小團圓), a novel Chang largely completed in 1976 but kept revising throughout her life. *Little Reunion* was published posthumously in 2009.

While it is evident, then, that Eileen Chang devoted much of her life to retelling the story of "What a Life!", this was far from the only example of Chang's complex aesthetic of revision and bilingualism.[4] She rewrote, for example, *Eighteen Springs* (十八春, 1950) into *Half a Life* (半生緣, 1968); and translated "Stale Mates: A Short Story Set in the Time When Love Came to China" (1956) into Chinese (五四遺事, 1958).[5] As I have discussed elsewhere, another of Chang's English novels, *The Rouge of the North* (1967), also went through multiple incarnations.[6] Chang started out with the novella "The Golden Cangue" (金鎖記) in 1943; she translated the novella into English in the 1950s and expanded it into the full-length novel *Pink Tears* in 1956. She rewrote *Pink Tears* twice in the 1960s, finally turning it into *The Rouge of the North*. Meanwhile, she translated *The Rouge of the North* back into Chinese, under the title "Embittered Woman" (怨女, 1968). Thus, over a span of twenty-four years, in two languages, Chang wrote "The Golden Cangue" at least six times.[7]

One can discern in Chang's rewritings a Freudian impulse—to overcome her childhood trauma by explaining it away. The multiple versions of her story can be read as various accounts of her family romance, each revealing bits and pieces of a past that Chang tried in vain to exorcise. On the other hand, one can equally detect Chang's unique feminist intent, which prompts her to challenge the *master* plot of her family story by retelling it. As if she could no longer trust the (Father's) law of narrative, Chang experiments with languages, genres, and modes, such that she undermines the monolithic discourse of a patriarchal society. Her engagement with bilingual writing particularly intimates a polemic, treating English as no more alien a medium than Chinese for transmitting, or translating, her already alienated existence in the Chinese environment.

Above all, Eileen Chang conceived of rewriting as both a ritual of exorcism and a form of incantation. The way in which Chang "repeats" herself by traversing rhetorical, generic and linguistic boundaries has given rise to a peculiar philosophy of writing. To write, as she would have it, is not to represent but to approximate bygone experiences; it is an intermittent plunge into the cavern of memory, throwing different light on its sunken passages. More provocatively, to write is to translate memory into art, an effort to remember, and re-member, pieces of the past in a mediated form. In the exploratory art of writing and rewriting, recovery of the past may bring new pain and pleasure, not just catharsis and banishment.

Chang was the most popular writer in Japanese-occupied Shanghai during the Second World War. At a time when nationalist discourse and propaganda literature prevailed, Chang distinguished herself by writing (in both English and Chinese) stories and essays that portrayed historical contingencies and human frailties. Her non-conformism was also reflected in her short-lived marriage to Hu Lancheng (胡蘭成, 1906–81), a flamboyant intellectual and collaborator in the Nanjing puppet regime. For her noncommittal political status and idiosyncratic style, Chang was boycotted by fellow writers after the end of the war; worse, she was forced to the margins of literary respectability after the new China was founded in 1949.

Chang fled China in 1952. During her three-year sojourn in Hong Kong, she wrote and published two English language novels—*The Rice-Sprout Song* (1955) and *Naked Earth* (1956). By 1956, she had settled in the United States. Various factors, including the desire to continue her career as a writer as well as the need to secure a living, compelled her to continue to write in English. She completed *Pink Tears* in 1956, and started a new project a year later. According to Chang's correspondence with her close friends Stephen and Mae Soong, this new project would chronicle her personal experience from childhood up to her romance with Hu Lancheng.[8] In 1961, Chang began to refer to the work by its formal title—*The Book of Change*. By 1963, the first half of the novel, which she had for some time considered long enough to be published separately, became known as *The Fall of the Pagoda*.

As discussed above, *Pink Tears* was never published until it had been through a series of revisions and given the new title *The Rouge of the North*. The journey of *The Book of Change* (and *The Fall of the Pagoda*) was even more arduous than that of *Pink Tears*. In her letters to Stephen Soong (宋淇) in 1964 Chang expressed increasing frustration after the manuscript was rejected several times in a row; in the meantime, she found it difficult to conclude the work according to her original intent. As it stands, the final version of *The Book of Change* hardly touches on Chang's life with Hu Lancheng; instead, it narrates Chang's student years in Hong Kong (1939–42), ending with her return to Shanghai after Pearl Harbor and the fall of Hong Kong to Japanese troops.

After 1964, Chang seemed to have given up all hope of publishing *The Book of Change*. But she was obviously mindful that her project remained unfinished. She continued to write, this time in Chinese. The draft of *Little Reunion* came out more than a decade later as a full, Chinese version of the story that *The Book of Change* once promised to tell but never did. Neither *The Book of Change* nor *Little Reunion*, however, was published during Chang's lifetime.

With this understanding in mind, we can now turn to *The Fall of the Pagoda* and ponder its meaning in light of its previous and subsequent incarnations such as "What a Life! What a Girl's Life!", "Whispers," and *Little Reunion*. The novel starts with a four year-old Lute, Chang's alter ego, watching her mother Dew and Aunt Coral leaving for Europe. It then follows every stage of Lute's childhood up to the point where she has an intense quarrel with her father and stepmother and is locked alone in a room for six months. With the assistance of her nanny Dry Ho, Lute finally runs away from home. The novel ends with Lute getting ready to study overseas and bidding farewell to Dry Ho, who is retiring.

For readers of Chang's earlier works, the above summary should sound familiar. With a few minor changes in characterization and plotting, the novel is derived largely from "Whispers" and other writings about Chang's childhood and adolescence. But *The Fall of the Pagoda* is not merely a fictionalized account of Eileen Chang's early autobiographical writings. When she wrote "What a Life! What a Girl's Life!", Chang had just survived her ordeal to testify to a horrific case of paternal abuse; when she wrote "Whispers," she was a rising star in the literary circle of wartime Shanghai who was charged with an impulse to lay bare her past. It was in writing *The Fall of the Pagoda*, twenty years after her traumatic experience and self-exiled from her home and country, that Chang finally gained a temporal/spatial and emotional distance at which to reflect on her early life. A few other factors may also have been in play. Chang's mother died in 1957, the year in which Chang started to write the novel, and her father had passed away four years earlier. Thus, *The Fall of the Pagoda* could be read as Chang's first attempt at telling her family story with a newly acquired (fictional) freedom.

In terms of literary mode, *The Fall of the Pagoda* begins as a comedy of manners and gradually evolves into a gothic thriller. Lute's father Elm Brook and mother Dew both come from reputable backgrounds. They were betrothed in childhood, but their marriage proves to be a mismatch. Elm Brook's sister Coral, however, becomes Dew's closest friend; they travel to Europe together and finally form an alliance against Elm Brook. The families of Lute's parents branch out into different houses, which interact with each other, generating a dense network of relationships. In these moments, the novel adopts an anthropological posture; at its most compelling its narrative brings to mind scenes from *The Plum in the Golden Vase* (金瓶梅), and more particularly, *Dream of the Red Chamber*, Chang's favorite work.

But Chang is keenly aware of the fact that the time that lends substance and intelligibility to these family sagas is long gone. Contradictions and aberrations are the norm in Lute's family. This is a household immersed in a decaying grandeur amid the intoxicating smell of opium, but it never hesitates to pursue new and exotic things, from automobiles to movies. Desolation and decadence rule. Lute's father indulges himself in debauchery while her mother cannot wait to become a Nora of New China. Nevertheless, both share the disposition to squander the family fortune recklessly; children are their last concern. The Russian Revolution, the creation of Manchukuo, and the Second Sino-Japanese War take place one after another in the novel, but except for momentary disturbances, nothing affects this family, which has already been engulfed by its own corruption.

Chang views these characters with an ironic sympathy, but she is unsparingly sarcastic about their collective complacency and lack of self-awareness. Whereas Elm Brook and other male relatives are lagging pathetically behind the times, Dew and Coral appear somewhat foolish in their overzealous pursuit of new womanhood. One can only sigh when one comes across passages that describe how Dew is swimming or skiing heroically despite her "liberated" bound feet, or how Elm Brook and Honor Pearl, Lute's stepmother, experiment with home economics by raising geese in their desolate garden—an abject carnival indeed.

Lute's life becomes difficult after the arrival of her stepmother Honor Pearl, a peevish woman who is hostile to Lute from the outset. Due to Honor Pearl's manipulation of the family dynamic, Lute gradually finds herself estranged from her father and brother; she feels most humiliated when ordered to wear her stepmother's used clothes at school, an actual incident that Chang would remember for the rest of her life. When Dew returns to Shanghai at the outbreak of the War and has Lute stay with her for a brief period, Honor Pearl is given a new excuse to punish Lute. What follows is a by now familiar episode: Lute is badly beaten by her father and imprisoned in a barren room; she almost dies from pneumonia and finally runs away from home before suffering a nervous breakdown.

We can hardly miss Chang's employment of gothic elements here, from a ghostly house to nightmarish incarceration, from a vulnerable girl to an evil stepmother. What impresses us is that Chang's narration retains its aloofness even at the most dramatic moments, due partly to her English style and partly to the emotional distance she cultivates throughout the novel.

The novel's plot has one additional twist. Whereas Lute barely escapes her father's house, it is Hill, Lute's quiet, feeble brother, who turns out to be the last casualty of the family horror story. Hill's sudden death from tuberculosis represents *The Fall of the Pagoda*'s most conspicuous deviation from other, more "truthful" accounts of Chang's experience. However, this imagined loss is where Chang asserts her power as a fiction writer. She must have concluded that she could not spell out the demonic magnitude of her own trauma without the death of Hill, Lute's only sibling and the last male descendent of her family.

Towards the end of the novel, Lute is afforded the opportunity to study abroad. But readers of Chang's early works know this is a false hope, and that more trials are to befall Lute. The war has broken out. Any expectation is doomed to be dashed, a theme on which Chang would elaborate in *The Book of Change*. The last chapter of *The Fall of the Pagoda* therefore opens with a suggestive statement—"Lute was always leaving things around or losing them." Indeed, this scene, with its focus on loss, can serve as a metaphor for the novel. Lute's story is ultimately one of loss—the loss of innocence, the loss of childhood, and above all, the loss of one's mother. The novel starts with Lute bidding farewell to her mother, and ends with her saying goodbye to her nanny, her surrogate mother. Thus concludes the first part of a Chinese female *bildungsroman* of the most heartbreaking kind.

The Fall of the Pagoda adopts a much more leisurely pace than "Whispers" in narrating the story of Chang's or Lute's childhood and adolescent years. Perhaps unsure of her target audience's capacity to understand a Chinese subject, Chang tries to recount a distinct episode in each of the novel's twenty-four chapters; to that effect the novel's structure may appear a little rigid; particularly so, in view of the mercurial, free, and indirect style Chang dwells on later in *Little Reunion*. Chang must also have intended to increase the novel's exotic appeal by giving her characters quaint English names, presumably equivalents to their Chinese names, such as Elm Brook and Pussy Willow, and by highlighting stock oriental subjects, such as concubinage and foot-binding. Even the novel's title, *The Fall of the Pagoda*, refers to the popular Chinese folktale of the White Snake. These efforts, however, struggle to relay the psychological nuance and stylistic expertise characteristic of Chang's Chinese writings to the English context.

For our purposes, the most salient feature of the novel is that Chang adopts a child's point-of-view to tell her story, as if she after all did not want to part with the role she should have hated to relive. This child's perspective effectively differentiates *The Fall of the Pagoda* from either "What a Life!" and "Whispers", or *Little Reunion*. Through Lute's eyes, Chang reviews those scenes that brought her so much pain in her early years, and tries to come to terms with things she once failed to understand. Critics trained in psychoanalysis could argue about Chang's complex mentality: she seeks to redeem her childhood trauma by re-enacting it, or more intriguingly, to "inhabit" her trauma by ostensibly denouncing it. Either way it bespeaks the deep-seated ambivalences in Chang's portrait of an artist as a young girl.

To be sure, Chang was not the first modern Chinese woman writer to draw upon childhood experience. Others who come to mind are Bing Xin 冰心 (1900–99), who describes her childhood in idyllic and nostalgic prose; Xiao Hong 蕭紅 (1911–42), who reminisces about her lonely formative years in Northern Manchuria; and Ling Shuhua 凌叔華 (1900–90), who relates her early life in an old, scholarly family in her English memoir *Ancient Melodies* (1953). Incidentally, Ling Shuhua's memoir was released to warm reviews; its success may have given Chang the impetus to write along similar lines. Still, *The Fall of the Pagoda* deserves to be read on its own terms. The world in which Eileen Chang grows up has little of the aura of pastoral innocence that characterizes Bing Xin's or Xiao Hong's writing; nor does it partake of the kind of elite self-esteem underlying Ling Shuhua's memory. Chang is more concerned about a girl who is thrown into an adult milieu in such a way that she becomes old even before coming of age.

Although Chang adopts a child's viewpoint to describe an early modern Chinese family in crisis, the way in which she *narrates* Lute's eyewitness account betrays a much more sophisticated tonality. Chang complained to Stephen Soong that the use of a child's point-of-view limits the novel's realistic subtlety, but the fact is that it helps bring about a different, paradoxical thrust. When Lute's fascination with Disney cartoons is juxtaposed with her father's mediocre taste for prostitutes, or when Lute's yearning for maternal love is offset by Dew's hesitation even to hold her daughter's hand when crossing the street, Lute's (or Eileen Chang's) ironic undertone is unmistakable. Delinquent parenthood is at the core of Chang's diagnosis of her unhappy life. Resounding are Eileen Chang's words in her essay "Making People" (造人, 1944): "Children aren't as muddleheaded as we imagine them to be. Most parents don't understand their children, while most children are able to see through their parents and understand what sort of people they are."[9]

For all their morbidities, the adult characters in *The Fall of the Pagoda* are not always agents of sheer malevolence. Eileen Chang indicates at various points that her parents and their generation too were once children, only becoming grotesques and perverts as a result of their own parents' negligence and incompetence. Chang also understands that this generation of Chinese grew up at a most volatile moment of modern Chinese history, challenged alternately by old and new values. Lucky were the few who ended up becoming wholesome modern beings. Like Lute's and Chang's parents, most Chinese nevertheless paid an enormous price as they reached in vain for social and ethical identities. As such, the names Chang gives to her characters, such as Prudent Pool, Honor Pearl, Pillar, Hill, Aim Far, Prosper, and so on, take on a sardonic dimension, insinuating the outrageous inconsistency between naming and reality, one's parents' expectations and one's lived experience.

At stake here is the problem of marriage. Chang casts a pathological look at *all* marital relationships in the novel, and treats them as the origin of endless gossip, resentment, conspiracies, and scandals. Elm Brook and Dew hardly share a happy moment together; their children Lute and Hill become bitter fruits of their wedlock. Other characters, from Elm Brook's half-brother to Dew's brother and their spouses, are no better off. Whereas husbands seek alternatives by patronizing prostitutes, committing adultery, or owning concubines, wives are left to become "embittered women." Even servants are not exempt from the bleak consequences of marriage.

The Fall of the Pagoda invites an extra-lingual reading of Chang's own failed marriage before it is fully recounted in *Little Reunion*. When writing "Whispers" in the summer of 1944, Chang was on intimate terms with Hu Lancheng and had yet to experience the downside of their romance. Chang and Hu were married in August, 1944, and broke up three years later, in part because of Hu's repeated infidelity. When she began to work on *The Fall of the Pagoda* in 1957, Chang had been divorced from Hu for a decade and had just remarried. She was no longer the vulnerable girl in "Whispers" who watched helplessly as her parents quarreled, but a woman who had learned first-hand the harsh lesson of marital betrayal.[10]

In this sense, the most telling case is not that of Lute's parents but that of her stepmother, Honor Pearl. Daughter of a concubine who has lost her master's favor, Honor Pearl starts life as a meek girl. In response to the May Fourth call for romantic freedom, she defies an arranged marriage and falls in love with a poor cousin. The couple eventually decides to commit suicide due to the lack of family approval. But Honor Pearl's sweetheart reneges on their death pact; worse, he runs away as Pearl takes her share of the poison. Honor Pearl survives the suicide attempt but is sent into confinement by her father, finding solace only in opium. After being married off to Elm Brook, she becomes a shrewish wife, a bed-ridden opium smoker, and a murderous stepmother—a bitter compensation for her lover's betrayal.

The characterization of Honor Pearl may be a composite of Cao Qiqiao (曹七巧) and Jiang Chang'an (姜長安) of "The Golden Cangue," the arch villain-ess and her vulnerable daughter in Chang's fictional world. Honor Pearl has almost crossed the threshold of May Fourth Enlightenment, only to be cast back into the edifice of feudal cannibalism. Honor Pearl's downfall compels one to ponder the path that Chang herself could have taken in the aftermath of her betrayal by Hu Lancheng. One might even wonder whether Chang's failed marriage to Hu represents a fiasco of modern free love or the curse of a stale talent-beauty romance.

Chang's misgivings about marriage in either new or old form do not stop here. In another episode, she has Dew and Coral chat about a murder that was committed in Lake Grasmere, England. A newly-wed couple who were over-seas Chinese students were honeymooning in the resort, but the wife was found dead one day, "barefoot but with one of her silk stockings around her neck," still holding her parasol. The killer turned out to be her husband. The morality tale seems to suggest that not only does marriage hurt; it kills. It would take Chang many more years to unveil the lethal undercurrent of her relations with Hu Lancheng. In *Little Reunion*, when their marriage turns sour, murderous desire surfaces even at just a touch between the husband and wife.

Finally, a few more words about the novel's title, *The Fall of the Pagoda*. Chang makes it clear in her correspondence with Stephen Soong that the Pagoda in question is the Leifeng Pagoda, the site where the beautiful White Snake is said to have been caged eternally for her determination to love a human.[11] Young Lute first hears this story from her nanny and is fascinated by its haunting beauty. The episode does not occur in either Chang's autobio-graphical essays or her Chinese language writing. By invoking a legend that has obvious exotic overtones, Chang may have consciously been pandering to non-Chinese readers. Still, the reference to the Pagoda provides a poignant mytho-logical subtext to Chang's own experience of incarceration and escape.

More significantly, the Pagoda takes us into the intertextual world of modern Chinese literature. Most noticeable perhaps is Lu Xun's (魯迅, 1881–1936) famous essay "On the Fall of the Leifeng Pagoda" (論雷鋒塔的倒掉, 1924). In the essay Lu Xun lashes out at the stifling moral strictures of Chinese society, considering it as not only preventing anyone from yearning for true love but also fostering a culture of hypocrisy. Thus he welcomes the news of the fall of the Leifeng Pagoda, and sneers at those who are still trying to safeguard its debris.[12] Chang may or may not have had Lu Xun or his essay in mind when writing her novel. The point is that, like Lu Xun, Chang finds in the fall of the Pagoda a series of associations—from the collapse of a phallic symbol to the tumbling of patriarchal authority; from Chinese feudalism to Chinese nationalism—and brings them to bear on her own concerns. Almost all of the male characters in her novel are cast in a negative light. As male power proves to be an eroding construct, hollowing out from within, so does the traditional family system. One may also note that Lu Xun's essay was first published in 1924, which coincides with the time when Chang's mother and aunt went overseas. Their decision certainly thwarted the towering dignity of a male-centered society.

The invocation of the Pagoda also brings to mind two other texts of Chinese New Literature, Yin Fu's (殷夫, 1909–31) poem "Children's Pagoda" (孩兒塔, 1930) and Bai Wei's (白薇, 1893–1987) play *Fighting Out of Ghost Pagoda* (打出幽靈塔, 1927). Children's Pagoda refers to a tower built for the purpose of storing the bones of children who die young; hence it is a space that hosts underdeveloped bodies and prematurely stunted souls. A disciple of Lu Xun, Yin Fu writes the poem to reiterate the cry of Lu Xun's Madman, "Save the Children!" In history, Yin Fu was the youngest of the five leftist writers executed by the Nationalist Party in the notorious "Incident of Five Martyrs."[13] Bai Wei is a particularly provocative woman writer of the post-May Fourth era. In her play, the Ghost Pagoda refers to a prison where virgin girls are confined in order to satisfy the sexual needs of an evil landlord. At the center of the play is an orphan girl being coerced to marry the landlord, only to discover at the last moment that she is his illegitimate daughter; meanwhile, the girl has fallen in love with a young man who turns out to be her half-brother. When the revolutionaries come to the girl's rescue, it is too late. Incest taboo and revolutionary totem clash in the play, demanding the girl's life as sacrifice.

Read in this light, *The Fall of the Pagoda* is not a singular case but a belated variation of the "structure of feeling" that occupied modern Chinese writers. Chang, however, has a different take when it comes to the aftermath of the fall of the Pagoda. Lu Xun, Bai Wei, and Yin Fu all belong to the revolutionary camp of writers. As much as they may have wanted to topple the pagoda of feudal China, they shared a wish to see a new pagoda erected in its place. In this new construct, the modern pagoda can take the form of revolution, party, liberation, or nation. To that end, they are also "pagoda builders," like those revolutionary figures of the fiction volume *Pagoda Builders* (建塔者, 1931) by Tai Jingnong 臺靜農 (1903–90), Lu Xun's close friend and a founder of the League of Leftist Writers in the north.

Eileen Chang does not share this vision. An individualist and arch-cynic at heart, she was always skeptical about any claim made in the name of sublime figures. Therefore, if "the fall of the pagoda" marks an apocalyptic moment in the modern Chinese cultural imaginary, it makes sense to Chang only in decadent terms. Writing *after* the fall of the pagoda means to reflect on the illusory ambition that leads to the initial building of the pagoda, to observe the ghostly forces unleashed amid the ruins of the fallen pagoda and, most unexpectedly, to "celebrate" an eerie, desolate atmosphere that has enshrouded the Chinese land ever since.

Writers and critics of the revolutionary discourse did not welcome Chang's vision. But Chang need not serve only as a reactionary example insofar as her writing entertains a negative dialectic of history and progress. It has become a cliché in the field of modern Chinese literary studies to discuss the dubious agency of modernity in terms of Walter Benjamin's Angel of History, who is blown by the wind of the modern backwards toward the future while facing the debris of the past.[14] But instead of the Angel, one can discern an alternative vision in Chang's White Snake, the charming, monstrous female creature banished to the underground of the Leifeng Pagoda because of her desire and sacrifice for human frailties and cruelties. It is by calling on the ancient legend and its uncanny return in modern times that Chang recapitulates her thought in "Writing of One's Own" (自己的文章, 1944):

> This era sinks away from us like a shadow, and we feel we have been abandoned . . . we seek the help of an ancient memory, the memory of a humanity that has lived through every era, a memory clearer and closer to our hearts than anything we might see gazing far into the future. And this gives rise to a strange apprehension about the reality surrounding us. We begin to suspect that this is an absurd and antiquated world, dark and bright at the same time.[15]

I would therefore argue that Chang's *Fall of the Pagoda* projects an involutionary discourse, in that it points to an introverted tendency, a move that expands not through the increasingly efficient use of new inputs but through the replication and elaboration of an inherited pattern of thoughts and deeds.

It curls in such a way as to turn inward upon itself. Reactionary as this reading may seem, Chang has nevertheless offered a most sobering perspective from which to detect the specter—or the Snake—that looms underneath every new, *man-made* tower.

And in the 1950s, what project could have been more elevating than the construction of New China? Chang, however, chose at this time to leave her country for good. She voluntarily withdrew from any kind of nationalist cause, retreating instead into the dark niche of memories. Yet she never ceased exploring Chinese humanity at its most convoluted; to that end she took a serpentine path to the "absurd and antiquated world," exposing a reality that is "both dark and bright at the same time." Thus, in the late 1950s, in a most nonconformist way, Chang began to map out a story of (dis)enchantment with China, by observing not the rise of any soaring construct, but the fall of the pagoda.

The Book of Change

Eileen Chang arrived in Hong Kong from Shanghai in the summer of 1939 and enrolled in the University of Hong Kong as a student of English Literature. Chang had hoped to study in England, but the outbreak of the Second World War foiled this plan. War interfered with her studies anyway: the Japanese invaded Hong Kong on December 7, 1941, the same day they launched the attack on Pearl Harbor. After eighteen days of resistance, the British colonial government surrendered on December 25. The University of Hong Kong shut down in the aftermath of the surrender, and its students were forced to evacuate.

Like many other students who went to study in Hong Kong, Chang found herself stranded on the island in the subsequent months of the Japanese occupation. During this period, communication with mainland China and other areas was interrupted and travel became extremely hectic. Chang was forced to take on clerical and nursing jobs in order to make a living. Eventually, she was able to secure a seat on a refugee ship to Shanghai. When she finally made it home, it was already the summer of 1942.

This Hong Kong experience was a turning point in the life and career of Eileen Chang. Before she went to Hong Kong, Chang was a runaway, estranged from her father and stepmother as well as her biological mother. By comparison, Chang's student life at the University of Hong Kong was a happy time that the war brought to a sudden end.

The Japanese takeover of Hong Kong represented a cataclysmic moment in history, and taught Chang a lesson about the brutality of war and the gratuitousness of any human attachments. This lesson would prove to be all the more poignant after she returned to Shanghai and witnessed the transformation of this city, which was also now under Japanese occupation. It was at this juncture that Chang decided to begin her writing life in earnest.

It therefore comes as little surprise that Chang should draw heavily on her Hong Kong experience when writing her early stories. The most famous piece is "Love in a Fallen City" (傾城之戀, 1943), a novella about a romance between a divorced Shanghai woman and an overseas Chinese playboy against the backdrop of wartime Hong Kong. The couple both start the affair with selfish motives, but end up finding true love with each other because of the fall of Hong Kong. Thus, a historical catastrophe serves unexpectedly as a catalyst for romance, turning a rendezvous into a lifelong marital pact. As Chang wryly observes, thousands of lives were lost during the war, as if only for the purpose of making one mediocre couple's romance possible.[16] Such a bemused look at the contingencies of history and human fate was to become a constant theme of Chang's writings. To that end, Hong Kong takes on a metaphorical dimension as a city where changeability and normalcy, individual desire and societal fate, interact with each other in a mercurial way.

Equally notable is Chang's essay "From the Ashes" (燼餘錄, 1944). This is an extraordinary piece in Chang's oeuvre, not only because it gives a first-hand account of life in Hong Kong immediately after the Japanese invasion but also because it provides a unique view of the meaning of war and life during war. Under Chang's pen, the fall of Hong Kong did not bring about remarkable deeds of sacrifice or heroism so much as it revealed the cowardice and selfishness of humanity. Chang is quick to tell us that she is one of those people her essay sets out to satirize: first shocked by the disorder of the war, but quickly becoming accustomed to the new order of life. She describes herself as indifferent to the accidental deaths in the air raids and absent-minded on rescue mission; what concerns her most is food. Moreover, she calls attention to the grotesque behavior and "bizarre wisdom" that can be prompted by the instinct to survive. Mixing black humor with self-mockery, her exposé is both scathing and hauntingly nonchalant, such that it gives rise to an effect of muted festivity.

And yet Chang is also aware of the fact that although this behavior appears inhuman, it is only too predictably human. Behind her portrait of the anomalous manners and morals of wartime lurks a deep pathos about humanity's limitations. This is a moment of historical catastrophe (亂世), as she calls it elsewhere, a time when all core values dissolve and human endeavor becomes meaningless. Her writing, accordingly, is nothing but a feeble, belated testimony, rescued from "the ashes." Hence the famous conclusion to "From the Ashes":

> The vehicle of the time drives inexorably forward. We ride along, passing through thoroughfares that are perhaps already quite familiar. Against a sky lit by flames, they are capable nevertheless of shaking us to the core. What a shame that we occupy ourselves instead searching for shadows of ourselves in the shop windows that flit so quickly by—we see only our own faces, pallid and trivial. In our selfishness and emptiness, in our smug and shameless ignorance, every one of us is like all the others. And each of us is alone.[17]

For readers who are familiar with Eileen Chang's writings in Chinese, the storyline of *The Book of Change* may first impress as an English language fictional rewrite of "From the Ashes." We have discussed in relation to *The Fall of the Pagoda* Chang's penchant for rewriting in bilingual and cross-generic terms. *The Book of Change* provides yet another example of this. Chang wrote the novel in the late 1950s as if intending to revisit her wartime experience in a different linguistic and generic medium. Almost all of the events in "From the Ashes" are adapted for inclusion in this novel, and episodes are even expanded to discrete, full-length chapters. By taking up the form of the novel, Chang presumably sought to release the dramatic power inherent in her biographical essay. However, from a critical perspective, *The Book of Change* may not read as compellingly as "From the Ashes." Although the novel format allowed for more dramatic latitude in terms of narrating her wartime ordeal, as a literary text, it fails to evoke the same kind of psychological and moral intensity that made "From the Ashes" such a complex reflection of and on the war. Missing are the subtexts that made the earlier essay a modern classic: tension between historical catastrophe and everyday trivia, nationalist calls to arms and individual desires for survival, and the ubiquitous threat of death and youthful insouciance.

Nevertheless, *The Book of Change* does tell us something else about Chang's life and creative vision. For one thing, it reveals for the first time Chang's ambivalent relationship with her mother; it also brings to light how Chang manages to return to Shanghai months after her entrapment in Hong Kong. These additional details help to enrich the context of "From the Ashes," pointing to a different direction in Chang's "plotting" of history and personal memory.

The Fall of the Pagoda, one might recall, had been conceived as the first part of *The Book of Change*. Lute, Chang's alter ego, is a sensitive, unhappy girl growing up in a decaying aristocratic family. Lute's mother, Dew, leaves her husband and children to pursue greater freedom overseas, and by the end of the novel she has returned to Shanghai as a self-styled socialite. After a falling out with her father, Lute finds temporary shelter in her mother's apartment and prepares to study in England at the latter's suggestion.

The Book of Change takes up where *The Fall of the Pagoda* leaves off. Comprising twenty-two chapters, the novel starts with Lute's initiation into her mother's flamboyant lifestyle in Shanghai, followed by her decision to study in Hong Kong rather than England due to the war, and her brief reunion with her mother on the colonial island. This portion of the novel covers ten chapters, and ends with Dew's departure for India on the eve of the Japanese invasion.

The Book of Change devotes its final chapters to Lute's journey home. At a time when maritime transportation was mostly suspended, Lute at first considers it unlikely that she will be able to return to Shanghai. But through a case of mismanagement at the hospital where she works, she "persuades" her superior to find a few seats for her and her classmates. She ends up boarding a ship authorized by none other than the Japanese Commander-in-Chief in Hong Kong, Rensuke Isogai, to send refugees with connections or means back to China. As Lute notes, the passengers include such celebrities as Mei Lanfang (梅蘭芳), the superstar of Peking opera.

From this brief summary, we can now better gauge the relationship between "From the Ashes" and *The Book of Change*. While "From the Ashes" concentrates on Chang's experience of the war at its most intense, *The Book of Change* offers a prolonged narrative about Lute's struggle for survival. Whereas "From the Ashes" relates how Chang is shocked to an epiphanic revelation of the war and its nihilist thrust, *The Book of Change* "domesticates" Lute's apprehensions by literally encrusting the war with familial concerns. While Lute has been deprived of parental love since childhood, Shanghai remains the space she feels attached to and readily calls home. *The Book of Change* begins with Lute's departure from Shanghai and culminates in her return. Both thematically and formally, this circular journey contrasts with the symbolism of total meltdown suggested by "From the Ashes."

The above observations become more significant when we examine the novel's title, *The Book of Change*, in the framework of an allusion. Chang no doubt draws her inspiration from the esoteric Chinese classic, *The Book of*

Change (*Yi Jing*). In the novel, Chang narrates a scene in which Lute, working at a makeshift hospital, discovers a heap of discarded books and "hopes to find a copy of *The Book of Change*":

> It was philosophy based on the forces of *yang* and *yin*, light and darkness, male and female, how they wax and wane, grow and erode, with eight basic diagrams by which fortunes could be told with tortoise shells. She had never read it. It was the most esoteric of the five classics and not taught in the classroom because of its obscurity and more important, its mention of sex.[18]

Chang herself has never been known for her knowledge of the *Yi Jing*. By adopting the title of the classic for her own novel, Chang inevitably prompts one to ponder her motivations. She may intend to capitalize on the classic's exotic appeal in order to attract her prospective readers' attention; to construe Lute's or her own fate in light of ancient wisdom; or to launch a subtle attack on her former husband Hu Lancheng who takes pride in being an interpreter and practitioner of the *Yi Jing*. These possibilities aside, I argue that, vacillating between the appeal of Orientalism and a divinatory contemplation of personal life, Chang seeks to elicit from (the title of) *The Book of Change* a philosophy of writing, one that both testifies to the transience of life and plays with the transformative power of fiction.

To begin with, in view of the rich implication of the word "change" in *The Book of Change* in the Chinese original, *yi* (易), which could denote transience, simplicity, transformation, and transaction, among other things,[19] Chang may very well have brought it to bear on her own multifaceted experience. Although the novel is structured around the fall of Hong Kong and the heroine's return to Shanghai, by the time Chang began the project—the late 1950s—she must have already been conscious of the unpredictable changeability governing all forms of retrospective writing. By then, Chang had experienced first-hand another national crisis—the fall of China to the Communists in 1949. This new crisis forced her to flee Shanghai for Hong Kong in 1952, via a reversal of the route she took ten years earlier when she escaped Hong Kong. After a three-year sojourn in Hong Kong, she immigrated to the United States. During this period, Chang was involved in two romances. Her clandestine marriage to Hu Lancheng ended in 1947; and in 1956, she met and married Ferdinand Reyher (1891–1967). Finally, writing in the US in the late 1950s, Chang was an author twice removed from her homeland, struggling to establish a career in a language other than her mother tongue. Looking back at her adventures since

1938, she had every reason to reflect on the changes she had been through and to contemplate the meaning of the changeability of one's fate.

At a deeper diction level, the title of *The Book of Change* as Chang uses it points to the paradox of change inherent in temporal flux and human vicissitudes. Scholars have pointed out that when change is understood as a constant factor in cosmic movement, of which human ups and downs are only one part, a different implication arises: change yields a perennial, repetitive pattern, thereby implying unchangeability.[20] As Lute comments, the ancient text teaches how "the forces of *yang* and *yin*, light and darkness, male and female . . . wax and wane, grow and erode." It is the mutual implication between apparently opposing forces, and the cyclical, dialectic pattern that comes into existence as a result, that manifests the Way of change. For all the complexities of interpretation, this Way should inform a simple truth that is accessible to all.

Accordingly, time should not only signify a linear flow but also a "spatial flux," in which change and no change, exchange and interchange interact with each other and give rise to multiple configurations. This leads to the third level of implication of "change." That is, as a force that disturbs the status quo, change always contains an unceasingly transformative—indeed generative—momentum. Hence "production and reproduction is what is called (the process of) change" (生生之謂易).[21] Change constitutes the basic principle that enacts the cosmology of life. It is in the context of this metaphysical tradition that one comes to appreciate the nonconformist aspect of Eileen Chang's penchant for rewriting. Repetition, as she would have it, indicates neither a dull duplication of that which is extant nor a return to the starting point. Rather, it refers to a subtle dis-placement of the origin, a phantasmal re-presentation of the identical.[22]

To return to "From the Ashes" and *The Book of Change*, one discerns an array of reciprocal relations between the two works, such as autobiographical testimonial and fictional account, trauma and its displacement, history as prescience and history as hindsight. These elements work on each other's premises and attributes, generating new and unexpected meanings. Above all, the fact that Chang chooses English to rewrite her wartime experience calls attention to the chameleon nature of language as a vehicle for remembering things past. Accordingly, one can talk about Chang's treatment of time, history, and language as an exercise in isomorphism. With the fall of Hong Kong as its subject, "From the Ashes" casts an eschatological spell on humanity while *The Book of Change*, as its title suggests, projects a return and regeneration of life, for good or ill. Chaos and contingency are after all underlain by persistence and rejuvenation.

As suggested by Chang's *The Book of Change*, the concept of change continues to manifest its power in her writings from subsequent years. In 1976, Chang completed the draft of her Chinese novel *Little Reunion*. The novel is intended as a full account of Chang's life from childhood to her divorce from Hu Lancheng; as such, it completes what Chang had tried to do in her two English language biographical works of fiction, *The Fall of the Pagoda* and *The Book of Change*. Interestingly enough, the narrative of *Little Reunion* is framed by Chang's (or her heroine's) recollection of her Hong Kong experience, particularly the Japanese attack on Hong Kong that coincided with her final exam day at the University of Hong Kong. Such a structural arrangement makes *Little Reunion* a chiasmic counterpart to *The Book of Change*, which, as discussed above, frames Chang's Hong Kong experience with her Shanghai memories. As such, the mutual contextualization of Shanghai and Hong Kong provides a spatial analogy to Chang's rumination on the poetics of change and interchange in a cyclical way.

The Book of Change opens with the initiation of Lute into her mother's world: "Lute has never seen an artichoke before." As it is, Lute's first "encounter" with the exotic vegetable at Dew's dining table is ripe with symbolism. For Dew, the artichoke conveys the taste "of Paris," her beloved city, while for Lute it embodies the alienated relationship between the mother and daughter: something whose heart one gets to one leaf at a time but that may be unpalatable in the end.

In a way typical of Eileen Chang's ironic style, this "artichoke" incident serves as a mock-heroic prelude to a novel that chronicles a girl's search for adulthood in the midst of a historical disaster. Just as Dew and Coral, Lute's aunt, are engaged in the art of eating artichoke hearts, the war is looming large. "Fighting may break out anytime," Dew notes. But even before the war besets her, Lute is already witnessing the breakdown of all values on the home front.

The estrangement between Lute and Dew was touched upon in *The Fall of the Pagoda*, but as Chang herself admitted, in that earlier work the relationship was mostly seen from the perspective of Lute as a child. Now an eighteen-year-old girl, Lute is ready to unpack the layers of her mother's psyche. Lute has left her father's house for good, only to find herself a misfit in her mother's apartment. She is awkward at social gatherings, to the point where her mother calls her a "pig." As she gradually peels away the layers of mystery surrounding her mother's elegant circle, she becomes increasingly amazed by the seediness of the gossip and scandal. She overhears that her mother and aunt may have been in a lesbian relationship; her aunt goes to bed with her cousin; her mother is dating more than one non-Chinese boyfriend at the same time; and, more stunningly, her uncle Pillar is not her real uncle but a changeling bought from a beggar couple.

Given her self-centered lifestyle and capricious attitude towards her daughter, Dew may come across as a textbook example of the "evil mother." But a closer reading suggests that her changeability corresponds to the theme of *The Book of Change*. A victim of traditional marriage, Dew wants Lute to acquire a new style of life, but she also entertains the prospect that she may be able to capitalize on her daughter's future marriage. She never hides her snobbery with regard to things new and foreign, claiming that she is able to appreciate China more because she is able to adopt a foreigner's perspective. Chang refers several times to the agency of the "female" principle in the novel, citing the common wisdom of *yin* versus *yang*. To that end, her mother should be a role model. Both aloof and pragmatic, both persistent and unpredictable, this female principle as embodied by Dew, as Chang would have it, can ignite one's survival instinct when least expected. But it can also hurt because it is free of any *man-made* decorum.

We thus come to the first turning point in the novel, when Lute is unexpectedly awarded a private scholarship by her history professor Mr. Balisdell. She brings the good news and money to Dew, only to arouse the latter's suspicion that she has exchanged her body for a monetary reward. Worse still, Lute later discovers that Dew has gambled away her scholarship money in a mahjong game. This leads to the falling out between the mother and daughter. With Dew squandering her scholarship, Lute feels she has "paid back" her mother's investment in her. She no longer "owes" Dew anything.

As such, Chang gives the implication of "change" an economic twist: as one gloss for the Chinese original *yi* suggests, change means not only interchange or exchange but also *jiaoyi* (交易, transaction).[23] In view of the tension between Lute and Dew, one finds that, where ethical and emotional binding shortchanges, the calculus of give and take sets in. The mother's selfishness and the daughter's pragmatism read like a nightmarish supplement to the conventional feminist view of mother-daughter bonding. Nevertheless, Chang would have retorted: Isn't such an instinct for exchange/transaction germane to an understanding of our capacity for perseverance, something that particularly helps to validate the female principle of survival and self-sufficiency?

When Lute bids a bitter farewell to Dew at the end of Chapter 10, she has unknowingly learned a crucial lesson from her mother—the importance of being *not* earnest. With her mother's lesson in mind, Lute is able to quickly acquire the necessary self-interest and independence to survive the worst moments of the fall of Hong Kong. Indeed, she could not have obtained her ticket to Shanghai had she not exercised shrewdness and calculation. In real life, Chang never saw her mother after a brief reunion in postwar Shanghai. In the fictional account, however, she would continue to re-enact the love-hate relationship between mother and daughter until the end of her career.

In the middle chapters, the novel focuses on the fall of Hong Kong in 1941. Lute and her classmates were nervously preparing for their finals on the morning they heard the news of the Japanese attack. Instead of feeling fear and panic, the students are excited. They know little of war, while the cancellation of the exams, followed by the shutdown of the school, means an unexpected escape from the routines of life. Some immediately start to worry about a proper wardrobe as they seek a safe shelter from the bombing. Chang describes the students' untimely jubilation in an indulgent manner, for she knows that in a few days they are going to be tested by the trials of starvation, exodus, and death. Even then, however, she is skeptical that the students have the capacity to learn from their harsh experience. Chang does not hold the residents of Hong Kong in high esteem either. For her, this colonial island "had never seen war, not even the Opium War that created the city."[24] It merely serves as a space for showcasing the naiveté, cowardice, and selfishness of human beings at a time of drastic change.

Such a cynical attitude frees Chang from the formulaic discourse that would come to dominate modern Chinese literature during the Sino-Japanese War. She observes the responses of people around her with wonder, discerning in them a striking mixture of horror and humor. One such example is Lute's friend Bebe Sastri,[25] an Indian girl who is also from Shanghai. Bebe ventures out to a cartoon movie in downtown Hong Kong in the midst of a bombing, and bathes and sings in the dorm while a bomb drops on a neighboring dorm. Lute herself fares no better. Upon hearing of the surrender of Hong Kong to the Japanese, she and several classmates eagerly await the first opportunity to leave school in search of ice cream, completely undaunted by the prospect of stumbling over corpses scattered in the streets.

There is one occasion when Lute meets the threat of death face to face. In Chapter 14, she goes downtown by tram to register as an Air-Raid Precaution volunteer, only to be caught in an air raid. Along with the other passengers, she jumps off the tram and is barely able to find a shelter before the bombs fall. When this ordeal is over, she realizes that she would have been killed had the bombs landed on her side of the street. However, what truly strikes her is the fact that even in the midst of the bombing, the sky is as bright and blue as ever, and that the now empty tram stands still in the middle of the street, filled with pleasant sunshine. Moments after the bombing, the tram is again filled with passengers; everything quickly returns to normal. Lute is suddenly struck by an awareness of her desolate circumstances:

> The bombing moved away. She took the same tram home. Walking up she suddenly realized that there was no one to tell it to. Bebe was gone. And not just in Hong Kong but in the whole world, who was there? . . . She would tell Aunt Coral someday although she would not expect her aunt to be greatly stirred to hear that she had nearly gotten killed. Bebe would miss her if she had died but Bebe was always happy.[26]

This sense of transience and gratuitousness is compounded by the news that Lute's history professor Balisdell has been shot dead, not by Japanese soldiers but by friendly fire. Professor Balisdell, one might recall, was the professor who gave Lute a private scholarship. Up to that point Lute had never cared much about her history class; she now learns her lesson at the expense of her teacher's death.

Despite the threat of death, what truly concerns Lute is daily survival. Food becomes the most pressing need. Lute observes the irony that the fear of food shortage increases her classmates' appetites; that food rationing creates a new economy of smuggling or hoarding of private supplies; and that numerous food vendors pop up immediately after the fall of Hong Kong. In one episode at the hospital, Lute and her fellow nurses bake a tray of dinner rolls one night using the coconut oil otherwise only used for making soap. They have a wonderful snack together despite—or perhaps because of—the patients who are dying amid incessant groaning and screaming just a few feet away.

Lute also observes that romance flourishes during wartime. People fall in love for the sake of either seeking protection or simply fending off loneliness. As Chang narrates, these romances would not have formed during peaceful times. When the desire for companionship and the desire for convenience are conflated, the libidinous drive of human beings finds an unlikely alliance with an anarchist impulse. Adultery, cohabitation, and abortion all become understandable. After all, this is a time of chaos, a moment in which the extraordinary has become the ordinary. In Chang's view, in order to survive such a time, people are driven to grasp at anything that is tangible. Physical intimacy, like food, becomes a poignant index that conveys the primordial need of humanity.

But what Chang wants to explore is not merely the ethical or political outcome of the war; she impresses us more with her inquiry into the *economics* of the war. At a time when all values break down, Chang tells us, people become more rather than less calculating. Food and sex, accordingly, are as fundamental to human needs as tokens of exchange, facilitating a wide range of motives from survival to opportunism. Chang's novella of the 1940s, "Love in a Fallen City," provides a most compelling example in this regard. But if "Love in a Fallen City" still valorizes the residual axiology of true love in a time of war, *The Book of Change* brings the transaction of food, sex, marriage, and ideology, among other things, down to the level of day-to-day negotiation. However devastating, the change brought by the Japanese occupation is quickly naturalized by people in exchange for a more manageable form of existence.

Bearing this insight in mind, I argue that Lute is able to adapt to the status quo thanks to the experience she has had living with both her father and mother. Since childhood, she has been immersed in the abacus of human relationships, and she learns to become supersensitive to money after moving to live with her mother. The fall of Hong Kong creates an "ideal" venue, where Lute puts her knowledge of change, and exchange, into practice. Ultimately, she manages to leave Hong Kong by striking a deal with her superior.

The Book of Change ends happily as Lute makes a safe return to Shanghai. But this narrative closure is clearly tongue-in-cheek because Lute manages to overcome her obstacles not through any socially recognized virtue such as patriotism or heroism but by an investment of bad faith at the right moment. While this may be the price Lute has to pay for growing up, I suspect that Chang entertains a deeper layer of cynicism. This brings to mind the theme of "Love in a Fallen City," that thousands of lives were sacrificed gratuitously in the war as if only to consummate one mediocre couple's romance. Likewise, the denouement of *The Book of Change* insinuates that for all the mishaps resulting from the fall of Hong Kong, at least one girl prevails. Lute's triumph is predicated on nothing more than the law of untenability of human constancy. This paradox drives home the dialectics of (ex)change of Chang's novel.

Thus far, we have discussed Eileen Chang's *The Book of Change* in light of her personal and fictional experience as well as her paradoxical tribute to the ancient classic of the same title. I argue that by invoking the title *The Book of Change*, Chang sets in motion an endless interplay of thematic axes such as depth and surface, obscurity and simplicity, history and autobiography, philosophical rumination and fictional experiment, and most intriguingly, change as transformation and change as transaction. As a way of concluding my reading of the novel, I call attention to a specific derivative tendency that arises from Chang's writings in the mid-twentieth century.[27]

In my discussion of *The Fall of the Pagoda*, I introduce involutionary poetics as a principle of Chang's writing, by which I mean a narrative practice that replaces a linear, progressive sequence with an inward turn to itself. With *The Book of Change*, I argue that on top of the involutionary inclination, Chang is playing with a derivative poetics—derivative, in the sense that her narrative does not emphasize originality so much as a capacity for continued, figurative replacement and transformation, thereby subverting any claim to authenticity. To reiterate the point, Chang's *The Book of Change* is both a re-configuration of the "traces" left by "From the Ashes" and a preview of *Little Reunion*, her tell-all fictional memoir. Moreover, insofar as the novel is a belated spin-off of Chang's earlier writings, it generates its own derivatives and doubles. Chang's *The Fall of the Pagoda*, now published independently, was originally part of *The Book of Change*.

Chang is also conscious of the derivative inclination of her writing, to the extent of elaborating on it at both structural and conceptual levels. As early as the second chapter of *The Book of Change*, Lute encounters Zeng Pu's (曾 樸, 1872–1935) *A Flower in the Sea of Sins* (孽海花, 1907), the most famous roman à clef in early twentieth-century China. A panoramic exposé of late Qing politics and history, Zeng's novel achieved enormous popularity, in part because the text was replete with thinly-disguised representations of contemporary figures, incidents, and anecdotes. The guessing game became so much of the reading experience that a glossary appeared to help readers identify the characters and their actual counterparts. For instance, the romance of Lute's grandparents (or Chang's grandparents, Zhang Peilun [張佩綸, 1848–1903] and Li Juou [李菊藕, 1866–1912]), which is otherwise not covered in orthodox historiography, is featured in the novel.

Lute's discovery of *A Flower in the Sea of Sins* prompts her to launch a parallel survey of (family) history and its fictitious doubles. She is so fascinated with the phantasmal duplicities arising from the novel that she concludes:

> These were people she could admire. She admires her mother and aunt but they came and went, more like friends. Her grandparents would never leave her because they were dead. They will never disapprove or get angry, *they would just lie quietly in her blood and die once more when she died.*[28]

For readers familiar with Chang's oeuvre, the italicized part of the quote reappears, in Chinese, in Chang's autobiographic photo album *Mutual Reflections: Looking at My Old Photo Album* (對照記：看老照相簿, 1994). In other words, the way in which Chang recycles a textual line from one work to another parallels her effort to resuscitate a family line from one generation to another.

This example also intimates the thrust of Chang's "self-writing" as a lifelong project that stems as much from her confessional urge as from her desire for self-fictionalization. Through Lute's story, Chang seems to suggest that if she could only learn her family history through a novel such as *A Flower in the Sea of Sins*, it makes equal sense that she could write her own experience back into fictional forms.

The circular, derivative inclination in Chang's writings has at least two more models. It is well known that Chang was fascinated by Han Bangqing's (韓邦慶, 1856–94) *The Sing-song Girls of Shanghai*, a courtesan novel based on its author's own adventures in the pleasure quarters of fin-de-siècle Shanghai. Han's novel has never been popular, but Chang likes it because, against the generic tradition of the courtesan novel, it downplays the glamor of the demimonde, presenting instead an ambiance full of mundane goings-on and mediocre personalities. Hence it is a forerunner of modern Chinese realism. Both *The Fall of the Pagoda* and *The Book of Change* bear the imprints of *The Sing-song Girls of Shanghai* in ornamenting (family) history with everyday trivia while discerning a total desolation underneath any human pursuit of vanity.[29]

In turn, *The Sing-song Girls of Shanghai* derives its structure and characterization from Cao Xueqin's (曹雪芹, 1724?–63) *Dream of the Red Chamber*, the *magnum opus* of classical Chinese fiction and the ultimate source of Chang's inspiration. Chang first read *Dream of the Red Chamber* at the age of eight; as early as 1934, she attempted to create a modern version of it in "Modern Dream of the Red Chamber" (摩登紅樓夢).[30] The masterpiece's exposé of an aristocratic household in decline must have struck the young Chang as similar to her own family's fate, and its emphasis on the ephemeral nature of youth, femininity, and dreams, and vertiginous interplay of attachment and transcendence would have resonated further.

More pertinent to our concerns is the fact that, as she grew older, Chang became increasingly conscious of the pain and pleasure in Cao Xueqin's continued revision—rewriting—of his manuscript throughout his life. Cao Xueqin "worked on it for ten years, in the course of which he rewrote it no less than five times" (披閱十載，增刪五次), while leaving it unfinished in the end.[31] *Dream of the Red Chamber* is a project that ceaselessly transforms itself along with the progression of its author's life. To that effect, it is a *Book of Change* of its own kind.

It may therefore not be a coincidence that when rewriting her life stories in the last four decades of her career, Chang was engaged in two parallel projects. She translated *The Sing-song Girls of Shanghai* from the Wu dialect into Mandarin Chinese, and from Chinese into English; and she undertook a close reading of *Dream of the Red Chamber* by means of textual analysis, philological verification, and biographical research, a project later published as *The Nightmare in the Red Chamber* (紅樓夢魘, 1977). These three projects (creation, exegesis, translation) cannot be separated from each other; rather, they form an intertextual, cross-generic, and translingual network, pointing to the multiple terms of Chang's derivative poetics.

Upon completing her Mandarin translation of *The Sing-song Girls of Shanghai*, Chang sarcastically observes, "Whereas modern Chinese readers had overlooked *The Sing-song Girls of Shanghai* three generations in a row, Eileen Chang had closely read *Dream of the Red Chamber* as many as five times in recent years."[32] Implied here is not merely Chang's critique of the fate of two masterpieces, but her idiosyncratic agenda of writing and reading. Moving from English (*The Book of Change, The Fall of the Pagoda*) to Chinese (*Little Reunion*), from fiction to pictorial representation (*Mutual Reflections*), and from translation to critical annotation, Chang takes writing as a continuum of metamorphoses. She harbors little "anxiety of influence" and almost no "politics of interpretation." She would have sneered at these as symptoms of Western poetics. When she conflates exegesis with creative writing, she re-enacts the subtle hermeneutic circle of "relate/transmit" (述) and "create" (作). When she engages in translating her own works and those of others, she does not align herself with "translingual practice," a theory haunted by the fear of incommensurability in meaning and power, but instead finds an analogy in "changing fashions," an exercise enacted as much by political motivations as by gendered, intimate desires and material innovations. "A Chronicle of Changing Clothes" (更衣記, 1944), it will be recalled, is Chang's Chinese translation of her own

"Chinese Life and Fashions" (1943), and one of the earliest examples of her bilingual writings.[33] To that extent, translation or *yi* (譯) can also be taken to resonate with the broader, epistemological dynamics of change and exchange, *yi* (易).

In this chapter I have described the metamorphosis of *The Book of Change* in detail in order to stress the tortuous path Chang took in writing it. I argue that *The Book of Change*, as its title implies, epitomizes a writing project that cannot stop transforming itself until its author's life comes to an end. Each incarnation of this writing project points to Chang's changing attitude towards her early experience as well as her renewed tactic of storytelling. As such, Chang writes as if undertaking her own *à la recherche du temps perdu* (remembrance of things past). She demonstrates that the "things past" are not locked in the passage of time, waiting to be retrieved, any more than they are active ingredients in one's memory, ever ready to interact with things that are happening in the present.

Conventional wisdom has it that Chang's creativity suffered a precipitous decline after she left China in 1952. This may be the conclusion if one defines creativity narrowly in terms of originality, novelty, and iconoclasm, notions that are the by-products of the age of Romanticism and high modernism. But a project such as *The Book of Change* encourages one to re-evaluate Chang's creative output. At a time when most Chinese writers were tirelessly exploring the new and unprecedented in the May Fourth brand of modernist spirit, Chang opted to dwell on what many critics deem decadent and ideologically problematic. She points nevertheless to a genealogy in which revolution is underlined by involution, and revelation presupposes derivation. And it is not until the dawn of a new century that we have finally come to realize that where most of her fellow writers performed the least modern of modernities, Chang managed to bring about the most unconventional of conventionalities.

Afterword

Leo Ou-fan Lee

The quality and range of the papers in this volume speak for themselves. What remains for me to do in this Afterword is to ask the inevitable question—what next? What is to be done when a writer and her works have received too much, not too little, attention, especially in the Chinese-speaking world?

However, it must be acknowledged that in spite of C. T. Hsia's high praise of Eileen Chang's fiction in his classic *A History of Modern Chinese Fiction, 1910–1957* (1961), Western scholars have not responded with equal enthusiasm to this talented writer. As Kam Louie indicates in his Introduction, so far there is yet to be a full-length study in English or any other foreign language of Chang's life and works, although a smattering of translations have appeared. This seeming lack of interest contrasts sharply with the situation in Taiwan, where Chang has been a legend for decades, and more recently in post-Mao China, where a flood of works of all kinds have poured out steadily and Eileen Chang "fever" has continued to rage to the present day, with no signs of abating. This phenomenon itself merits some comparison and reflection: What accounts for this "Eileen Chang fever"? Does her legendary status satisfy some collective psychological need or fit better with the present-day mood of the so-called "Bobos" (Bourgeois bohemians) in urban China? Nicole Huang, Esther Cheung, and Shuang Shen have detailed their quests to answer some of these questions in Chapters 3 to 5, exploring the trajectories of the mundane, fashion, gender, and betrayal with Taiwan, Japan, Shanghai, and China as backdrops.

Notwithstanding these excellent explorations of Chang's craft, it must be stated that part of her recent popularity is due to the commercial success (at least in Chinese-speaking regions) of Ang Lee's film, *Lust, Caution* (色，戒, 2007) which is a creative adaptation of one of Chang's stories of the same title. The ideological furor it has generated has led me to write a small book about the film and the story.[1] This film, in turn, has renewed our interest in other films that are based on Chang's stories, such as *Love in a Fallen City* (傾城之戀, dir. Ann Hui, 1987) and *Red Rose, White Rose* (紅玫瑰白玫瑰, dir. Stanley Kwan, 1994) (both directed by Hong Kong directors), as well as Chang's own film scriptwriting. The relationship between text and image is a topic worth pursuing side by side with a reconsideration of Chang's place in modern Chinese literature. These are tasks for all serious scholars, past and present, Chinese and Western. The papers collected in this volume represent a welcome advance in scholarship. In particular, the chapters by Gina Marchetti (Chapter 7) and Hsiu-Chuang Deppman (Chapter 8) deal with Ang Lee's filmic treatment of Chang's text in great detail, while Jessica Li (Chapter 2) discusses the renewed interest in "Love in a Fallen City" (1943) as seen through a new stage adaptation.

The issue that captures my own interest is Eileen Chang's bilingualism, which is triggered directly by the recent publication of three newly discovered works of fiction: *Little Reunion* (小團圓, 2009), *The Fall of the Pagoda* (2010) and *The Book of Change* (2010), the latter two forming a sequence of two autobiographical novels originally written by Chang in English (which are then translated into Chinese). Indeed, these three novels are the focus of attention in the last three chapters of this book.

In the field of cultural studies, bilingualism is by no means a side issue; in fact, it occupies the very center of theoretical concern. Scholars in Hispanic and Chicano/Chicana studies in the United States are especially keen to address this issue, perhaps more so than their colleagues in Asian-American and Chinese studies. The recent work of Doris Sommer, for instance, is a case in point, in which she attempts to extricate the complexities of the socio-cultural effects of bilingual writing and speech common in the Hispanic minorities in the US.[2] One of Sommer's central arguments relates to how this language practice as a collective cultural habit is embedded in a certain "double consciousness" that the early Afro-American scholar and writer W. E. B. DuBois once attributed to black Americans. Can one say the same about Eileen Chang?

My tentative answer is that we can't. For I find that her efforts at English fiction writing still reveal a singular "obsession with China"—not only in her personal memory and consciousness but in her English language as well.[3] In *The Fall of the Pagoda* in particular, Chang's writing style is still quite "Chinese": it shows traces of a conscious attempt to find English equivalents to the Chinese modes of expression in order to explain her Chinese world to Western readers of her time (presumably in middle-class America). As is well known, despite many revisions, Chang failed to find an American publisher. Somehow her "Chineseness" stood in the way. This is a problem shared of course by many non-Western writers whose works have proved untranslatable. But then there are also others—Vladimir Nabokov comes readily to mind—who are capable of writing in two languages and show a stylistic mastery of both. In my view, Eileen Chang's English, though excellent, fails to match the supple and sophisticated style of her Chinese writings. (On the other hand, her own Chinese translations of American literary classics such as Emerson and Hemingway have proved to be more successful and enduring.) Perhaps, as Xiaojue Wang argues in Chapter 6, Chang deliberately attempts to create a China that does not meet her Western readers' Orientalist expectations, "She [Eileen Chang] is well aware of the constructedness of China and Chineseness in the eyes of the West. Her fiction never lacks moments satirizing characters who fall in love with a China fabricated by their own imaginations."

Is this necessarily a defect in her bilingual aesthetics? For scholars, it points to the related issue of what might be called "self-translation," an implicit bilingual practice in which the language used in the text occupies only the surface layer, beneath which a deeper linguistic operation stemming from the mother tongue is also under way. In Eileen Chang's case, while the surface language is English, deep down she is still writing in Chinese, which at least in part controls and shapes her English style. In my review of *The Fall of the Pagoda* for a bilingual journal based in Hong Kong, I have commented on this in some detail by citing several passages from her first English language novel. The implication is that only when Chang temporarily departs from her Chinese base does her English style take flight. Still, even in such passages her English is still occasionally awkward and reads like a translation. Indeed, we could look at Chang not simply as translator, but as Shuang Shen does in Chapter 5, as a performer and her act of "self-translation" as an identity performance and "impersonation": "The fact that Chang did not present herself as a translator in most cases, but intended for her texts, whether published in English or in Chinese, to be read as originals, suggests that there is an issue of 'masking' in her self-translation and bilingual practice." I hope such insights will open up new terrain for research and analysis by interested scholars in the field of translation studies or by those readers who are themselves bilingual. (The latter includes most, if not all, contributors to this volume).

Eileen Chang's two English novels obviously maintain a close and intricate relationship with her Chinese novel, *Little Reunion*, as they draw on the same autobiographical material. This begs a further question: why was Chang so consistently absorbed with her own life, particularly in her last thirty years in America, where she had become a self-imposed recluse? Was she intent on doing a kind of "*à la recherche du temps perdu*" like Proust? Or for that matter has she ever read Proust, aside from the likes of Somerset Maugham, Stella Benson, and J. P. Marquand—all second-class writers? The subject seems old-fashioned, but nevertheless worth exploring. Yet to pursue this further would call for a comparative method and approach informed by cultural history, a method that I am not fully qualified to employ. Again I leave this to younger and more adventurous colleagues. For example, Xiaojue Wang, Shuang Shen and Tze-lan Sang have shed much light on re-evaluations of Chang's creative activities in the decades after her relocation to the US.

Most significantly, in his perceptive analysis of these two novels in Chapter 11, David Wang addresses a similar question from a more literary and theoretical angle by introducing two interrelated concepts. The first of these, "involutionary poetics," Wang derives from *The Fall of Pagoda* and defines as "a narrative practice that replaces a linear, progressive sequence with an inward turn to itself." In relation to *The Book of Change*, he argues that on top of this involutionary inclination, Chang is playing with a "derivative poetics" in the sense that "her narrative does not emphasize originality so much as a capacity for continued, figurative replacement and transformation, thereby subverting any claim to authenticity." Wang's two concepts provide a fitting counterpoint and corrective to the excessive preoccupation among Chinese readers and critics with reading Chang's novels as merely indexes to her private life. Wang rightfully points the way toward technique and style. He interprets Chang's "self-writing" as "a lifelong project that stems as much from her confessional urge as from her desire for fictionalization." One could say the same of Proust— or even Virginia Woolf, whose fiction also shows an involutionary "inward turn." If so, how do we measure Chang's talent and greatness in the company of these literary giants? Or do we seek only her uniqueness as a Chinese creative writer? I hope these questions may serve to enlarge the scope of research and thinking among Eileen Chang specialists.

One way of following Wang's theoretical trek is to look more closely into the ways in which such a re-configuration of traces left by an earlier work is worked out by Chang's deployment of a different language and style. Does the use of English help to transform the fragments of personal memory to which she returns again and again and bring new insights? If so, how?

My own reactions are somewhat varied. If all three recent novels are examples of "derivative poetics," Chang's Chinese novel, *Little Reunion*, is more revelatory than her two English works, of which the writing of the second volume, *The Book of Change*, appears to be more sure-footed. This is not the place to go into detailed analysis, as several chapters of this volume have done. Suffice to say that whereas Chang still maintains a high degree of emotional involvement in her Chinese work, her English novels show a certain narrative distance without much irony. (The first novel adopts the point-of-view of a young girl.) If Chang has purposely chosen to recycle "a textual line from one work to another," the reader naturally expects to find a little more nuance and a different angle of vision in the recycled text. It is in this regard that I find her English works, particularly *The Fall of the Pagoda*, somewhat disappointing. If originality is no longer a crucial issue, what about narrative technique? If "self-writing" has become rewriting, issues of language (whether Chinese or English) and style become, it seems to me, even more crucial. It is in this respect that scholars, rather than common readers, can gain deeper insights and therefore make a greater contribution to the veritable cultural industry of Eileen Chang. This volume has made a start in discussing some of these issues; I hope my brief Afterword also serves to encourage more scholars to engage in such endeavors.

Notes

Introduction

1. Eva Hung, "Editor's Page," *Renditions: A Chinese-English Translation Magazine.* Special Issue on Eileen Chang 45 (1996): 4.

2. Su Weizheng 蘇偉貞, *Copying: On the Generations of Taiwanese Chang School Creative Writers* 描紅：臺灣張派作家世代論 (Taipei: Sanmin shuju, 2006).

3. C. T. Hsia, *A History of Modern Chinese Fiction, 1917–1957* (New Haven: Yale University Press, 1961), 389.

4. See Yu Qing 于青, *Biography of Eileen Chang* 張愛玲傳 (Guangzhou: Huacheng chubanshe, 2008), 15.

5. Jin Kai-jun 金凱筠 (Karen Kingsbury), "Eileen Chang's 'Cenci de duizhao' and Eurasian Culture-Creation," 張愛玲的《參差的對照》與歐亞文化的呈現, ed. Yang Ze 楊澤, *Reading Eileen Chang: Collected Essays from the "International Conference on Eileen Chang Research"* 閱讀張愛玲：張愛玲國際研討會論文集 (Taipei: Maitian, 1999), 311.

6. Eileen Chang, "The Unfortunate Her" 不幸的她, *Eileen Chang: Writings, Supplement* 《張愛玲：文集，補遺》, ed. Zi Tong 子通 and Yi Qing 亦清 (Hong Kong: Cosmos Books, 2003), 270–72.

7. Chang, "The Unfortunate Her," 272.

8. Eileen Chang, "Comments on the Reprint of *Romances*" 《傳奇》再版的話, reprinted in *Complete Essays of Eileen Chang* 張愛玲散文全集, ed. Wu Danqing 吳丹青 (Zhengzhou: Zhongguo nongmin chubanshe, 1996), 439.

9. Lin Zou, "The Commercialization of Emotions in Zhang Ailing's Fiction," *The Journal of Asian Studies*, 70, 1 (2011): 29–51.

10. Eileen Chang, "Whispers," trans. Janet Ng, *Renditions* 45 (Spring 1996): 43–44.

11. Zhang Zijing 張子靜 and Ji Ji 季季, *My Sister: Eileen Chang* 我的姐姐張愛玲 (Changchun: Jilin chuban jituan, 2009), 133.

12. Originally published in 1944. Reprinted in "Sayings of Yanying" 炎櫻語錄 in *Complete Essays of Eileen Chang* 張愛玲散文全集, 307–9.

13. The essay was collected in the volume 《流言》 in 1945, which was later translated as *Written on Water,* trans. Andrew F. Jones, co-ed. with an introduction by Nicole Huang (New York: Columbia University Press, 2005), 53–55.

14. Hsia, *A History of Modern Chinese Fiction,* 398.

15. Zhang Zijing, *My Sister: Eileen Chang,* 198–203.

16. These essays are collected in *Written on Water.*

17. Leo Ou-fan Lee, *Shanghai Modern: The Flowering of a New Urban Culture in China, 1930–1945* (Cambridge: Harvard University Press, 1999), 289.

18. 〈自己的文章〉, translated as "Writing of One's Own," in *Written on Water,* 15–22.

19. Hu Lancheng 胡蘭成, "On Eileen Chang" 論張愛玲, published in 1944, reprinted in Hu Lancheng, *Writing in the Age of Turbulence* 亂世文談 (Hong Kong: Cosmos Books, 2007), 30.

20. Hu Lancheng, "Eileen Chang and the Leftists" 張愛玲與左派, published in 1945, reprinted in *Writing in the Age of Turbulence,* 36.

21. Eileen Chang, *The Rice-Sprout Song,* first published in 1955, reprinted in *The Rice-Sprout Song: A Novel of Modern China* (Berkeley: University of California Press, 1998).

22. Eileen Chang, *Naked Earth* (Hong Kong: Union Press, 1956).

23. Translated in Eileen Chang, "Lust, Caution," trans. Julia Lovell, in *Lust, Caution and Other Stories* (London: Penguin, 2007), 1–37.

24. Cai Dengshan 蔡登山, *Eileen Chang: "Lust, Caution"* 張愛玲：色戒 (Beijing: Zuojia chubanshe, 2007).

25. For example, Leo Ou-fan Lee 李歐梵, *Looking at Lust, Caution: Literature, Cinema, History* 睇色，戒：文學 · 電影 · 歷史 (Oxford: Oxford University Press, 2008).

26. Lee Haiyan, "Enemy under My Skin: Eileen Chang's *Lust, Caution* and the Politics of Transcendence," *PMLA* 125, 3 (2010): 640–56.

27. For selected correspondence between Chang and relevant people such as Stephen Soong about the publication of the novel, see Song Yilang 宋以朗 (Roland Soong), Preface to Eileen Chang's *Little Reunion* 小團圓 (Hong Kong: Huangguan, 2009), 1–17.

28. For a very interesting discussion of the implications of the publication of the novel on Eileen Chang's relationship with her readership in Taiwan and Hu Lancheng's impact there, see Peter Lee, "Eileen Chang's Fractured Legacy," Online AsiaTimes, April 29, 2009. http://www.atimes.com/atimes/China/KD29Ad01.html.

29. C. T. Hsia, "Preface," in Sima Xin 司馬新, *Eileen Chang in America* 張愛玲在美國 (Shanghai: Shanghai wenyi chubanshe, 1996), 14.

Chapter 1

1. Lu Xun 魯迅, "My Views on Chastity," 我之節烈觀 in *Silent China: Selected Writings of Lu Xun,* ed. and trans. Gladys Yang (Oxford: Oxford University Press, 1973), 143.

2.　Zhang Junli 張鈞莉, "The Masculine World in Eileen Chang's Fiction" 張愛玲 小說中的男性世界, in *Eileen Chang's Fictional World* 張愛玲的小說世界, ed. Zhang Jian 張健 (Taipei: Taiwan xuesheng shuju, 1984), 55.

3.　Kam Louie, *Theorising Chinese Masculinity: Society and Gender in China* (Cambridge: Cambridge University Press, 2002), 100–11.

4.　Eileen Chang, "Writing of One's Own" 自己的文章, in *Written on Water* 流言, trans. Andrew F. Jones, co-ed. with an introduction by Nicole Huang (New York: Columbia University Press, 2005), 18.

5.　Eileen Chang, "Red Rose, White Rose," in *Love in a Fallen City*, trans. Karen Kingsbury (New York: New York Review Books, 2007), 255.

6.　Chang, "Love in a Fallen City," in *Love in a Fallen City*, 130.

7.　Louie, *Theorising Chinese Masculinity*.

8.　Xun Yu 迅雨 (Fu Lei's pen name), "On Eileen Chang's Short Stories" 論張愛玲 的小說, first published in 1944, appendixed in Tang Wenbiao 唐文標, *On Eileen Chang* 張愛玲研究 (Taipei: Lianjing chuban shiyegongsi, 1976), 113–35.

9.　Yu Guanying 余冠英, trans. and annotator, *Selections from The Book of Songs* 詩經 選 (Beijing: Renminwenxue chubanshe, 1982), 22–23.

10.　Eileen Chang, "Love in a Fallen City" 傾城之戀, in *Complete Works of Eileen Chang,* Volume 5 張愛玲全集‧五 (Hong Kong: Huangguan chubanshe, 2007), 216.

11.　Eileen Chang, "Writing of One's Own," in *Complete Essays of Eileen Chang* 張愛玲 散文全集 (Zhengzhou: Zhongyuan nongmin chubanshe, 1996), 314.

12.　Chang, "Love in a Fallen City", 148.

13.　Ibid.

14.　Leo Ou-fan Lee, "Eileen Chang: Romances of a Fallen City," in Lee, *Shanghai Modern: The Flowering of a New Urban Culture in China, 1930–1945* (Cambridge: Harvard University Press, 1999), 299.

15.　Yu, *Selections from the Book of Songs,* 28.

16.　Bob Hodge and Kam Louie, *The Politics of Chinese Language and Culture* (London: Routledge, 1998), 103.

17.　Chang, "From the Ashes" 燼餘錄, in *Written on Water,* 45.

18.　Chang, "Love in a Fallen City," 149.

19.　Luo Xiaoyun 羅小雲, Appendix 2: Examining Eileen Chang's Attitudes to Life in "Love in a Fallen City" 附錄2：從〈傾城之戀〉看張愛玲對人生的觀照, in *Collected Critical Essays on Eileen Chang's Short Stories* 張愛玲短篇小說論集, ed. Chen Bingliang 陳炳良 (Taipei: Yuanjing chubanshe shiye gongshi, 1983), 154.

20.　Luo, Appendix 2, 155.

21.　Lee, "Eileen Chang: Romances of a Fallen City," 292–93.

22.　Chang, "Red Rose, White Rose," 255.

23.　Chang, "Red Rose, White Rose," 256.

24.　Rey Chow, "Seminal Dispersal, Fecal Retention, and Related Narrative Matters: Eileen Chang's Tale of Roses in the Problematic of Modern Writing," *Differences: A Journal of Feminist Cultural Studies* 11, 2 (1999): 163.

25. See Chen Bingliang 陳炳良, "The Narcissus and the Rose—on Red Rose, White Rose 水仙與玫瑰——論〈紅玫瑰與白玫瑰〉中的佟振保, in *Collected Critical Essays on Eileen Chang's Short Stories* 張愛玲短篇小説論集, 73–85, for further discussion on this distinction.

26. Chang, "Red Rose, White Rose," 256.

27. Chang, "Red Rose, White Rose," 259.

28. Chang, "Red Rose, White Rose," 262.

29. Chang, "Red Rose, White Rose," 262.

30. Ibid., 312.

31. Eileen Chang, "Frank Comments on 'Love in a Fallen City'" 關於〈傾城之戀〉的老實話, in *Information on Eileen Chang Old and New* 舊聞新知張愛玲, ed. Xiao Jin 肖進 (Shanghai: Huadong shifan daxue chubanshe, 2009), 42.

Chapter 2

1. In the film adaptation, the conflicts in the Shanghai household are not depicted in very much detail, but the battle against the Japanese in Hong Kong with the help of British soldiers is recounted at length. The film was released in 1984, after the signing of the agreement between the People's Republic of China and Britain confirming that the sovereignty over Hong Kong would return to China in 1997. Ann Hui declared that the film was dedicated to the nostalgic history of Hong Kong, and sought to reproduce Hong Kong's past before it vanished.

2. Linda Hutcheon, *A Theory of Adaptation* (New York and London: Routledge, 2006), 177.

3. Hutcheon, *A Theory of Adaptation*, 177.

4. Eileen Chang, "Reflections on 'Love in a Fallen City'" 回顧傾城之戀, in *Complete Works of Eileen Chang,* Volume 18 張愛玲全集・十八 (Hong Kong: Huangguan wenxue chubanshe, 2005), 16. Eileen Chang, "Shanghainese, After All" 到底是上海人, in *Written on Water* 流言, trans. Andrew F. Jones, co-ed. with an introduction by Nicole Huang (New York: Columbia University Press), 16.

5. Eileen Chang, *Little Reunion* 小團圓 (Hong Kong: Huangguan chubanshe, 2009), 45.

6. Eileen Chang, "Frank Comments on 'Love in a Fallen City'" 關於《傾城之戀》的老實話, in *Mutual Reflections: Looking at My Old Photo Album* 對照記：看老照相簿 in *Complete Works of Eileen Chang,* Volume 15 張愛玲全集・十五 (Hong Kong: Huangguang chubanshe, 2000), 103.

7. Eileen Chang, "Love in a Fallen City," in *Dragonflies—Fiction by Chinese Women in the Twentieth Century,* trans. and ed. Shu-ning Sciban and Fred Edwards (Ithaca, New York: East Asia Program, Cornell University, 2003), 39.

8. George Bluestone, "The Limits of the Novel and the Limits of Film," in *Novels into Film* (Berkeley: University of California Press, 1957), 47.

9. Fredric Mao 毛俊輝 and Leo Ou-fan Lee 李歐梵, "Sophistication Made in Hong Kong—Dialogue between Lee Ou-fan and Mao Junhui" 香港製造的上海世

故──李歐梵與毛俊輝對談, *(New) Love in a Fallen City* (program) (Hong Kong: Hong Kong Repertory Theatre, 2006), 21.

10. Hoyan Hangfeng 何杏楓 has analyzed in detail the singing and dancing elements in her essay, "Tonight What Songs Are You Singing?—On Hong Kong Repertory Theatre's *(New) Love in a Fallen City*"「今夜你們唱甚麼歌」──論香港話劇團的《(新)傾城之戀》, in *Hong Kong Drama Journal* 香港戲劇學刊, no. 4 (2006): 252.

11. Eileen Chang, "Love in a Fallen City," trans. Karen Kingsbury, *Renditions* 45 (Spring 1996): 82.

12. Chang, "Frank Comments on 'Love in a Fallen City,'" 103.

13. Chang, "Love in a Fallen City," 58.

14. Before the production opened, several popular Toronto newspapers reported that Leung had greeted 500 fans in Market Village, a Chinese Canadian shopping mall in Toronto. For example, the *Toronto Sun* published a close-up of Leung's face with many fans taking photographs of him, under the heading, "Fans Love Chinese Idol—Big Welcome for Top Actor" (April 27, 2006); *Metro* displayed a close-up of Leung's smiling face as he shook someone's hand under the title, "Fans Fall for Tony" (April 27, 2006); and *Ming Pao* used the caption, "The King of Movies Arrives in Toronto" (April 26, 2006). Similarly, *Singtao Weekly* printed the heading, "Newly Born Movie King Arrives in Honor" (April 29, 2006).

15. For example, *Singtao Daily News* published the news that "Leung Kar-fai arrived to celebrate 'Hong Kong Culture & Heritage Day'" (April 27, 2006), which is a celebration proclaimed by the Toronto City Council and held on April 26. To further promote *NLFC* in Toronto, Leung donated a pair of "Bruno Magli—Love" shoes he wore in the French film *L'Amant* (*The Lover*, dir. Jean-Jacques Annaud, 1992) to Mrs. Sonja Bata, the Founding Chair of the Bata Shoe Museum in Toronto. The Hong Kong Economic Trade Office released a report that "Tony Leung presents footwear for Museum's 'Walk of Fame'" (April 27, 2006), which was carried by newspapers such as *Singtao Daily News* (April 28, 2006), *Today Daily News* (April 28, 2006) and *Ming Pao* (April 30, 2006). Furthermore, the money generated by the show was donated to the Yee Hong Community Wellness Foundation. Newspapers carried photographs of Leung chatting and joking with seniors (*The Mirror*, April 28, 2006) and laughing with the president of the Foundation and a resident of the Yee Hong Centre (*Singtao Daily News*, April 28, 2006). The *Toronto Sun* also published a photograph of Leung receiving a kiss from a seventy-seven-year-old woman (April 28, 2006).

16. Hutcheon, *A Theory of Adaptation*, 126.

17. Rey Chow, "Against the Lures of Diaspora: Minority Discourse, Chinese Women, and Intellectual Hegemony," in *Gender and Sexuality in Twentieth-Century Chinese Literature and Society*, ed. Tonglin Lu (Albany: State University of New York Press, 1993), 41.

18. Sigmund Freud, "The Uncanny," in *The Norton Anthology of Theory and Criticism,* ed. Vincent B. Leitch (New York and London: W. W. Norton & Company, Inc., 2001), 934.

19. Chang, "Love in a Fallen City," 51.

20. Homi K. Bhabha, *The Location of Culture* (London and New York: Routledge, 1994), 13.

21. Bhabha, *The Location of Culture,* 54.

22. Bhabha, *The Location of Culture,* 2.

23. Eileen Chang, "Writing of One's Own," in *Written on Water,* 17.

24. Chang, "Writing of One's Own," 17.

25. Hutcheon, *A Theory of Adaptation,* 92.

26. Mao and Lee, "Sophistication Made in Hong Kong," 20.

27. Yanyan Guo 郭莛莛, "Hong Kong Repertory Theatre Artistic Director Fredric Mao—Untangled Fate of Drama in This Life" 香港話劇團藝術總監毛俊輝—— 這一世解不開的戲劇緣, *Toronto City Newspaper,* May 12, 2006, 32.

28. Ban, Gu 班固, "Biographies of the Empresses and Imperial affinities," no. 67a, 外戚傳‧第六十七上, in *History of the Former Han Dynasty,* Volume 97a 前漢書‧卷九十七上. http://www.xysa.net/a200/h350/02qianhanshu/t-097.htm.

29. Chang, "Love in a Fallen City," 70.

30. Julia Kristeva, "Woman Can Never Be Defined," trans. Marilyn A. August, in *New French Feminisms: An Anthology,* ed. Elaine Marks and Isabelle de Courtivron (New York: Schocken Books, 1981), 137.

31. Chang, "Love in a Fallen City," 70.

32. Chang, "Shanghainese, After All," 55.

33. The crew of the Hong Kong Repertory Theatre for the stage production *NLFC* consisted predominantly of Hong Kong people. Although Fredric Mao was born in Shanghai, he grew up in Hong Kong and most of his theatrical career unfolded in that city. The playwrights who worked on the production included Chan Koochung, who was born in Shanghai and grew up in Hong Kong, and Nick Yu, who was from Shanghai and was recruited to add a feeling of that city. The actors and actresses came mainly from Hong Kong or from Mainland China via Hong Kong.

Chapter 3

1. Hu Lancheng 胡蘭成, "A Woman of the Republican Era: On Eileen Chang" 民國女子：張愛玲記, in *This Life, These Times* 今生今世 (Taipei: Yuanjing, 1996), 167–200.

2. Ikegami Sadako 池上貞子 is the only scholar who has written on the subject. See Ikegami Sadako, "Eileen Chang and Japan" 張愛玲和日本, in *Reading Eileen Chang: Collected Essays from the "International Conference on Eileen Chang Research"* 閱讀張愛玲：張愛玲國際研討會論文集, ed. Yang Ze 楊澤 (Taipei: Maitian, 1999), 83–102.

3. See "A Gathering of Summer Cooling" 納涼會記, *The Miscellany Monthly* 雜誌月刊 15, 5 (August 1945): 67–72. The photo in question appears on page 71. The

image is also included in Chang's *Mutual Reflections: Looking at My Old Photo Album* 對照記：看老照相簿, the last work to be published before the author's death in 1995. In the captions that accompany the photo, the date is wrongly given as 1943. Perhaps even Chang herself could not fathom the fact that the photo was taken on the eve of Japan's defeat. See *Mutual Reflections: Looking at My Old Photo Album* (Taipei: Huangguan, 1994), 65–66.

4. See Yiman Wang, "Between the National and the Transnational: Li Xianglan/ Yamaguchi Yoshiko and Pan-Asianism," *IIA Newsletter* 38 (September 2005): 7. For a study of Li Xianglan's role in Japan's colonial film industry, see Shelley Stephenson, "'Her Traces Are Found Everywhere': Shanghai, Li Xianglan, and the 'Greater East Asian Film Sphere'," in *Cinema and Urban Culture in Shanghai, 1922–1943*, ed. Yingjin Zhang (Stanford: Stanford University Press, 1999), 222–45. See also Yamaguchi Yoshiko's own account in Li Xianglan, *The First Half of My life* 我的半生, trans. Jin Ruojing (Hong Kong: Baixing wenhua shiye, 1992), and Ri Ko-ran and Tanaka Hiroshi et al., "Looking Back on My Days as Ri Ko-ran," *Sekai* (September 2003): 171–75. Translated by Melissa Wender, the interview is located at http://www.zmag.org/znet/viewArticle/7000 (accessed August 13, 2009).

5. For an analysis of the film, see Poshek Fu, *Between Shanghai and Hong Kong: The Politics of Chinese Cinemas* (Stanford: Stanford University Press, 2003), 110–18. See also Zhiwei Xiao, "The Opium War in the Movies: History, Politics and Propaganda," *Asian Cinema 11*, 1 (Spring/Summer 2000): 68–83.

6. Paul Pickowicz, in his comments on an earlier version of this chapter, noted this peculiar phenomenon.

7. Chang, *Mutual Reflections: Looking at My Old Photo Album*, 65–66.

8. Chang, *Mutual Reflections: Looking at My Old Photo Album*, 65.

9. The legend goes that this was the dress that earned Chang her reputation as a public figure with a particular taste for "strange costumes" (奇裝異服). Zhang Zijing, Eileen Chang's younger brother, wrote about her dress sense. Pan Liudai, another woman writer of the time who was not particularly friendly with Chang, also wrote of Chang's penchant for setting fashion trends. See Zhang Zijing 張子靜, *My Sister Eileen Chang* 我的姊姊張愛玲 (Shanghai: Wenhui chubanshe, 2003).

10. The group photo is an index to important cultural figures in occupied Shanghai. Chen Binhe (1897–1945), considered an enigmatic figure in modern Chinese history, had many ties with the Leftist movement early in his career. He had been an editor at *Shenbao* 申報 since the early 1930s, and was known as a fierce critic of Chiang Kai-shek's Nationalist government. In 1936 he fled to Hong Kong, only to reappear in 1941 in Shanghai, where he was transformed into a promoter of pan-Asian projects and ideologies. When the war ended, he fled to Japan, dying a mysterious death in a mental institution in 1945. Jin Xiongbai (1904–85), a well-known figure in Shanghai's newspaper circle, became a key member of the Wang Jingwei government during the occupation. When the war ended, he was prosecuted, and was imprisoned for a period of time but released in 1948. He lived out the second

half of his life in Hong Kong and was the author of a series of memoirs about his newspaper career and the vicissitudes of the Wang Jingwei administration.

11. See "A Roundtable Discussion on Sai Shoki's Dance" 崔承喜舞蹈座談, *The Miscellany Monthly 12*, 2 (November 1943): 33–38. For a discussion of Choe's wartime activities, see Sang Mi Park, "The Making of a Cultural Icon for the Japanese Empire: Choe Seung-hui's U.S. Dance Tours and 'New Asian Culture' in the 1930s and 1940s," *positions: east asia culture critique 14*, 3 (2006): 597–632. See also Wen-hsun Chang, "Choi Seung-Hee and Taiwan: 'The Joseon Boom' in Taiwan of the Pre-war Period," *Platform Anthology: Asia Culture Review* (September 2009): 28–32, and a short documentary on Choe titled *Choi Seunghee: The Korean Dancer*, produced and directed by Won Jong-sun (West Long Branch, NJ: Kultur, 1998).

12. For a study of Chang's essay writing, see Nicole Huang, *Women, War, Domesticity: Shanghai Literature and Popular Culture of the 1940s* (Leiden: Brill, 2005), 122–58. For a Chinese version of the relevant section, see *Writing against the Turmoil: Eileen Chang and Popular Culture of Occupied Shanghai* 亂世書寫：張愛玲與淪陷時期上海文學及通俗文化, trans. Hu Jing (Shanghai: Shanghai Sanlian Press, 2010), 149–92.

13. Original text in "Written on Water" 流言, 1945, 7–8. The paragraph here is translated by Andrew F. Jones, in *Written on Water*, co-ed. with an introduction by Nicole Huang (New York: Columbia University Press), 7–8.

14. See examples in Jacqueline Atkins, ed., *Wearing Propaganda: 1931–1945: Textiles on the Home Front in Japan, Britain, and the United States* (New Haven: Yale University Press, 2005).

15. My gratitude to Wen-hsun Chang, who shared her readings of these two portraits with me.

16. See *Written on Water*, 53–54.

17. See David Schimmelpenninck van der Oye, "The Genesis of Russian Sinology," *Kritika: Explorations in Russian and Eurasian History 1*, 2 (Spring 2000): 355–64. See also Schimmelpenninck van der Oye's new book entitled *Russian Orientalism: Asia in the Russian Mind from Peter the Great to the Emigration* (New Haven: Yale University Press, 2010), in which he again traces Russian interest in the Orient to well before the Revolution of 1917. The long history of the Institute of Oriental Manuscripts in St. Petersburg, which can be traced to Peter the Great in the 1700s, testifies to the genesis of Russian studies of Asia. By the 1860s, the acquisition of various Asian languages had become of paramount importance to the Russian Empire. See http://www.orientalstudies.ru/eng/ (accessed February 19, 2010). My gratitude to Louise Young and David MacDonald for suggesting these sources.

18. See *Written on Water*, 30. Eileen Chang's knowledge of the Japanese language seems to have stayed with her in the later stages of her life. In Qiu Yanming's 1987 interview with Wang Chen-ho 王禎和, Wang reminisces about the time when Chang visited Taiwan in the fall of 1961 and briefly stayed at Wang's parents' home in Hualian. Wang mentions that Eileen Chang could speak Japanese, and that her conversations with Wang's mother were often conducted in Japanese. See Qiu

Yanming 丘彥明, "Eileen Chang in Taiwan" 張愛玲在台灣, in *The World of Eileen Chang* 張愛玲的世界, ed. William Tay 鄭樹森 (Taipei: Yunchen, 1989), 21.

19. See *Written on Water*, 141. Chang's essay was originally published in *Miscellany Monthly* in August 1944.

20. My translation.

21. See *Sankashū zenchūkai* (*The Complete and Annotated Poems of a Mountain Home*, 山家集全註解) (Tokyo: Kazama shobō 風間書房, 1971), 142. I am grateful to Charo D'Etcheverry who located the original poem for me.

22. Zhou's original Chinese translation is: "夏天的夜，有如苦竹，竹細節密，不久之間，隨即天明"; rendered in English, it is almost identical to the revised text by Shen Qiwu. See Zhi An 止庵, "On the 'Bitter Bamboo' Poem" 苦竹詩話, *Southern Weekly* 南方週末, April 3, 2008.

23. *Written on Water*, 143. My translation.

24. See Shen Qiwu 沈啟無, "Random Notes from My Southbound Journey" 南來隨筆, *Bitter Bamboo 2* (November 1944): 11–12. My translation.

25. See *Written on Water*, 165–56.

26. See Ikegami Sadako, "Eileen Chang and Japan," in *Reading Eileen Chang*, 86.

27. See *Written on Water*, 186.

28. See *Written on Water*, 185.

29. Tōhō's touring schedule is cited in Ikegami Sadako, "Eileen Chang and Japan," *Reading Eileen Chang*, 89–92.

30. Source cited in Yau Shuk-ting 邱淑婷, *The Filmic Relations between Hong Kong and Japan: In Search of the Origin of the Pan-Asian Film Sphere* 港日電影關係：尋找亞洲電影網絡之源 (Hong Kong: Tiandi tushu, 2006), 54. An English edition of Yau's book was published as *Japanese and Hong Kong Industries: Understanding the Origins of East Asian Film Networks* (New York: Routledge, 2009).

31. The most recent remake of the Tanuki Goten story was directed by Suzuki Seijun 鈴木清順 in 2005, and was also a musical, starring Zhang Ziyi as Princess Racoon.

32. See "On Dance," in *Written on Water*, 189.

33. For a discussion of wartime transnational Japanese film culture in general, see Michael Baskett, *The Attractive Empire: Transnational Film Culture in Imperial Japan* (Honolulu, HI: University of Hawaii Press, 2008).

34. A list of Japanese films shown in Shanghai can be found in Yau Shuk-ting, *The Filmic Relations between Hong Kong and Japan: In Search of the Origin of the Pan-Asian Film Sphere*, 191–99.

35. See Yiman Wang, "Screening Asia: Passing, Performative Translation, and Reconfiguration," *positions: east asia cultures critique 15*, 2 (2007): 319–43.

36. See C. T. Hsia 夏志清, "Letters from Eileen Chang to Me" 張愛玲給我的信件, *Unitas* 聯合文學 150 (April 1997): 155–58. My translation.

37. See Su Weizhen 蘇偉貞, ed., *The World of Eileen Chang, Sequel* 張愛玲的世界，續編 (Taipei: Yunchen, 2003), 185–86. My translation.

38. "A Return to the Frontier," *The Reporter* (March 1963): 38–39.

39. See *Crown Magazine* 皇冠雜誌 650 (April 2008): 70–91. My translation.

40. My translation. The essay was first published in *Heaven and Earth Monthly* 天地雜誌 18 (March 1945); reprinted in *Lingering Melodies* 餘韻 (Taipei: Huangguan, 1987), 49–63. The title implies a clever pun. The phrase *shuangsheng* 雙聲, meaning two or more characters with the same initial consonant, is often used in conjunction with *dieyun* 疊韻, meaning two or more characters with the same vowel formation. It is a linguistic terminology that suggests the basic rhyming principles in the Chinese language, but can also imply a sense of harmony. For a discussion of the roundtable talk as an important cultural genre in Shanghai of the 1940s, see Nicole Huang, *Women, War, Domesticity: Shanghai Literature and Popular Culture of the 1940s,* 75–76.

41. *Lingering Melodies,* 58–59. My translation.

Chapter 4

1. See Huang Ziping 黃子平, "'Changing Clothes' and 'Mutual Reflections': Images of Clothes and Ornaments in Eileen Chang's Writings" 更衣對照亦惘然——張愛玲作品中的衣飾, in *Re-reading Eileen Chang* 再讀張愛玲, ed. Liu Shaoming 劉紹銘, Leung Ping-kwan 梁秉鈞, and Xu Zidong 許子東 (Hong Kong: Oxford University Press, 2002), 132–39; and Rey Chow, "Modernity and Narration—in Feminine Detail," in *Woman and Chinese Modernity: The Politics of Reading between West and East* (Minneapolis: University of Minnesota Press, 1991), 84–120.

2. See Chang Hsiao-hung 張小虹, "Fetish and Eileen Chang: Sex, Commodity and Colonial Charm" 戀物張愛玲：性、商品與殖民迷魅, in *Reading Eileen Chang: Collected Essays from the "International Conference on Eileen Chang Research"* 閱讀張愛玲：張愛玲國際研討會論文集, ed. Yang Ze 楊澤 (Taipei: Maitian, 1999), 177–210; and Li Xiaohong 李曉紅, *Eileen Chang: In the Face of Tradition* 面對傳統的張愛玲 (Kunming: Yunnan People's Publishing House, 2007).

3. See Nicole Huang, *Women, War, Domesticity: Shanghai Literature and Popular Culture of the 1940s* (Leiden: Brill, 2005).

4. Huang, *Women, War, Domesticity,* xxiv.

5. See Leo Ou-fan Lee 李歐梵, "Eileen Chang: Romances of a Fallen City," in *Shanghai Modern: The Flowering of a New Urban Culture in China, 1930–1945* (Cambridge: Harvard University Press, 1999), 267–303; and "Historical Associations 2" 歷史的聯想 (二), in *Reading Lust, Caution: Literature, Film, and History* 睇色，戒：文學、電影、歷史 (Hong Kong: Oxford University Press, 2008), 87–96.

6. See Harry D. Harootunian, *History's Disquiet: Modernity, Cultural Practice, and the Question of Everyday Life* (New York: Columbia University Press, 2000), 5.

7. Walter Benjamin, *Reflections: Essays, Aphorisms, Autobiographical Writings,* ed. Peter Demetz, trans. Edmund Jephcott (New York: Schocken Books, 1978), 182.

8. Quotation from Walter Benjamin, cited in Richard Wolin, *Walter Benjamin, An Aesthetic of Redemption* (Berkeley: University of California Press, 1994), 130.

9. Huang, *Women, War, Domesticity,* 51.

10. Huang, *Women, War, Domesticity,* 128.

11. See Lim Chin Chown 林幸謙, *Eileen Chang's Discourse: Writing of Female Subjectivity and Castration* 張愛玲論述：女性主體與去勢模擬書寫 (Taipei: Hungyeh Publishing, 2000), in which he argues that Chang's fiction reveals a dual consciousness. While Chang reveals how women in her time are subordinated to tradition and patriarchy, she insists on a subversive attitude toward oppression.

12. Paul de Man, "Literary History and Literary Modernity," in *Blindness and Insight: Essays in the Rhetoric of Contemporary Criticism* (Minneapolis: University of Minnesota Press, 1983), 157.

13. Charles Baudelaire, *The Painter of Modern Life and Other Essays,* ed. and trans. Jonathan Mayne (London: Phaidon Press, 1964), 13.

14. The translation is taken from Eileen Chang, "Writing of One's Own," in *Written on Water* 流言, trans. Andrew F. Jones, co-ed. with an introduction by Nicole Huang (New York: Columbia University Press, 2005), 17.

15. *Romances* 傳奇增訂本 (Shanghai: Shanhe tushu, 1946) was published two years after the first edition. The enlarged edition contained five new fictional works and an epilogue "Days and Nights of China" by Chang. In the preface, Chang revealed that "Days and Nights of China" was developed from a poem of the same title that she had written earlier.

16. Walter Benjamin, "Theses on the Philosophy of History," in *Illuminations,* ed. Hannah Arendt, trans. Harry Zohn (New York: Schocken Books, 1969), 258.

17. C. T. Hsia, *A History of Modern Chinese Fiction, 1917–1957* (New Haven: Yale University Press, 1971), 389.

18. Hsia, *A History of Modern Chinese Fiction,* 398.

19. Hsia, *A History of Modern Chinese Fiction,* 396.

20. Hsia, *A History of Modern Chinese Fiction,* 414.

21. In Wang Guowei's critical essay "On the *Dream of the Red Chamber*" (紅樓夢評論, 1904), he proposes two ways of classifying Chinese literature. *Peach Blossom Fan* deals with history, politics, and the nation while *Dream of the Red Chamber* tends toward the universal and the philosophical. See "On the *Dream of the Red Chamber,*" in *Wang Guowei's Three Literary Treatises* 王國維文學論著三種 (Beijing: The Commercial Press Library, 2001): 1–24.

22. See Liu Zaifu, "Eileen Chang's Fiction and C. T. Hsia's *A History of Modern Chinese Literature,*" trans. Yunzhong Shu, MCLC Resource Center, July 2009. http://mclc.osu.edu/rc/pubs/liuzaifu.htm (accessed February 19, 2010). The original Chinese essay was first published in *Re-reading Eileen Chang.*

23. Liu, "Eileen Chang's Fiction and C. T. Hsia's *A History of Modern Chinese Literature.*"

24. Chang, "Writing of One's Own," in *Written on Water,* 17–18.

25. Chang, "From the Ashes," in *Written on Water,* 52.

26. Chang, "Writing of One's Own," 17.

27. Chow, *Woman and Chinese Modernity,* 85.

28. Liu, "Eileen Chang's Fiction and C. T. Hsia's *A History of Modern Chinese Literature.*"

29. Liu, "Eileen Chang's Fiction and C. T. Hsia's *A History of Modern Chinese Literature.*"

30. See Rey Chow's *Woman and Chinese Modernity;* and Hu Lancheng 胡蘭成, "On Eileen Chang" 論張愛玲 (1944) and "Eileen Chang and the Leftist" 張愛玲與左派 (1945), in *Writing in the Age of Turbulence* 亂世文談 (Hong Kong: Cosmos Books, 2007), 12–30 and 31–37.

31. See Henri Lefebvre, *Critique of Everyday Life,* trans. John Moore (London: Verso, 1991–2005).

32. Rob Shields, *Lefebvre, Love and Struggle: Spatial Dialectics* (London and New York: Routledge, 1999), 65.

33. Harootunian, *History's Disquiet,* 55.

34. See Benjamin, "Theses on the Philosophy of History," 261–63.

35. Peter Osborne, *The Politics of Time: Modernity and Avant-garde* (London: Verso, 1995), 196.

36. Chang, "Epilogue: Days and Nights of China," in *Written on Water,* 214.

37. See Georg Simmel, "The Metropolis and Mental Life," in *The Blackwell City Reader,* ed. Gary Bridge and Sophie Watson (Malden, MA: Blackwell Publishers, 2002), 11–19.

38. Chang, "On the Second Edition of *Romances,*" in *Written on Water,* 199.

39. Chang, "On the Second Edition of *Romances,*" 199.

40. See Lee, "Eileen Chang: Romances of a Fallen City" for his discussion of decadence in Chang's fiction.

41. Chang, "On the Second Edition of *Romances,*" 199.

42. Richard Lehan, *The City in Literature* (Berkeley and Los Angeles: University of California Press, 1998), 73.

43. Osborne, *The Politics of Time,* 189.

44. See Sapajou with R. T. Peyton-Griffin, *Shanghai's Shemozzle* (Hong Kong: China Economic Review Publishing, 2007). The publication collates the cartoons crafted by Russian army-lieutenant-turned-cartoonist Georgii Avksent'ievich Sapojnikoff, who also went under the artistic alias of Sapajou. Sapojnikoff became a refugee in Shanghai in 1920, and for fifteen years, beginning in 1925 and through the Japanese occupation, published daily cartoons in the *North-China Daily News,* the most influential English language newspaper of the time.

45. Chang, "Epilogue: Days and Nights of China," 215.

46. Franz Kafka, *The Diaries of Franz Kafka, 1910–23,* ed. Max Brod, trans. Joseph Kresh and Martin Greenberg (Harmondsworth: Penguin Books, 1964), 301.

47. Chang, "Writing of One's Own," 16.

48. Chang, "Writing of One's Own," 17.

49. Chang, "Writing of One's Own," 18

50. Chang, "Epilogue: Days and Nights of China," 214.

51. This translation is taken from Eileen Chang, "Preface to the Second Printing of *Romances,*" trans. Karen S. Kingsbury and Chang, *Love in a Fallen City and Other Stories* (London: Penguin, 2007), 2.

52. Chang, "Steamed Osmanthus Flower: Ah Xiao's Unhappy Autumn," trans. Simon Patton, ed. Eva Hung, *Traces of Love and Other Stories* (Hong Kong: Research Center for Translation, CUHK, 2009), 60.
53. Tao Fangxuan 陶方宣, *Colorful Clothing of Eileen Chang* 霓裳──張愛玲 (Hong Kong: Joint Publishing, 2009).
54. Eileen Chang, *Mutual Reflections: Looking at My Old Photo Album* 對照記：看老照相簿 (Hong Kong: Huangguan, 1994).
55. Chang, "Epilogue: Days and Nights of China," 218.
56. Chang, "Chinese Life and Fashions," *Unitas* 聯合文學 5 (1987): 71. The essay was originally in English and published in *The XXth Century* 4 (January 1943): 54–61. Chang later expanded it into a Chinese essay entitled "A Chronicle of Changing Clothes" (更衣記, 1944).
57. See Chang, "Yanying's Catalogue of Clothes" 炎櫻衣譜, *Ming Pao Daily News* (December 25, 2009): D06. The essay was originally published in April 1945 in *Li Bao*, a Shanghai tabloid.
58. See http://online.sfsu.edu/~wenchao/translation/nora.pdf for Li Wenchao's new translation of Lu Xun's "After Nora Walks Out, What Then?" (accessed February 19, 2010).
59. Chow, *Woman and Chinese Modernity*, 85.

Chapter 5

1. Based on the files of the poet Nie Gannu, which have recently been opened to the public, writer Yu Zhen wrote a long article on the persecution of Nie before and during the Cultural Revolution. The article contains many detailed descriptions of the spying activities carried out by Nie's friend, artist Huang Miaozi, whose reports to the authorities caused Nie to be sentenced as "an anti-revolutionary element." This article was published in the lesser-known journal *The Chinese Writer* 中國作家 in February 2009. On March 18, 2009, the popular essayist Zhang Yihe's article "Who Sent Nie Gannu to Jail?" appeared in *Southern Weekly* 南方週末. She later wrote several other articles that revealed that the translator Feng Yidai had been sent by the authorities to spy on her father Zhang Bojun. All of these articles were widely circulated on the Internet after their publication, prompting many discussions and debates in the public sphere.
2. The Taiwan and Hong Kong editions of *Little Reunion* 小團圓 were published in February 2009. The mainland Chinese edition of the novel did not come out until April 2009, but many people had read sections of the novel on the Internet by the time the mainland version was published.
3. For mainland criticism of Ang Lee's film and Chang's short story, see the website "Utopia" (http://www.wyzxsx.com/), which organized a discussion forum on both texts. Many articles included in this forum had previously been published in the print media. See Huang Jisu's articles, "'Lust, Caution' and Eileen Chang," "'Lust, Caution' and Ang Lee," and "China Has Stood Up, but People Like Ang Lee Are

Still Kneeling Down," all of which can be found on "Utopia" as well as many other websites.

4. Conventional interpretations of Eileen Chang's works portray her as an aesthetic writer not concerned with major political issues. One can trace the origin of this line of criticism to C. T. Hsia's *A History of Modern Chinese Fiction* (1961), which was the first academic endeavor to seriously consider Chang's work in the context of modern Chinese literary history.

5. See my manuscript "Betrayal and Historical Representation in Zhang Ailing's 'Little Reunion,'" under review by MCLC.

6. Crystal Parikh, *An Ethics of Betrayal: The Politics of Otherness in Emergent U.S. Literatures and Culture* (New York: Fordham University Press, 2009), 10.

7. Parikh, *An Ethics of Betrayal*, 10.

8. See Shuang Shen, Introduction, *Cosmopolitan Publics: Anglophone Print Culture in Semi-Colonial Shanghai* (New Brunswick: Rutgers University Press, 2009).

9. For a discussion of May Fourth cosmopolitanism, see Chapters 2 and 3 of Shu-mei Shih's book *The Lure of the Modern: Writing Modernism in Semi-Colonial China, 1917–1937* (Berkeley: University of California Press, 2001). Here I am using "May Fourth tradition" to refer to the literary production in the post-May Fourth period that consciously followed the legacy of the May Fourth and New Culture movements.

10. See Rey Chow's *Woman and Chinese Modernity: The Politics of Reading between East and West* (Minneapolis: University of Minnesota Press, 1991) for a discussion of the Mandarin Ducks and Butterflies School and its relationship to May Fourth discourse.

11. For a critique of some current discourses of Chinese cosmopolitanism from a diasporic perspective, see Ien Ang, *On Not Speaking Chinese* (London: Routledge, 2001).

12. Quoted by Martin K. Doudna in *Concerned about the Planet: The Reporter Magazine and American Liberalism, 1949–1968* (Westport, CT: Greenwood Press, 1977), 94.

13. Parikh, *An Ethics of Betrayal*, 12.

14. In *Asia/Pacific as Space of Cultural Production*, Rob Wilson and Arif Dirlik have tried to rethink the space "Asia Pacific" as not just "formulated by market planners and military strategists" but a "space of cultural production" (Durham: Duke University Press, 1995, 6). Yunte Huang uses the term "transpacific" as a place of "history, literature, counterpoetics," as indicated in the title of his book *Transpacific Imaginations: History, Literature and Counterpoetics* (Cambridge, Mass.: Harvard University Press, 2008).

15. Parikh, *An Ethics of Betrayal*, 32.

16. For a definition of "Sinophone," see Shu-mei Shi's discussion in *Visuality and Identity: Sinophone Articulations Across the Pacific* (Berkeley: University of California Press, 2007), 23–39.

17. Yunte Huang argues in his book *Transpacific Imaginations: History, Literature, Counterpoetics* that the trans-Pacific has to be narrated from the perspectives of "both shores." In fact, the "trans-Pacific" has more than two shores. The strategic role played by an urban locale such as Hong Kong—a city of refugees and diasporic peoples of various kinds—in the Cold War imagination complicates the portrayal of the trans-Pacific as just consisting of the United States and China.

18. In her analysis of Chang's translation of her own story "Stale Mates" (1956) into the Chinese "Wusi yishi" 五四遺事 (1957), Jessica Tsui Yan Li finds that Chang's translation manages to "represent" the source text without "reproducing" it faithfully, and that there is a relationship of interdependence between the source text and the translated text, the author and the translator. "This interdependent relationship breaks through the boundaries between the source texts and translations as well as between author and translator. The two works cannot substitute one another; this renders the significance of the two texts as a whole greater than that of the texts seen in isolation," according to Jessica Tsui Yan Li in "Politics of Self-Translation: Eileen Chang," *Perspectives: Studies in Translation 14*, 2 (2006): 101. Li's reading emphasizes the "whole" that is "greater" than the text in each language, which sounds a lot like Benjamin's notion of the "suprahistorical kinship" among languages and his understanding of translation and the original as "fragments." However, not only is the unalienated "whole" an idealistic notion, but in Chang's case, what is the original is already open to question.

19. Tina Chen, *Double Agency: Acts of Impersonation in Asian American Literature and Culture* (Stanford: Stanford University Press, 2005), 14.

20. Judith Butler, "Betrayal's Felicity," *Diacritics 34*, 1 (2004): 82.

21. Klaus Mehnert, "Shoulder Straps—And Then?" *The XXth Century*. 6, 2 (February 1944): 81.

22. Eileen Chang, "Chinese Life and Fashions," *The XXth Century* (January 1943): 54.

23. Eileen Chang, "A Chronicle of Changing Clothes" 更衣記, in *Written on Water* 流言, trans. Andrew F. Jones, co-ed. with an introduction by Nicole Huang (New York: Columbia University Press, 2005), 65.

24. Eileen Chang, "Peking Opera through Foreign Eyes," in *Written on Water,* 105.

25. Chang, "Peking Opera through Foreign Eyes," 111.

26. This manuscript was published in the March 2008 issue of *Muse* (Hong Kong), 64–72.

27. John G. Cawelti and Bruce A. Rosenberg, *The Spy Story* (Chicago: The University of Chicago Press, 1987), 20.

28. Cawelti and Rosenberg, *The Spy Story*, 21.

29. Chang, "The Spyring," 67.

30. Chang, "The Spyring," 67.

31. Chang, "The Spyring," 72.

32. Cawelti and Rosenberg, *The Spy Story,* 55.

33. Walter Benjamin, *The Arcades Project,* trans. Howard Eiland and Kevin McLaughlin (Cambridge: The Belknap Press of the Harvard Press, 2003), 420.

34. Chen, *Double Agency*. See Chapter 6 for a discussion of Chang-rae Lee's *Native Speaker*.
35. Chang, "The Spyring," 70.
36. Chang, "The Spyring," 70.
37. Chang, "The Spyring," 70.
38. Chen, *Double Agency*, 15.
39. Chen, *Double Agency*, 15.
40. Doudna, *Concerned about the Planet*, 127.
41. Eileen Chang, *A Return to the Frontier* 重返邊城 (Taipei: Huangguan chubanshe, 2008), 63.
42. Chang, *A Return to the Frontier*, 64.
43. Chang, *A Return to the Frontier*, 64.
44. Chang, *A Return to the Frontier*, 66.
45. Chang, *A Return to the Frontier*, 74.
46. Chang, *A Return to the Frontier*, 74.
47. Sidonie Smith and Julia Watson, *Reading Autobiography* (Minneapolis: University of Minnesota Press, 2001), 150.

Chapter 6

1. For a reading that focuses on Chang's special destruction of political orthodoxy in these two anti-Communist novels, see David Der-wei Wang, "Three Hungry Women," in *The Monster That Is History: History, Violence, and Fictional Writing in Twentieth-Century China* (Berkeley, Los Angeles, and London: University of California Press, 2004), 117–47; and his preface to the reprint of Eileen Chang's *The Rice-Sprout Song* (Berkeley, Los Angeles, and London: University of California Press, 1998), xii–xxv.
2. Kenny K. K. Ng, "Romantic Comedies of Cathay-MP&GI in the 1950s and 60s: Language, Locality, and Urban Character," *Jump Cut: A Review of Contemporary Media 49* (Spring 2007, www.ejumpcut.org/archive/jc49.2007/text.html).
3. Stephen Soong later became Eileen Chang's lifetime friend. It was actually with Soong's support that she was able to obtain the opportunity to write screenplays for MP&GI during the 1950s and 60s, and screenwriting became her main source of income. For further discussion on the MP&GI screen committee, see Poshek Fu, "Modernity, Diasporic Capital, and 1950's Hong Kong Mandarin Cinema," *Jump Cut: A Review of Contemporary Media 49* (Spring 2007, www.ejumpcut.org/archive/jc49.2007/text.html); Law Kar, "A Glimpse of MP&GI's Creative/Production Situation: Some Speculations and Doubts," and Shu Kei, "Notes on MP&GI" in *The Cathay Story*, ed. Wong Ain-ling (Hong Kong: Hong Kong Film Archive, 2002), 58–65; 66–81.
4. For a study of Eileen Chang's film scripts, see Leo Ou-fan Lee, "Eileen Chang: Romances in a Fallen City," in *Shanghai Modern: The Flowering of a New Urban Culture in China, 1930–1945* (Cambridge, MA: Harvard University Press, 1999),

276–80; William Tay 鄭樹森, "Eileen Chang and Two Film Genres," 張愛玲與兩個片種 in *INK* (印刻文學生活誌) 2, 1 (September 2005), 154–55.

5.   Eileen Chang, "Preface," in *Nightmare in the Red Chamber* 紅樓夢魘 (Taipei: Huangguan, 1976), 10.

6.   Wang Kai 王愷, "The Birth of the Yue Opera *Dream of the Red Chamber*," 越劇《紅樓夢》的誕生 in *Sanlian Weekly* 三聯週刊 (July 9, 2009), 56–65.

7.   Adaptations of *Dream* on the big screen continued in the 1970s. The production with the greatest circulation was the Shaw Brothers' *Dream of the Red Chamber* 金玉良緣紅樓夢 (1977), which starred Brigette Lin Qingxia and Sylvia Zhang Aijia and was directed by Li Hanxiang.

8.   For a detailed examination of the 1955 "Criticize Hu Shi Campaign," see, for instance, Jerome Grieder, "The Communist Critique of Hunglou meng," *Papers on China* (Harvard University, East Asian Research Center) 10 (October 1956): 142–68. For a discussion of the "New Redology" (New Hongxue) of the early twentieth century, see Louise Edwards, "New Hongxue and the 'Birth of the Author': Yu Pingbo's 'On Qin Keqing's Death,'" *Chinese Literature: Essays, Articles, Reviews (CLEAR)* 23 (December 2001): 31–54.

9.   Mao Zedong 毛澤東, "Speech on Philosophical Issues," 關於哲學的講話 (1964) in *Long Live Mao Zedong Thought* 毛澤東思想萬歲 (n.p., 1969), 549.

10. Su Qing was implicated in the ensuing anti-Hu Feng campaign in 1955 and was imprisoned in the same year as a member of the Hu Feng cohort, which precipitated the virtual disappearance of the opera excerpt from the theater repertoire. The excerpt "Baoyu and Daiyu" originally starred the opera diva Yin Guifang.

11. For a brief discussion of Su Qing's Yue opera reworking of *Dream,* see Wang Yixin 王一心, *They Three: Zhang Ailing, Su Qing, Hu Lancheng* 他們仨：張愛玲，蘇青，胡蘭成 (Shanghai: Dongfang chuban zhongxin, 2008), 130–41.

12. The original lyrics composed by Xu Jin reads: "拋卻了莫失莫忘通靈玉，掙脫了不離不棄黃金鎖。離開了蒼蠅競血骯髒地，撇開了黑蟻爭穴富貴窠。"

13. See Eileen Chang's letters to Ferdinand Reyher, collected in Zhou Fengling 周芬伶, *Turquoise Blues: A Biography of Zhang Ailing* 孔雀藍調：張愛玲評傳 (Taipei: Maitian, 2005), 179–206.

14. Eileen Chang, "Postscript to Mandarin Translation of *Sing-song Girls*," in Han Bangqing, *Mandarin Translation of The Sing-song Girls of Shanghai* 《海上花開》,《海上花落》, trans. and annotated by Eileen Chang (Taipei: Huangguan, 1983), 639.

15. For related research on this genre in Hong Kong film history, see, for instance, Chen Weizhi 陳煒智, *I Love Huangmei Tune: Classic Impressions of Traditional China—A Preliminary Study of Hong Kong and Taiwan's Huangmei Opera Films* 我愛黃梅調：絲竹中國，古典印象——港臺黃梅調電影初探 (Taipei: Muchun, 2005); Ng Ho 吳昊, *Period Drama, Huangmei Opera* 古裝，俠義，黃梅調 (Hong Kong: Joint Publishing, 2004).

16. Haun Saussy, "The Age of Attribution: Or, How the 'Honglou meng' Finally Acquired an Author," *Chinese Literature: Essays, Articles, Reviews (CLEAR)* 25

(December, 2003): 129. In this article, Saussy provides an important perspective on the theory of *Dream*'s authorship.

17. Chang, *Nightmare in the Red Chamber,* 10.

18. Xiaojue Wang, "*Stone* in Modern China: Literature, Politics, and Culture," in *Approaches to Teaching The Story of the Stone (Dream of the Red Chamber),* ed. Andrew Schonebaum and Tina Lu (Modern Language Association, forthcoming), 662–91.

19. Chang, *Nightmare in the Red Chamber,* 6.

20. Guo Yuwen 郭玉雯, "*Nightmare in the Red Chamber* and Redology"《紅樓夢魘》與紅學, in *Studies on Dream of the Red Chamber: From Red Inkstone to Eileen Chang* 紅樓夢學：從脂硯齋到張愛玲 (Taipei: Liren, 2004), 341–68.

21. There have been few studies of Eileen Chang's *Nightmare in the Red Chamber.* Some articles worth noting are Guo Yuwen, "*Nightmare in the Red Chamber* and Redology," and "On *Nightmare*'s Textual Analysis and Its Value"《紅樓夢魘》的考證意見與價值, in Guo, *Studies on Dream of the Red Chamber,* 341–68, 369–415; Kang Laixin 康來新, "Mutual Reflections: Eileen Chang and *Dream of the Red Chamber*" 對照記：張愛玲與《紅樓夢》, in *Reading Eileen Chang: Collected Essays from the "International Conference on Eileen Chang Research"* 閱讀張愛玲：張愛玲國際研討會論文集, ed. Yang Ze 楊澤 (Taipei: Maitian, 1999), 29–58; Zhao Gang 趙岡, "Eileen Chang and Redology" 張愛玲與紅學, *United Daily News* 聯合報, November 21, 1995.

22. Zhou Ruchang 周汝昌, *She Must Have Been a Character in Dream of the Red Chamber: Eileen Chang and Dream of the Red Chamber* 定是紅樓夢裡人：張愛玲與紅樓夢 (Beijing: Tuanjie chubanshe, 2005).

23. In his 1921 treatise "Textual Research on *Dream of the Red Chamber,*" 紅樓夢考證 Hu Shi first identified Cao Xueqin as *Dream*'s author. More importantly, he utilized historical pragmatism as a critical method, providing a new point of departure for the study of *Dream,* and launched a new school of Redological studies—the kaozheng school. See Hu Shi, "Textual Research on *Dream of the Red Chamber,*" in *Selected Writings of Hu Shi* 胡適文存 (Taipei: Yuandong tushu gongsi, 1953), 575–620. Among recent *Dream* research, Anthony C. Yu's *Rereading Stone: Desire and the Making of Fiction in Dream of the Red Chamber* (Princeton, NJ: Princeton University Press, 1997) is particularly noteworthy.

24. Eileen Chang, "Remembering Hu Shi" 憶胡適之, in *Chang's View* 張看 (Taipei: Huangguan, 1996), 152.

25. A main hypothesis Eileen Chang proposes in this regard is about the character Xiren. She maintains that Gao E has deliberately distorted the image of Xiren and projected his own failed relationship with his maid-cum-concubine Wanjun onto the persona of Xiren. See Eileen Chang, "An Anecdote about *Dream*: Gao E, Xiren, and Wanjun" 紅樓夢插曲之一：高鶚、襲人與畹君, in *Nightmare in the Red Chamber,* 57–68.

26. Chang, "The Incomplete *Dream of the Red Chamber,*" in *Nightmare in the Red Chamber,* 22.

27. Chang, *Nightmare in the Red Chamber,* 9.

28. Eileen Chang, "From the Mouths of Babes," 童言無忌, in *Written on Water* 流言 (Taipei: Huangguan, 1991), 12.

29. Eileen Chang, "The Fifth Close Reading of *Dream of the Red Chamber*: The Original Authentic Version" 五詳紅樓夢：舊時真本, in *Nightmare in the Red Chamber,* 333.

30. Chang, "The Fifth Close Reading of *Dream of the Red Chamber*," 333.

31. Chang, "The Fifth Close Reading of *Dream of the Red Chamber*," 333.

32. Chang, "The Fifth Close Reading of *Dream of the Red Chamber*," 333.

33. Eileen Chang, "Preface," in *Nightmare in the Red Chamber,* 10.

34. Eileen Chang, "Writing of One's Own" 自己的文章, in *Written on Water,* trans. Andrew F. Jones, co-ed. with an introduction by Nicole Huang (New York: Columbia University Press, 2005), 19.

35. Eileen Chang, *Nightmare,* 329. The English word "Ms. Know-all" is from Chang's original text.

36. Lu Xun 魯迅, "On the Historical Evolution of Chinese Fiction" 中國小説的歷史的變遷, in *The Complete Work of Lu Xun,* vol. 9 魯迅全集・九 (Beijing: Renmin wenxue, 1991), 338.

37. Eileen Chang, "The Religion of the Chinese" 中國人的宗教, in *The Lingering Cadence* 餘韻 (Taipei: Huangguan, 1991), 17. The English translation was quoted from David Pollard, ed. and trans., *The Chinese Essay* (New York: Columbia University Press, 2000), 284.

38. For instance, see Leo Ou-fan Lee, "Eileen Chang: Romances in a Fallen City," in *Shanghai Modern*; and Rey Chow, "Modernity and Narration: In Feminine Detail," in *Woman and Chinese Modernity: The Politics of Reading between West and East* (Minneapolis, Minnesota: University of Minnesota Press, 1991), 84–120.

39. Chang, "Writing of One's Own," 19.

40. Wang Guowei 王國維, "A Critique of *Dream of the Red Chamber*" 紅樓夢評論, in *Critical Materials on the Chinese Novel by Twentieth-Century Chinese Scholars* 二十世紀中國小説理論資料, vol. 1, 1897–1916, eds. Chen Pingyuan 陳平原 and Xia Xiaohong 夏曉虹 (Beijing: Beijing University Press, 1989), 96–115.

41. Qian Min 錢敏, "Eileen Chang and Her *Nightmare in the Red Chamber*" 張愛玲和她的《紅樓夢魘》, *Dushu* 讀書 11 (2000): 110–11.

42. Huang Xincun 黄心村, "Dreaming in the Red Chamber, Writing in a Different Age" 夢在紅樓，寫在隔世, in *Eileen Chang Degree Zero* 零度看張：重構張愛玲, ed. Shen Shuang 沈雙 (Hong Kong: The Chinese University Press, 2010), 99–118.

43. Zhou Ruchang, *She Must Have Been a Character in Dream of the Red Chamber,* 30.

44. For Hu Shi's letter to Eileen Chang, see Chang, "Remembering Hu Shi," in *Chang's View,* 141–54. For Hu Shi's article on *The Sing-song Girls of Shanghai,* see Hu Shi, "Preface" to Han Bangqing, *The Sing-song Girls of Shanghai* 海上花列傳 (Taipei: Guangya, 1984), 8. This remark was originally proposed by Lu Xun.

45. Ye Zhaoyan 葉兆言, "Laughter in the Besieged City," 圍城裡的笑聲 *Shouhuo* 收穫, no. 4 (2000): 149.

46. For an exploration of how the McCarthyistic anti-Communist campaign affected cultural production in the United States in the Cold War era, see Frances Stonor Saunders, *The Cultural Cold War: The CIA and the World of Arts and Letters* (New York: The New Press, 1999).

47. See Eileen Chang's letter to C. T. Hsia on October 16, 1964, collected in C. T. Hsia 夏志清, "Eileen Chang's Letters to Me," 張愛玲給我的信件 in *Unitas* 聯合文學 13, 11 (September 1997): 69–70.

48. Hsia, "Eileen Chang's Letters to Me," 70–71.

49. For an examination of the construction of China imageries in Chinese American literature, theater, and film, see, for instance, Sau-ling Cynthia Wong, *Reading Asian American Literature: From Necessity to Extravagance* (Princeton, NJ: Princeton University Press, 1993); Weijie Song 宋偉傑, *Images of China in American and Chinese-American Novel and Drama* 中國，文學，美國：美國小説戲劇中的中國形像 (Guangzhou: Huacheng Press), 2003; Shan Dexing 單德興, *Inscriptions and Representations: Chinese American Literary and Cultural Studies* 銘刻與再現：華裔美國文學與文化論集 (Taipei: Maitian, 2000).

50. See Eileen Chang's letter to C. T. Hsia on December 31, 1965, collected in C. T. Hsia, " Eileen Chang's Letters to Me," in *Unitas* 聯合文學 13, 6 (April 1997): 52–53.

51. Ye Zhaoyan, "Laughter in the Besieged City," 149.

52. Ye Zhaoyan, "Laughter in the Besieged City," 149.

53. The English translation of "The Golden Cangue" by the author herself is collected in Joseph S. M. Lau, C. T. Hsia, and Leo Ou-fan Lee, eds., *Modern Chinese Stories and Novellas, 1919–1949* (New York: Columbia University Press, 1981), 530–59.

54. David Wang, "Foreword," in Eileen Chang, *The Rouge of the North* (Berkeley, Los Angeles, London: University of California Press, 1998), xi–xii.

Chapter 7

1. Eileen Chang, Wang Hui-ling, and James Schamus, *Lust, Caution: The Story, the Screenplay, and the Making of the Movie* (New York: Pantheon, 2007).

2. Chen Lin, "The Real Story behind Lust, Caution Revealed," China.Org, http://www.china.org.cn/english/entertainment/224552.htm (accessed September 14, 2007).

3. Lung Ying-tai on *Lust, Caution,* East South West North, http://www.zonaeuropa.com/20070915_1.htm (accessed September 18, 2011).

4. Anita Mui portrays her in Eddie Fong's *Kawashima Yoshiko—The Last Princess of Manchuria* (Hong Kong, 1990).

5. See Nicole Huang, *Women, War, Domesticity: Shanghai Literature and Popular Culture of the 1940s* (Leiden: Brill, 2005).

6. See, for example, Ann Hui 許鞍華, *Love in a Fallen City* 傾城之戀 (1984); Stanley Kwan 關錦鵬, *Red Rose, White Rose* 紅玫瑰與白玫瑰 (1994); Ho Hsiao-Hsien

侯孝賢, *Flowers of Shanghai* 海上花 (1998); and Fred Tan 但漢章, *The Rouge of the North* 怨女 (1989).

7. Leo Ou-fan Lee 李歐梵, *Watching Lust, Caution: Literature, Cinema, History* 睇色，戒：文學・電影・歷史 (Oxford: Oxford University Press, 2008). See also Leo Ou-fan Lee, "Ang Lee's *Lust, Caution* and its Reception," *boundary 2* 35, 3 (2008): 223–38.

8. Quoted in Poshek Fu, "The Ambiguity of Entertainment: Chinese Cinema in Japanese-occupied Shanghai, 1941 to 1945," *Cinema Journal* 37, 1 (Autumn 1997): 66–84 (see p. 74).

9. See Eileen Chang, *The Rice-Sprout Song* (Berkeley: University of California Press, 1998), originally published in 1955 with another edition in 1967, and *The Naked Earth* (Hong Kong: Union Press, 1956).

10. Geoffrey Macnab, "'I Had to Get to the Heart of Darkness': An Interview with Ang Lee," *The Guardian*, December 14, 2007. http://www.guardian.co.uk/film/2007/dec/14/1.

11. Robert Stam and Ella Shohat, "Film Theory and Spectatorship in the Age of the 'Posts,'" in *Reinventing Film Studies*, ed. Christine Gledhill and Linda Williams (London: Oxford University Press, 2000), 381–401 (see p. 390).

12. Michael Wood, "At the Movies: *Lust, Caution*," *London Review of Books* 30, 2 (January 24, 2008): 31. http://www.lrb.co.uk/v30/n02/wood01_.html (accessed September 18, 2011).

13. James Schamus, a film professor at Columbia University, may need to have a particularly good command of Hollywood and Shanghai screen classics to teach his courses there.

14. Corrado Neri, "The Enemy within: A Comparative Reading of *Lust, Caution* and *Daybreak*" (conference paper), a conference on "Locality, Translocality, and De-Locality: Cultural, Aesthetic, and Political Dynamics of Chinese Language Cinema," University of Shanghai, July 12, 2008.

15. Miriam Hansen, "Fallen Women, Rising Stars, New Horizons: Shanghai Silent Film as Vernacular Modernism," *Film Quarterly* 54, 1 (2000): 10–22 (see p. 19).

16. Fu, "The Ambiguity of Entertainment," 80.

17. Nicole Huang gives a fascinating account of the reception of *Gone with the Wind* (1939) in *Women, War, Domesticity*.

18. Stam and Shohat, "Film Theory and Spectatorship," 398.

19. Slavoj Žižek, *Enjoy Your Symptom! Jacques Lacan in Hollywood and out* (New York: Routledge, 1992), 44.

20. Žižek, *Enjoy Your Symptom*, 34.

21. Žižek, *Enjoy Your Symptom*, 53. Emphasis in original.

22. Bernardo Bertolucci later cast Giovanna Galletti as a prostitute in *Last Tango in Paris*, 1972.

23. Susan Sontag, "Fascinating Fascism," *New York Review of Books*, February 6, 1975. Reprinted online at http://www.history.ucsb.edu/faculty/marcuse/classes/33d/33dTexts/SontagFascinFascism75.htm.

24. Sontag, "Fascinating Fascism."
25. Nicole Sperling, "Ang Lee and James Schamus Get Frank," *Entertainment Weekly*, March 19, 2008. http://www.ew.com/ew/article/0,,20185085,00.html (accessed September 18, 2011).
26. Leo Lee has noted the connection to *The Conformist* (confirmed in a conversation Lee had with Ang Lee). However, the connection, in my view, extends far beyond that particular film.
27. Chang, *Lust, Caution*, 34.
28. Karsten Witte, Barbara Correll, and Jack Zipes, "Introduction to Siegfried Kracauer's 'The Mass Ornament,'" *New German Critique* 5 (Spring 1975): 59–66 (see p. 66).
29. Macnab, "'I Had to Get to the Heart of Darkness.'"

Chapter 8

1. When "Lust, Caution" was first published in the "Literary Supplement" of the *China Times* in 1978, Yu Wai-ren (the pen name of the famous science fiction writer Zhang Xiguo) wrote a scathing review that criticized Chang's immorality for "lauding a Chinese traitor." A month later, Chang published a response that defended her position and accused Yu Wai-ren of misinterpreting her story. See Cai Dengshan 蔡登山, *Lust, Caution, Eileen* 色戒愛玲 (Taipei: INK Publishing, 2007); and Eileen Chang, *The Sequel* 續集 (Taipei: Huangguan, 1997).
2. Cai Dengshan's *Lust, Caution, Eileen* suggests that Chang's story might be based on a true historical incident that implicated KMT's spy Zheng Ruping and her unsuccessful assassination of Ding Mocun, the spy chief in Wang Jingwei's puppet government in 1939. In *Looking at Lust, Caution: Literature, Cinema, History* 睇色，戒：文學．電影．歷史 (Oxford: Oxford University Press, 2008), Leo Ou-fan Lee 李歐梵 offers an insightful comparison of Chang's and Lee's different characterizations. Gina Marchetti's essay "Eileen Chang and Ang Lee at the Movies: the Cinematic Politics of *Lust, Caution* (Chapter 7 in this anthology) argues that adaptation is both a form of translation and an act of "betrayal." Peng Hsiao-yen 彭小妍 examines the ways in which *Lust, Caution* uses woman as "metaphor" to "deconstruct the fundamental ideals of patriotism and romance." See "Woman as Metaphor: the Historical Construction and Deconstruction in *Lust, Caution*" 女人作為隱喻：《色｜戒》的歷史建構及解構, *Journal of Theater Studies* Vol. 2 (2008): 209–36. Chang Hsiao-hung 張小虹 draws attention to the complex cultural connotations of the two concepts "lust" and "caution" in "Wide Open Lust Caution—from Ang Lee to Eileen Chang" 大開色戒——從李安到張愛玲 in *China Times'* "Literary Supplement," September 28–29, 2007, E7. Lee Haiyan uses the notion of "contingent transcendence" to argue that Chang's fiction allows women to "locate [their] ethical and political agency in the domain of the social, the everyday, and the feminine" ("Enemy under My Skin: Eileen Chang's *Lust, Caution* and the politics of Transcendence." *PMLA: Publication of Modern Language Association* 125.3 (2010): 640–56. Finally, Robert Chi analyzes

the reception of the movie in "Exhibitionism: 'Lust, Caution,'" *Journal of Chinese Cinemas* 3, 2 (2009): 177–87.

3. From Yuan Qiongqiong to Zhong Xiaoyang and from Zhu Tianwen to Hou Xiaoxian, Chang's life and work have inspired writers, dramatists, and directors in Hong Kong, Taiwan, overseas Chinese communities, and China. See Yvonne Sung-sheng Chang, "Yuan Qiongqiong and the Rage for Eileen Zhang among Taiwan's Feminine Writers," in *Gender Politics in Modern China: Writing and Feminism,* ed. Tani Barlow (Durham: Duke University Press, 1993), 215–37.

4. Eileen Chang, *The Sequel,* 3. If not noted otherwise, all translations of Chang's non-fiction writings are mine.

5. Michael Berry, *Speaking in Images: Interviews with Contemporary Chinese Filmmakers* (New York: Columbia University Press, 2005), 155.

6. Chang's experience in the film industry has been well documented. In addition to seeing many of her stories adapted as stage plays and movies, she wrote several film scripts and collaborated with the renowned Hong Kong director Sang Hu in 1947. See William Tay 鄭樹森, ed., *From the Modern to the Contemporary* 從現代到當代 (Taipei: Sanmin, 1994); William Tay, *The World of Eileen Chang* 張愛玲的世界 (Taipei: Yunchen, 1994); and Liu Shu 劉澍 and Wang Gang 王綱, eds., *Eileen Chang's Space of Light and Shadow* 張愛玲的光影空間 (Beijing: Shijie zhishi chubanshe, 2007).

7. Both Rey Chow and Leo Ou-fan Lee have analyzed Chang's writing in light of her cinematic vision. See Chow's *Woman and Chinese Modernity: The Politics of Reading between West and East* (Minneapolis: University of Minnesota Press, 1991) and Lee's *Shanghai Modern: The Flowering of a New Urban Culture in China, 1930–1945* (Cambridge: Harvard University Press, 2001).

8. Michael Berry, *Speaking in Images,* 340.

9. Shui Jing 水晶, *The Art of Eileen Chang's Novels* 張愛玲的小說藝術 (Taipei: Dadi, 2000), 38.

10. See Ma Ning, "Symbolic Representation and Symbolic Violence: Chinese Family Melodrama of the Early 1980s," in *Melodrama and Asian Cinema,* ed. Wimal Dissanayake (Cambridge: Cambridge University Press, 1993), 29–58; and Chris Berry, "Wedding Banquet: A Family (Melodrama) Affair," in *Chinese Films in Focus: 25 New Takes,* ed. Chris Berry (London: British Film Institute Publishing, 2003), 183–90.

11. Cai, *Lust, Caution, Eileen,* 20.

12. Ang Lee, "Afterword," in *Lust, Caution,* trans. Julia Lovell (New York: Anchor Books, 2007), 59.

13. See, for instance, Leo Ou-fan Lee's *Shanghai Modern* and Poshek Fu's *Between Shanghai and Hong Kong: The Politics of Chinese Cinemas* (Stanford: Stanford University Press, 2003).

14. Cai, *Lust, Caution, Eileen,* 24–27 ; Zhang Zijing, *My Sister Eileen Chang* 我的姊姊張愛玲 (Taipei: Shibao, 1996), 220–21.

15. Chang, *The Sequel,* 4.

16. Chang, *Lust, Caution,* trans. Julia Lovell (New York: Anchor Books, 2007), 3.

17. Lee, "Afterword," 60.

18. Chang, *Lust, Caution,* 19.

19. Lee, "Afterword," 59.

20. A good example is Lee's *Crouching Tiger, Hidden Dragon* (2000), where he opens a martial arts film with a five-minute expositional conversation between the two main characters, Yu Xiulian and Li Mubai.

21. Chang, *Lust, Caution,* 39–40. I have modified Lovell's translation substantially here. See Chang's original text in *The Story of Regret* (惘然記), 27.

22. Chang, *Lust, Caution,* 45–46. Again, I have modified Lovell's translation of this passage.

23. Chang, *Lust, Caution,* 26.

24. Jean Baudrillard, *Seduction,* trans. Brian Singer (New York: St. Martin's Press, 1990), 81.

25. Critics have various interpretations of why Jiazhi lets down her guard at this critical moment. Haiyan Lee, for example, suggests that Chang's Jiazhi is touched by the image of Yi's vulnerability: "In the film, her utterance of 'Run' seems activated by bodily memories—an instance of speaking sexual truth to power, as it were. In the story, by contrast, it is the face of a man whose eyelashes are likened to ethereal moth wings that take Jiazhi to the beyond." See Lee's "Enemy under My Skin: Eileen Chang's Lust, Caution and the Politics of Transcendence," *PMLA* 125, 3 (May 2010): 648.

26. Jean Baudrillard, *Seduction,* 69. Original italics.

27. Chang, *Lust, Caution,* 39

28. Lee, *Looking at Lust, Caution,* 24.

Chapter 9

1. Eileen Chang, *Little Reunion* 小團圓 (Hong Kong: Huangguan, 2009), 276. All page references to *Little Reunion* are drawn from the first Chinese edition. All English translations are my own.

2. Hu Lancheng 胡蘭成, *This Life in This World* 今生今世 (Taipei: Yuanjing, 1996), 173.

3. Chang, *Little Reunion,* 218.

4. Su Tong 蘇童, "Eileen Chang Reminds Me of Lin Daiyu" 張愛玲讓我想起了林黛玉, *Wanxiang* 萬象 February 2001, 3, 2: 127–29.

5. Eileen Chang loved *Dream of the Red Chamber,* and wrote a book about it, entitled *Nightmare in the Red Chamber* 紅樓夢魘 (Hong Kong: Huangguan, 1996). But in the book there is scant description of Lin Daiyu, revealing Chang's own lack of interest in this character.

6. Related letters, as well as Roland Soong's own explanation, are reproduced in the introduction to *Little Reunion.*

7. I choose to refer to the characters by the anglicized names Julie, Rachel, and Jody rather than using Chinese pinyin because I think Chang intended these characters (and almost everyone in the colonial city) to have Western names.

8. Although Zhiyong went to Shanghai often, his own family was in Nanjing, and he also ran a newspaper and literary magazine in central China, where he met Ms. Kang. Zhiyong, like Hu Lancheng, collaborated with the Japanese government during the Second World War, and was accused of being a traitor after the war, which meant he had to flee urban areas and hide in the countryside.

9. Chang, *Little Reunion*, 277.

10. Zhi An 止庵, "Only a Floating Life for Xiao tuanyuan" 浮生只合小團圓, *Wen Wei Po* 文匯報, March 23, 2009, http://trans.wenweipo.com/gb/paper.wenweipo.com/2009/03/23/BK0903230001.htm (accessed April 16, 2009).

11. Chang, *Little Reunion*, 325.

12. Hu, *This Life in This World*, 177.

13. This dream of children might be remotely connected to her abortion, depicted earlier in the book, and which I will discuss in the next section.

14. Chang, *Little Reunion*, 256.

15. Chang, *Little Reunion*, 262–64.

16. Chang, *Little Reunion*, 171.

17. Chang, *Little Reunion*, 284.

18. Sang Hu 桑弧 is a film director whose creative life spanned the Republican and socialist eras. Among the thirty-plus films he directed are *Everlasting Love* (不了情, 1947) and *Viva the Wife* (太太萬歲, 1948); Eileen Chang wrote the scripts for both films.

19. Chang, *Little Reunion*, 287.

20. Chang, *Little Reunion*, 179.

21. Chang, *Little Reunion*, 265.

22. This idea was raised in a letter Soong wrote to Chang in 1976, after he finished reading *Little Reunion*. The letter appears in the introduction to Chang's novel (*Little Reunion*, 11).

23. Chang, *Little Reunion*, 155.

24. Chang, *Little Reunion*, 221.

25. Chang, *Little Reunion*, 248.

26. Chang, *Little Reunion*, 89.

27. Chang, *Little Reunion*, 294.

28. Eileen Chang describes *Little Reunion* thus in a letter to Stephen Soong: "This is a story full of passions. I want to articulate the many meandering pathways romantic love engenders; even when love is completely disillusioned, there is still something left." The letter is quoted in the introduction to *Little Reunion*, 10.

29. This has been observed in another autobiographical work by Chang, *Mutual Reflections: Looking at My Old Photo Album* 對照記：看老照相簿 (Hong Kong: Huangguan, 1994). See Laikwan Pang, "Photography and Autobiography: Eileen

Chang's Mutual Reflections: Looking at My Old Photo Album," *Modern Chinese Literature and Culture* 13, 1 (Spring 2001): 73–106.

30. Chang, *Little Reunion*, 265.

31. Chang, *Little Reunion*, 129.

32. Chang, *Mutual Reflections: Looking at My Old Photo Album*, 6.

33. Mladen Dolar, "At First Sight," in *Gaze and Voice as Love Object*, ed. Reneta Salecl and Slavoj Žižek (Durham, NC, and London: Duke University Press, 1996), 135.

34. Chang, *Little Reunion*, 187–88.

35. As Jean Baudrillard has pointed out, distance can no longer be conceptualized in this global world, where advanced communication technology erases the existence of strangers. We have simply lost the ability to accept and respect the state of "incomprehension." This inability to come to terms with otherness is therefore not only an attribute specific to some persons, but a social phenomenon permeating our global society. See Jean Baudrillard and Marc Guillaume, *Radical Alterity*, trans. Ames Hodges (Los Angeles: Semiotext[s], 2008), 113–31.

36. Chang, *Little Reunion*, 177.

37. Chang, *Little Reunion*, 180.

38. Chang, *Little Reunion*, 324.

39. For a pertinent reading of the relationship between pain and self, see Jane Kilby, "Carved in Skin: Bearing Witness to Self-Harm," in *Thinking through the Skin*, ed. Sara Ahmed and Jackie Stacey (London: Routledge, 2001), 124–42.

40. For an elaborate discussion of the use of the notion of "otherness" in contemporary critical discourse, see Tamise Van Pelt, "Otherness," *Postmodern Culture* 10, 2 (January 2000). http://muse.jhu.edu/journals/postmodern_culture/v010/10.2vanpelt. html (accessed September 18, 2011).

41. As Van Pelt reminds us in the aforementioned article, Lacan's theory develops from his earlier mirror stage theory to the later theory of the registers: in the former, Lacan attempts to explain the dynamics of an intrapsychic alterity in interpersonal terms; it is only in his later theory of the registers that he focuses primarily on intrapsychic dynamics, thereby moving from the (imaginary) other to the (symbolic) Other.

42. Jessica Benjamin, *The Bonds of Love: Psychoanalysis, Feminism, and the Problem of Domination* (New York: Pantheon Books, 1988), 20.

43. Benjamin, *The Bonds of Love*, 21.

44. Jessica Benjamin, *Shadow of the Other: Intersubjectivity and Gender in Psychoanalysis* (New York: Routledge, 1998), 86.

45. Joseph S. M. Lau, a long-time Eileen Chang scholar and personal friend, finds this book second-rate compared to the works Chang created in her golden age— the 1940s. For Lau, the value of *Little Reunion* lies mostly in its autobiographical nature, in the sense that we can better understand Chang and her works through this piece. Liu Shaoming 劉紹銘 (Joseph Lau), "No Little Reunion Yet" 小團未 圓, *Ming Pao* 明報, March 16, 2009. In fact, this position coincides with the *Little Reunion*-mania in the Chinese-speaking world. Immediately after its publication

in February 2009, comments on the work abounded, both in print and online, by lay readers and devoted scholars, and the pirated and imported versions were widely read in mainland China in the mere two-month gap before its official simplified Chinese version was published in April 2009. Not surprisingly, an enormous amount of readerly and critical effort has been devoted to matching the characters in the book to actual persons, as well as to the reconstruction of Chang's own life, which has attracted so much curiosity. Some fans claim to be able to trace the identities of even the most minor characters. See, for example, Meidusha's 美杜莎 blog, "Little Reunion and Its Characters" 小團圓，以及出場人物, March 2009, http://schlafen.pixnet.net/blog/post/22868102 (accessed April 15, 2009). Because of the book, the personal lives of past literary figures such as Hu Lancheng (as Zhiyong), Sang Hu (as Yanshan), and even Ke Ling 柯靈 (as Xunhua) have enjoyed renewed popular attention.

46. Benjamin, *Shadow of the Other,* 90.
47. Chang, *Little Reunion,* 181–83.
48. Chang, *Little Reunion,* 189–90.
49. Chang, *Little Reunion,* 190.
50. Martin Heidegger, "The Age of the World Picture," in *The Question Concerning Technology and Other Essays,* trans. William Lovitt (New York: Harper and Row, 1977), 115–54.
51. Benjamin, *Shadow of the Other,* 93.

Chapter 10

1. Chang lived in the United States from 1955 to 1995. She spent a short time in Hong Kong in 1961 to write film screenplays and made a brief visit to Taiwan later that year, but otherwise spent all her time in the United States.
2. The title of the novel has been variously translated into English as "Little Reunion" and "small reunion." Song Yilang (Roland Soong), son of Song Qi and the executor of Chang's literary estate, states that he originally translated the title as *Little Reunion* but now believes that the title should be translated as *Small Reunions.* He cites Chang's usage of the same phrase 小團圓 in something she wrote on August 13, 1991 that described the trajectory of her childhood and adolescence as resembling "bamboo sections," in that it consisted of four periods—each four years long—demarcated by the departures and returns of her mother. Following these was a five-year period that ended in Chang's return from Hong Kong to Shanghai (in 1942) to be reunited with her aunt. In her own words, she experienced "several small reunions" (幾度小團圓) following periods of separation; see Song, "A Blog about *Little Reunion*" 《小團圓》的 BLOG, Post 30 (May 19, 2009), at http://zonaeuropa.com/culture/c20090419_1.htm#016 (accessed September 30, 2009). Although Song's discovery is illuminating, I will use the less awkward *Little Reunion* as the translation for 小團圓, to be consistent with other contributing authors of this volume.

3. Eileen Chang comments on the connection between *Little Reunion* and *The Book of Change* in a letter dated March 14, 1976 to Song Qi, excerpted in Song Yilang 宋以朗, "Preface to *Little Reunion*" 小團圓前言, in Eileen Chang, *Little Reunion* 小團圓 (Taipei: Huangguan, 2009), 6. According to Song Yilang, Chang began to work on *The Book of Change* in 1957 ("A Blog about *Little Reunion*," Post 16, May 4, 2009, at http://zonaeuropa.com/culture/c20090419_1.htm#016, accessed September 30, 2009).

4. A year after the publication of *Little Reunion*, Chang's two English autobiographical novels were released by Hong Kong University Press in the spring and fall of 2010. I regret not being able to delve into them here due to space limitations. Suffice it to say that, as texts written for the purpose of courting an English-speaking audience, Chang's English novels should be situated in the literary and cultural contexts of mid-century America, which deserves a full study of its own. For a related discussion, see Shuang Shen's chapter in this volume, which interprets Chang's shorter English writings in terms of Cold War politics and her struggle to find a place for herself and her works while in exile. For a reading of Chang's repeated rewriting of her life story as epitomizing a poetics of "involution and derivation," focusing especially on Chang's English autobiographical novels, see David Wang's chapter in this volume. My own chapter is dedicated to understanding Chang's self-fashioning textual performances directed at Chinese reading publics as her mirror and audience.

5. Eileen Chang, "On Reading" 談看書, in *Chang's View* 張看 (Taipei: Huangguan, 1991), 155–97. "On Reading" was followed by a shorter essay, "An Afterword to 'On Reading'" 〈談看書〉後記, in the same year. Publication years are based on the chronology included at the end of Huangguan's 2001 collector's edition of *Eileen Chang's Collected Works:* 張愛玲典藏全集 (Taipei: Huangguan, 2001), 14: 247–54. For the dates of composition, see Eileen Chang, *The Story of Regret* 惘然記 (Taipei: Huangguan, 1991), 4; and Song, "Preface to *Little Reunion*," 3–17.

6. The 1970s also saw Chang devote considerable energy to a textual study of *Dream of the Red Chamber*, which deserves separate consideration.

7. Chang, "On Reading," 189.

8. Zhang Xiaohong 張小虹, "Legally Pirating Eileen Chang—There Will Never Be a Reunion Hereafter" 合法盜版張愛玲，從此永不團圓, *United Daily* 聯合報, February 27, 2009.

9. Chang, *Little Reunion*, 3.

10. Song, "Afterword to *Little Reunion*" 小團圓後記, http://www.zonaeuropa.com/culture/c20090305_1.htm (accessed September 30, 2009).

11. Chang, *Little Reunion*, 15–16.

12. Chang, *Little Reunion*, 4, 5.

13. Chang, *Little Reunion*, 6.

14. Chang, *Little Reunion*, 8.

15. Chang, *Little Reunion*, 8.

16. 妨礙 in modern Chinese usually means hindrance or interference. However, here it seems to be used interchangeably with 礙語, or inappropriate words, an expression that appears in another letter Chang wrote (dated July 18, 1975) commenting on her revisions (Chang, *Little Reunion*, 4).

17. Du Yu 杜預, et al., annotated, *The Three Biographies of The Spring and Autumn Annals* 春秋三傳 (Shanghai: Shanghai guji chubanshe, 1987), 144.

18. If the deceased held an official title or if the family was affluent, it was common for their family to commission an eminent writer to write a lavishly embellished biography based on a draft provided by the family; see Pei-yi Wu, *The Confucian's Progress: Autobiographical Writings in Traditional China* (Princeton: Princeton University Press, 1990), 24, 58. See also Denis Twitchett, "Chinese Biographical Writing," in *Historians of China and Japan*, ed. W. G. Beasley and E. G. Pulleyblank (London and New York: Oxford, 1961), 95–114.

19. Paul de Man, "Autobiography as Defacement," *MLN* 94, 5 (1979): 919–30; Philippe Lejeune, *On Autobiography* (Minneapolis: University of Minnesota Press, 1989), 13.

20. Quoted in Song, "Preface to *Little Reunion*," 13. The English words "unconventional" and "unsympathetic" appear in the Chinese original.

21. See, for example, Sima Wensen 司馬文森, *A History of Cultural Traitors' Crimes* 文化漢奸罪惡史 (Shanghai: Shuguang chubanshe, 1945). It is difficult to ascertain Sima's identity and relationship to the returning Nationalist government. The label "cultural traitor," though ill defined, was common in popular media at the time and was adopted by the state in its prosecution of certain prominent writers and intellectuals who had held administrative positions during the Japanese era. Chang never held any position, so she was never prosecuted by the state despite suffering virulent personal attacks in the press. For further discussion, see Xia Yun, "Traitors to the Chinese Race (Hanjian): Political and Cultural Campaigns against Collaborators during the Sino-Japanese War of 1937–1945," Ph.D. dissertation, University of Oregon, 2010, especially Chapters 4–5.

22. Lejeune, *On Autobiography*, 3–21.

23. Lejeune gives a basic definition of autobiography thus: "Retrospective prose narrative written by a real person concerning his own life, where the focus is his individual life, in particular the story of his personality" (Lejeune, *On Autobiography*, 4). This definition describes *Little Reunion* well, even if formally it is not what Lejeune would call a classic autobiography.

24. Lingzhen Wang, *Personal Matters, Women's Autobiographical Practice in Twentieth-century China* (Stanford: Stanford University Press, 2004); Nicole Huang, *Women, War, Domesticity: Shanghai Literature and Popular Culture of the 1940s* (Leiden: Brill, 2005), Chapter 5; Amy Dooling, *Women's Literary Feminism in Twentieth-century China* (New York: Palgrave, 2005), especially discussion on Bai Wei; Ruihua Shen, "New Woman, New Fiction: Autobiographical Fictions by Twentieth-century Chinese Women Writers," Ph.D. dissertation, University of Oregon, 2003.

25. Sidonie Smith, *A Poetics of Women's Autobiography: Marginality and the Fictions of Self-Representation* (Bloomington: Indiana University Press, 1987), 45.

26. Compared with letters and diaries, poetry was a relatively public genre commonly used by late imperial Chinese women. For a taste of the common motifs of longing and sickness in late imperial women's poetry, see Kang-i Sun Chang and Huan Saussy, eds., *Women Writers of Traditional China: A Collection of Poetry and Criticism* (Stanford: Stanford University Press, 1999). Although women may have expressed their thoughts and feelings in less formulaic ways in their private letters and diaries, few such writings were published. One late imperial woman who wrote a very original public work about her life expressing frustration and discontentment with the lack of career opportunities for women was Wu Zao 吳藻, but she was a rare exception rather than the norm; see Wei Hua, "The Lament of Frustrated Talents: An Analysis of Three Women's Plays in Late Imperial China," *Ming Studies* 32 (1994): 28–42. It should also be noted that Wu Zao's work, *The Disguised Image* 喬影, though highly self-referential, is very different from a modern autobiography in that Wu speaks through a dramatic persona, and the plot concerns mainly the present, not the past.

27. Wang, *Personal Matters*, 61–139; c.f. Sally Lieberman, *The Mother and Narrative Politics in Modern China* (Charlottesville: University Press of Virginia, 1998).

28. Chang, *Little Reunion*, 30, 32, 136, 144–45, 149.

29. Dooling, *Women's Literary Feminism*, 3–6.

30. Chang, *Mutual Reflections*, 20.

31. Chang, *Little Reunion*, 138.

32. Sima, *A History of Cultural Traitors' Crimes*, 2–6, 49–50. See also Anonymous, *The Heinous History of Female Collaborators* 女漢奸醜史 (Shanghai: Dashidai shushe, ca. 1940s), 10. For Hu's recollection of his involvement in Wang's government, see Hu Lancheng 胡蘭成, *This Life in This World* 今生今世 (Taipei: Yuanjing, 2004), 173–257; this edition restores the chapter on Wang's regime that was excised from the 1976 Yuanjing edition. The complete version was first published in Japan in 1959 under the variant title 今世今生. For a collection of Hu's political writings during the war, see Hu Lancheng, *War Is Difficult, So Is Achieving Peace* 戰難和亦不易 (Shanghai: Zhonghua ribao guan, 1940).

33. Chang, *Little Reunion*, 64.

34. Chang, *Little Reunion*, 38, 104, 107, 110, 119–22, 197.

35. Chang, *Little Reunion*, 241.

36. Chang, *Little Reunion*, 8.

37. Eileen Chang, *Written on Water* 流言 (Taipei: Huangguan, 1991), 21.

38. Elsewhere, Chang tentatively translates the term 社會小說 into English as "the novel of manners" (Chang, "Remembering Hu Shi" 憶胡適之, in *Chang's View*, 153).

39. Chang, "On Reading," in *Chang's View*, 188.

40. Chang, "On Reading," 188.

41. Chang, "On Reading," 188.

42. Chang, "On Reading," 189.
43. Chang, "On Reading," 190.
44. Chang, "On Reading," 190.
45. Her excitement as a teenager upon discovering allusions to her paternal grandparents' lives in *A Flower in a Sea of Sin* is described in *Mutual Reflections*, 34–38; the incident also appears in *Little Reunion*, 119–22, but the novel's title is changed to *Record of a Clear Night* (清夜錄).
46. Chang, "On Reading," 185.
47. Chang, "On Reading," 184–85. New journalism was a style of news writing that arose against the background of the civil movement and anti-war protests in the US in the 1960s and 1970s, using some literary conventions then considered unconventional for news reporting. Representative writers included Truman Capote, Norman Mailer, Thomas Wolfe, Joan Didion, and Robert Christgau. See Thomas Wolfe, *The New Journalism: Conversations with America's Best Nonfiction Writers on Their Craft* (New York: Vintage Books, 2005); Michael L. Johnson, *The New Journalism: The Underground Press, the Artists of Nonfiction, and Changes in the Established Media* (Lawrence: The University Press of Kansas, 1971). Judging from Eileen Chang's reading list in "On Reading," she was well informed about cultural developments in the US. Her championing of factual representation in the Chinese social novel would make her a close ally of the American new journalists in their theoretical outlook. For instance, Truman Capote wrote *In Cold Blood* (1966) as a "nonfiction novel," and Norman Mailer advocated "history as the novel, the novel as history." However, based on her terse comments on new journalism, Chang apparently did not care for the strong political agendas of some new journalists.
48. Chang mentions that the story was based on some "material" she had obtained, which vaguely implies that it was inspired by a real incident (Chang, *The Story of Regret*, 4). Since the story's adaptation as a film by Ang Lee, there has been wide speculation that it is loosely based on the KMT underground agent Zheng Pingru's attempt to lure and assassinate the collaborationist intelligence chief Ding Mocun in 1939. On the Zheng Pingru incident, see Luo Jiurong 羅久蓉, "Historical Reality and Literary Imagination: Gender and the Discourse of the Nation in the Death of a Female Spy 歷史真實與文學想像：從一個女間諜之死看近代中國的性別與國族論述," *Research on Women in Modern Chinese History* 近代中國婦女史研究 11 (2003): 47–98; for an excellent study comparing the Zheng incident and Eileen Chang's story "Lust, Caution," see Guo Yuwen 郭玉雯, "A Study of Eileen Chang's 'Lust, Caution,'—Mentioning Also the Relevant Historical Records and Ang Lee's Screen Version of the Story 張愛玲〈色戒〉探析──兼及相關之歷史記載與李安的改編電影," *NTU Studies in Taiwan Literature* 台灣文學研究集刊 4 (2007): 41–76.
49. On Eileen Chang's comic screenplays, see Kenny K. K. Ng, "The Screenwriter as Cultural Broker: Travels of Eileen Chang's Comedies of Love," *Modern Chinese Literature and Culture* 20, 2 (Fall 2008): 131–84; Poshek Fu, "Eileen Chang,

Woman's Film, and Domestic Culture of Modern Shanghai," *Tamkang Review* 29, 4 (1999): 9–28.

50. Eileen Chang, *Lust, Caution and Other Stories*, trans. Julia Lovell (London: Penguin, 2007), 4. Citations of the story in English are based on this translation.
51. Chang, *Lust, Caution*, 3.
52. Chang, *Lust, Caution*, 20.
53. Chang, *Lust, Caution*, 29.
54. Chang, *Lust, Caution*, 40.

Chapter 11

1. *The Shanghai Evening Post* was run by Carl Crow (1884–1945), a Missouri-born newspaperman, businessman, and author. Carl Crow arrived in Shanghai in 1911 and made the city his home for a quarter of a century. For more information, see Paul French, Carl Crow, *A Tough Old China Hand: The Life, Times, and Adventures of an American in Shanghai* (Hong Kong: Hong Kong University Press, 2006). The title of Eileen Chang's essay was provided by newspaper editors.
2. C. T. Hsia was the first scholar to introduce Eileen Chang as a canonical writer to the English-speaking world. See Hsia's chapter on Chang in *A History of Modern Chinese Fiction, 1917–1957* (New Haven: Yale University Press, 1961).
3. Chang's letter to Stephen Soong, April 2, 1963.
4. For more comprehensive discussions of Chang's bilingualism and rewriting, see Liu Shaoming 劉紹銘 (Joseph Lau), "Transmigration: On the Shuttling of Eileen Chang's Bilingual Translations" 輪迴轉生：張愛玲的中英互譯; and Zhang Man 張曼 "The Flow of Culture in the Midst of Intertextual Flux" 文化在文本間穿行：論張愛玲的翻譯觀, in Chen Zishan 陳子善, *Re-reading Eileen Chang* 重讀張愛玲 (Shangahi: Shanghai shudian chubanshe, 2008), 214–33; 234–46.
5. According to Stephen Soong, Chang wrote the English version first. See also Kao Chuan-chih 高全之, *Eileen Chang Reconsidered* 張愛玲學 (Taipei: Maitian, 2008), 418.
6. See my introduction to *The Rouge of the North* (Berkeley: University of California Press, 1998), viii.
7. See Kao's analysis, 321–44.
8. Chang's letter to Stephen Soong 宋淇, September 5, 1957.
9. I am using Andrew F. Jones's translation. See *Written on Water* 流言, trans. Andrew F. Jones, co-ed. with an introduction by Nicole Huang (New York: Columbia University Press, 2005), 131.
10. It should also be noted that Chang married Ferdinand Reyher (1891–1967) in 1956. This marriage was nevertheless soon burdened by Reyher's health problems and the resultant financial strain. As with the writing of *The Fall of the Pagoda*, Chang wrote *The Book of Change* in the midst of worrying about Reyher and their future.

11. Chang's letters to Stephen Soong, June 23, 1963; January 25, 1964. In the 1963 letter Chang called her novel *The Leifengta Pagoda Has Fallen* 雷峰塔倒了; in the 1964 letter she called it *The Leifeng Pagoda* 雷峰塔.

12. For Lu Xun and contemporary literati's responses to *The Fall of the Pagoda*, see Eugene Wang's succinct analysis in "Tope and Topos: The Leifeng Pagoda and the Discourse of the Demonic," in *Writing and Materiality in China*, ed. Judith Zeitlin and Lydia Liu (Cambridge, MA: Harvard University Press, 2003), 517–35.

13. See T. A. Hsia's analysis in *The Gate of Darkness: Studies on the Leftist Literary Movement in China* (Seattle: University of Washington Press, 1968), Chapter 4.

14. Walter Benjamin, *Illuminations*, trans. Harry Zohn (New York: Schocken, 1969), 257–58.

15. Chang, "Writing of One's Own," *Written on Water*, 18.

16. Eileen Chang, "Love in a Fallen City": "Hong Kong's defeat had brought Liusu victory. But in this unreasonable world, who can distinguish cause and effect? Who knows which is which? Did a great city fall so that she could be vindicated? Countless thousands of people dead, countless thousands of people suffering, after that an earthshaking revolution… Liusu did not feel anything subtle about her place in history." Karen Kingsbury's translation, in *Love in A Fallen City* (New York: New York Review of Books, 2007), 167.

17. Chang, "From the Ashes," *Written on Water*, 52.

18. Eileen Chang, *The Book of Change* (Hong Kong: Hong Kong University Press, 2010), 230.

19. Cheng Zhongying 成中英, *Theory of Benti in the Philosophy of Yijing* 易學本體論 (Beijing: Beijing University Press, 2006), 3–34.

20. Cheng, *Theory of Benti in the Philosophy of Yijing*, 29.

21. "The Great Treatise I," Zhouyi 周易，繫辭上, trans. James Legge, *Chinese Text Project* 中國哲學書電子化計劃, http://chinese.dsturgeon.net/text.pl?node= 46908&if=gb&en=on.

22. Gilles Deleuze, *Difference and Repetition*, trans. Paul Patton (New York: Columbia University Press, 1995). See also J. Hillis Miller's discussion of repetition as an aesthetic principle of fictional creation, in *Fiction and Repetition* (Cambridge: Harvard University Press, 1982), Chapter 1.

23. Chang, *The Book of Change*, 10–11.

24. Chang, *The Book of Change*, 201.

25. This character is based on Chang's best friend at the time, Fatima Mohideen, a girl whose father was from Ceylon and her mother a native of Tianjin.

26. Chang, *The Book of Change*, 181.

27. For more definition of derivative aesthetics, see my discussion in *Fin-de-siècle Splendor: Repressed Modernities of Late Qing Fiction, 1849–1911* (Stanford: Stanford University Press, 1997), 76–80.

28. Chang, *The Book of Change*, 20.

29. See my discussion in *Fin-de-siècle Splendor*, 89–101.

30. This novel is a playful parody of Cao Xueqin's masterpiece. It was aborted by Chang after she composed the initial chapters and has never been published.

31. I am using David Hawkes' translation, *The Story of the Stone*, vol. 1 (New York: Penguin, 1973), 51.

32. "張愛玲五詳《紅樓夢》，看官們三棄《海上花》". Eileen Chang, "Afterword to the Mandarin Edition of *The Sing-song Girls of Shanghai*" 國語版《海上花》譯後記, in Chang, trans. with annotations, 國語海上花列傳, vol. II (Taipei: Huangguan chubanshe, 1995), 724.

33. By "translingual practice" I am referring to the theory of translated Chinese modernity developed by Lydia Liu, in *Translingual Practice: Literature, National Culture, and Translated Modernity—China, 1900-1937* (Berkeley: University of California Press, 1995). I am using the term in Chang's case anachronistically so as to stress Chang's alternative view of translation. Chang wrote her English essay "Chinese Life and Fashions" in 1943 for the English language journal *The XXth Century*. She translated and revised the piece for the Chinese language magazine *Past and Present* 古今, retitling it "A Chronicle of Changing Clothes" 更衣記. This piece was later included in Chang's collection "Written on Water" 流言. See Andrew F. Jones's triangulated translation into English of Chang's translation into Chinese in *Written on Water*, 65–77.

Afterword

1. Leo Ou-fan Lee 李歐梵, *Watching Lust, Caution: Literature, Cinema, History* 睇色，戒：文學‧電影‧歷史 (Oxford: Oxford University Press, 2008).

2. Doris Sommer, *Bilingual Aesthetics: A Sentimental Education* (Durham: Duke University Press, 2004); and *Bilingual Games: Some Literary Investigations* (New York: Palgrave, 2004).

3. See my reviews of these two novels: "Her English Problem" (review of *The Fall of the Pagoda*) and "Change and Chang" (review of *The Book of Change*), in *Muse* (Hong Kong) 41 (June 2010): 105–08; and 45 (October 2010): 89–93.

Index

*Page numbers in **bold type**, e.g. **31–40**, refer to detailed discussion of the topic. The entries under Chang, Eileen are divided into various categories, which are also indicated by **bold type**.*